38⁵⁰

ONCE
•
WAS
•
ENOUGH

by
William Torbert Leonard

The Scarecrow Press, Inc.
Metuchen, N.J., & London
1986

BOOKS BY WILLIAM TORBERT LEONARD:

MASQUERADE IN BLACK
BROADWAY BOUND
THEATRE: STAGE TO SCREEN TO TELEVISION
THE FUNSTERS*
HOLLYWOOD PLAYERS: THE THIRTIES*
HOLLYWOOD PLAYERS: THE FORTIES*
FILM DIRECTORS GUIDE: THE U.S.*

_____

*(Co-authored with James Robert Parish)

Library of Congress Cataloging-in-Publication Data

Leonard, William T.
  Once was enough.

  Includes indexes.
  1. Theater--New York (N.Y.)--Reviews. 2. Drama--
Stories, plots, etc. I. Title.
PN2277.N5L38 1986   792.9'5'097471   86-11855
ISBN 0-8108-1909-0

Copyright © 1986 by William Torbert Leonard
Manufactured in the United States of America

CONTENTS

Acknowledgments	v
Matinee	vii-xii
Broadway Takes a Brodie	xiii-xvii
THE PLAYS	1-208
Bombs in Season: Chronological Index	209-211
Actor Index	212-223
Choreographer Index	224
Composer Index	225-226
Costume Designer Index	227-229
Set Designer Index	230-232
Director Index	233-235
Lyricist Index	236-237
Playwright Index	238-241
Producer Index	242-246
General Index	247

ACKNOWLEDGMENTS

Research is a tedious pursuit ameliorated by ever helpful librarians. Special thanks for their assistance is made to Curator Dorothy Swerdlove and her staff of the Theatre Collection at the Library and Museum of the Performing Arts at Lincoln Center, New York; to various departments of the Free Library of Philadelphia: Geraldine DuClow and Elaine Ebo of the Theatre Collection; Bernard Pasqualini and staff of the Newspaper Department; Frederick Kent and staff of the Music Department; William Lang of Social Science and History Department, and many others. Appreciation for their assistance is also made to Gerald Bordman, G. Harold Hozey, Jean McRobert, Mimi Rosnow, and Alfred Simon. And to the community of Theatre Critics without whose appraisals, right or wrong, this book could not have been written.

MATINEE

Prior to the turn of the century new plays, including several of Henrik Ibsen's then controversial dramas, were tested on Broadway at special one-performance matinees. Actors occasionally assembled a cast of peers to test their talents in toga, buskin and blank verse without fear of critical bodkins. Repertory companies often included untried or foreign plays and rarely performed classics for a single performance. Special matinees relieved producers of the risk and cost of a road tryout and new playwrights were given Broadway exposure, albeit for one performance only. Later restrictions and requirements of the Actors' Equity Association, founded December 22, 1912, and the growing economical structure of the theatre, in addition to occasional shortage of theatres, by 1914 gradually dispensed with this practice. However, producer John D. Williams did experimentally produce Eugene O'Neill's first full-length play in 1920 (which he had optioned in 1918) for a special matinee.

Arnold Daly and Winchell Smith produced New York's first production of George Bernard Shaw's Candida for $350 at a special trial matinee at the Princess Theatre on December 9, 1903. Arnold Daly played Marchbanks to Dorothy Donnelly's Candida and the play's success extended to additional matinees. Candida opened a regular engagement at the Madison Square Theatre on January 4, 1904, to complete 133 performances. Richard Mansfield imported England's fine actress Janet Achurch for the title role in his production of Candida in 1895, but egotistical Mansfield abandoned the play during rehearsals when Miss Achurch "showed that she would act him off the stage."

Richard Bennett, while playing the leading role in Elmer Rice's drama For the Defense which opened on December 19, 1919, at the Playhouse Theatre, was eager to play the part of Robert Mayo in Eugene O'Neill's new play and determinedly goaded John D. Williams into producing Beyond the Horizon at the Morosco Theatre for a special matinee on February 3, 1920. A hybrid cast was assembled for Beyond the Horizon--from Rice's For the Defense, Louise Closser Hale, George Riddell, and Mary Jeffrey, and from Langdon McCormick's play The Storm (which had opened at the 48th Street Theatre on October 2, 1919), Edward Arnold and Helen MacKeller.

The experimental matinee of Beyond the Horizon was such a success that O'Neill's drama continued playing matinees at the Morosco Theatre until February 23rd when Arnold Bennett's play Sacred and Profane Love became the theatre's tenant. Beyond the Horizon moved to the Criterion Theatre where John D. Williams's production of Eugene Brieux's play The Letter of the Law was playing evening performances. The matinees continued until a regular run of Beyond the Horizon began on March 9, 1920, at the Little Theatre for 111 performances and Eugene O'Neill won the first of his four Pulitzer Prizes for his first full-length play.

A random sampling of these one-performance matinees includes the following:

Ghosts by Henrik Ibsen (Berkeley Lyceum Theatre, January 5, 1894); with Ida Jeffreys-Goodfriend, Courtnay Thorpe, Albert Lawrence

Mrs. Smith's Husband by Catherine Lewis (Herald Square Theatre, October 22, 1894); with Catherine Lewis, Walter Walker

The Little Hussar by Elizabeth Stagg and Emma Steiner (5th Avenue Theatre, December 21, 1894); with Ada Gilman, Frank Thropp

The Bathing Girl a musical comedy by Rupert Hughes and Robert Coverly (5th Avenue Theatre, September 2, 1895); with William Stephens, Grace Golden

Benedict Arnold by Echard Golden (5th Avenue Theatre, December 27, 1895); with Henry Jewett, Vincent Serrano

A Man and His Wife by George Fleming [Constance Fletcher] (Empire Theatre, March 6, 1897); with William Faversham, Robert Edeson, Viola Allen

John Gabriel Borkman by Henrik Ibsen (Criterion Theatre, November 18, 1897); with E. J. Henley, Ann Warrington

Hedda Gabler by Henrik Ibsen (5th Avenue Theatre, March 30, 1898); with Elizabeth Robins, Leo Ditrichstein, William Courtleigh

The Master Builder by Henrik Ibsen (Carnegie Lyceum Theatre, January 17, 1900); with John Steppling, Florence Kahn, William H. Pascoe

The Storm by Alexander Ostrovski (Carnegie Lyceum Theatre, March 2, 1900); with Frederick Lewis, Florence Kahn

The Weather Hen by Berte Thomas and Granville Barker (Manhattan Theatre, April 13, 1900; with John Bunny, George S. Probert, George Backus

The Heather Field by Edward Martyn (Carnegie Lyceum Theatre, April 19, 1900); with John E. Kellard, Jobyna Howland, J. Brandon Tynan

The Land of Heart's Desire by William Butler Yeats (Wallack's Theatre October 8, 1900); with Adelaide Thurston, Alphonz Ethier, John Glendinning; followed by In A Balcony by Robert Browning, with Otis Skinner, Eleanor Robson, Mrs. Sarah Cowell Le Moyne [These plays were repeated at special matinees at Wallack's Theatre on October 26, 1900, and at the Knickerbocker Theatre on May 6, 1901]

Sold and Paid For by John C. Dixon (Herald Square Theatre, December 7, 1900); with John C. Dixon, Alice Saunders, Lewis Wood

Cashel Byron by Harrison J. Wolfe, from George Bernard Shaw's novel Cashel Byron's Profession (Herald Square Theatre, December 27, 1900); with Harrison J. Wolfe, Billy Elmer, Grace Griswald

King Washington by Robert Lewis Wead (Wallack's Theatre, April 26, 1901); with David Murray, Maude Granger, Macey Harlam x / Matinee

Gypsy by Sidney Grundy (Garrick Theatre, December 30, 1903); with Guy Standing, Doris Keane, George Irving

The Triumph of Love by Martha Morton Conheim (Criterion Theatre, February 8, 1904); with Maclyn Arbuckle, George Backus, Carlotta Nielson

Love's Pilgrimage by Horace B. Fry (Wallack's Theatre, April 14, 1904); with Carlotta Nielson, Guy Bates Post, William S. Hart

Robert Burns by Clayton Mackenzie Legge (Carnegie Lyceum, January 28, 1905); with Clayton Mackenzie Legge, Rose E. Tapley, George H. Loane

The Player Maid by Louise Mallory (Liberty Theatre, October 13, 1905); with Charles Coburn, Elliott Dexter, Florence Davis

My Wife Won't Let Me a musical comedy by C. Baswitz and Herbert Dillea (Berkeley Lyceum Theatre, August 14, 1906); with Edgar A. Foreman, May Anderson, Charles Bassett

Dr. Wake's Patient by W. Gayer Mackay and Robert Ord (Garrick Theatre, November 19, 1907); with Bruce McRae, Charles Walcott, Effie Germon

Disengaged by Henry James (Hudson Theatre, March 11, 1909); with Dorothy Donnelly, Frank Gilmore, Louise Closser Hale

In the Long Run by Archer Jones (Comedy Theatre, December 3, 1909); with William H. Bonney, Irving Cummings, Caroline Harris

The Wedding Day by Jessie Trimble (Hackett's Theatre, December 10, 1909); with Jane Darwell, Jesse Bonselle, Sheldon Lewis

Know Thyself by Paul Hervieu (Berkeley Theatre, December 27, 1909); with Arnold Daly, Louise Ritter, Frederick Lewis

Olive Latimer's Husband by Rudolph Besier (Hackett Theatre, January 7, 1910); with Charles N. Grenne, Sheldon Lewis, Amelia Mayborn

Noah's Flood (author unrecorded) (New Theatre, March 27, 1911); with Ben Johnson, Pedro de Cordoba, Ferdinand Gottschalk; and Nice Wanton (author unrecorded), with Frank Gilmore, Cecil Yapp, Reginald Barlow

Tainted Philanthropy by Abraham Goldknopf (Belasco Theatre, November 26, 1912); with Teresa Maxwell Conover, Eugene O'Brien, Milton Sills; and The Poetasters of Ispahan by Clifford Bax, with Elizabeth Risdon, Walter Kingsford, Maurice Elvey; and Beauty and the Jacobin by Booth Tarkington, with Elizabeth Risdon, Walter Kingsford, Eva Leonard Boyne

Chains by Porter Emerson Browne (Criterion Theatre, December 16, 1912); with Olive Wyndham, Shelly Hull, Mrs. Thomas Whiffen

The Hundredth Man by Hutcheson Boyd (Wallack's Theatre, February 8, 1913); with Kate Mayhew, Ralph Stuart, William Fredericks

The Honeymoon by Arnold Bennett (Lyceum Theatre, February 24, 1913); with Laura Hope Crews, Howard Estabrook, Frank Reicher

Mary's Manoeuvres by Alice E. Ives (Lyceum Theatre, February 25, 1913); with Ida Waterman, Kenneth Hill, Minnette Barrett; and Revenge; or the Pride of Lillian Le Mar by Rachel Crothers, with Ben Greet, Jane Grey, Cyril Keightley

The Stronger by August Strindberg (48th Street Theatre, March 18, 1913); with Hedwig Reicher, Mabel Moore, Marjorie Edmondson; and Pariah by August Strindberg, with Frank Reicher and Walter Hampden

The Necken by Elizabeth G. Crane (Lyceum Theatre, April 15, 1913); with Kate Mayhew, Alberta Gallatin, William H. Post; and The Guilty Conscience by Robert H. Davis, with William H. Post, Alberta Gallatin, Frederick Perry

School by T. W. Robertson (Playhouse Theatre, December 16, 1913); with Alice Brady, Charles Cherry, Ernest Glendinning

A Woman Killed with Kindness by Thomas Hayward (Lyceum Theatre, March 30, 1914); with Eugene O'Brien, Frank Morgan, Charlotte Ives; and Granny Maumee by Ridgely Torrance, with Dorothy Donnelly, June Mathis, Lola Clifton

BROADWAY TAKES A BRODIE

The Brooklyn Bridge across the East River connecting the Island of Manhattan with the Borough of Brooklyn opened on Thursday, May 24, 1883. Designed by Muhlhausen, or German-born John Augustus Roebling, in 1867, the construction of the bridge was supervised by his son Washington Roebling following the death of John Augustus in New York on July 22, 1869. The Brooklyn Bridge with its 1,595-foot main span and its two 930-foot long side spans was then the longest suspension bridge in the world.

Late in the afternoon of May 19, 1885, a Washington swimming instructor, Emmett Odlum, lost his life by leaping from the bridge. Shortly after 2 P.M. on Saturday, July 24, 1886, at the bridge's New York pier, a tall, slim man from New York's Fourth Ward climbed into a lumber wagon entering the bridge. He gave the wagon driver two cents for his bridge fare. The twenty-eight-year-old passenger was an unemployed former Bowery newsboy, bootblack, and Coney Island lifeguard who lived with his two daughters and one son at 85 Chrystie Street. His name was Steve Brodie.

Some one hundred yards from the New York pier, slender, agile Brodie jumped from the lumber wagon to the bridge railing and climbed down to a lower girder where he could not be reached by pursuing Bridge Officer Lally. Tossing his coat and hat away and with his pants tightly tied at the ankles with rope, Brodie suspended himself on the girder, then quickly dropped feet first 120 feet into the East River. Mike Phelan, Tim Brennan, and two other Fourth Ward cronies rowed Phelan's boat to the floundering jumper and hauled him aboard. Bridge Officer Lally arrested Brodie for endangering his life by jumping off the Brooklyn Bridge, and Brodie was taken to the Oak Street police station, then transferred to the Tombs Police Court. Tombs Justice Kilbreth approved lawyer Francis V.S. Oliver's request for Brodie's release under $1,000 bail and the cocky, uneducated young Irishman left the Tombs to be hailed as a hero by a wildly cheering crowd.

Brodie won his $200 bet from Tim Brennan by completing his jump from the Brooklyn Bridge and his leap brought him a ten-week contract at $250-a-week for personal appearances at Nathan Morris's Bowery Museum. "Taking a Brodie" caught on and in 1886 Larry Donovan and a man named Barker jumped from the Brooklyn Bridge; another potential leaper, Collins, was arrested before he could complete his descent into the East River. Adventurous De Freitas made the jump in April, 1887, but the following month Ed Curry was arrested before he could accomplish what had become a presumed leap to instant fame and fortune.

Steve Brodie had suddenly become a hero of sorts and was acclaimed by the audience at Niblo's Garden on February 22, 1892, when he was featured in Steele Mackaye's melodrama Money Mad, portraying, of all things, a dedicated Chicago Clark Street bridgekeeper rescuing a drowning man. Brodie also headlined R. N. Stephens's melodrama On The Bowery on September 10, 1894, at the 14th Street Theatre for a week's engagement and made an extensive tour of major cities and hinterland one-night stands in the play. Steve's insatiable thirst for publicity continued with a marathon swim down the Hudson River and, advertised as "Steve Brodie, The Daring Bridge Jumper," he jumped from bridges across the country.

Steve opened a "sporting saloon" on the Bowery, gaining a large clientele and additional celebrity by offering free umbrellas to unprepared pedestrians on rainy days and paying funeral expenses for unidentified or indigent occupants of the City Morgue. In 1898 Brodie toured with Gus Hill's vaudeville sketch One Night in Brodie's Barroom. While appearing in Chicago with Gus Hill's company, Steve's passion for publicity produced bizarre headlines on March 31, 1898, when he hoaxed the country by telegraphing his wife and family, then living at 125 East 106th Street, a premature announcement of his death. The picaresque, legendary Steve Brodie, born on New York's East Side in 1858, died at the age of forty-three in San Antonio, Texas, on Thursday, January 31, 1901.

The first production of Joseph Schenck and Darryl F. Zanuck's newly formed motion picture company, Twentieth Century, was The Bowery, based on a novel by Michael L. Simmons and Bessie Ruth Solomon, directed by Raoul Walsh and released by United Artists on October 13, 1933. The climax of The Bowery was Steve Brodie's (George Raft) leap from the Brooklyn Bridge and thirty-two years later Brodie again leaped into questionable fame in a Broadway musical misadventure called Kelly.

Kelly has been documented and proclaimed by writers, theatre devotees, and members of the theatrical profession as the colossus of one-performance musical comedy flops on Broadway. There is certainly sufficient evidence to support the constant derogatory references to Kelly but there were many other Broadway one-performance disasters that, in retrospect, make Kelly seem like a minor masterpiece.

Ann Harding caustically commented after one Broadway performance in Abraham Cochrane, "Critics have made New York the only one-night stand in the country." The Dean of American Critics, The New York Times's Brooks Atkinson, once noted, "In the mythology of Broadway 'Critic' stands for assasin." New York's dwindling commune of critics has been accused of being the villainous executioner of many promising productions, but the sudden death of many productions was due to their being more villainous than promising.

Richard Maney in Fanfare, his perceptive account of show-business, wrote, "Critics have but one thing in common, suspicion of the sanity of their fellows. In lofty or gruesome fashion, their reviews reflect their prejudices, their taste and their familiarity, or scorn for, the English language. In an earlier day, a play charged with hokum or heroics, however poisonous to the reviewers, might develop into a mint." "Courageous producers in the past risked small fortunes to keep a show on the boards until an inconstant public believed it to be a production of merit. There is no explaining the fickle theatre public who as often as not embrace a play of deplorable dramaturgy or a non-musical musical comedy while ignoring productions of theatrical excellence."

Abie's Irish Rose and Tobacco Road were two of several plays which received no glowing benedictions from the critics but survived to become two of the longest running hits in the

history of the American theatre despite a critical chorus of
Dies Irae and venomous epithets. Today, however, as Maney
noted, "recovery from critical cudgeling is all but impossible."

Lehman Engel in his book The Critics (Macmillan, 1976)
briskly bisected three of New York's current appraisers
(Clive Barnes, Douglas Watt, and Martin Gottfried) qualifying
their merits and demerits and examining their reviews as the
"result of reaction rather than consideration" on the premise
that "one man's taste is most people's poison." The Season,
William Goldman's 1969 best-selling book, prescribed pillory
for the majority of New York's theatrical scribes. Years ago
Disraeli wrote: "Critics are men who have failed in literature
and art"; Dr. Johnson's analysis was that "Criticism is the
device by which one may grow important and formidable at the
expense of others," while Coleridge claimed reviewers were
"failed poets, historians, biographers, etc.--therefore they
turn critics." Lord Byron apotheosized, "A man must serve
time to every trade save censure--critics all are ready made."

Playwright Elmer Rice, after the critical clobbering and
failure of his plays Between Two Worlds and Judgement Day,
in 1934 addressed Professor John H. H. Lyon's Columbia University class. Rice's off-the-record remarks, which he later
described as "injudicious and ill-mannered," unexpectedly appeared that evening in The Sun. Rice deplored the crass
commercialism of the Broadway theatre which subordinated art
to business with its emphasis "on trivial, tasteless plays that
catered to the idle people" and then salvoed the critics with
"fostering the theatre of sterile entertainment and with discouraging innovators and rebels" calling them "stupid and illiterate. For the most part they are all men without intellect,
perception, sensitivity or background. They pander to the
tastes of the empty-headed, the bored, the insensitive and the
complacent."

Maxwell Anderson was enraged at the critical castration
of his 1946 play Truckline Cafe, which closed after thirteen
performances, and retaliated in a large advertisement in The
New York Times, "The public is far better qualified to judge
plays than the men who write reviews for our dailies. It is
an insult to our theatre that there should be so many incompetents and irresponsibles among them. There are still a few
critics who know their job and respect it, but of late years
all plays are passed on largely by a sort of Jukes family of

journalism who bring to the theatre nothing but their own hopelessness, recklessness and despair."

Despite the opinions and analysis of critics stated above, it clearly requires dedication to withstand the boredom, embarrassment, and disappointment of the opening and closing of so many productions after one performance, not only for the critics but for the first-night audiences and those players who bravely recovered from the slings and arrows of devastating reviews in plays they had to know were terminal.

There were no second nights. Once was enough!

ONCE WAS ENOUGH

ABRAHAM COCHRANE (Belasco Theatre, February 17, 1964). Produced by Walter Fried and Helen Jacobson; A drama by John Sherry; Production supervised by Harold Stone; Setting and Lighting, Robert O'Hearn; Costumes, Domingo A. Rodriguez; Production assistant, Wanda Davie; Company manager, Robert Kamlot; Stage managers, Richard Evans, Ian Cameron
    Bill Travers (Abraham Cochrane); Ann Harding (Myra Holliday); Nancy Wickwire (Helen Balcon); Peter Adams (Roger Balcon); John Griggs (Samuel Holliday); Franklin Cover (Brock Holliday); Jerome Collamore (Gregory Lawton); Audrey Ward (Alice); Richard Nicholls (Dr. Thomas Barrett); Olympia Dukakis (Anne Dowling)

    Abraham Cochrane, an uninhibited, free and independent spirit, visits the Holliday family in their palatial Eastern seacoast home. Middle-aged Myra Holliday has not revealed to her family Dr. Barrett's warning that she is in immediate danger of a coronary crisis. Myra's daughter, Helen, is tormented with a dreary marriage to Roger Balcon, a former Wall Street stockbroker recently returned from a year in a mental hospital. Sensuous Abraham, a self-proclaimed latter-day Don Juan, charms Myra and has an affair with vulnerable and willing Helen. But Abraham's carefully planned, unencumbered, carefree way of life is shattered when Myra dies, leaving him her sumptuous home, and Helen proudly announces she is pregnant with his illegitimate child.

    "There is an abundance of talk about life in <u>Abraham Cochrane</u> but very little of its breath and pulse," reported Howard Taubman (<u>The New York Times</u>), "--for all its atmosphere or urbanity, <u>Abraham Cochrane</u> is lifeless." Norman Nadel (<u>New York World-Telegram-Sun</u>) advised, "<u>Abraham Cochrane</u> is not a good play, and I shall suggest to the editors of the <u>World Almanac</u> that they include it, as of yesterday's date, in that fascinating section that catalogues the year's catastrophes."

    John Chapman (<u>Daily News</u>) added, "The play is an ever-so-elegant fiction--and if its characters can't get excited about it, why should I?" Walter Kerr (<u>Herald Tribune</u>) found "No one really survives the ordeal of reading author John Sherry's loftily literary lines --The program indicates that the play was undirected. The production bears this out."

Ruggedly handsome Northumberland, England-born Bill Travers's career spanned many motion pictures, including the international hit <u>Born Free</u> and several London stage appearances. Travers made his Broadway debut in Steven Gethers's play <u>A Cook for Mr. General</u> for twenty-eight performances in 1961 and returned to Broadway in the title role of <u>Abraham Cochrane</u>.

Famous actress Ann Harding, born Dorothy Walton Gatley on August 7, 1901, played 437 performances in the title role of Bayard Veiller's drama <u>The Trial of Mary Dugan</u> at Broadway's National Theatre during the 1927-1928 season, then had a notable film career spanning twenty-seven years. Ann Harding, who died at her Sherman Oaks, California, home at the age of seventy-nine on September 1, 1981, returned to the stage in London on February 10, 1937, in George Bernard Shaw's <u>Candida</u>. She returned to the Broadway stage on February 28, 1962, in Ira Levin's drama <u>General Seeger</u>, directed by George C. Scott who also played the title role for two quick performances, and the same year she appeared in Dore Schary's play <u>Banderol</u>, which closed on-the-road in Philadelphia on September 22, 1962. <u>Abraham Cochrane</u> was Ann Harding's last Broadway appearance.

John Sherry, a one-time Virginia dairy farmer, published his first novel, <u>The Departure</u>, in 1953. Thirty-nine-year-old John Sherry's aw'fully literary first play, titled <u>Abraham's House</u>, was retitled <u>Abraham Cochrane</u> and passed unmourned in spite of his high glossed rhetoric which failed to inject life into his still-born, old-fashioned characters.

* * *

ACCORDING TO LAW and A STRANGE PLAY (Mansfield Theatre, June 1, 1944). Produced and directed by Eugene Endrey; <u>According to Law</u> by Noel Huston; <u>A Strange Play</u> by Patti Spears; Settings by Harry Bennett; Lighting, Leo Kerz; General manager, Elias Goldin; Stage manager, P. A. Leonard

    According to Law: Don Appell (Ben Staggs); Gregory Robbins (Jim Nailey); Dayton Lummis (Senator Lawrence); Robert Harrison (Henry Terry); Windsor Bryan (Henry Yancey); Henry Wilson (George Randall); Lorraine MacMartin (Mrs. Harkness); Harvey Marlowe (Harvey); Burton Mallory (Luke); Wardell Saunders (Charlie Teague)

    A Strange Play: Ralph Clanton (William Douglas); Alicia Parnahay (Claire); Herbert Hayes (Paul Cartwright); Richard Gordon (Dr. Stephen Duryea); Byron Russell (James)

According to Law

Black Charlie Teague is unjustly accused of rape and framed by promiscuous Mrs. Harkness. The Southern court appoints a drunken lawyer named Ben Staggs to defend Teague. Teague appears in court in a wheelchair, having been shot by the sheriff's posse. Staggs valiantly tries to save Teague's life but the prejudiced judge and jury condemn the black man to die in the electric chair.

A Strange Play

Playwright Paul Cartwright is aware that Claire, the young wife of his best friend, elderly Dr. Stephen Duryea, is having a love affair in their Long Island home with a handsome young actor, William Douglas. Cartwright decides to use this knowledge as the basis for a new play, alternating the ending against the reaction of telling the cuckhold husband or having the best friend remain silent about the affair.

The critics praised Noel Huston's one-act curtain raiser, According to Law, winner of the 1939 American Civil Liberties Union prize, which was produced and directed by Eugene Endrey in 1940 at the Provincetown Playhouse. Patti Spears's two-act "drahma," A Strange Play, was unanimously greeted by the critics with long knives. The audience roared with laughter at Spears's dialogue and the emoting of the cast, and midway through the first act approximately one third of the audience remained in the theatre. Wilella Waldorf (New York Post) agreed that "The dialogue was the sort nobody wanted to listen to even once," and George Freedley (Morning Telegraph) called it "The year's dullest and silliest play."

Robert Garland (New York Journal-American) announced: "It's the worst play I ever saw. There ain't no such playwriting. There ain't no such playacting!" Herrick Brown (New York Sun) reported, "The Broadway theatre seldom offers quite the strange evening it did last night--a two-act play by Miss Patti Spears, most aptly named A Strange Play." Louis Kronenberger (PM) wrote "A Strange Play makes hardly a grain of sense and is couched in rather astonishing language. The acting is even worse, if that's possible, than the writing." John Chapman (Daily News): "The acting is terrible, and I won't bother you with the half of the plot I heard." Lewis Nichols (The New York Times) capsulated A Strange Play with "It grows tiresome. The acting is bad, too."

According to Law: Produced and directed by Eugene Endrey at the Provincetown Playhouse on March 19, 1940 (in conjunction with William Kozlenko's one-act play The Devil Is a Good Man and E. P. Conkle's one-act play What D'You Call It?). Setting by Edwin H. Vander Noot; Lighting, Edward C. Fitzgerald; Stage manager, Robert Hall
    Don Appell (Ben Staggs); Jay Barney (Henry Terry, District Judge); Henry Walden (Jim Nailey, County Attorney); Charles Newman, Jr. (Senator Lawrence, an Attorney); P. Jay Sidney (Charlie Teague); Richard O'Connor (Henry Yancey, Deputy Sheriff); Jon David (Court Reporter Harvey); Tom McGivern, Jr. (George Randall, Deputy Sheriff); Edmond Le Comte (Bailiff Luke) (Mrs. Harkness unlisted in original cast)

4 / Animals

* * *

ANIMALS (Princess Theatre, April 22, 1981). Produced by Steve Salvatore and Michael Jordan in association with Joel B. Leff; Written and directed by Eddie Lawrence; Scenery, John Wright Stevens; Lighting, Marc B. Weiss; Costumes, Marilyn Bligh-White; Elephant Head, Jane Stein; Duck Bill, Rodney Gordon; Sound, Christopher J. Chambers; Directorial assistant, Glenn Taranto; Wardrobe, Toni Baer; Hairstylist, Armand Bouton; Associate producers, Jeffrey Madrick, Steven Kent Goldberg, Anthony Mazzarella; Stage managers, Jack Timmers, Margaret Peckham

The Beautiful Mariposa: Cara Duff-MacCormick (Maid); Cecilia Flores (Maria Rios); Lazara Perez (Juan Ribera); Demo DiMartile (Manuelo Ribera); Ben Kapen, Victor Argo (State Troopers)

Louie and the Elephant: Dan Frazer (Louie Bengal); Barbara Erwin (Lulu Hopper); Victor Argo (Thaddeus); Joel Kramer (Elephant)

Sort of an Adventure: Jennie Wechsler (Harriet Greshaw); Ben Kapen (Eddie Greshaw); Barbara Erwin (Hester Cable); Cara Duff-MacCormick (Hedda Webb-Winters)

The Beautiful Mariposa

Spanish toreador Ribera plans to kill a bull in each of the United States but in Kansas he accidentally kills a mariposa-colored cow and he is pursued by state troopers.

Louie and the Elephant

A San Francisco elephant longs to become a man and be seen in Bay City restaurants with his fiancee.

Sort of an Adventure

Hedda Webb-Winters is a circus freak, half-duck, half-woman, and materializes into a complete and attractive woman after eating roast duck in her lover Eddie's Greenwich Village apartment.

Playwright-actor Eddie Lawrence's career began in vaudeville. He later developed a comic character, "The Old Philosopher," on radio and television and he was a comedy writer for Jack E. Leonard, Bert Lahr, and Sid Caesar. Lawrence appeared as Crook-finger Jake in 1955's revival of Kurt Weill and Bertolt Brecht's The Threepenny Opera and as the bookie Sandor in the Comden and Green/Jule Styne 1956 musical hit Bells Are Ringing. In James Lipton's 1967 musical-comedy adaptation of Kaufman and Hart's comedy The Man Who Came to Dinner into the short-lived Sherry!, Lawrence played Banjo, the caricature of Harpo Marx. But Mr. Lawrence's lasting claim to questionable fame was as the author of Kelly, Broadway's favorite monumental musical disaster in 1965.

Animals was originally produced under the title of Louis and the Elephant, at the Off-Broadway Sheridan Square Playhouse on November 2, 1971. Louis and the Elephant gave eight previews and never officially opened.

Louis and the Elephant. Produced by Edgar Lansbury, Stuart Duncan, Joseph Beruh, in association with Nan Pearlman; Director, John Marley; Settings and Lighting, William Pitkin; Costumes, Stanley Simmons; Sound, Gigi Cascio; Technical director, Don Hinds; General Manager, Al Isaac; Stage manager, Gail Bell

The Beautiful Mariposa: Liz Torres (Maria Rios); Hope Cameron (Maid); Jaime Sanchez (Juan Ribera); Harvey Solin (Manuelo); Josip Elic, Art Vasil (Policemen)

Louis and the Elephant: Dan Frazer (Louis Bengal); Louise Troy (Lulu Hopper); Josip Elic (Thaddeus Armstrong); Lee Richardson (The Elephant); Harvey Solin (Press Agent)

The Adventure of Eddie Greshaw: Lee Richardson (Eddie Greshaw); Louise Troy (Hedda Webb-Winters); Marge Redmond (Harriet); Hope Cameron (Hester)

Ten years later Louis and the Elephant became Animals and invaded Broadway where it exceeded its original flop record by nine previews and one performance.

"Mr. Lawrence has composed three long sketches that are unfunny, shapeless and, at times, incomprehensible," reported Frank Rich (The New York Times). "Animals is so detached from any known reality that the audience might just as well be staring in a void." Lawrence's staging was considered to be as deplorable as his writing, set against "tawdry sets in the histrionic, eye-bulging manner of old-time burlesque." To the actors caught in this theatrical trap, Rich expressed sympathy and appreciation of "just how much bravery it takes to pursue an acting career in New York." Clive Barnes recommended "Animals best kept in the pen" and declared "The actual writing is almost as bad as the concept."

Although Animals had flopped ten years prior to its invasion of Broadway, the first of the three cartoons, The Beautiful Mariposa had originally been produced on July 1, 1952, by the American Lyric Theatre at the Provincetown Playhouse. Lawrence's one-act fantasy shared the bill with Kurt Weill's charming one-act folk-opera Down in the Valley, staged by Tony Randall, with Eva Marie Saint and Pernell Roberts, which was followed by Gian Carlo Menotti's The Old Maid and the Thief.

Twenty-nine years had not improved the color nor writing of Mr. Lawrence's mariposa cow. Animals can be dismissed with actress June Buckridge's (formerly Sister George) withering acceptance of the decline of her career, reduced to playing a cow, at the close of Frank Marcus's fascinating 1966 comedy The Killing of Sister George: "Moo! God-Damn It! Moo!"

* * *

BEYOND EVIL (Cort Theatre, June 7, 1926). Produced by David Thorne; A drama by David Thorne; Director, Edward Massey; General manager, Frank Adams; Stage manager, Robert Horwood

Mary Blair (Madeline Robinson); Eduardo Sanchez (Tom Walker); Louis Ancker (John Robinson); Betty Sargent (Kitty Robinson); Helen Beresford (Ellen Robinson); Robert Horwood (Gustave Berg); Nat S. Jerome (Peter Chickov); Bee Morosco (Daisy Murray); Edward Reese (Richard Osborn)

Bored with her husband, John, Madeline Robinson mortgages their small-town drugstore and leaves for Harlem to live with mulatto Tom Walker. Threatened with financial ruin, Madeline poisons herself rather than return and resume life with her husband.

Beyond Evil was one show on which all critics were in accord. The gentlemen of the press applauded the audience rebellion which ran the "gauntlet of ridicule" and united in their exacerbation of David Thorne's publicized threat to Eugene O'Neill. "So unruly was the audience in its contempt for the entertainment that it became wolflike in its demeanor and worried them with savage howls of ridicule" reported Percy Hammond (Herald-Tribune), describing the drama as "a ludicrous display of scarlet merchandise in the basement of the theatre. It ought not to be allowed, and the punishment it got from last night's audience was merciful."

J. Brooks Atkinson (The New York Times), not easily aroused by the most obnoxious offerings, described the overture of tittering shortly after Beyond Evil began, which crescendoed into loud guffaws mingled with catcalls, cheers of the Bronx variety augmented with deprecating shrill whistles. When the final curtain mercifully came down on Beyond Evil the audience silenced a smattering of polite applause with a lusty chorus of boos, "usually reserved for the Yankee Stadium when Ruth strikes out with the bases full." Atkinson felt the audience reception of Beyond Evil was "less unique than the happenings that were set forth on the stage" and described Thorne's play as "disjointed, replete with meaningless expressions, and minor absurdities--Seldom, if ever, has a New York audience greeted a new play with such demonstrations of bantering disapproval as were accorded Beyond Evil."

Described by The New York Times as "a breathless bit of news," neophyte playwright David Thorne announced that he had written Beyond Evil as a direct challenge to Eugene O'Neill, who "treated the dangers of miscegenation in his play All God's Chillun Got Wings and made a failure of the presentation" adding that he had successfully accomplished what "O'Neill attempted and failed." Beyond Evil was ballyhooed as a satire on All God's Chillun Got Wings and Lulu Belle and was predicted to out-sex Mae West's contested play Sex. Unfortunately, Thorne's only claim to fame was to have written what was called "The World's Worst Play."

Against dire predictions of riots, fanned by inflammatory newspaper coverage and the ranting of leading moralistic orators, plus threats of reprisals from the Ku Klux Klan supported by opportunistic politicians, Eugene O'Neill's controversial play All God's Chillun Got Wings was bravely produced by Kenneth Macgowan at the Provincetown Playhouse on May 15, 1924. The agonized hue and cry preceding the opening of All God's Chillun Got Wings was all based on a white actress kissing the hand of her black husband. Paul Robeson was cast as the husband and Mary Blair, the beleaguered heroine of Beyond Evil, played his white wife. The lukewarm reviews disappointed and silenced the self-appointed protectors of public purity. Time magazine reported the play hardly lived up "to the provocative possibilities of the background." When All God's Chillun was revived fifty-one years later on Broadway, Eugene O'Neill's turgid dramaturgy was still considered "a very poorly written play."

It had been recorded that poet-novelist David Thorne's literary talents did not include those of playwright, but his second Broadway contribution, an adaptation of Oscar Wilde's The Picture of Dorian Gray, called Dorian Gray, opened at the Biltmore Theatre on May 21, 1928, to play sixteen performances, despite savage reviews. Only because Beyond Evil mercifully disappeared after its one performance, which equalled the rebellion of audiences against the presumptuous talent of Count Joannes during his beseiged nineteenth-century career, did it escape the wrath of the gods of censorship and damnation released against the Broadway stage.

During playboy Mayor James J. Walker's vacation, the corrupt Tammany Hall politicians, became, unbelievably, supporters for the suppression of vice, focused on blatant immorality on the Broadway stage. District Attorney Joab H. Banton first cited Bunk of 1926 for being iniquitous. An injunction prevented the closing of Bunk of 1926, which had opened on February 16, 1926, featuring actor Gene Lockhart, who had written the songs and sketches (with Percy Waxman); the revue completed 104 performances. Other shows on Banton's list of the salacious were Sholem Asch's God of Vengeance and Roland Oliver's play Night Hawk. Peter Glenn's comedy New York Exchange withstood objections for ten weeks, but William Francis Dugan's The Virgin Man was stopped at its sixty-third performance and the cast, including Dorothy Hall and Don Dilloway, and author Dugan were arrested and trundled off to jail. Dugan and his cast were fined $250 each and released under a suspended sentence, provided they would sin no more.

Mae West's first attempt at playwriting was The Albatross, written under the pseudonym of Jane Mast, which she retitled Sex. When the play was rejected by the Shuberts, Mae West and C. V. Morgenstern produced Sex at Daly's Theatre on April 26, 1926. The play astounded the supposedly sophisticated Manhattan press and public and newspapers refused advertisements for Miss West's Sex. Undulating Mae, starring in Sex as Margie LaMont, a Montreal prostitute keeping the British navy happy, was arrested on February 9, 1927. Judge Donnellan fined Mae $500 and packed her off to the Jefferson Market prison on Welfare Island. When she completed her ten-day sentence, Mae gave the prison library a gift of $1,000. The following year Mae West's salacious play Pleasure Man was closed by the police after two performances.

Edouard Bourdet's drama La Prisonnière, dealing with veiled lesbianism, opened at the Theatre Femina in Paris in March 1926, starring Mlle. Sylvia and Pierre Blanchar. The Parisian production was followed by Max Reinhardt's mounting of the play at Vienna's Josefstadt Theatre, with Helen Thimming and Ernest Deutsch. Arthur Hornblow, Jr. translated La Prisonnière for the English-speaking stage as The Captive, which opened at Broadway's Empire Theatre on September 29, 1926, starring Helen Manken and Basil Rathbone.

Police wagons arrived at the stage door of the Empire Theatre to transport director Gilbert Miller and the entire cast, including Helen Menken, Basil Rathbone, Ann Andrews, and Norman Trevor, to jail, after they had given 160 performances without noticeable damage to the morals of Manhattan. An agreement to voluntarily withdraw The Captive appeased the authorities and everyone was released.

Although The Captive was selected by New York's leading critics as one of the year's best plays, Burns Mantle, in his volume of Best Plays of 1926-27, declined to include the drama. Mr. Mantle was aware that an assigned play jury of twelve voted 7 to 5 for the play's continuance and that "audiences could not have been drawn to the theatre or satisfied in the theatre by any salaciousness traceable to either the text or the action of the Bourdet drama." Mantle, however, rationalized, "Inasmuch as The Captive has been condemned, however unjustly, by law and voluntarily withdrawn, without benefit of trial, from our stage, it ceases actively to figure as a history-making contribution to the current drama--and shall remain where fate and circumstances have placed it."

Under pressure from New York's Governor Alfred E. Smith, the hedonistic, gallivanting mayor of New York City, James J. Walker, warned theatre managers and producers to clean up their act. A committee of nine was formed, representing producers, playwrights, and actors, to act as their own censors. Although Walker had defeated a movement to censor novels with a wisecrack--"I have never yet heard of a girl being ruined by a book"--he invited all the leading Broadway producers to City Hall to attend his meeting dealing

with "War on Immoral Plays." With the exception of producers Florenz
Ziegfeld, George White, and Earl Carroll (whose revues were considered highly risqué), all of the invited producers attended.

New York State senator Republican Roger B. Wales, at the suggestion of New York District Attorney Banton and Brooklyn's District Attorney Charles H. Dodd, drafted legislation designed to purify
the wicked stage. The Wales Padlock Act, which was signed into law
by Governor Smith on April 7, 1927, sternly stated, "The license
authorities have power to padlock a theater for one year if the owner,
producer or manager or actor is convicted of permitting an obscene,
indecent, immoral or impure play."

The Messrs. Shubert capitalized on the Wales Padlock Act on
July 5, 1927, when they opened their revue Padlocks of 1927 at their
Broadway Shubert Theatre. The revue starred brassy, blonde Mary
Louise Cecelia Guinan, one-time movie star in early Westerns but more
famous as Texas Guinan, Broadway's notorious speakeasy hostess
greeting her customers with "Hello, Sucker," who became a regular
patron of Federal Prohibition raiders. The cast of Padlocks of 1927
included Lillian Roth, George Raft, and Jay C. Flippen, with star
Guinan making her entrance on a white horse.

The first casualty of the Wales Padlock Act was Simon Gantillon's
play Maya, translated by Ernest Boyd. Maya, produced by the
Actor-Managers, Inc., opened at the Comedy Theatre on February
21, 1928, but shuttered after fifteen performances under threat of
padlock. A fine actress, Aline MacMahon, played a French prostitute
dispensing philosophical support to her clients while neglecting her
professional calling.

Eugene O'Neill was awarded his third Pulitzer Prize for Strange
Interlude in 1928. District Attorney Banton declined censoring
Strange Interlude on the rather wobbly basis that, although it did
offend good taste, "The District Attorney, as an official, is not concerned with matters affecting good taste." Additionally, the advisory
board for the Pulitzer Award arbitrarily removed Joseph Pulitzer's
final stipulation that the prize be given for "raising the standards
of good morals, good taste and good manners."

Walter Kerr's April 7, 1950, essay in The Commonweal succinctly
clarified the irrelevant moral judgments of art in the theatre by
quoting St. Thomas: "If beauty demands that the whole of nature
be imitated, and if, for instance, sin is to be found in nature, then
sin must be found in art." Brooks Atkinson observed, "Like life
in general, the theatre is not remarkable for its good taste," but "it
is a good deal chaster than it was in the time of the Restoration
dramatists, who were morbidly filthy. For real bawdy, go to the
Elizabethans."

BICYCLE RIDE TO NEVADA (Cort Theatre, September 24, 1963). Produced by Roger L. Stevens and Herman Shumlin, in association with Nelson Morris and Randolph Hale; A drama by Robert Thom, based on Barnaby Conrad's novel Dangerfield; Director, Herman Shumlin; Settings and lighting, Howard Bay; Costumes, Edith Lutyens Bel Geddes; Production assistant, Raymond A. League; General manager, Victor Samrock; Company manager, Robert Alex Baron; Stage managers, Michael Thoma, Joseph Brownstone
    Franchot Tone (Winston Sawyer); Richard Jordan (David Sawyer); Lois Smith (Lucha Moreno); Ron Leibman (Rip Calabria); Leona Powers (Phoebe Fletcher); Paul McGrath (Victor); Lulumae Hubbard (Elizabeth); John Marriott (Austin); Leslie Redford (Basil); Barbara Mostel (Sally Dawn); John Boruff (Bentley); Guy Repp (Chandler); Violet Dunn (Miriam Cooper Clyde, known as Mrs. Tiggy-Winkle)

    Legendary, aging, alcoholic, prize-winning novelist Winston "Brick" Sawyer has composed his "homey" acceptance speech in anticipation of receiving the prestigious British Shavian Award for his latest novel. Adding to Sawyer's frustrations is the antagonistic reunion, after many years, with his 22-year-old son, David, and the unexpected arrival of his 26-year-old mistress, actress Lucha Moreno, who hoped to ease the trauma to volatile Sawyer should his anti-Catholic novel, The Prelate, fail. Sawyer's friends, aware of the physical and creative decline of the once-celebrated author and chronicler of his era, who mirrored regional foibles and pretentions of America, gather in his Santa Barbara home to celebrate the publication of his first book in nine years. The reviews of The Prelate are devastating. Nervously sober for several years, alcoholic Sawyer returns to drinking and vents his rage on his friends. Realizing that his pretense of continued creative writing has been revealed and becoming aware of the mutual attraction of his son and young mistress, Sawyer then learns he did not receive the Shavian award. He collapses and dies.

    "This script purported to be based on the antics of an alcoholic, prize-winning novelist. In the event that audiences should not catch on that the hero was Sinclair 'Red' Lewis, the character was nicknamed 'Brick.' Audiences caught on all too fast with the result that the opening night also turned out to be the closing" (Theatre Arts). Howard Taubman (The New York Times) reported, "For one searing scene at the end of the second act Bicycle Ride to Nevada looks, sounds and behaves like drama. The rest of the evening it is, like its principal figure, a hollow shell," adding, "One wishes one could welcome Bicycle Ride to Nevada more warmly, for its aspirations are as honorable as they are serious."

    British author George Dangerfield, winner of the 1953 Pulitzer Prize for History for The Era of Good Feelings, his study of the administrations of James Monroe and John Quincy Adams (which also won Columbia University's 1953 Bancroft prize for "distinguished writing in American History") had given his friend Barnaby Conrad permission to use his name as the title of his novel based on Sinclair Lewis. Prior to the start of rehearsals for the play at the Ethel Barrymore Theatre on August 21, 1963, Dangerfield protested his name being used for the dramatization. The Sawyer character in the play, hopelessly striving to get himself in shape, furiously pedals an immobile cycle, claiming he could "ride it to Nevada." Playwright Robert Thom, who had spent eight months adapting Conrad's novel Dangerfield, retitled his drama Bicycle Ride to Nevada, which played nine performances in New Haven prior to opening on Broadway.

The New Haven Register critic reported, "The author's spiritual bicycle ride to Nevada, taken in a sweat suit on an exercise cycle, remains monotonously alcohol-scented and full of dramatic huffing and puffing." Sam Zolotow's New Haven prediction was "It is going to take considerable pedaling to keep Bicycle Ride to Nevada on Broadway, if it ever gets there." The symbolic pedaling lasted only one performance at a loss of $178,000.

Author Barnaby Conrad was, for a short time in 1947, secretary to the literary firebrand Sinclair Lewis. Conrad's novel Dangerfield, "A Novel About a Great American Author" published by Harper and Brothers in 1961, was reviewed by V. P. Hass (Chicago Sunday Tribune, October 15, 1961): "Conrad, of course, does not identify Lewis, but the flaming red hair, the ugly pockmarked face, the endless mimicry, the iconoclastic novels, and the alcoholism of his Dangerfield coupled with his own intimate association with Lewis leave little doubt." William Hogan (San Francisco Chronicle), having greatly admired Mark Schorer's recent definitive biography of Sinclair Lewis, felt that "Conrad made a mistake on this brief and always predictable story. It was a good idea that simply did not come off."

Unfortunately, neither did Robert Thom's play Bicycle Ride to Nevada.

* * *

BILLY (Billy Rose Theatre, March 22, 1969). Produced by Bruce W. Stark, in association with Joseph Shoctor; A musical suggested by Herman Melville's Billy Budd; Book by Stephen Glassman; Music and Lyrics, Ron Dante and Gene Allan; Settings, Ming Cho Lee; Lighting, Martin Aronstein; Costumes, Theoni V. Aldredge; Director, Arthur A. Seidelmann; Musical sequences staged by Grover Dale; Orchestrations, Ronald Frangipane; Dance music arranged by Coleridge Perkinson; Incidental music and special arrangements by Wally Harper; Associate designer, Leigh Rand; Production assistants, Ellen Young, Kate Draper; Sound, Admins, Ltd.; A Vanark Enterprise, Ltd. Production; Musical director, Jack Lee; Company manager, Peter Neufield; Stage managers, Tom Porter, Frank Rembach, Simm Landres, Pascual

Vaquer
  Robert Salvio (Billy Budd); Laurence Naismith (Captain Edward
  Vere); John Beal (Dansker); Dolph Sweet (Whiskers); William
  Countryman (Lt. William Radcliffe); John Devlin (John Claggart,
  Master-at-Arms); Michael Tartel (Lt. Roger Mordant); Alan Weeks
  (Boscombe); Simm Landres (Cpl. John Bernard); Igors Gavon
  (Boyer); Al Cohen (Gilbert); Peter De Maio (Donald Taff); Danny
  Carroll (Rawley); Joseph Dellasorte (John Thorp); Barbara Monte
  (Molly); Bill Schustik (Stafford); Pascual Vaquer (Fallon); Howard
  Girven (Smithy); Laried Montgomery (Stoker); Steven Boockvor
  (Rush); Christopher Chadman (Potter); Michael Peters (Roper);
  Tim Ramirez (Marsten); Ron Tassone (Harker); Frank DeSal (Seeger); DeWayne Oliver (Grimer); Laried Montgomery, Danny Villa
  (Marine Corporals); George Marcy (Campbell)
SONGS: Chanty; Molly; Watch Out for Claggart; Work; Shaking
Hands with the Wind; Billy; Whiskers' Dance; It Ain't Us Who Make
the Wars; The Bridge to Nowhere; In the Arms of a Stranger; The
Night and the Sea; My Captain; The Fiddlers' Green; Requiem;
Afraid; There in the Dark. (Original Cast Album--ABC Records)

Handsome, uneducated, guileless Billy Budd is assigned as a
seaman to the Royal Navy frigate H.M.S. Indomitable, engaged in
warfare with Napoleon's French fleet in 1798. Sadistic master-at-
arms John Claggart, hated by the crew, resents the crew's affection
for virtuous Billy and is enraged by the favorable impression the
young seaman has made on the ship's officers. Claggart unjustly
accuses Billy of inciting mutiny and ridicules Billy's nervous stutter
and inarticulation in defending the charge. Billy hits Claggart and
kills him. Officers and crew feel Billy was justified in hitting Claggart
but the naval code demands a court-martial trial. Although aware of
Claggart's treachery and sympathetic to Billy, Captain Edward Fair-
fax Vere strictly adheres to British Naval Law and, against his own
moral beliefs and concept of justice, sentences Billy Budd to be hanged
for hitting a superior officer. Captain Vere is completely unnerved
when Billy, trying to prevent a possible mutiny before his hanging,
cries out, "God bless Captain Vere!"

Billy, claimed Clive Barnes (The New York Times), "had honest
aspirations, but although it tried hard, it sank with all hands--a victim of under-intelligence and sub-achievement." Stephen Glassman's
adaptation was viewed as reducing Melville's original story "to the
level of pulp adventure" and "If the book is unfair to Melville, the
music and lyrics positively insult his genius. They are graffiti on
the wall of literature" and "Billy is the perfect example of the axiom
that nothing kills a show so effectively as lack of talent." Edwin
Newman (NBC-TV) said "Take it all in all, Billy is a compelling piece
of theatre."

Richard Watts, Jr. (New York Post) wrote, "The difficulty with
Billy is that it is a noisy and physically energetic musical drama in
which the sound and fury signify virtually nothing" and he felt the

original work had been "tickered and scuttled" by author Stephen Glassman, who "merely managed to flatten out all the dramatic possibilities inherent in the conflict and make it almost meaningless." John Chapman (Daily News) considered Billy a brave show for Broadway" and although billed as a musical, "a long one-act tragic opera." Leonard Harris (WCBS-TV) reported, "It starts as a handsome musical, but handsome is as handsome does, and Billy doesn't."

Billy, performed without intermission, had seven previews and one performance.

In 1949 Louis O. Coxe and Robert Chapman adapted Herman Melville's posthumously published 1924 novella, Billy Budd, Foretopman, as a two-act play titled Uniform of Flesh, which was produced by the Experimental Theatre under the sponsorship of the American National Theatre and Academy at the Lenox Hill Playhouse in New York on January 29, 1949, for seven performances. Chandler Cowles and Anthony B. Farrell produced a revised version of the play, retitled Billy Budd, at the Biltmore Theatre on February 19, 1951.

Melville's tale of a confrontation between a paragon of virtue and the vindictive purveyor of evil was based on an incident that occurred in the nineteenth-century American navy. Brooks Atkinson (The New York Times) reported, "Mr. Coxe and Mr. Chapman have written an extraordinarily skillful play." John Chapman (Daily News) compared the Melville tale to a tragic H.M.S. Pinafore, dismissing it with "I thought Billy was silly," whereas William Hawkins (World-Telegram) considered the play, "an absorbing work, with its share of wry humor, and is unquestionably memorable theatre." John McClain (Journal-American) disliked the drama and "was bored with golden-boy Billy Budd's staunch preoccupation with holiness."

Composer Benjamin Britten was commissioned by the Arts Council of Great Britain to compose an opera based on Billy Budd, which premiered at the Royal Opera House, Convent Garden in London, on December 1, 1951, with Theodor Uppman in the title role and Peter Pears as Captain Vere. The first performance of Britten's opera in America was NBC's television production aired on October 19, 1952, and the opera's American stage debut was at Bloomington, Indiana, on December 5, 1952.

In 1962 Peter Ustinov produced, directed, and, with De Witt Bodeen and Robert Rossen, adapted to the screen the Coxe-Chapman stage version of Melville's story, with Terence Stamp as Billy Budd and Peter Ustinov as Captain Vere. The play was also produced several times for television. CBS's Playhouse of Stars televised the play on January 11, 1952, with Charles Nolte as Billy and Walter Hampden as Captain Vere. Pond's TV Theatre on March 10, 1955, featured Geoffrey Horne as Billy and Luther Adler as Captain Vere. DuPont's Show of the Month's television production of the play on May 25, 1959, had Don Murray as Billy Budd, James Donald as

14 / Billy

Captain Vere, and Alfred Ryder quickly substituted for ill Jason Robards, Jr. as the evil Claggart.

Previous Productions

<u>Uniform of Flesh</u> (Lenox Hill Playhouse, January 29, 1949--7 performances). Produced by the Experimental Theatre under the sponsorship of the American National Theatre and Academy; A play by Louis O. Coxe and Robert H. Chapman, based on Herman Melville's novel <u>Billy Budd</u>; Director, Norris Houghton; Scenery and costumes, Paul Morrison; Musical arrangements and direction, Lehman Engel; Technical director, Howard Jondi; Production consultant, Lincoln Kirstein; Stage manager, John Holden; Assistant stage managers, Everett Dwight, Wynn Handman

> Charles Nolte (Billy Budd); Tom McDermott (Captain Edward Fairfax Vere); Peter Hobbs (John Claggart); Martin Brandt (The Dansker); Anthony Carr (Kincaid); Winston Ross (Philip Michael Seymour); Preston Hanson (Lieutenant Ratcliffe); Robert McQueeney (Lieutenant Wyatt); John Fisher (Gardiner); Everett Dwight (Rea); Carl Shelton (Surgeon); Lee Marvin (Payne); Sherman Lloyd (O'Daniel); Guy Tane (Butler); Wynn Handman (Hallam); Walter Thompson (Messboy); Carl Shelton (Duncan); Ken Sutton (Talbot); Charles Holt (Evans); Curly Schatz (Bugler); Charles Argile (Drummer boy); Paul Anderson (Jenkins); Charles Fade, Peter Ostroff, Allen Schepper (Sailors); Sven Holst, Paul Mario (Tenors); John Salter, Earl Seyfert (Baritones)

<u>Billy Budd</u> (Biltmore Theatre, February 10, 1951--105 performances). Produced by Chandler Cowles and Anthony B. Farrell; Director, Norris Houghton; Scenery, Paul Morrison; Costumes, Ruth Morley; Production associate, Benet Segal; General manager, Paul Groll; Stage managers, Ben Margulies, William Armitage

> Charles Nolte (Billy Budd); Dennis King (Captain Edward Fairfax Vere); Torin Thatcher (John Claggart); James Daly (succeeded by Judson Pratt) (Talbot); Jeff Morrow (Jenkins); Lee Marvin (Hallam); Guy Spaull (Philip Michael Seymour); George Fells (The Dansker); Bertram Tanswell (Jackson); Leonard Yorr (Butler); Kenneth Paine (Kincaid); Judson Pratt (succeeded by Charles Carshon) (Payne); Walter Burke (O'Daniel); Charles Hudson (Messboy); Bernard Kates (Squeak); Robert McQueeney (Duncan); Winston Ross (Surgeon); Jack Manning (Gardiner); Henry Garrard (Rea); Preston Hanson (John Ratcliffe); Norman Ettlinger (Bordman Wyatt); Charles Carshon (succeeded by Robert Dudley) (Stoll); Martin Brandt (Byron); David Long (Drummer); Robert Dudley (succeeded by Bill Froelich) (Sailor); Bill Froelich (Sailor)

Opera

<u>Billy Budd</u> (Covent Garden, London, December 1, 1951). Produced by Basil Coleman; Composer, Benjamin Britten; Libretto (based on Herman Melville's novel), E. M. Forster, Eric Crozier; Designer,

John Piper; Musical conductor, Benjamin Britten; Chorus master, Douglas Robinson; Vocal score, Erwin Stein; Covent Garden orchestra leader, Thomas Matthews

    Theodor Uppman (Billy Budd); Peter Pears (Captain Vere); Frederick Dalberg (Claggart); Hervey Alan (Mr. Redburn); Geraint Evans (Mr. Flint); Michael Langdon (Lt. Ratcliffe); Anthony Marlowe (Red Whiskers); Bryan Drake (Donald); Inia Te Wiata (Dansker); William McAlpine (Novice); David Tree (Squeak); Ronald Lewis (Bosun); Rhydderch Davies (First Mate); Hubert Littlewood (Second Mate); Emlyn Jones (Maintop); John Cameron (Novice's Friend); Alan Hobson (Arthur Jones); Peter Flynn (Cabin Boy); Brian Ettridge, Kenneth Nash, Peter Spencer, Colin Waller (Four Midshipmen)

<u>Billy Budd</u> (Metropolitan Opera House, New York, March 31, 1979). Produced and directed by John Dexter; Designed by William Dudley; Lighting, Gil Wechsler; Conductor, Raymond Leppard; Chorus Master, David Stivender; Assistant stage directors, Brian Gray, Bruce Donnell; Musical preparation, Donald Foster, William Vandice; Prompter, William Vandice

    Richard Stilwell (Billy Budd); Peter Pears (Captain Vere); James Morris (Claggart); Peter Glossop (Redburn); David Ward (Mr. Flint); John Cheek (Lt. Ratcliffe); Robert Nagy (Red Whiskers); Andrew Foldi (Dansker); James Atherton (Novice); Andrea Velis (Squeak); Morley Meredith (Bosun); Andrew Smith (First Mate); Gene Boucher (Second Mate); John Carpenter (Maintop); John Davies (Novice's Friend); Nico Castel (Arthur Jones); Scott Rigby (Cabin Boy); Richard Firmin (Gunner's Mate); Hal Roberts (Sailor); Robert Goodloe (Donald); Jeremy Pearce, Mark Freiman, Stephen White, Michael Carter (Midshipmen)

<u>NBC-TV Opera</u> (October 19, 1952) NBC. Produced by Samuel Chotzinoff; Director, Kirk Browning; Associate producer, Charles Polachek; Music director, Peter Herman Adler; Settings, William Molyneaux; Composer, Benjamin Britten

    Theodor Uppman (Billy Budd); Andrew McKinley (Captain Vere); David Williams, Paul Ukena, Robert Holland, Leon Lishner, Kenneth Smith, and Robert Gross

Screen

<u>Billy Budd</u> (released October 30, 1962): Produced by Allied Artists, Executive producer, A. Ronald Lubin; Producer, Director, Peter Ustinov; Screenplay, DeWitt Bodeen, Robert Rossen, Peter Ustinov; Photography, Robert Krasker; Production designer, Don Ashton; Art director, Peter Murton; Costumes, Anthony Mendelson; Assistant directors, Michael Birkett, Claude Watson; Music and music director, Anthony Hopkins; Special effects, George Blackwell; Assistant cameramen, John Harris, Kelvin Pike; Editor, Jack Harris

    Terence Stamp (Billy Budd); Peter Ustinov (Captain Edward Vere); Robert Ryan (John Claggart); Melvyn Douglas (The Dansker);

16 / Blood Red Roses

Ronald Lewis (Jenkins); David McCallum (Lt. Wyatt); John
Neville (Lt. Ratcliffe); Paul Rogers (Lt. Seymour); Lee Montague
(Squeak); Thomas Heathcote (Payne); Ray McAnally (O'Daniel);
Robert Brown (Talbot); John Meillon (Kincaid); Cyril Luckham
(Hallam); Neil MacGinnis (Captain Graveling); Victor Brooks, Barry
Keegan (Seamen)

Television

Playhouse of Stars (January 11, 1952) CBS: Produced and directed
by William H. Brown, Jr.; Television adaptation of the play by Louis
O. Coxe and Robert H. Chapman by Don Ettinger; Settings, Al Os-
trander; Music, Glen Osser
    Charles Nolte (Billy Budd); Walter Hampden (Captain Vere); Peter
    Hobbs (Claggart); Wolfe Barzell (Dansker); Guy Spaull (Philip
    Michael Seymour)

Pond's Theatre (March 10, 1955) ABC
    Geoffrey Horne (Billy Budd); Luther Adler (Captain Edward Vere);
    Joseph Wiseman (John Claggart)

DuPont Show of the Month (May 25, 1959) CBS: Director, Robert
Mulligan; Television adaptation, Jacqueline Babbin and Audrey Gellen;
Settings, Bob Wade; Produced by David Susskind
    Don Murray (Billy Budd); James Donald (Captain Edward Vere);
    Alfred Ryder (replaced Jason Robards, Jr.) (John Claggart);
    Roddy McDowall (Squeak); Eric Berry (Seymour); Thayer David
    (Ratcliffe); George Ebeling (Dansker); Tim O'Connor (Jenkins);
    James Valentine (Wyatt); Tom Clancy (Talbot); John McLiam (Kin-
    caid); Pat Malone (O'Daniel); Robert Blossom (Jackson)

* * *

BLOOD RED ROSES (John Golden Theatre, March 22, 1970). Pro-
duced by Seymour Vall and Louis S. Goldman in association with Rick
Mandell and Bjorn T. Swanstrom; A musical comedy with Book and
Lyrics by John Lewin; Music, Michael Valenti; Director, Alan Schnei-
der; Settings, Ed Wittstein; Lighting, Tharon Musser; Costumes,
Deidre Cartier; Musical numbers staged by Larry Fuller; Musical
director, Milton Setzer; Orchestrations, Julian Stein and Abba Bogin;
Production assistant, Wendy Chernis; Assistant director, Joan Thorne;
Assistants to producers, Maggie Vall, Janet Burton; Company mana-
ger, Paul Groll; Stage managers, Richard Thayer, Louis Pulvino
    Sydney Walker (Fitzroy Somerset, Lord Raglan, Commander-in-
    Chief); Jeanie Carson (Alice Crabbe, a bawd; Florence Nightin-
    gale; Queen Victoria); Ronald Drake (Prince Albert); Jess Rich-
    ards (Pvt. William Cockcroft); Philip Bruns (Pvt. John Smalls);
    Jay Gregory (W. H. Russell, London Times); Charles Abbott
    (Russian Soldier); Lowell Harris (Cornet Edwin May); William Tost,
    Bill Gibbens (Grenadier Guards)
SONGS: The Cream of English Youth; A Garden in the Sun; Song

of How Mucked Up Things Are; Song of Greater Britain; Black Dog Rum; In the Country Where I Come From; The English Rose; Soldiers' Prayer; Blood Red Roses; The Fourth Light Dragoons; Song of the Fair Dissenter Lass

    Blood Red Roses was a plotless musical. A program note indicated that "Like World War I and America's Vietnam adventure, the Crimean War was a triumph of futility and brutalization. Its inept conduct and questionable purpose were opposed by the editor of the London Times and his able correspondent, William Howard Russell. The aristocratic military establishment in England was headed by such figures as Lord Raglan, the political establishment by hawks such as Lord Palmerston and by the Queen and Prince Albert. Conservatism was firmly entrenched in spite of the efforts of such mildly revolutionary groups as the Chartists. The Crimean War is best remembered for the charge of the Light Brigade and the work of Florence Nightingale at the Scutari base hospital."

    Brendan Gill (The New Yorker) suggested offering a prize to Blood Red Roses as "the most unlikely theatrical enterprise of the year" calling the musical "the most ineptly written show of the year" and playwright/lyricist John Lewin, "simply a bad writer." Clive Barnes (The New York Times) called Blood Red Roses "a very bloodthirsty entertainment" which was closer "to Carnaby Street than mid-Victorian England" and felt the author had not "done a great deal of historical research on the project."

    The symbolic futility and stupidity of war had been given a more satirical treatment in George S. Kaufman's innovative book, set to music by George Gershwin with lyrics by his brother Ira, called Strike Up the Band, which opened on September 5, 1927, in Philadelphia, Pa., and closed there on September 17, 1927. Morrie Ryskind revised Kaufman's book and the musical was recast. Strike Up the Band opened at the Times Square Theatre on Broadway on January 14, 1930. Six years later Paul Green's fantastic fable of World War I, Johnny Johnson, with a musical score by Kurt Weill, was a succès d'éstime when produced by the Group Theatre at the 44th Street Theatre on November 19, 1936.

    The progression of the questionable delights and blatant horror of war reached its apex in England's musical satire Oh! What a Lovely War, compiled by the Theatre Workshop in a treatment adapted from the British radio show The Long, Long Trail. The World War I satire was originally produced at Stratford on March 19, 1963, and Oh! What a Lovely War enjoyed a great success when it opened at London's Wyndham's Theatre on June 20, 1963, for a run of 507 performances. David Merrick and Gerry Raffles presented Joan Littlewood's English production of Oh! What a Lovely War on Broadway at the Broadhurst Theatre on September 30, 1964, for 125 performances.

    The Crimean War had been dramatized in many and varied forms in the theatre and in motion pictures. Reginald Berkeley's drama Lady With a Lamp opened at London's Garrick Theatre in January 1929, featuring Edith Evans as Florence Nightingale, for 176 performances but transferred to Broadway at the Maxine Elliott Theatre on November 19, 1931. Miss Evans and the play departed after twelve performances. Lytton Strachey's biography of Nurse Nightingale was disastrously filmed by Warner Brothers-First National as The White Angel in 1936, starring Kay Francis. Eric Linklater's English comedy Crises in Heaven, produced and directed by John Gielgud, with decor by Cecil Beaton, at London's Lyric Theatre on May 10, 1944, featured Josephine Middleton as Florence Nightingale with little success.

Fascination with the Battle of Balaklava and the charge "into the valley of death" by "the brave 600" of Lord Cardigan's Light Brigade on October 25, 1853, was the subject of several motion pictures, beginning with Thomas A. Edison's 1912 short film The Charge of the Light Brigade. Sono Art-World Wide Pictures produced The Charge of the Light Brigade (also known as Jaws of Hell) in 1931 and Alfred Lord Tennyson's epic poem was again the basis for Warner Brothers 1936 motion picture The Charge of the Light Brigade. Great Britain's 1968 Woodfall production of The Charge of the Light Brigade, directed by Tony Richardson, attempted to record the true history of the Crimean War and, although it was more historically and politically accurate, the American version in 1936 starring Errol Flynn was far more exciting. The 1968 British Crimean Brigade saga was the fifth film released in England dealing with the events at Balaklava.

Richard Attenborough's 1969 film version of Oh! What a Lovely War, adapted to the screen by Len Deighton, featured the elite of Britain's stage and screen but did not recapture the sardonic bite of the stage production. British critic David Wilson singled out the film's finale with its "stunning visual metaphor for a wasted generation. A pastiche of Jerome Kern's 'They Didn't Believe Me' fades from the soundtrack as the camera slowly pulls away from a hillside to reveal an infinity of white crosses." Wilson correctly described the variance between the successful stage production and the overblown film version which, although retaining the general format of the stage presentation, lost "the hard, simple anger of the original" and was replaced by "an elaborate charade."

A year after Attenborough's Oh! What a Lovely War, John Lewin's caustic cantata caroling the bloodthirsty waste of war--Blood Red Roses (which was originally titled The Blood of an Englishman)-- appeared. The $175,000 production of Blood Red Roses was top-priced at $9.50 with drastically reduced prices for its nine previews. Producer Seymour Vall had little luck with war plays. In March of the previous year his production of Roger O. Hirson's comedy World War 2½ at Off-Broadway's Martinique Theatre sustained 13 previews and one performance.

The subject of man's inhumanity to man has been given wide

coverage for centuries in both theatre and literature, but George Santayana's prediction that unless we learn from history we shall be forced to repeat it never has registered with world powers nor most of their subjects. Blood Red Roses did not advance the cause with its caricatured characters and, with all due respect to Mr. Santayana, will not, it is hoped, be repeated.

* * *

BREAK A LEG (Palace Theatre, April 29, 1979). Produced by Stephen R. Friedman, Irwin Meyer, and Kenneth D. Laub in association with Arthur Mogull, Jerold J. Rubinstein, and Warner Plays, Inc.; A comedy by Ira Levin; Director, Charles Nelson Reilly; Scenery, Peter Larkin; Lighting, Marc B. Weiss; Costumes, Theoni V. Aldridge; Production assistant, Chip Neufeld; Technical coordinator, Arthur Siccardi; Wardrobe, Warren Morrill; Assistant director, Timothy Helgeson; Production associate, Claire Nichtern; Hairstylist, Ray Iagnocoo; Producer's assistants, Ellen Segal, Wendy Harris; General managers, R. Tyler Gatchell, Jr., Peter Neufeld; Stage managers, Peter Lawrence, Fred Chalfy, James Wooley; Company manager, James G. Mennen

Julie Harris (Gertie Kessel, an actress); Rene Auberjonois (Johann Schiml, a critic); Jack Weston (Dietrich Merkenschrift, a theatrical manager); David Margulies (Imre Laszlo, a playwright); Michael Connolly (Pepi Lubauer, a scenic designer); Joseph Leon (Freitag, Merkenschrift's assistant); Patricia O'Connell (Mitzi Karlowe, a singing sweetheart/Cleaning woman/Wardrobe mistress/Usher/Actress); James Cahill (Carlo Mizzi, a singing sweetheart/Coachman/Usher/Actor/Painter); Timothy Lewis (Stagehand/Actor); Natalie Norwick (Actress)

"Long ago in Vienna, or Berlin, or Prague, or Buda-Pesth. Anyway it's not New York and not now" but somewhere in Mittel-Europe at the turn of the century, pompous and narcissistic, vitriolic critic Johann Schiml's savage review of actress Gertie Kessel's performance as Ophelia recommended that she follow Hamlet's advice and hie herself to a nunnery. After Gertie spends a year in self-imposed exile, producer Merkenschrift persuades her to leave the nunnery and use her talent and womanly wiles to seduce the despised critic in retaliation for egocentric Schiml's constantly slashing reviews. Using a script prepared by inept playwright Laszlo, Gertie unfortunately falls in love with the acerbic critic and marries him. Gertie also discovers that the critic is highly vulnerable to personal criticism. Merkenschrift enlists the services of other actors damned in print by Schiml to read playwright Laszlo's caustic lines. Disguised as ordinary citizens, they damn Schiml within his hearing. The deluded, sensitive critic rabidly records every critical and vicious remark made about him until he loses his mind.

One of many theatrical superstitions is the opening-night ersatz euphemistic advice to "Break a Leg" for fear of disaster by wishing a player "Good Luck"! Ira Levin's comedy Break a Leg, reputedly based on the character of New York magazine's dreaded critic John Simon plus another "in" gag created by casting, as the comedy's playwright actor David Margulies--which happens to be the real name of producer David Merrick--needed all the good luck it could muster. It was, claimed Glenne Currie (United Press International), "By far the worst play of the season, also the worst waste of talent in years."

Clive Barnes (New York Post) added, "To suggest that Break a Leg needs a splint would be to offer it an unjustifiable hope of recovery. Even wholesale surgery could not help its terminal case of mediocrity--The sheer ineptitude of the play is quite astonishing-- The characters are cartoons, the writing feeble, and the situations only intermittently diverting. It should never have come to Broadway." Richard Eder (The New York Times) reported, "Ira Levin has written a comedy about a critic who finds fault with everything, and in this case, I'm afraid there's nothing for it but to step right into the role. Break a Leg has one large funny joke in the first act, and one little but appealing joke in the second."

Following native-born New Yorker Ira Levin's first play, a hilarious adaptation of Mac Hyman's novel No Time for Sergeants, which opened on October 20, 1955, and closed September 15, 1957, after 798 performances, and his 1960 delightfully successful comedy Critic's Choice which completed 189 performances, he experienced five straight flops: Interlock (1958); General Seeger (1962); Drat! The Cat (1965); Dr. Cook's Garden (1967); and Veronica's Room in 1973. Levin's thrilling play Deathtrap opened on February 26, 1978, and closed on June 13, 1982, completing 1,793 performances. His best-selling novels, transferred to the screen, include Rosemary's Baby, The Stepford Wives, and The Boys from Brazil. Break a Leg, described at its best as "witless, clumsy and offensive," was a failed farce.

Ira Levin wrote Break a Leg in one month during 1974. The 1979 production of the farce was tested at the American Shakespeare Theatre at Stratford, Connecticut, on April 3, 1979, and, after twelve previews at Broadway's Palace Theatre, it opened and closed there on April 29, 1979, at a loss of approximately $425,000. Charles Nelson Reilly, who had increased the laughter level on Broadway in Bye, Bye, Birdie, Hello, Dolly, How to Succeed in Business Without Even Trying, and Skyscraper, won praise for his direction of Julie Harris as poet Emily Dickinson in William Luce's solo-comedy Belle of Amherst and also staged Phillip Hayes Dean's mono-drama Paul Robeson starring James Earl Jones in 1978. Reilly resigned from directing his first large-cast production, Break a Leg, prior to the Broadway opening, replaced by Frank Dunlap.

Levin's farce had originally been produced by U.R.G.E.N.T. Theatre (15th floor of 151 West 46th Street) in May of 1974. Directed by Sheldon Patinkin, the experimental tryout of Break a Leg had the

following cast:
  Barbara Dana (Gertie Kessel, leading actress); Timothy D. Lewis (Johann Schiml, a critic); Paul Dooley (Dietrich Merkenschrift, a producer); Frank Bongiorno (Lazzlo, a playwright); Richard Manheim (Pepi Lubauer); Martin Harvey Friedberg (Freitag, a producer's assistant); Linda Russell (Mitzi Karlowe); Glenn Zeitler (Carlo Mitzi) (The Singing Sweethearts); Christopher Camille Walsh, Linda Chase (Stagehands); Richard Fay (An Inventor)

* * *

THE BRIDAL CROWN (Vanderbilt Theatre, February 5, 1938). Produced by Experimental Theatre, Inc., (Peggy Fears, Felix Rolo, and Nathan Zatkin); A drama by August Strindberg based on Edwin Bjorkman's translation; Director, Andrius Jilinsky; Settings, Eugene Dunkel; Costumes and Marionettes by Stasy Uskinsky; Madame Balieff, Mary Towner, and the New York Players Workshop
  Aurora Bonney (Kersti); Dehner Forkum (Mats); Aletta Stever (Midwife-Witch); Anne Gerlette (Mother of Kersti); Richard Kronold (The Grandfather); Jane MacDwyer (The Grandmother); Wesley Towner (The Father); Sylvia Blumberg (The Mother); Marion Rahill (Brita); Elizabeth Edwards (Anna); Rosalind Carter (Lit-Karen); Mildred Loscht (Lit-Mats); Sey Bochner (Stig Matsson); Willard Duckworth (The Verger); Alexander McLaughlin (The Soldier); Edith Charles, Lilian Walden, Jeanne Fagen, Adela Engel (The Bridesmaids); Nikita Soussanin (The Pastor); Alexander Basset (The Wanderer); Lee Kresel (The Headsman); Arthur H. Menkin (The Guard); Ralph Portnow, David Slayton, Anita Haas, Martha Mattey, Henry Shereshefsky (Kersti's Relatives); Lee Kresel, Ralph Norton, Harold Heifer, Leah Margulies, May Bolhower (Mats' Relatives); Raymond Brown (The Voice of the Water Spirit); Karen Johnston (The Voice of the Child in White); Mildred Loscht (The Voice of the Mocker); Leafie Wilbur, Anne Martin, Masha Pankevich, Karen Johnston (The Servants)

Kersti gives her illegitimate child by Mats to a midwife-witch in return for a bridal crown worn only by virgins at their wedding. After Kersti and Mats are married, Kersti tosses her bridal crown into a millrace. A search is made for the crown but only the drowned body of Kersti's bastard child is found. Banished to an island, Kersti is persecuted until she dies.

Pupils of Andrius Jilinsky's New York Players Workshop paraded their training for critical scrutiny in Swedish dramatist Strindberg's arty fable. The Bridal Crown made its Broadway debut but it was best left to more experienced professionals or in the repertory of Europe's art theatres. "Although Mr. Jilinsky's pupils give it a respectable student performance, they give it nothing more. For it is plain that the fable and mood of Strindberg's tone poem are foreign to their experience," wrote Brooks Atkinson (The New York Times).

* * *

BRIGHTOWER (John Golden Theatre, January 28, 1970). Produced by Michael Byron and Mel Weiser; A drama by Dore Schary; Director, Mel Weiser; Settings, Tom Munn; Lighting, John Gleason; Costumes, Noel Taylor; Production assistant, Sally Goldwater; Hairstylist, Kenneth; Produced by B/W Productions; General manager, Richard Seader; Stage managers, Harry Young, Andy M. Rasbury
    Robert Lansing (Daniel Brightower); Geraldine Brooks (Sara Brightower); Paul McGrath (Nick Hagen); Will Hussung (Jess); Arlen Dean Snyder (Clay Benson); Martha Galphin (Lori Granger); Richard Buck (Bill Canfield)

    Legendary author Daniel Brightower, winner of three Pulitzer Prizes, has led a hard-drinking, hell-raising, womanizing, and adventurous life. Aware he is losing his mind, Brightower commits suicide by leaping from a mountain cliff. His widow, Sara, considers the arrival of Brightower's eager Biographer, Clay Benson, at their remote Vermont home as an invasion of privacy. Encouraged by the friendship and understanding of publisher Nick Hagen, Sara refuses to cooperate with Benson to supply personal data for his proposed definitive biography. Sara prefers to preserve the fiction of her famous husband's death as accidental.

    Dore Schary's success as a playwright was rewarded with a 1958 Tony Award for his superb play based on the early life of Franklin Delano Roosevelt, Sunrise at Campobello. Schary's play Banderol, which dramatized the behind-the-scenes power struggle between Louis B. Mayer and Nicholas Schenck and associates for control of the Metro-Goldwyn-Mayer studio in Hollywood, opened and closed in Philadelphia in September 1962. Brightower was obviously based on the final days and ultimate suicide of novelist Ernest Hemingway. Beyond the Hemingway reference, Brightower utilized the same theme as Ida Alexa Ross Wylie's novel Keeper of the Flame and Diana Morgan's play The Starcross Story (first performed in England as After My Fashion).

    Clive Barnes (The New York Times) found that "The structure of the play is a strangely mottled affair" and "The writing takes mediocrity to new heights and depths of levelness." Barnes considered the acting only slightly better than the play, adding, "If you want to know why serious drama is dying on Broadway, take Brightower as an object lesson. Its pompous noodle is filled with illusions of artistry, and its quality of writing wouldn't make an agony column." Emory Lewis (The Record) described Brightower as "a bland, old-fashioned, static and dull preachment," and William Glover (Associated Press) claimed "Brightower constantly promises more than it delivers, and that is just too bad." Leonard Harris (CBS-TV) recorded, "The story outline of Dore Schary's new play is not bad. The play is a failure." Edwin Newman (NBC-TV) said, "Brightower is Hemingway, or a reasonable facsimile. Dore Schary's play about him is interesting without being very good." Brendan Gill (The New Yorker) found

Brightower "was intended to be a neatly dovetailed little bandbox of a play [but] became, instead, an all too commodious coffin."

* * *

BROADWAY FOLLIES (Nederlander Theatre, March 15, 1981). Produced by Edgar Lansbury, Joseph Beruh, and James Nederlander; Concept and direction by Donald Driver; Music and lyrics, Walter Marks; Choreography, Arthur Faria; Scenery, Peter Larkin; Lighting, Roger Morgan; Costumes, Alvin Colt; Sound, Abe Jacob; Musical direction, vocal and dance arrangements, Marvin Laird; Orchestrations, Bill Byers; Talent coordinator, Gilbert Miller; Production supervisor, Robert Straus; Directorial assistant, Nina Faso; Production assistants, Kim Larimore, John Nassivera; General manager, Marvin K. Krauss; Wardrobe, Peter J. FitzGerald; Assistant to producers, Darrell Jonas; Hairstylists, Joe Tubens, Calvin Trahan; Stage managers, John Actman, Joel Tropper
    Robert Shields, Lorene Yarnell, Tessie O;Shea, Michael Allen Davis, Milo and Roger, Los Malambos, Gaylord Maynard and Chief Bearpaw, Scott's Royal Boxers (Principals); Stephen Bourneuf, Kitty Kuhn, Mark Martino, Nancy Meadows, Brad Miskell, Alice Anne Oakes, Aurelio Padron, R. J. Peters, D'Arcy Phifer, Marh Ruhala, Karen Teti, Suzanne Walker (Singers, Dancers)
NUMBERS: Broadway Follies; Vaudeville; Wonderful U; Piccadilly; The Pampas; The Oasis; The Toyshop; The Paper Bag Rag; The Barnyard; At Home with the Clinkers; The Saloon; Tap My Way to the Stars; The Rest of Michael Davis; Grand Parade

    Broadway Follies was, according to Mel Gussow (The New York Times), "a small brash vaudeville show--an unconnected series of seven vaudeville acts" at which "P. T. Barnum would have blushed at the flimflammery."

    The hit of this pastiche was self-deprecating, dead-pan comic juggler Michael Allen Davis. Tessie O'Shea of the British music halls and several Broadway musicals performed several songs and persuaded the audience to remove paper bags enclosed in the program and play them as banjos to her "Paper Bag Rag." Los Malambos, a trio of bola-swinging gauchos from Argentina; Milo and Roger, a comic magic-act from the Crazy Horse Club in Paris with their duck Spiro; Scott's Royal Boxers from Britain playing a game of ball with balloons; Gaylord Maynard and his well-trained horse, Chief Bearpaw, feigning drunkenness; and top-billed former San Francisco street performers and television mimes Shields and Yarnell, performing five routines backed by a chorus of twelve, comprised the rest of the bill. Other than Michael Davis, who was one of the winners of the 1981 Theatre World Awards, and nostalgic Tessie O'Shea, the acts were considered "limited in talent" and the show not worth "the high-powered, top dollar ticket."

    Robert Shields, born Robert Schildkraut, a cousin to the late, great actor Joseph Schildkraut, briefly studied the art of pantomime with Marcel Marceau in Paris. He first gained recognition as a street performer in 1970 on San Francisco's Union Square where he was frequently arrested as a public nuisance. Shields and Lorene Yarnell, a sister of the late musical-comedy and television actor Bruce Yarnell, were married-in-mime in San Francisco's Union Square. Shields and Yarnell, who had their own television variety show during the summer of 1977 for CBS, made their Broadway debut in Broadway Follies but were not considered sufficiently talented to carry a Broadway show.

Welsh-born (Caerdydd, March 13, 1918) "Two-Ton" Tessie O'Shea was a long-time favorite headliner of the British music halls, and she made her Broadway debut in 1963 as Ada Cockle in Harry Kurnitz's adaptation of Terence Rattigan's comedy The Sleeping Prince, retitled The Girl Who Came to Supper, with music and lyrics by Noel Coward. Tessie O'Shea stopped the show for 112 performances with her zestful singing and dancing of "London is a Little Bit of All Right." Michael Allen Davis, born in San Francisco on August 23, 1953, transferred from Broadway Follies to delight audiences in the long-running smash hit Sugar Babies, starring Mickey Rooney and Ann Miller.

Edgar Lansbury and Joseph Beruh's success with The Magic Show, featuring young Canadian magician Doug Henning, which opened at the Cort Theatre on May 28, 1974, and closed on December 31, 1978, after 1,859 performances, inspired them to substitute vaudeville for magic on Broadway. Broadway Follies had been in the planning stage for five years and Lansbury scouted Europe for the show's talent, but Follies magic evaporated quickly.

That venerable mecca of vaudeville known as the Palace at Broadway and 47th Street opened on March 24, 1913. The last week of two-a-day vaudeville began on July 9, 1932, followed by combining motion pictures with reduced variety acts until ultimately the Palace became a motion picture theatre in November. Undistinguished vaudeville bills attempted a comeback at the Palace in 1949, combined with a minor screen attraction. Only such stars as Judy Garland, in 1951, and another great entertainer, Betty Hutton, intermittently brought a resurgence of interest in what had become a nostalgic-but-doomed phase of show business. In 1953 Danny Kaye brought to the Palace renewed hope for vaudeville's revival, a hope that was increased by Garland's return on November 26, 1956. Jerry Lewis's appearance in 1957 had critics optimistically predicting "vaudeville is not dead," and Harry Belafonte recaptured the Palace's stage with his one-man show from December 1959 until March 1960.

For the next five years, the Palace continued to regress into another seedy Manhattan movie-grind house, until Detroit's Nederlander family became owners of the theatre in August 1965. Under the direction of stage designer Ralph Alswang, James Nederlander beautifully repaired and refurbished the old, decrepit Palace, which reopened as a glowing legitimate theatre on January 29, 1966, with Gwen Verdon starring in the delightful musical comedy Sweet Charity.

James Nederlander was one of the producers of Broadway Follies, which would not have been booked into the Palace during its heyday. The resurrection of vaudeville did occur on television, where variety shows with top talents flourished for several years, until overexposure on competing networks brought about public apathy and disinterest. Theatregoers accustomed to seeing vaudeville in various disguises in their home on television were reluctant to pay $30 to see a less-than-video attraction on Broadway. After fourteen previews, Broadway Follies left the Nederlander Theatre after one performance.

Joe Laurie, Jr. wrote a eulogy for America's once great entertainment in his 1953 history Vaudeville: From the Honky-Tonks to The Palace: "The vaudeville we knew from the turn of the century to 1932 when the Palace closed its stage door and practically tacked up a sign reading 'Vaudeville Dispossessed'; the real, honest, vital vaudeville of the old two-a-day of the Palace (and other big-time vaude) will never return" but he added, "Like reincarnation, vaude will keep coming back in other forms. But big-time vaude is now just a sweet memory." Over the years prior to television, efforts to revive vaudeville, by mounting productions on the Broadway stage featuring former two-a-day name-acts, had meagre runs and were only mildly successful. Beyond television's overproduced variety shows, however, vaudeville remained consigned to Valhalla.

Producers Paul Small and Fred Finklehoffe's program pronouncement for their Broadway vaudeville show Laugh Time at the Shubert Theatre on September 8, 1943, read, "We have never conceded the corpus delicti. We have disbanded the pallbearers, halted the requiem, on the laudable suspicion that Laugh Time will demonstrate that the burial of vaudeville circa 1932 was premature." Laugh Time accumulated 126 performances and included the talents of Frank Fay, Ethel Waters, Bert Wheeler, Buck and Bubbles, and others. Encouraged by the reception of Laugh Time, Small opened his vaudeville show Startime at the Majestic Theatre on September 12, 1944, which featured Lou Holtz, The DeMarcos, Berry Brothers, and Benny Fields for 120 performances.

Frank Fay's Vaudeville opened at the 44th Street Theatre on March 2, 1939, starring perennial master-of-ceremonies Fay, Elsie Janis, Eva Le Gallienne, and Smith and Dale, with tickets priced at 55¢ to $2.20. In 1938 nightclub impressario Clifford C. Fischer's success with an ersatz French vaudeville, Folies Bergere (which would have been stoned in Paris), at San Francisco's Golden Gate International Exposition, prompted him to bring the show to Broadway on December 25, 1939, where it remained at the Broadway Theatre for 121 performances.

Fischer convinced the Messrs. Shubert the time was ripe for the renascence of vaudeville and, with their backing, produced Priorities of '42 at the 46th Street Theatre on March 12, 1942, scaled at $2.00 top in the evening and $1.00 for matinees. The vaudeville program included Willie Howard, Lou Holtz, Phil Baker, Paul Draper, Hazel Scott, and others for an astonishing 353 performances. The unanticipated success of Priorities quickly spawned a second two-a-day unit, called Keep 'Em Laughing, at the 44th Street Theatre on April 24, 1942, headlined by William Gaxton, Victor Moore, Hildegarde, Paul and Grace Hartman, and with Zero Mostel and Jack Cole--tickets at 50¢ to $2.00. Keep 'Em Laughing closed after 77 performances and reopened on May 29, 1942, as Top Notchers, led by Gracie Fields, with Al Trehan, Walter O'Keefe, The Hartmans, Argentinita and others, through 48 showings.

Intrigued with the apparent rebirth of vaudeville, Ed Sullivan and Noble Sissle produced an all-black variety show called Harlem Cavalcade at the Ritz Theatre on May 1, 1942, featuring in the cast Flournoy Miller, Amanda Randolph, Tim Moore, Noble Sissle, and the Delta River Boys. Harlem's entry faded after 49 performances. "The Perfect Fool" Ed Wynn brought his Laugh, Town, Laugh into the Alvin Theatre on June 22, 1942, with the perfect clown Ed Wynn as master of ceremonies to Smith and Dale, Jane Froman, Señor Wences, and Carmen Amaya for 65 performances ticketed at 55¢ to $2.20 on a regular legitimate-theatre performance schedule.

Peripatetic Clifford C. Fischer returned again with his New Priorities of 1943 on September 15, 1942, at the 46th Street Theatre. The bill included Harry Richman, Bert Wheeler, Carol Bruce, Henny Youngman, Hank Ladd, and Harrison & Fisher and there were 54 performances with tickets priced at 50¢ to $2.50. The following night Showtime arrived at the Broadhurst Theatre starring George Jessel, Jack Haley, Ella Logan, and the De Marcos. Showtime played eight performances weekly at a scale of $1.00 to $2.75 and remained for a season's run of 342 performances. Frank Veloz and Yolanda Casazza, advertised as "Veloz and Yolanda, the Lunts of the Dancing World" opened their vaudeville dancing entry, featuring guitarist Vincente Gomez, on February 5, 1942. After eleven performances at the Mansfield Theatre the "Lunts of the Dancing World" departed.

Barbara Walters' father, Lou, produced a variety show, Take a Bow (originally called Slap Happy), at the Broadhurst Theatre on June 15, 1944, starring Chico Marx with Jay C. Flippen, Pat Rooney, and Gene Sheldon for a quick twelve performances. All of these vaudeville extravaganzas had box-office prices comparable to and often less than Broadway's motion picture houses. Nearly four decades later Broadway Follies confronted prospective audiences, already sated with television's variety, with a roster of talents inferior to those of the forties for a top ticket of $27.50 on week nights and $30.00 for weekends. Broadway Follies lost its weekends--in one night.

* * *

A BROADWAY MUSICAL (Lunt-Fontanne Theatre, December 21, 1978).
Produced by Norman Kean and Garth G. Drabinsky; A musical with
Book by William F. Brown; Music, Charles Strouse; Lyrics, Lee
Adams; Director, Gower Champion; Settings, Peter Wexler; Lighting,
John DeSantis; Costumes, Randy Barcelo; Musical conductor, Kevin
Farrell; Assistant conductor, Tim Stella; Orchestrations, Robert M.
Freedman; Musical supervision and vocal arrangements, Donald Pippin;
Dance arrangements, Donald Johnston; Co-choreographer, George
Bunt; Sound, Abe Jacob; Production coordinator, Barbara Mae
Phillips; Associate producer, Maria Di Dia; Production associate, Jacob
Weisbarth; Dance assistant, Calvin McRae; Production assistants,
David Thalenberg, Robert G. Adams; Wardrobe, Toni Baer; Associate
to producer, Arnold Gottlieb; Hairstylist, Ronald DeMann; Assistant
to director, Barry Moss; Associate scenic designer, Hal Tine; Assistant to producer, Connie Dash; Stage managers, Sherry Cohen,
David Rubinstein, Judy Binus
 Warren Berlinger (Eddie Bell); Gwyda DonHowe (Stephanie Bell);
Anne Francine (Shirley Wolfe); Larry Marshall (Richie Taylor);
Patti Karr (Maggie Simpson); Tiger Haynes (Sylvester Lee);
Irving Allen Lee (James Lincoln); Jo Ann Ogawa (Richie's Secretary); Sydney Anderson, Michael Gallagher (Richie Taylor's Lawyers); Alan Weeks (Stan Howard); Larry Riley (Lonnie Paul);
Christina Kumi-Kimball (Kumi-Kumi); Gwen Arment (Rehearsal
Pianist); Reggie Jackson (Louie); Martin Rabbett (Jake); Albert
Stephenson (Big Jake); Robert Melvin (Junior); Nate Barnett
(Nathaniel/Policeman); Maris Clement, Loretta Devine, Jackee Harry
(Smoke and Fire Back-Up Singers); Sydney Anderson, Maris Clement, Loretta Devine (Theatre Party Associates); Albert Stephenson,
Robert Melvin, Martin Rabbett (Male Dancers); Jackee Harry (Melinda Bernard); Sydney Anderson, Gwen Arment; Nate Barnett,
Maris Clement, Prudence Darby, Don Edward Detrick, Loretta
Devine, Sharon Ferrol, Michael Gallagher, Scott Geralds, Maggy
Gorrill, Jackee Harry, Leon Jackson, Reggie Jackson, Carleton
Jones, Christina Kumi-Kimball, Michael Kubala, Robert Melvin,
Jo An Ogawa, Karen Paskow, Martin Rabbett, Albert Stephenson,
Marilynn Winbush, Brad Witsger (Ensemble)
SONGS: Broadway, Broadway; A Broadway Musical; I Hurry Home
to You; Smoke and Fire; Lawyers; Yenta Power; Let Me Sing My Song;
The 1934 Hot Chocolate Jazz Babies Revue; It's Time for a Cheer-Up
Song; You Gotta Have Dancing; What You Go Through; Don't Tell
Me; Together

 Crass, high-pressure Broadway producer Eddie Bell inveigles
young, neophyte, black playwright James Lincoln, from Ohio, into
turning his serious play The Final Point, a basketball locker-room
drama exposing the exploitation of human beings, into an upbeat
black musical called Sneakers. The rehearsals are a shambles, augmented by the temperament of the musical's Las Vegas nightclub star
Richie Taylor and by his brace of lawyers. Bell is low on taste and

lower on financing when Shirley Wolfe's theatre-party bookings are canceled. Sneakers stumbles into Washington, D.C., for a pre-Broadway tryout and the critics savagely destroy it. Obnoxious rock-star Taylor walks out on the show, and desperate producer Bell goads young playwright Lincoln into taking the lead. Lincoln proves to be a sensational performer and Sneakers becomes a sensational hit.

"It is a musical that by its own definition has to pretend to be a flop--and succeeds only too effortlessly," reported Clive Barnes (The New York Post). "A Broadway disaster--We are being shown-- very effectively--the anatomy of a Broadway failure--A grotesquely wrongheaded venture, and one can only feel a decent sympathy for the very talented people who have somehow gotten themselves involved in it." Douglas Watt (Daily News) felt the "season is still in bad need of a Broadway musical--Although William F. Brown's book is impossible, allowing for a cynical line or two, Charles Strouse's score and Lee Adams' lyrics are frequently engaging." Mel Gussow (The New York Times) saw the show as "not so much directed--or written --as glued together from spare parts" and "a framework for a string of slack tunes and show-business wisecracks.... Probably the people who would be most offended by this enterprise are those who continue to be hopeful about the state of the Broadway musicals."

Producer Norman Kean claimed to have caught the idea for A Broadway Musical while watching the auditions for the all-black revival of Frank Loesser's Guys and Dolls in 1976. Playwright William F. Brown had been represented on Broadway in 1967 with four performances of his play The Girl in the Freudian Slip and he provided sketches, dialogue, and continuity to Leonard Sillman's New Faces of 1968. Off-Broadway, Brown's play How to Steal an Election had 89 performances in 1968 but his most successful theatrical venture was adapting L. Frank Baum's The Wonderful Wizard of Oz to the stage as the musical The Wiz, which racked up 1,672 performances.

A Broadway Musical was first tested at the Theatre of the Riverside Church, New York, under the direction of George Faison. Julius La Rosa and Helen Gallagher headed the cast, which included Larry Marshall, Anne Francine, Alan Weeks, Gwyda DonHowe, Ron Ferrell, Larry Riley, Julia Lemae, and others. Director George Faison was replaced by Gower Champion. Julius La Rosa and Helen Gallagher left the cast, and A Broadway Musical, reshaped by Champion, after fourteen previews and an investment of approximately $900,000, gave one performance on Broadway.

Forty-nine-year-old New York composer Charles Strouse and fifty-four-year-old Ohio lyricist Lee Adams had first collaborated on The Shoestring Revue in 1955 and then in The Littlest Revue in 1956. The team's first Broadway success was with Gower Champion's debut as a director of a book musical on April 14, 1960, Bye, Bye, Birdie. Strouse and Adams returned to Broadway on March 19, 1962, with 80 performances of the musical All-American and in 1964 Sammy Davis,

Jr. starred in their musical version of Clifford Odet's play <u>Golden Boy</u>, which ran for 569 performances. <u>It's a Bird--It's a Plane--It's Superman!</u> was set to music by Strouse and Adams in 1966 for a flight of 129 performances. Their greatest success on Broadway was in collaboration with Betty Comden and Adolph Green on 1970's <u>Applause</u>, which scored 896 performances. <u>A Broadway Musical</u> added nothing to their past laurels.

* * *

<u>BROTHERS</u> (Music Box Theatre, November 9, 1983). Produced by Noel Pearson, in association with Orion Television, Inc. and Carnan Productions, Inc.; A drama by George Sibbald; Director, Carroll O'Connor; Setting, Thomas A. Walsh; Lighting, Craig Miller; Costumes, Merrily Murray-Walsh; Technical supervisor, Jeremiah Harris; General managers, Joseph P. Harris, Peter T. Kulok, Steven E. Goldstein; Company manager, Steven H. David; Wardrobe, Anthony Karniewich; Props, Joseph Harris, Jr., Clyde Churchill, Jr.; Production assistant, Roma Friedman; Stage managers, Hugh O'Connor, Bethe Ward
    Carroll O'Connor (Jim); Frank Converse (Harry); Dennis Christopher (Tommy); Pat McNamara (James); Gary Klar (Earl)

    Widowed Scottish immigrant Jim MacMillan installed his four sons as workers in a shipyard where he is the dedicated president of the local union. Son Harry soon left to become a successful lawyer in Boston and perpetual student Earl returned to college in his midthirties to get a teaching degree. Son James is a recovering alcoholic and youngest son, Tommy, is debilitated by a kidney disease, surviving only with dialytic treatments. The family reunites for the Connecticut union's annual Labor Day picnic. Lawyer Harry has agreed to donate a kidney as transplant for his brother Tommy, but he reneges on his promise, rationalizing that since their mother died of kidney failure, it is possible one of his children might one day require the operation, plus he basically dislikes his younger brother. Jim's blustering insistence that brothers should take care of one another and "without the union, we're nothing" fails to alter the situation. Harry returns to his lucrative Boston law practice, Earl to his perpetual studies, and James resumes drinking after years of sobriety. Jim, left alone with Tommy, assures his terminally ill youngest son they will somehow survive.

    Carroll O'Connor, born on Saturday, August 2, 1924, in New York City, gained national fame as the stupid, loudmouth bigot Archie Bunker on Norman Lear's monumentally successful half-hour CBS television comedy series <u>All in the Family</u>, which premiered on January 12, 1971, until it was superseded by <u>Archie Bunker's Place</u> on September 23, 1979. Carroll O'Connor started his acting career with the Abbey Theatre in Dublin in 1950 and later transferred to Hilton Edwards and Micheal MacLiammòir's prestigious Dublin Gate Theatre Company. He first appeared on the New York stage in Burgess Meredith's expertly directed production of Marjorie Barkentin's adaptation of James Joyce's Ulysses in Nighttown at the Off-Broadway Rooftop Theatre on June 5, 1958. In 1960 O'Connor was headed for Broadway in a supporting role in Harry F. Travin's comedy Goodwill Ambassador, but the play closed in Boston on March 26, 1960. Consequently Brothers became Carroll O'Connor's rather brief Broadway debut. [Carroll O'Connor returned to Broadway at the Royale Theatre on January 2, 1985, co-starring with Frances Sternhagen in James Duff's drama Home Front, which received mixed notices and closed on Saturday, January 12, 1985.]

Besides displaying little affection for Sibbald's Brothers, the community of critics also pounced on O'Connor for playing a Scottish character with a pronounced Irish brogue. Douglas Watt (Daily News) reported "Brothers is not what Archie needed--a dreary play about a dreary family--it is hard to see why Carroll O'Connor should have chosen to star in it and, worse, to stage it, for his directorial hand lies stiffly on an already dull script--Better direction would certainly have helped a bit, but better writing was more seriously needed."

Clive Barnes (The New York Post) felt that Brothers was "almost defiantly old-fashioned. It could--dirty language apart--have been written forty years ago--It is a play of machinations and mechanism rather than blood and heartbeat" but he added cryptically, "Yet the play--and O'Connor--are staple Broadway fare." Frank Rich (The New York Times) wrote, "Brothers lacks the one ingredient that was even more crucial than Mr. O'Connor to the success of All in the Family, laughter."

George Sibbald's Brothers had its world premiere at Costa Mesa, California, produced by David Emmes with the following cast: George Murdock (Jim MacMillan); David Ralphe (Harry); Joe Pantoliano (Tommy); Jonathan Terry (James) and Dennis Franz (Earl). Metropolitan Opera employee, Scots-born George Sibbald's other plays include The All-American Sweepstakes; The Dodge Boys; Interstate 76; Nobody Likes Stephen Sondheim West of Tenth Avenue.

Plays titled Brothers have had small success in the theatre, beginning with Publius Terentius' (known as Terence) (185-159 B.C.) The Brothers (also known as Adelphi), while Fyodor Mikhailovitch Dostoievsky's unfinished 1881 novel The Brothers Karamozov was dramatized with only moderate success. Herbert Ashton, Jr.'s 1928 drama Brothers was a possible exception. Ashton's Brothers, dealing with twin brothers played by Bert Lytell for 255 performances on Broadway during the 1928-1929 season, and by Hartley Power in London the following season, was successful. Barry Litvak's 1929 folk-opera Brothers (Frank and Jesse James) never made it to Broadway. Stephen White's Brothers had one performance at Theatre Four in New York on February 13, 1972. Christopher Gore's Brothers failed Off-Broadway but was revised by Gore and set to music by David Spangler as the musical Nefertiti which, Broadway bound, opened and closed in Chicago in 1977. Eric Krebs' drama of sibling rivalry failed in 1977, as did Kathleen Collins' drama of black Brothers in 1982.

And Cain and Abel were never much of a hit.

* * *

CHILDREN! CHILDREN! (Ritz Theatre, March 7, 1972). Produced by Arthur Whitelaw and Seth Harrison in association with Ben Gerard; A thriller by Jack Horrigan; Director, Joseph Hardy; Setting and lighting, Joe Mielziner; Costumes, Ann Roth; Hairstylist, Romaine Greene; Portrait, Stanley Roseman; Producers' assistants, John Clement, Dina Alkalay; Production assistant, Steven Kronovek; General manager, Marvin A. Krauss; Stage managers, Victor Straus, Philip Cusack

Dennis Patrick (Philip Collins); Gwen Verdon (Helen Giles); Elizabeth Hubbard (Evelyn Collins); Elaine Hyman (Peg Yaeger); Josef Sommer (Dr. Karl Yaeger); Shawn Campbell (Mark Collins); Ariane Munker (Susan Collins); Johnny Doran (Bobby Collins)

Wealthy Philip Collins and his wife, Evelyn, join Dr. Karl and Peg Yaeger for a New Year's Eve party, leaving their incorrigible children in the care of babysitter Helen Giles in their luxurious Manhattan home. Helen, recently recovered from a nervous breakdown, is no match for the three diabolic Collins children, who have murdered a former babysitter by frightening her into a fatal heart attack. The children proceed to sadistically torment Helen. One of the young boys makes sexual advances to her and his sister, Susan, attempts a lesbian confrontation. When the children's parents return, Helen hysterically relates the evening's horrors but she is unable to convince them of their children's guilt, discovering that Philip and Evelyn are as vicious as their children when they declare her insane.

Clive Barnes (The New York Times) disclaimed playwright Horrigan's description of Children! Children! as "a thriller," calling it about "as thrilling as cornflakes on fog" with "the blatant monstrosities of this quite insulting play, insulting to the intelligence that is" comparable to the acting which "was so indescribably bad that I do not intend to attempt to describe it." William Glover (Associated Press) recessed Children! Children! as "another Broadway boo-boo." Douglas Watt (Daily News) wrote, "This play by Jack Horrigan is one of the clumsiest attempts at a thriller yet witnessed." Richard Watts (New York Post) considered Children! Children! "a serious disappointment as an evening of spine-tingling" but admired the dramatic debut of Gwen Verdon: "Miss Verdon is a fine actress, and her portrayal of a trapped woman is believable and appealing."

The malevolence of children and their creative, if often psychopathic, mayhem had been well documented in several plays prior and far superior to Children! Children!. Lillian Hellman's taut 1934 drama The Children's Hour and Hagar Wilde and Dale Eunson's 1942

melodrama Guest in the House both examined the havoc wrought by
a pathological young female liar. Edwin Bronner's failed thriller
The Intruder (which closed on the road in 1952) and Maxwell Anderson's absorbing 1954 drama The Bad Seed were studies in the diabolical and murderous behavior of young girls. In 1950, William
Archibald's The Innocents, an adaptation of Henry James's 1898
classic story The Turn of the Screw, dramatized a governess's frantic
efforts to save the souls of two children possessed by the evil spirits
of their late former governess and her dead lover. The only common
bond between Children! Children! and The Innocents is that both were
performed without an intermission.

Forty-seven-year-old Gwen (Gwyneth Evelyn) Verdon became an
established Broadway musical-comedy star through her brilliant performances in Can-Can (1953); Damn Yankees (1955); New Girl in Town
(1957); Redhead (1959) and Sweet Charity in 1966. Children! Children! was Gwen Verdon's debut as a dramatic actress. In 1975 the
redheaded, supremely talented Gwen returned to Broadway in her
own métier, the musical comedy, in Chicago. Playwright Jack Horrigan
was a former actor, employed in 1972 by Manufacturer's Hanover
Trust Company in Manhattan. After Children! Children! Mr. Horrigan
undoubtedly remained in the more lucrative banking business.

* * *

CLEAVAGE (Playhouse Theatre, June 23, 1982). Produced by Up
Front Productions: Braxton Glasgow III, William J. O'Brien III,
Morgan P. O'Brien, David E. Fite; A musical with book by Buddy
and David Sheffield; Music and lyrics, Buddy Sheffield; Director,
Rita Baker; Musical numbers staged by Alton Geno; Musical conductor
and musical arrangements, Keith Thompson; Sets, Morris Taylor;
Lighting, scenery, and costume supervision, Michael Hotopp, Paul
DePass; Costumes, James M. Miller; Assistant to producer, Catherine
A. Adams; Technical supervisor, Jeremiah Harris; Wardrobe, Bruce
Catt; Sound, Theodore Jacobi; General manager, Theatre Now; William
Court Cohen, Eddie Davis, Norman E. Rothstein, Ralph Roseman,
Charlotte W. Wilcox
    Daniel David; Tom Elias; Marsha Trigg Miller; Jay Rogers; Sharon
    Troyer Scruggs; Dick Sheffield; Mark Fite; Terese Gargiulo; Pattie
    Tierce
SONGS: Cleavage; Puberty; Only Love; The Thrill of the Chase;
Surprise Me; Reprise Me; Believe Me or I'll Be Leavin' You; Lead
'Em Around by the Nose; Give Me an And; Just Another Love Song;
Sawing a Couple in Half; Bringing Up Badger; Voices of the Children;
All the Lovely Ladies; Living in Sin; Boys Will be Girls
ORCHESTRA: Keith Thompson (Conductor/Keyboards); Philip Fortenberry (Piano/Synthesizer); Jeff Myers (Bass); Howard Joines (Drums)

This witless and interminably boring fiasco was generally, and
justifiably, ignored. The sketches dealt with the marriage, personal
relationships, and separation of couples old and young. The unani-

mous critique for Cleavage was that it should have been cleaved in Biloxi, Mississippi, where the amateurish mish-mash originated. After six previews and one performance, Cleavage was gone.

* * *

THE CUBAN THING (Henry Miller Theatre, September 24, 1968). Produced by Ivor David Balding and Associates, Ltd.; A drama written and directed by Jack Gelber; Setting, Robin Wagner; Lighting, Jules Fisher; Costumes, Patricia Quinn Stuart; Documentary film, Lee Lockwood; Film sequences, P.G.L. Productions; Production supervisor, Richard Scanga; Associate producer, Samuel Bronstein; Sound, Val Peters; General manager, Michael Brandman; Stage managers, Roger Johnson, Jr., Joel Walker

    Rip Torn (Roberto); Raul Julia (Chan); Jane White (Barbara); Maria Tucci (Alicia); Harold Scott (Juan); Conrad Bain (Appleby); Michael Wager (Carlos); Jenny Egan (Mamma); Robert Fields (Paco); Harry Packwood (O'Hara); Rose Gregorio (Daisi); Jeanne Kaplan (Cuqui); Henry Proach (Angel); Richard Steel-Reed (Ray); Carla Pinza (Billi)

    Decadent, wealthy businessman Roberto's sexy, pretentious wife, Barbara, deplores his excesses and his passion for showing pornographic films to his family and friends. Roberto has made secret contributions to Fidel Castro's guerillas in the Sierra Maestra of the Oriente Province, supporting the revolutionary movement against Cuban President Folgencio Batista, who flees Cuba in December, 1958, leaving Castro to become the island's dictator. Eight years later, the family butler, Chan, a strong supporter of the revolution, has become Castro's overlord in charge of Roberto's home and is married to his idealistic, Sarah Lawrence-educated daughter, Alicia. Their former visitors, American newspaper and television correspondents Appleby and O'Hara, have been replaced by proletarian prostitutes Daisi, Billi, and Cuqui, and Roberto's lovely Havana home has been reduced to a deplorable barracks where food is scarce. Roberto and his wife have descended to servant status but Roberto is proud to have been accepted as a member of Castro's Revolutionary Party.

    Richard Watts, Jr. (New York Post) found the revolution tedious and reported, "Perhaps as a salute to Fidel, the play seems as long as one of his speeches" and that playwright Gelber had written a "chronicle of a dull, unattractive family group living lives of tedious desperation without adding anything of dramatic or thoughtful value concerning the revolution in which they are caught--It really isn't pro-Castro, but I'm afraid it is anti-drama."

    Clive Barnes (The New York Times) reported "It was a tribute to American freedom that a pro-Castro play should be produced in New York; unfortunately, Mr. Gelber's work proved less of a tribute to the American theater." Richard P. Cooke (The Wall Street Journal)

conceded "Mr. Gelber is entitled to his political views (and fortunate to be able to freely present them)" but "Mr. Gelber's sympathetic treatment of the Castro revolution is poorly conceived and written." John Chapman (Daily News) described The Cuban Thing as being an "excessively talky and quite undramatic drama."

Far more exciting and dramatic than anything on-stage was the near-riot outside Henry Miller's Theatre during the play's thirteen previews, when anti-Castro factions gathered en masse to protest Gelber's play. On Thursday, September 19, 1968 three canisters of tear gas were released in the balcony and orchestra areas of the theatre, despite surveillance of undercover agents in the audience. The theatre was quickly invaded by uniformed New York policemen waving nightsticks, and the audience stumbled out into 43rd Street, staggering about, gassed to the eyeballs. The street was further congested with two ambulances, four squad cars, a fire truck, and an oversized paddy wagon.

The Cuban Thing, on Tuesday, September 24, 1968, according to The Christian Science Monitor, "stirred up a lot of people at its opening, but virtually none of them was in the audience. Anti-Castro demonstrators chanted audibly on the street during the performance. A few broke into Henry Miller's Theatre, causing Rip Torn to call out 'Hold It' from the stage--The work was not dramatically effective enough to have promoted any cause and, in fact, it was not so much promoting a cause as showing a human context as it is affected by the revolutionary changes." About forty anti-Castro demonstrators tried to storm police barricades on 43rd Street between 6th and 7th Avenues and fights broke out between them and some sixty policemen. As soon as the audience cleared the theatre, police had the marquee lights turned off, darkening the play's advertisement showing a woman smoking a cigar and wearing a soldier's cap.

Fifty-three-year-old former United Nations nightshift mimeograph operator, Chicago-born Jack Gelber received acclaim for his first play, The Connection, dealing with the drug sub-culture. It was produced by the politicized Living Theatre Repertory Company at their Off-Broadway theatre on July 15, 1959. Kenneth Tynan (The New Yorker) called The Connection "The most exciting new play that Off-Broadway has produced since the war." Played in repertory with other plays, including 64 performances of Gelber's play The Apple in 1961, The Connection, when it closed in 1963, had amassed 742 performances.

The Establishment Theatre Company, Inc. produced Gelber's play Square in the Eye at Off-Broadway's Theatre De Lys on May 20, 1965, for 31 performances. Gelber put in time writing unproduced scripts in Hollywood and directed Arnold Wesker's Off-Broadway 1966 play The Kitchen, and he also staged Arthur Kopit's drama Indians for the Royal Shakespeare Company in London in April, 1968. Norman Mailer's novel Barbary Shore was adapted and directed by Gelber

Dance a Little Closer/ 35

for the New York Shakespeare Festival Public Theatre's production on January 10, 1974, featuring Rip Torn and Estelle Parsons for 48 performances. Gelber also directed The Repertory Company of Lincoln Center's 1971 production of Merle Molofsky's drama Kool Aid.

The American Place Theatre produced Gelber's play Sleep and there, in 1972, he directed Robert Coover's comedy The Kid and Frank Chin's play The Chickencoop Chinaman. At The American Place Theatre in October 1976, Gelber directed his play Jack Gelber's New Play: Rehearsal and there, on February 25, 1979, he staged Sam Shepard's drama based on Howard Hughes, called Seduced, with Rip Torn. While teaching playwriting at Columbia University and later at Brooklyn College, Gelber wrote, in 1982, a drama based on the lost idealists of the sixties called Starters, which tried-out on the road.

The Connection, however, remains Jack Gelber's only successful play and, due to the unwarranted pyrexic protestations, his most publicized one was his only Broadway adventure, The Cuban Thing.

* * *

DANCE A LITTLE CLOSER (Minskoff Theatre, May 11, 1983). Produced by Frederick Brisson, Jerome Minskoff, James Nederlander, and the Kennedy Center, Roger L. Stevens, Chairman; A musical with Book, Lyrics, and Direction by Alan Jay Lerner; Based on Robert E. Sherwood's play Idiot's Delight; Music, Charles Strouse; Musical staging and choreography, Billy Wilson; Settings, David Mitchell; Lighting, Thomas Skelton; Costumes, Donald Brooks; Musical direction, Peter Howard; Orchestrations, Jonathan Tunick; Dance music, Glen Kelly; Technical supervisor, Jeremiah Harris; Sound design, John McClure; Production supervisor, Stone Widney; Assistant to producer, Dwight Frye; Assistant conductor, Les Scott; Assistants to Mr. Lerner, Judy Insel, Ellen Walter; Wardrobe, Jennifer Bryan, Irene Bunis; Props, Paul Biega; Skating staged by Blair Hammond; Hairstylist, Joe Tubens; Associate producer, Paul N. Temple; Production assistants, Marty Erskine, Martin Shelby; Company manager, Mitzi Harder; Stage managers, Alan Hall, Steven Adler, Dianne Trulock; General management, Joseph P. Harris, Peter T. Kulok, Steven E. Goldstein, Nancy Simmons
    Len Cariou (Harry Aikens); Liz Robertson (Cynthia Brookfield-Bailey); George Rose (Dr. Josef Winkler); Don Chastain (Roger Butterfield); David Sabin (Johannes Hartog); Elizabeth Hubbard (Countess Carla Pirianno); Diane Pennington, Cheryl Howard, Alyson Reed (The Delights: Shirley, Bebe, Elaine); Noel Craig (Captain Mueller); Brent Barrett (Charles Castleton); Jeff Keller (Edward Dunlop); I. M. Hobson (Reverend Oliver Boyle); Joyce Worsley (Hester Boyle); Joseph Kolinski (Heinrich Walter); Robin Stephens (Cynthia's Double); Philip Mollet (Bellboy/Harry); Brian Sutherland (Waiter/Harry's Double/Harry); James Fatta (Rink Attendant/Violinist/Harry); Colleen Ashton (Ice Skater); Colleen Ashton, Candy Cook, Mary Dale, James Fatta, Philip Mollet, Linda

Poser, Robin Stephens, Brian Sutherland, Peter Wandel (Hotel Guests)
SONGS: It Never Would've Worked; Happy, Happy New Year; No Man Is Worth It; What Are You Going to Do About It?; A Woman Who Thinks I'm Wonderful; Pas de Deux; There's Never Been Anything Like Us; Another Life; Why Can't the World Go and Leave Us Alone?; He Always Comes Home to Me; I Got a New Girl; Dance a Little Closer; There's Always One You Can't Forget; Homesick; Mad; I Don't Know; Auf Wiedersehen; I Never Want to See You Again; On Top of the World

During "the avoidable future" guests are seemingly trapped in the Barclay-Palace Hotel in the Austrian Alps when a confrontation between the NATO forces air armada and the Soviet Union's threat of further invasion nearly precipitates a nuclear war. Second-rate song-and-dance man Harry Van and his three chorus girls, The Delights, entertain the guests, singing a homesick paeon to America, Three Mile Island, and Love Canal. Harry meets mysterious Cynthia Brookfield-Bailey, the elegant mistress of European-born, egocentric, American diplomat Dr. Josef Winkler, whose credo is "the best we can hope for is fear of each other." Harry recognizes Cynthia as a former nightclub singer named Cindy Brooks with whom he had a one-night affair in Omaha's Ramada Inn. While Cynthia refuses to recognize Harry and nervous guests ice-skate, Pan Am employees Charles Castleton and Edward Dunlop try to persuade Church of England Reverend Oliver Boyle to marry them, over the great objections of the cleric's wife, Hester Boyle. The threat of nuclear holocaust is canceled and the guests depart. Cynical, hedonistic diplomat Dr. Winkler deserts gold-digging Cynthia, who is reluctantly reunited with Harry.

When Robert Sherwood's Idiot's Delight was revived in Los Angeles in 1970, The New York Times's critic Mel Gussow noted "This is one play that might benefit from musical expansion." Dance a Little Closer, as devised by Alan Jay Lerner, was not benefited. Frank Rich (The New York Times) called the Lerner musical version "a huge, extravagant mishmash" where "The message--is lost," adding, "Dance a Little Closer is one of those musicals that seems to have taken on a rampaging, self-destructive life of its own; an initially shaky premise is steadily dismantled by errors of judgement on all fronts." Alan Jay Lerner's staging of Dance a Little Closer was called "static," "heavy," and torpid." Charles Strouse's music and Lerner's ever-listenable lyrics were excellent.

Alan Jay Lerner had toyed with the adaptation of Idiot's Delight for some twelve years. He told the press "What I've tried to do is preserve the fundamental structure of the play and to replace some characters who would not be relevant today with characters I think are." Consequently, Sherwood's wealthy munitions mogul, Achille Weber, became Dr. Josef Winkler, European-born, American diplomat based on Henry Kissinger. The newlyweds, Mr. and Mrs. Cherry, of Sherwood's play became two Pan Am homosexuals seeking wedlock, and ersatz Russian Countess and former vaudevillian Irene was reincarnated as a phony English aristocrat and former nightclub singer Cindy Brooks. Lerner added, "I wanted to write an anti-nuclear play. Even though it does have a rather serious background, it is still a love story and a romantic comedy in a strange way." Rehearsals began on March 7, 1983, and previews started on Saturday, April 16th. After twenty-seven previews Dance a Little Closer opened and closed on Wednesday, May 11, 1983, to become a $2.5 million dollar non-nuclear holocaust.

Dance a Little Closer was the Broadway debut of Liz Robertson who had charmed and dazzled London as Eliza Doolittle in 1979's revival of Lerner and Loewe's musical classic My Fair Lady. Liz Robertson, the daughter of a London policeman, grew up in Ilford, where the famous Thompson-Bywaters 1922 murder case had occurred (later dramatized in the plays People Like Us and A Pin to See the Peepshow). At the age of twenty-six Liz Robertson became the eighth wife of sixty-three-year-old Alan Jay Lerner, in August 1981. The other Mrs. Alan Jay Lerners were Ruth O'Day Boyd (1939-1942); Marion Bell (1947-1949); Nancy Olson (1950-1957); Micheline Muselli Posso di Borgo (1957-1960); Karen Gundersen (1966-1974); Sandra Payne (1974-1976); and Nina Bushkin (1977-1980).

Despite the failure of Dance a Little Closer, Alan Jay Lerner's theatrical successes far outdistanced his marriages. Although he had written an uneven book and uneasy lyrics for Kurt Weill's music in 1948's Love Life, Lerner's greatest success in the theatre was with composer Frederick Loewe, with whom he first collaborated in 1942 by writing the book for a musical version of Barry Connor's comedy The Patsy, with Earle Crooker creating the lyrics. Called The Life of the Party, the musical closed in Detroit.

Lerner wrote the libretto and lyrics to Loewe's music for What's Up (with Arthur Pierson cooperating on the book in 1943); The Day Before Spring (1945); Brigadoon (1947); Paint Your Wagon (1951); My Fair Lady (based on George Bernard Shaw's play Pygmalion) (1956); Camelot (based on T. H. White's novel The Once and Future King) (1960); and 1958's Best Picture of the Year, Metro-Goldwyn-Mayer's superb Academy Award-winning musical Gigi, which was transferred to the Broadway stage in 1973 and reappeared in London in 1985 to dismal reviews. Lerner received an Academy Award for his adaptation of Colette's novel Gigi and for the film's title song. His story and screenplay for Metro-Goldwyn-Mayer's 1951 Academy Award Best Picture of the Year, An American in Paris was heralded as a masterpiece, with music and lyrics by George and Ira Gershwin, and he received an Oscar.

After Loewe's regrettable retirement, Lerner collaborated with other composers on less notable musicals. He wrote the book and lyrics for On a Clear Day You Can See Forever in 1965, with music by Burton Lane. This project was originally a collaboration between Lerner and composer Richard Rodgers under the title of I Picked a Daisy but it was abandoned. Lerner's libretto and lyrics for Coco in 1969 were set to music by music by Andre Previn. Two years later Lerner adapted Vladimir Nabokov's novel Lolita to the stage, with music by John Barry, but Lolita, My Love closed on the road.

A monumental misadventure was Lerner's 1976 pretentious and pedestrian libretto and lyrics for 1600 Pennsylvania Avenue, with a Leonard Bernstein score, dubbed by theatre wags How Black Was Our White House? 1600 Pennsylvania Avenue braved Broadway for seven performances before being evicted. Gerald Bordman (American Musical Theatre) wrote about 1600 Pennsylvania Avenue, "Lerner's continuing inability to write well-constructed librettos from original ideas undermined the entertainment." Despite this truth, Lerner's poetic, literate, witty, and elegant lyrics are challenged today only by Stephen Sondheim among his peers. Carmelina, Lerner and Joseph Stein's adaptation of the film Buona Sera, Mrs. Campbell, with a delightful score by Burton Lane and charming lyrics by Lerner, deserved a better Broadway reception than it received in its meagre seventeen performances.

Dance a Little Closer's music was by Charles Strouse, who composed the scores for Bye, Bye Birdie (1960); All-American (1962); Golden Boy (1964); Applause (1970), and the ever lovin' Annie in 1977.

Early on, in 1981, Hollywood's James Coburn had expressed interest in playing the part of Harry Van. Luckily he remained in California. Len Cariou, a gifted actor and director who appeared to advantage in the Broadway musicals A Little Night Music, Applause, and Sweeney Todd, was cast as the song-and-dance-man but was strangely ineffective. Douglas Watt (Daily News) considered Charles Strouse's contribution to Dance a Little Closer one of his better scores but deplored the musical play as lacking sense; "Simply put, it is a chilly, charmless and foolhardy musical--Ironically, while Lerner's book--which he has also and probably unwisely, directed himself--is a generally disagreeable patchwork, and his lyrics show signs of strain." Clive Barnes (New York Post) reported "It looks like a good idea half-baked--the whole show has gone subtly but awfully wrong. Everything about it could work, but nothing does."

The Theatre Guild, Inc.'s production of Robert E. Sherwood's Idiot's Delight opened at the Sam S. Shubert Theatre on March 24, 1936, to play 299 performances. Directed by Bretaigne Windust, the production was conceived and supervised by Alfred Lunt and Lynn Fontanne. Miss Fontanne's clothes designed and executed by Valentina; Chorus costumes by Irene Sharaff; Dances staged by Morgan Lewis; Setting designed by Lee Simonson; Company manager, Lawrence Farrell; Stage manager, George Greenberg; Assistant stage managers, Le Roi Operti and Bates Smith

Alfred Lunt (Harry Van); Lynn Fontanne (Irene); Francis Compton (Achille Weber); Richard Whorf (Quillery); Sydney Greenstreet (Dr. Waldersee); Edward Raquello (Captain Locicero); George Meader (Dumptsy); Edgar Barrier (Auguste); S. Thomas Gomez (Pittaluga); Bretaigne Windust (Mr. Cherry); Jean McIntyre (Mrs. Cherry); Barry Thomson (Donald Navadel); Jacqueline Paige (Shirley Laughlin); Connie Crowell (Beulah Tremoyne); Frances Foley (Edna Creesh); Etna Ross (Francine Merle); Marjorie Baglin (Elaine Messiger); Ruth Timmons (Bebe Gould); Stephan Sandes (Signor Palota); Le Roi Operti (Signor Rossi); Ernestine De Becker (Signora Rossi); Giogio Monteverde (succeeded by Gordon Nelson) (Major); Alan Hewitt (succeeded by Charles Ansley (1st Officer); Winston Ross (2nd Officer); Gilmore Bush (3rd Officer); Tommaso Tittoni (succeeded by David Selva) (4th Officer); Una Val (Anna); Gerald Kunz, Max Rich, Joseph Knopf (Musicians)

PROGRAM NOTE: The Theatre Guild wishes to thank Irving Berlin for the use of some of his songs and for the special lyric for 'Swanee River,' sung by Mr. Lunt, and for invaluable suggestions in the staging of the musical number in Act II.

"The following musical numbers are played or sung during the action of the play by permission of the copyright owners: 'June in January'; 'When My Baby Smiles at Me'; 'Waters of the Minnetonka'; 'Putting on the Ritz'; 'Pardon My Southern Accent'; 'Valencia.'"

Brooks Atkinson (The New York Times) found that Sherwood's "anxiety about world affairs" and "love of a good time" result in one of his most likeable entertainments. While considering Sherwood's play "a robust theatre charade," Atkinson also added, "the discussion of war is inconclusive and the mood of the play is somewhat too trivial for such a macabre subject, it is probably taking Idiot's Delight much too seriously."

Robert Sherwood began writing Idiot's Delight, his 1936 Pulitzer Prize play, in 1933, completing the script in 1935. As had several playwrights before him, Sherwood read his anti-fascist play to totally paralyzed playwright Edward Sheldon, accepting Sheldon's comments and constructive criticism before winning the approval of the Lunts, for whom he had written Reunion in Vienna in 1931 and in 1940 would write his Pulitzer Prize drama There Shall Be No Night, a tribute to Finland's heroism during World War II. Sherwood dedicated the published play of Idiot's Delight to the Lunts, who had made constructive suggestions for rewriting and had played the leading roles to perfection, taking nineteen curtain calls on the opening night at Broadway's Shubert Theatre.

Production on Idiot's Delight began in January, 1936, and two hundred chorus girls arrived to audition for Harry Van's six chorines called "Les Blondes." The casting call was finally reduced to twelve girls who were auditioned by Sherwood, Alfred Lunt, producer Vinton Freedley, and playwright Russel Crouse, then the Theatre Guild's press agent.

Sherwood's play was set in the Hotel Monte Gabrielle in the Italian Alps where untalented song-and-dance man Harry Van and his troupe of six chorus girls arrive en route to another European engagement. Harry meets Russian Countess Irene, mistress of wealthy munitions manufacturer Achille Weber, and recognizes her as a former vaudevillian with whom he had had a steaming affair ten years before, in Room 974 of the Governor Bryan Hotel in Omaha, Nebraska. Irene's League of Nations passport is unacceptable to Italian authorities and Weber deserts her to leave with the other hotel guests for the safety of Switzerland at the outbreak of war. Harry remains in the deserted hotel with Irene during a massive air raid and as they watch bombs destroying the world around them they sing "Onward Christian Soldiers."

Idiot's Delight successfully toured the United States following the Broadway run of 299 performances until the production reached Omaha where Mayor Dan Butler denounced the proposed opening of the play, citing the lascivious liaison between Harry and Irene in Omaha's fictitious Hotel Governor Bryan. Mayor Butler vigorously denounced Sherwood's play as outrageously immoral and demanded sixteen deletions from the script. One more intelligent wag suggested changing the title to Idiot's Delete without a justifiable sub-title for hizonor, the Mayor of Omaha-ha-ha (as the city was pronounced by Lynn Fontanne in the play). Idiot's Delight opened intact and uncut to sold-out performances in the Nebraska metropolis with no noticeable degeneration of, nor threats to, the population's morality.

England's Lord Chamberlain had a more diplomatic approach to censorship, suggesting the removal of all references to dictatorship and fascists in the dialogue to ward off "any complaint from the continent" although Mussolini's black shirt Fascists and Hitler's brown shirt Nazis were doing some pretty fancy and ominous sabre rattling. Mussolini had invaded Ethiopia on October 3, 1935. Ethiopia's Haile Selassie sought an uneasy asylum in England and the League of Nations retained little more than a memory of its original purpose. Franco's military revolt in Spain on July 16, 1936, began the Spanish Civil War and the dress rehearsal for World War II. Herr Hitler invaded Austria on March 11, 1938, and on March 22, 1938, Sherwood's timely and perceptive play opened at London's Apollo Theatre, directed by Raymond Massey. Idiot's Delight later transferred to London's His Majesty's Theatre on October 24, 1938, to complete 230 performances.

Raymond Massey (succeeded by Lee Tracy) (Harry Van); Tamara Geva (succeeded by Tatiana Lieven) (Irene); Hugh Miller (Achille Weber); Carl Jaffe (Quillery); Franklin Dyall (Dr. Waldersee); Terence Neill (Captain Kirvlin); Ralph Roberts (Dumptsy); Cecil G. Calvert (Auguste); Charles Paul (Pittatek); Valentine Dyall (Mr. Cherry); Janet Johnson (Mrs. Cherry); Richard Rudi (Donald Navadel); Pat Denny (Shirley); Peggy Hamilton (Beulah); Joan Clarkson (succeeded by Elaine Murray) (Edna); Audrey Boyes (Francine); Eileen McCarthy (Elaine); Carol Dexter (Bebe); Benjamin Wright (Mr. Preva); Kara Shera (Mrs. Preva); Reginald Atkinson (Major); Elizabeth Adair (Maid); Peter Gyll (1st Officer); Edward Stuart (2nd Officer); Robert Beatty (3rd Officer); Patrick Jenkins (succeeded by Ambrose Day) (4th Officer); Jack Jacobs (Orchestra Leader); Tony Hatley, Bert Jacobs, Len Johnson (Members of Orchestra)

By arrangement with the New York Theatre Guild, the London production was produced by Raymond Massey and Henry Sherek by arrangement with Alec L. Rea; Setting by Lee Simonson; Mechanical effects by Alexander Black; Costumes by Motley, Karinska and Max Weldy; Company manager, Stanley Brightman; Stage managers, Peter Gyll, Ambrose Day

The New York City Theatre Company produced Idiot's Delight at New York's City Center Theatre for a limited run of sixteen performances beginning May 23, 1951. Directed by George Schaefer; Setting and Lighting by Eldon Elder; Costumes by Emiline Roche; Choreography by Ted Cappy; Artistic supervisor, Maurice Evans; Company manager, Edward A. Haas; Stage managers, Thelma Chandler, Tom Hughes Sand
    Lee Tracy (Harry Van); Ruth Chatterton (Irene); Stiano Braggiotti (Achille Weber); Emmett Rogers (Quillery); Stefan Schnabel (Dr. Waldersee); Louis Borell (Captain Locicero); John C. Becher (Dumptsy); Theodore Tenley (Auguste); Rock Rogers (Pittaluga); Winston Ross (Mr. Cherry); Sybil Baker (Mrs. Cherry); Chester Stratton (Donald Navadel); Irene Dailey (Shirley); Gretchen Houser (Beulah); Nancy Pearson (Edna); Rita Barry (Francine); Joanne Woodcock (Elaine); Lillian Udvardy (Bebe); John Weaver (Signor Rossi); Martine Bartlett (Signora Rossi); Alan Furlan (Major); Dan Rubinate (First Officer); Scott Fielding (Second Officer); Felice Orlandi (Third Officer); Bruce Jewell (Fourth Officer); Sarah Marshall (Anna); Max Marlin, Michael DuChesne, Sidney Rich, Phil Salomon (Musicians)

The Center Theatre Group of the Music Center of Los Angeles, Elliot Martin, Producer, revived Sherwood's anti-fascist drama from March 17, 1970, through April 25, 1970. Director, Garson Kanin; Setting, Harry Horner; Lighting, H. R. Poindexter; Costumes, Lewis Brown; Choreographer and associate director, Wally Strauss; Production supervisor, David Pardoll; Assistant choreographer, Bill Richards; Sound technician, Glenn Hayes; Interpolated music by John Uhler Lemmon, III; Musical arranger, John Guarnieri; Company manager, Charles Mooney; Stage manager, Dom Salinaro
    Jack Lemmon (Harry Van); Rosemary Harris (Irene); Sandor Szabo (Achille Weber); Pierre Olaf (Quillery); Sam Jaffe (Dr. Waldersee); Anthony Caruso (Captain Locicero); Leon Askin (Dumptsy); Reuben Singer (Auguste); Remo Pisani (Pittaluga); Terence Scammel (Mr. Cherry); Flora Plumb (Mrs. Cherry); John Myhers (Don Navadel); Marti Rolph (Shirley); Trayce Johnson (Beulah); Linda Gandell (Edna); Trish Mahoney (Francine); Corinne Carroll (Elaine); Lisa

42 / Destruction

Pharren (Bebe); Peter Brocco (Signor Rossi); Beppy De Vries (Signora Rossi); John Guarnieri (Paleta); Sam Scar (Major); Dom Salinaro, Colin Higgins, Leo Morrell, Michael Sevareid (Italian Officers); Jennifer Moore (Anna); George Auld (Saxophonist); Dick Berk (Drummer); Shirley Connell (Violinist); Susan Ohman (Flower Girl)

Metro-Goldwyn-Mayer paid Robert E. Sherwood $135,000 for the screen rights to Idiot's Delight, for which he wrote the screenplay. Filmed in 1938, Idiot's Delight starred Norman Shearer and Clark Gable, directed by Clarence Brown; Photography, William Daniels; Art director, Cedric Gibbons; Gowns, Adrian; Recording director, Douglas Shearer; Editor, Robert J. Kern; Music director, Herbert Stothart; Choreography, George King; Assistant art director, Wade B. Rubtoom; Set decorator, Edwin B. Willis; A Hunt Stromberg Production

Norma Shearer (Irene Fellara); Clark Gable (Harry Van); Edward Arnold (Achille Weber); Charles Coburn (Dr. Waldersee); Joseph Schildkraut (Captain Kirvline); Burgess Meredith (Quillery); Pat Paterson (Mrs. Cherry); Peter Willes (Mr. Cherry); Skeets Gallagher (Donald Navadel); Fritz Feld (Pittatek); Edward Raquello (Chiari); William Edmunds (Dumptsy); Paula Stone (Beulah Tremoyne); Virginia Dale (Francine Merle); Joan Marsh (Elaine Messiger); Bernadene Hayes (Edna Creesh); Lorraine Kreuger (Bebe Gould); Frank Orth (Benny Zinsser); George Sorel (Major); Hobart Cavanaugh (Frueheim, theatre manager); Adolph Milar (Fellara); Clem Bevans (Jimmy Barzek); Claire McDowell (Mother); Joe Yule (Comic); Emory Parnell (5th Avenue Cop); Robert Middlemass (Hospital commandant); Mitchell Lewis (Indian); Evelyn Knapp (Nurse); Eddie Gribbon (Cop); Jimmy Colin (Stagehand); Buddy Messinger (Usher); Charles Judels (Greek restaurant owner); Paul Panzer (Greek Chef); E. Alyn Warren, (Grand Hotel Clerk); Frank Faylen (Ed); Lee Phelps (Train Announcer); Francis McDonald (Flight Captain); Gary Owen (newsstand man); Bernard Suss (Auguste); William Irving (Sandro); Harry Strang (Sergeant); Bud Geary (Ambulance Driver); Gertrude Bennett (Woman with Powders); Bonita Weber (Woman with Catsup); Rudolf Myzet (Czech Announcer), Laura Hope Crews (Madame Zuleika).
SONGS: How Strange (Kahn/Stothart); Puttin' on the Ritz (Berlin); Onward Christian Soldiers (Sullivan)

Metro-Goldwyn-Mayer went further than England's Lord Chamberlain, removing all references to fascists or dictators and obscuring the identity of all military uniforms and the country of origin of raiding aircraft, despite Herr Hitler's establishment of his Nazi regime in Austria in March, 1938.

* * *

DESTRUCTION (Chanin Auditorium, June 30, 1932). Produced by the American Clasic Players; A tragedy by Bertha Wiernik; Director, Howard Sinclair

Claude Tonsick (Eleazur Amon); Kirk Brown (Josiah Amon); Joseph King ("Dr. Porzowsky"); Kathleen Costa (Della); Ruth Gion (Mira); Harry Tebbutt (Comrade Crown); Diana Park (Mrs. Kerlington); Virginia Dean (Rita); Louis Milner (Butler)

Minister Josiah Amon's son Eleazur is indoctrinated into communism by "Dr. Porzowsky." At a communist party rally Eleazur denounces God and capitalism. Josiah invades the Reds meeting and takes Eleazur home where the boy repents.

Destruction, rather preposterously described as "the play that would unite the world" was presented on the 50th floor of the Chanin Building and was described by The New York Times as "a futile, maundering play, as rhetorical and pretentious as a keynote speech, which is far too amateurish both in its writing and acting to warrant any attention." Billboard called Destruction "one of those earnest little dramas--so earnest it hurts--which are so incompetent that anybody but a theory-mad fanatic would realize their utter dramatic hopelessness at first glance."

* * *

DON'T CALL BACK (Helen Hayes Theatre, March 18, 1975). Produced by Charles Bowden, Slade Brown and Jim Milford; A "Thriller" by Russell O'Neil; Director, Len Cariou; Setting, Oliver Smith; Lighting, John Gleason; Costumes, Whitney Blausen; Miss Francis's gown by Egon von Furstenberg; Sound, Ken Guilmartin; Wardrobe supervisor, Cindy Chock; Production associate, David Hadden; Associate producer, Morgan Holman; General manager, James Walsh; Stage managers, Donald Christy, Frank Di Elsi, James Weaver
    Arlene Francis (Miriam Croydon); Dorian Harewood (Clarence); Stanley Grover (Gregory Schaeffer); Richard Niles (Jason Croydon); Robert Hegez (Trucker); Mark Kologi (Crowbar); Catherine Byers (Claire)

Actress and television personality Miriam Croydon returns to her duplex Park Avenue apartment after a road tour with her co-star and lover Gregory Schaeffer. Gregory leaves and Miriam discovers her apartment has been taken over by a trio of ghetto hoodlums fleeing from a couple of murders. The young criminals have been provided sanctuary by Miriam's son, Jason, who has impregnated the sister of the trio's black leader, Clarence. The invaders steal $5,000 from Miriam and rape her secretary, Claire. Clarence and his nervous cohorts demand $200,000 from New York's mayor and a jet plane at Kennedy Airport to take them to freedom. Clarence is shot and killed and his two stupid henchmen are shot trying to escape. Jason vindictively plans to kill his mother, holding her responsible for the deaths of his criminal cronies. Gregory, perplexed by Miriam's telephone warning not to call back, returns to the apartment where Miriam sees her son apprehended, and damns him as a living, breathing regret.

Don't Call Back had mixed reviews, once defined by George S. Kaufman as "good and lousy." Arlene Francis gave a taut performance considered by Clive Barnes (The New York Times) as "supremely natural," which held the play together, and Dorian Harewood's performance as Clarence was "perfectly matched." Barnes wrote about Harewood, "This is a performance I shall remember long after, I suspect, I will have forgotten the play"; and about the play, "Len Cariou has directed the play very well indeed, with nice melodramatic groupings, and some decently terse playing."

Richard Watts, Jr. (New York Post) called Don't Call Back "exquisitely trashy. O'Neil calls his play "a thriller," though the only thing thrilling about it is the novelty of stage bigotry" and it "is clumsily written, obviously directed and superficially performed." The Daily News critic Douglas Watt judged the ninety-minute play "unbearable" saying, "it is so ineptly manipulated and the dialogue is so atrocious that there are moments when it seems as though the author is attempting a travesty of the form. But no."

Two days after the closing of the $165,000 production of Don't Call Back, which survived thirteen previews and one performance, Arlene Francis told Anthony Mancini of The New York Post, "The critics' influence is what has killed the theatre in New York. I think it's dead now, except for musicals. They are entitled to say that a play didn't appeal to them or that they didn't care for certain performances, but I see no reason for them to be gratuitously vicious. The theatre's having a hard enough time surviving at all."

Don't Call Back was originally tested at Massachusetts Falmouth Playhouse for a week, beginning July 8, 1974. Directed by Anthony Perkins; A "thriller" by Russell O'Neil; produced by Sidney Gordon, Setting by Michael Sharp; Lighting by Michael Wheeler; A Charles Bowden and Morgan Holman production
 Arlene Francis (Miriam Croydon); Ernest Thomas (Clarence); Jay Doolittle (Gregory Schaeffer); Michael Mullins (Jason Croydon); Bruce Prieto (Trucker); Mark Kologi (Crowbar); Mary Cooper (Claire); Alan Pochi (Elevator Man); Terence Beasor (Police Captain); Kenneth Olin, David Stewart (Policemen)

It was announced that Don't Call Back would open at the Helen Hayes Theatre on February 10, 1975, produced by Charles Bowden and Ronald S. Lee, with Anthony Perkins as director.

Novelist Russell O'Neil was born in Conshohocken, Pa. on March 6, 1927, and had written two-minute spots for Arlene Francis on her NBC radio shows "Monitor" and "Emphasis." Miss Francis (Mrs. Martin Gabel) had interviewed O'Neil on the publication of each of his eight novels: Jonathan (1959); Climate of Violence (1961); The Devil's Profession (1963); The Most Beautiful Girls in the World (1970); The Alcatraz Incident (1971); Neighbors (1972); and Location and The Need (1974). Arlene Francis asked O'Neil to write a play for her and in January, 1974, the novelist (who had written three unproduced plays) started his "thriller," then titled Call Me Back, which he completed in March.

Don't Call Back was inevitably measured against more successful plays with variations of the same theme. Edward Chodorov's Kind Lady, based on Hugh Walpole's story The Silver Casket, opened at the Booth Theatre on April 23, 1935, to play 102 performances. Mary Herries was the "Kind Lady" held hostage in her London townhouse by a gang of thieves who systematically sell her valuable art collection until they are cornered and Mary is freed. Marie Baumer's melodrama Little Brown Jug, which opened at the Martin Beck Theatre on March 6, 1945, for a brief run of five performances, related the blackmailing of Irene Haskell and her daughter Carol for the accidental death of Carol's husband, as they are held hostage in their home by handyman Ira.

Mel Dinelli's suspense drama The Man, which opened at the Fulton Theatre on January 19, 1950, for 92 performances, dramatized the gradual imprisonment of Mrs. Gillis in her home by another handyman. A telephone repair man arrives to fix the out-of-service telephone and finds handyman, homicidal maniac Howard Wilton, has killed Mrs. Gillis. Alexander Graham Bell's invention was used to signal a hired assassin to kill Margot Wendice when she answered the telephone but her husband Tony was eventually trapped for murder in Frederick Knott's thrilling play Dial "M" for Murder which opened on October 29, 1952, at the Plymouth Theatre and completed 552 performances. Joseph Hayes's taut drama The Desperate Hours appeared at the Ethel Barrymore Theatre on February 10, 1955. For 212 performances escaped convicts Glen and Hal Griffen held the Hilliard family hostage in their suburban Indianapolis home until the brothers Griffen are killed by police.

Unfortunately, as William Glover (Associated Press) described Russell O'Neil's first produced play, "Don't Call Back is a wrong number."

* * *

FAME (John Golden Theatre, November 18, 1974). Produced by James J. C. Andrews and Tony Zanetta for Mainman; A comedy written and directed by Anthony J. Ingrassia; Setting, Douglas W. Schmidt; Lighting, Martin Aronstein; Costumes, Jeffrey B. Moss; Hairstylist and makeup concept, Hari Van Wyngerge; Wig styles, Hector Garcia; Wardrobe supervisor, Mallory Abramson; Associate producer, Shirley Rappaport; Sound, Chuck London; General manager, Norman Kean; Stage managers, R. Derek Swire, Peter von Mayrhauser
    Ellen Barber (Diane Cook); Nancy Reardon (Madge; Louella O. Parsons; Helen Harvey); Kawrie Driscoll (Bill; Ned; Milton; Sonny); Bibi Besch (Eunice; Eva; Luba); Robert Miano (Makeup Man; Young Gable; Richard Ronson; Young Priest); Jeremy Stevens

(Ed Aimes; Private Dick; Danny Grant; Walter; Sam; Newspaper Reporter); Rudy Hornish (Louis B. Mayer; Studio Official; Tadlock; TV News Reporter); Christine Lavren (Established Movie Actress in TV; Meg; An Established Actress; Telephone Operator; Woman with Fur at Party; Mrs. Hodges)

Illegitimately born Diane Cook, a sexy, insecure, overly ambitious Hollywood actress, learns early on to advance her career by using her natural beauty and body. Her rise to fame in motion pictures is beset by three troubled marriages--to a young mechanic, a temperamental prizefighter, and a famous intellectual but ineffective novelist. Diane is nationally acclaimed as a sex symbol rather than a serious actress and deeply depressed by the headlined failure of her personal life. She commits suicide by taking an overdose of sleeping pills.

Martin Gottfried (New York Post) reported, "Had Fame been offered to an off-off Broadway company, it would have been rejected as just another campy Marilyn Monroe story with Lana Turner dialogue" and described the play as "simply an amateur night version of a Hollywood novel." Clive Barnes (The New York Times), unwilling to nominate the worst play of the season after the one-performance debacle of Robinson Jeffers's Medea and Jason on October 2, 1974, at the Little Theatre, opted for Fame as the season's "worst." Mr. Barnes found "The best part of this limp rag of a comedy, based on the life and times of Marilyn Monroe, came at the intermission" watching stagehands shift furniture while recordings of Johnny Ray singing "Cry" and Eartha Kitt belting "I Want to Be Evil" were played. The Times's critic saw the play as "a mistake--It withered a long, slow death" and "The cast was not unduly distinguished, even though they may have been understandably embarrassed." Douglas Watt (Daily News) called Fame "Pure-White Idiocy. Watching a cow chew cud for two hours on end would prove more rewarding, both intellectually and artistically, than last night's Fame." Mr. Watt also listed the names of the author-director and the producers with a warning, "They are names to beware of."

The only well-defined, perceptive portrait of Marilyn Monroe was disguised as Maggie, the very beautiful, very insecure, self-destructive actress in Arthur Miller's autobiographical cathartic drama After the Fall, the first production of the newly formed Repertory Company of Lincoln Center, directed by Elia Kazan at the ANTA Washington Square Theatre on June 23, 1964, which performed 208 times. Nine years after Fame resisted fortune, another attempt to glorify Marilyn arrived on Broadway at the Minskoff Theatre on November 20, 1983. Marilyn: An American Fable, written by Patricia Michaels, with music and lyrics by Jeanne Napoli, Doug Frank, Gary Portnoy, Beth Lawrence, and Norman Thalheimer, was directed by Kenny Ortega and it survived sixteen performances. Frank Rich (The New York Times) described Marilyn: An American Fable as being "Incoherent to the point of being looney" and reported that the production "looks as if it suffered a bombing during previews."

Fame's transparent masking of living persons prominent in Marilyn's life included the substitution of a belligerent prizefighter for baseball's gentle giant Joe DiMaggio and a less-than-successful novelist masquerading as the brilliant playwright Arthur Miller. Norma Jean Baker, known as Marilyn Monroe, born on June 1, 1926, had three husbands: James Dougherty (1942-1946); Joseph DiMaggio (1954-1955) and Arthur Miller (1956-1961). Marilyn supposedly committed suicide at the age of thirty-six on August 5, 1962.

* * *

FATHER'S DAY (John Golden Theatre, March 16, 1971). Produced by Joseph Kipness and Lawrence Kasha; A comedy by Oliver Hailey; Director, Donald Moffat; Setting and lighting, Jo Mielziner; Costumes, Ann Roth; Production associate, Phyllis Dukore; General manager, Philip Adler; Company manager, Joseph M. Grossman; Stage managers, Phil Friedman, Gene Tyburn
   Brenda Vaccaro (Louise); Marian Seldes (Marian); Jennifer Salt (Estelle); Biff McGuire (Tom); Donald Moffat (Richard); Ken Kercheval (Harold)

During their children's outing with their fathers, aristocratic, leftist Marian and girlish Estelle join their outspoken, hard-bitten, ex-actress neighbor in her posh New York high-rise apartment to give each other moral support on Father's Day. The three divorcées shakily defend their new, proud independence and perversely invite their former husbands to their Father's Day party for cocktails, reminiscences, and recriminations. Prim and proper Marian still maintains sexual relations with her former husband, Richard, and perpetual orphan Estelle tries to adjust to her bisexual ex-mate Harold's marriage to a "poor" duPont. For all her brittle sophistication and forced vulgarity, embittered Louise still loves her ex-husband Tom. The three lonely divorcées are left alone at the end of Father's Day to compare themselves to Chekhov's Three Sisters.

Clive Barnes (The New York Times) viewed Father's Day as taking "a very harsh view of the woman's lot in divorce, and supports it with a few modestly amusing wisecracks and enormous gushes of hard-bitten feminine self-pity" while offering "no insights on marriage or divorce," calling it "an essentially static play." Richard Watts (New York Post) found the play "absorbing, intelligent and steadily entertaining," recommending that "To the disturbingly brief list of good new American plays of the season, I would emphatically add Father's Day." Douglas Watt (Daily News) called Father's Day "a tough-minded little comedy" which "gets to you" and "you stay hooked."

T. E. Kalem (Time magazine, March 29, 1971) deplored the producers sundering of Hailey's "fine comedy," based solely on Clive Barnes's negative review, "Barnes," wrote Kalem, "was born and reared in England, and while he likes to think that he understands

American comedy, it frequently leaves him nonplused." Kalem admired Hailey's comedy as "an evening in the theater suffused with stinging, gut-aching laughter." George Oppenheimer (Newsday) reported "Oliver Hailey has coated his comedy of divorce with so much veneer that it is practically impossible for reality to get inside either the story or the characters."

Joseph Kipness, affluent New York restaurant tycoon (Joe's Pier 52, Dinty Moore's and Hawaii Kai) and theatrical producer (La Plume de Ma Tante, High Button Shoes, and others) and Lawrence Kasha, producer of Hadrian VII and director of Bajour, Lovely Ladies, Kind Gentlemen had produced Comden and Green's adaptation of the film All About Eve, set to music by Charles Strouse and Lee Adams as Applause at Broadway's Palace Theatre on March 30, 1970. The enormously successful Tony Award-winning Applause would run 896 performances, starring Lauren Bacall, succeeded by Anne Baxter and Arlene Dahl, considerably enlarging the coffers of Messrs. Kipness and Kasha.

On the basis of a meagre advance sale and lack of theatre parties bookings, Kipness and Kasha reacted to Clive Barnes's negative review and closed Father's Day after sixteen previews and one performance. Kipness had raised $150,000 for the production, of which $35,000 was invested by Johanna Ventures, Inc. Co-producer Kasha contributed $9,000 and the play was reportedly sold to Martin Poll, representing Columbia Pictures, prior to production. Brendan Gill (The New Yorker) felt the closing of Father's Day was premature; "It was an imperfect play, but there were good things in it."

Father's Day had its world premiere in Los Angeles, produced by the Center Theatre Group at the New Theatre for Now in 1970. The play was directed by Michael Montel and designed by Robert Moor, Michael Garrett and Jeffrey Jones with the following cast: Barbara Colby (Louise); Diana Webster (Marian); Ellen Geer (Estelle); Donald Moffat (Richard); Lawrence Pressman (Harold); John Saxon (Tom). George Keathley produced and directed Father's Day at the Ivanhoe Theatre in Chicago in October, 1973, featuring Chita Rivera, Julie Adams, and Carol Ruth as the divorcées and Clifford David, Mark Le Mura, and Robert Elston as their ex-husbands.

The most successful production of Hailey's comedy was produced by Barbara Rush, in association with James A. Doolittle and the Greek Theatre Association in Los Angeles in 1974. The Rush production enjoyed a successful run on the West Coast and a six-city tour with a six-week engagement in Chicago. The play was directed by Tom Troupe and the cast included: Barbara Rush (Marian); Carole Cook (Louise); Gwynne Gifford (succeeded by Laura Wallace) (Estelle); Paul Kent (Richard); Jordan Rhodes (Harold) and Tom Troupe (Tom). Sylvia Drake (Los Angeles Times) reported, "It's funny--clever--so sly in wit. Barbara Rush gives a beautiful, richly layered performance."

Father's Day returned to New York on June 21, 1979, but Off-Broadway, at the American Place Theatre where it completed 101 performances: Produced by James Cresson, Christopher Ohman and Sam Crothers, in association with Edward Merkow; Director, Rae Allen; Setting, Christine Weppner; Costumes, Jane Greenwood; Lighting, John Gisondi; Stage manager, Herb Vogler; with the following cast: Susan Tyrrell (Louise); Tammy Grimes (Marian); Mary Beth Hurt (Estelle); Lee Richardson (Richard); Graham Beckel (Harold); John Cunningham (Tom). Richard Eder (The New York Times) in his review of the 1979 production commented that "I am afraid that it is essentially a limp and stilted play whose occasional amusing or touching lines are bright minutes caught in two mediocre hours."

Oliver D. Hailey, Jr., born July 7, 1932, graduated from the University of Texas and the Yale School of Drama, and he has written several plays. His comedy Hey You, Light Man! opened Off-Broadway at the Mayfair Theatre on March 1, 1963, to play 52 performances. Hailey's first Broadway-produced play was First One Asleep, Whistle, which opened and closed on February 26, 1966. Who's Happy Now? was an Off-Broadway production on November 17, 1969, and his comedy I Won't Dance was another one-performance Broadway casualty. His plays Continental Divide; For the Use of the Hall; And Where She Stops Nobody Knows; Animal; Crisscross; Red Rover, Red Rover; Tryptich; and I Can't Find It Anywhere have been produced by resident repertory companies in various states. For television Hailey wrote the pilot film Sidney Shorr, which he developed into the TV series Love, Sidney, starring Tony Randall.

Barbara Rush, who successfully produced and played Hailey's Father's Day, had a brief career on Broadway in 1984's A Woman of Independent Means, a solo-drama adapted from the novel by Elizabeth Forsythe Hailey, who is Mrs. Oliver Hailey.

* * *

FICKLE WOMEN (Nora Bayes Theatre, December 15, 1937). Produced by S. Mario Castagna and Irving E. Bizman; A drama written and directed by Murray Brown
    Virginia Elliott (Betty Stewart); Emilie Elden (Billie Bronson); Naomi Ravelle (Edna Walker); S. Mario Castagna (Marty Bronson); Mildred Rowlette (Alice Bronson); Edgar Winslow (Captain Morgan); Garri Rose (Detective Woods); Jerry Guardino (Tony Marillo); William Pharr (John Keenan); Caprice Petite (Dolores); Murray Brown (Ralph Walker)

Prostitute Betty Stewart leaves her profession to take care of Billie Bronson, the daughter of white slave victim Alice Bronson. Through Betty's assistance the police raid Edna Walker's bordello, where Betty shoots and kills white slave king-pin Marty Bronson. Alice is reunited with her daughter, Billie, and Betty is jailed for murder.

50 / First One Asleep, Whistle

Fickle Women was scheduled for a one-night performance with mad hopes of extending its Broadway run. The critics' lashing reviews cancelled the producer's presumptuous plans. Burns Mantle (Daily News) reported, "Fickle Women is as bad as a play can be, but not bad enough to be consistently amusing." John Mason Brown (New York Post) wrote, "One trouble with Mr. Brown as a dramatist is that he writes as if he had never been inside a theatre." Richard Lockridge (New York Sun) added, "Fickle Women is pretty funny, in its unique incompetence, if you don't mind laughing at incompetence," while Robert Coleman (Daily Mirror) doubted that worse things had been presented on the stage than Brown's Fickle Women. Coleman described the drama as an "amazing conglomeration of bunkum and hokum. Those of us who sat through the entire three acts of Fickle Women are, we think, entitled to citations for bravery under fire." John Anderson (New York Journal-American) claimed "as a play, it has a certain similarity to La Grippe in that it leaves its victims restless and dejected if not wishing they were dead. It is so bad that it is not even funny!"

* * *

FIRST ONE ASLEEP, WHISTLE (Belasco Theatre, February 26, 1966). Produced by Edgar and Bruce Lansbury; A comedy by Oliver Hailey; Director, John Berry; Setting and Lighting, Lloyd Burlingame; Costumes, Theoni V. Aldridge; Stage managers, Gigi Cascio, Sam Waterston; General manager, Joseph Beruh; Company manager, M. Weinberg
    Salome Jens (Elaine); Frank Converse (David); Marya Zimmet (matinees--Elissa Leeds) (Susan); Louise Shaffer (Esther)

Actress Elaine supports her illegitimate seven-year-old daughter, Susan, in their Manhattan apartment, by appearing in television commercials. Elaine's new lover is David, an unemployed married actor working in a Doubleday bookstore, and she is once again pregnant. Independent, self-sufficient Elaine has had an impressive string of lovers and she refuses David's proposal to divorce his wife in order to marry her. Elaine will maintain her independence and have another illegitimate child.

"The audience deserves an apology" reported Stanley Kauffmann (The New York Times) who described Hailey's comedy as "devoid of wit, insight and feeling. It is full of labored humor, magazine-fiction precepts and cuteness." Norman Nadel (New York World Telegram-Sun) labeled the play "Asleep--from bed to worse. If this were Europe, the audience would have hissed and thrown things, and more power to them. We spineless Yankees just sit there, suppressed by boredom and too meek to take our vengeance." Richard Watts, Jr. (New York Post) called the comedy "Little ado about not much. There have been worse plays than Oliver Hailey's First One Asleep, Whistle, but it is difficult to think of another that comes closer to sheer nothingness--Mr. Hailey's comedy has little to say and doesn't say it well enough to conceal the scantiness."

Playwright Oliver Hailey, whose comedy Hey You, Light Man! was praised during its 52 performances at Off-Broadway's Mayfair Theatre in 1963, was making his Broadway debut with First One Asleep, Whistle. Handsome young Frank G. Converse was also making his Broadway debut after two seasons playing minor parts with the American Shakespeare Festival. John McClain (Journal American) felt First One Asleep, Whistle should not have opened, calling it "an abysmal bust" and pondering why the Lansbury brothers and director John Berry tackled Hailey's comedy "with any hope of success--They should have blown the whistle out of town."

* * *

FRANK MERRIWELL (OR HONOR CHALLENGED) (Longacre Theatre, April 24, 1971). Produced by Sandy Farber and Stanley Barnett in association with Nate Friedman; A musical comedy with book by Skip Redwine, Larry Frank, Heywood Gould; Music and lyrics by Skip Redwine and Larry Frank; Director and choreographer, Neal Kenyon; Settings, Tom John; Lighting, John Gleason; Costumes, Frank Thompson; Musical director and vocal arrangements, Jack Lee; Orchestrations, Arnold Goland; Conductor and dance arrangements, Jack Holmes; Assistant choreographer, Bonnie Ano; Production coordinator, Don Eckstein; Associate producer, Aaron Ziegelman; General manager, Elias Goldin; Company manager, Barry Hoffman; Stage managers, Don Lamb, James Bernardi

Larry Ellis (Frank Merriwell); Linda Donovan (Inza Burrage); Bill Hinnant (Manuel); Peter Shawn (Bart Hodge); Neva Small (Belinda Belle Snodd); Thomas Ruisinger (Professor Burrage); Larry Ross (Ned); Lori Cesar (Snella Jean); Liz Sheridan (Mrs. Snodd); Jennifer Williams (Esther Carmichael); J. J. Jepson (Clyde); Walter Bobbie (Hugh); Gary Keith Steven (Tad Jones); Ellie Smith (Una Marie)

SONGS: There's No School Like Our School; Howdy, Mr. Sunshine; Prim and Proper; Inza; Look for the Happiness Ahead; I'd Be Crazy to Be Crazy Over You; Now It's Fall; The Fallin' Out-of-Love Rag; Frank, Frank, Frank; In Real Life; The Broadway of My Heart; Winter's Here; The Pure in Heart; Don't Turn His Picture to the Wall; Manuel Your Friend

Upright and stalwart all-American boy Frank Merriwell arrives at Fardale College in 1897, when Spain was agitating for war. Frank immediately floors bully Bart Hodge for attacking an unsuspecting Tad with a cowardly blow. Frank becomes the college hero, excelling at sports and falling in love with Inza Burrage, the daughter of chemistry professor Burrage, inventor of a bomb to destroy the world and sought by a Spanish spy. Merriwell saves Inza from various perils, including her entrapment by Spanish spy Manuel in an abandoned mine shaft in the Fardale Caves. Frank swings from the mine's cracking timbers and rescues Inza before Manuel's dynamite explodes.

Douglas Watt (Daily News) reported "Frank Merriwell, or Honor

Challenged is a dog. The show is so incredibly silly from start to finish that it makes It's Superman seem, in retrospect, like a masterpiece." Clive Barnes (The New York Times) recorded,"Frank Merriwell is a musical even though the music is the least admirable aspect of a modestly deplorable venture--It is all too forgettable for description. The book was worse. It was too descriptive to be forgettable." Walter Kerr (The New York Times) on May 9, 1971, reflected, "The evening was without wit or period feeling or panache, and it effectively disposed of the current notion that nostalgia works automatically, without help from men of talent and taste."

Neal Kenyon had directed and choreographed Dames At Sea, which opened Off-Broadway on December 20, 1968, and had completed 575 performances when it closed on May 10, 1970. George Oppenheimer (Newsday) noted, "It is hard to believe that the same Mr. Kenyon attended to the same chores in Dames At Sea the merry spoof of the musical films of the '30s," adding, "Unhappily, Frank Merriwell, or Honor Challenged--must be proclaimed a dud." Coupling the book and music and the colorless scenery and costumes together, Oppenheimer continued, "and its direction and choreography by Neal Kenyon only add to the blandness and amateurishness of the proceedings."

Singled out by all of the critics for his standout performance as Manuel, the Spanish spy, was Bill Hinnant who had been the original lovable Snoopy in John Gordon and Clark Gesner's long-running musical adaptation of Charles M. Shulz's comic strip Peanuts, called You're a Good Man, Charlie Brown in 1967. Richard Watts (New York Post) agreed that Hinnant stole the show but, about the Merriwell Broadway adventure, he conceded, "the inescapable fact is it is an embarrassingly amateurish concoction--neither the book nor the music can succeed in doing enough to carry on the vogue of nostalgia as the new American entertainment craze." Bill Hinnant drowned while vacationing in the Dominican Republic on February 17, 1978, at the age of forty-two.

Handsome six-footer George William Patten (who changed his given name of George to Gilbert) followed publisher Osmond W. Smith's suggestion to write a series of adventures based on an All-American, athletic, adventurous schoolboy and, using the pseudonym of Burt L. Standish, wrote his first 20,000-word Frank Merriwell story in four days. Burt L. Standish's Frank Merriwell stories were published by Street and Smith at five cents a copy. The first of 986 installments of Frank Merriwell adventures appeared on April 18, 1896, titled Frank Merriwell; or First Days at Fardale, and the first of 208 paperback Merriwell adventures, Frank Merriwell's School Days, was the basis for 1971's Frank Merriwell (Or Honor Challenged).

Patten, as Standish, ground out a complete Merriwell adventure of 20,000 words every seven days at $50 per week. Although his salary increased to $150 weekly, Patten never realized one cent of royalty for his monumental Merriwell output, which sold an estimated 124 million copies over seventeen years. Patten later acquired the copyright to his cleancut, chivalrous creation and Frank appeared in comic strips and was heard three times weekly on radio in 1934. NBC's Saturday-morning radio broadcast of The New Adventures of Frank Merriwell began on October 5, 1946, written by William Welch with Ruth and Gilbert Brann and featuring Lawson Zerbe as Frank, Elaine Rost as Inza Burrage, and Hal Studer as Bart Hodge. The second Merriwell radio series ended in 1949.

Gilbert Patten was married three times--to Alice Gardiner (1886-1898); Mary Nunn (1900-1916); and Carol Kramer (1918-1939). In 1941 he published his last tale of his then middle-aged hero, Mr. Frank Merriwell. The prolific writer and creator of Frank Merriwell, born at Corinna, Maine, on Thursday, October 25, 1866, died at the age of seventy-eight, in poverty and obscurity, at Vista, California, on Tuesday, January 16, 1945. Patten's autobiography, Frank Merriwell's "Father," edited by Harriet Hinsdale and Tony Clondon, was published by the University of Oklahoma Press in 1964.

Frank Merriwell (Or Honor Challenged) was given its world premiere at Hendrix College in Conway, Arkansas, in the early part of 1971. The "True-Blue Musical" by Skip Redwine, who graduated from Hendrix College in 1949 as Wilbur Redwine, was directed and choreographed by Larry Ellis; Musical direction by Wilbur "Skip" Redwine; Scenery by the N.J. Mirage Company; Technical adviser, Kenneth Gilliam; Costumes, Judy White; Vocal consultants, Robert McGill, Harold Thompson; Stage managers, Denny Farley, Mitch Jansonious; Assistant director, Buzz Albright; produced by Ella Myrl Shanks for the Division of Fine Arts of Hendrix College
Larry Ellis (Frank Merriwell); Marilela Pence (Inza Burrage); Randy Blyth (Bart Hodge); Joe Mays (Manuel and Joey, Jr.); Elizabeth Ann See (Belinda Belle); Jack Little (Professor Burrage); Ned Penney (Ned); Mary Lester (Snella Jean); Jan Gordon (Mrs. Snodd); Joyce Meggerson (Esther Carmichael); Rick Johnson (Clyde); Robert Armstrong (Hugh Basbridge); Jan Barger (Tad Jones); Nancy Brawner (Una Marie); Buzz Albright (Station Master); Barbara Baker (Lucy Nell); Judy Baker (Chole Myrtle); Adele Baldridge (Georgeanne); Beverly Cook (Miss Rhynas); Guy Couch (Walter Burrage); Martha Crofoot (Martha Joe); John Crofoot (Junior Jones); Hank Henley (Leslie); Mike McCully (Pepe); Robert Merriwether (Dean Gordon); Lucy Penix (Old Lady); Janna Sorrells (Mrs. Haskell); Fred Strebeck (Harvey)

In addition to the enlarged and later edited cast, the premiere production featured songs deleted from the Broadway production: "Ladies Auxiliary Steering Committee"; "Only Our Love"; "Be a Friend"; "Only Yesterday" and "Chili and Beans".

On December 25, 1971, the Drury Theatre produced Frank Merriwell (or Honor Challenged) at The Playhouse in Cleveland, Ohio.

54 / Frankenstein

Director, George Touliatos; Settings, Richard Gould; Costumes, Estelle Painter; Lighting, Jeffrey Dallas; Choreography, Anne McClusky; Musical Director, Donna Renton; Scenic art, Barbara Leatherman; Properties, David Smith; Director's assistant, Jim O'Connor; Stage manager, Richard Oberlin; Assistant stage managers, Ben Letter, Larry Tarrant

John Everson (Frank Merriwell); Kathleen Krizner (Inza Burrage); Bob Moak (Manuel); David O. Frazier (Bart Hodge); Mary Shelley (Belinda Belle Snodd); Robert Allman (Professor Burrage); Jon Beryl (Ned); Stephanie Lewis (Snella Jean); Edith Owen (Mrs. Snodd); Carolyn Younger (Esther Carmichael); John Buck, Jr. (Clyde); William Watson (Hugh); Peter Ostrum (Tad Jones); Paula Duesing (Una Marie); Stephen Randolph (Ephraim); Gail Oscar (Ida Day); Margaret Lunsford (Helen Bramble); Kate AuWerter (Elly True)

Frank Merriwell (Or Honor Challenged) did establish a "first" on Broadway. It was the first Broadway show to be produced under a "limited gross" contract by agreement with the theatrical unions and the League of New York Theatres. Nine musicians doubled in the pit, unions worked below scale and actors at scale of $164.50. Orchestra seats were $5; first mezzanine seats, $4; and second mezzanine seats, $3. The balcony of the Longacre Theatre was closed to maintain the weekly gross at $25,000. This admirable experiment of rolling back the price of theatre tickets for a Broadway musical to the level of the late thirties and early forties unfortunately could not prove itself after seven previews and one performance of Frank Merriwell (Or Honor Challenged).

* * *

FRANKENSTEIN (Palace Theatre, January 4, 1981). Produced by Terry Allen Kramer, Joseph Kipness, James M. Nederlander, Stewart F. Lane in association with Twentieth Century-Fox Productions; General management, Marvin A. Krauss Associates; A drama by Victor Gialanella based on the novel by Mary Wollstonecraft Shelly, Frankenstein; or the Modern Prometheus; Director, Tom Moore; Scenery, Douglas W. Schmidt; Costumes and puppets, Carrie F. Robbins; Arctic sequence puppets by Bil Baird; Lighting, Jules Fisher; Special effects and sound, Bran Ferren (Special effects equipment designed and built by Associates and Ferren: Chuck Harrison, Jim Shelly, Justin Scerbo, Philip Cullum, Jim Gheritty, Liza Hiltz, Ken Wisner, Steve Schultz, Jerry Nathanson); Music, Richard Peaslee; Organ recorded at St. Paul's Chapel, Columbia University organist George Stauffer; Music supervisor, Bruce Coughlin; Music coordinator, Earl Shendell; Makeup Design, John Caglione, Jr.; Makeup Technician, Linda Schultz; Fight coordinator, B. H. Barry; Puppet master, Peter Baird; Puppet consultant, Rebecca Bondor; Special effects director, William McDonough; Dog owner and trainer, William Berloni; Soundman and wardrobe, Peter J. FitzGerald; Hairstylists, John Quaglia, Debra Provenzano; Master soundmen, Allan Steeb,

James Limberg, James Travers; Assistant to Mr. Schmidt, Vicki Paul; Assistant to director, Nancy Robbins; Production assistant, Kathleen C. Shannon; Production associate, Charlotte Dicker, Associate producer, Marvin A. Krauss; Assistants to Robbins, Margarita Delgado, Roberta Favant, Debra Stein, Deborah Van Wettering; Master propertymen, Munro Gabler, Al Steiner; Propertyman, Charles Zuckerman; Stage managers, Michael Martorella, John Fennessy, Stephen Van Benschoten; Impalement effect by Foy Inventerprises, Inc.

David Dukes (replaced William Converse-Roberts) (Victor Frankenstein, a Young Scientist); John Glover (Henry Clerval, Victor's Friend); Dianne Wiest (Elizabeth, Victor's adopted "Cousin"); Keith Jochim (The Creature); John Carradine (DeLacey, a Blind Hermit); Douglas Seale (Alphonse Frankenstein, Victor's Father); Scott Schwartz (William Frankenstein, Victor's younger Brother); John Seitz (Hans Metz, a Villager); Dennis Bacigalupi (Peter Schmidt, a Villager); Jill P. Rose (Justine Moritz, a Maidservant); Richard Kneeland (Lionel Mueller, The Local Magistrate); Kate Wilkinson (Frau Mueller, his Wife); Champion McCallum's Pips Gadabout (Fritz, the Dog)

In the mid-nineteenth century, after long experimentation, scientist Dr. Victor Frankenstein develops a living creature from bits and pieces of dead bodies stolen from graveyards. During a violent electric storm over the tower laboratory of his Geneva, Switzerland, chateau, Dr. Frankenstein hysterically exclaims, "It's alive! There's a pulse!" The horribly freakish creature escapes from Frankenstein's laboratory, killing off the Doctor's younger brother and his dog and a blind hermit who has befriended him, plus other innocents. The creature destroys his creator's laboratory and kills the man playing God, Dr. Victor Frankenstein.

Mary Wollstonecraft Shelley's novel <u>Frankenstein; or The Modern Prometheus</u> was published on March 11, 1818, and was first dramatized by Richard Brinsley Peake as <u>Presumption; or The Fate of Frankenstein</u>, which opened on July 28, 1823, at London's English Opera House (Lyceum Theatre) with James Wallack as Dr. Frankenstein and Thomas Potter Cooke as the Creature. Five different dramatizations of the novel appeared in London in 1823 and Merle and Anthony's French dramatization, <u>Le Monstre et le Magicien</u>, was seen in a Paris Grand Guignol production in 1826. H. M. Milner's play <u>Frankenstein; or The Man and the Monster</u> opened at London's Royal Coburg Theatre on July 3, 1826. Richard Henry (Richard Butler and H. Chane Newton) burlesqued <u>Frankenstein</u> at London's Gaiety Theatre on December 23, 1887, with Nellie Farren as the addled Doctor and comedian Fred Leslie as the Monster. Peggy Webling's more literal adaptation of the novel featured Henry Hallat as Dr. Frankenstein and Hamilton Deane as the Monster at London's Little Theatre on February 10, 1930. None of the stage adaptations of <u>Frankenstein</u> could be called successful. Only Hollywood attained success and profit with Mrs. Shelley's novel.

Peggy Webling's play and Mrs. Shelley's book were adapted for the screen by John L. Balderston whose script was replaced by another scenario by Robert Florey and Garrett Fort. The Florey-Fort script was revamped by director James Whale with scriptwriters Francis Edwards Faragoh and Garrett Fort. In 1931 Frankenstein was superbly directed by James Whale for Universal Pictures, with Colin Clive as Dr. Frankenstein and Boris Karloff as the Monster. Whale's Frankenstein has become the film classic of the horror genre. But Frankenstein, or films relating to the Doctor and his Creature, proliferated to the brink of boredom for over forty years, into and including the era of television.

Possibly encouraged by the impressive, successful revival of Hamilton Deane and John Lloyd Balderston's 1924 dramatization of Bram Stoker's 1897 novel, Dracula, highlighted by Edward Gorey's striking settings and costumes and a virtuoso performance by Frank Langella, which opened on October 20, 1977, at the Martin Beck Theatre and closed on January 6, 1980, after an astonishing 925 performances (the original 1927 production of Dracula starring Bela Lugosi remained on Broadway for 261 performances), presumably a successful revival of Frankenstein appeared feasible.

The American public has been saturated and desensitized by mayhem and horror for many years. Hollywood's annual crop of ersatz, insensate horror films and television's daily macabre offerings (to say nothing of the news media and the daily evening news) had, by the decade of the eighties, relegated Frankenstein to classic camp. A bad play is seldom improved or redeemed when set to music or plied with excessive special effects. "The Play's the Thing" and no amount of theatrical tricks, pyrogenic hyperbole, or monetary investment can change that, although Broadway stubbornly attempts the impossible each season and Hollywood has persisted in the pursuit for years.

Victor Gialanella's first play was a dramatization of Frankenstein, originally tested by the Loretto-Hilton Repertory Company in St. Louis for a five-week run. Gialanella, then production manager for the Loretto-Hilton Repertory Company, was aware that Universal Pictures' adaptation drastically altered the novel, not only in the switching of characters' names but in making Frankenstein's Creature completely mute. Gialanella returned to Mrs. Shelley's tale for his script, augmented by special effects later designed for cinematic literature. "The novel is very different," Mr. Gialanella explained, "not only in its treatment of the Creature but also in its treatment of science at the time--It's never really been done, a first class American stage production. It's a helluvah vehicle, just presentationally and storywise. That, actually, was the genesis of it for me."

Joseph Kipness acquired Casablanca Records as his coproducer and engaged Tom Moore, who had directed Grease, Broadway's longest-running musical (3,388 performances), to direct Gialanella's horror opus, budgeted at $500,000 (later capitalized at $1.25 million) with an opening scheduled for December 18, 1980. Following Casablanca Records' fiscal problems, Kipness became coproducer with James M. Nederlander and Mrs. Terry Allen Kramer, joined later by Stewart F. Lane and Twentieth Century-Fox Productions. Two of Tom Moore's compatriots from <u>Grease</u> contributed--Douglas W. Schmidt was engaged to design eight sets arranged on a large turntable for the play's prologue and ten scenes and Carrie H. Robbins to create the costumes and puppets. The production's premier artiste was Hollywood special effects expert Bran Ferren, who had created the spectacular special effects for Ken Russell's film <u>Altered States</u> and Broadway's 1978 play <u>The Crucifer of Blood</u>.

Keith Jochim, who had created Gialanella's Creature in St. Louis, was engaged to reprise the monster role and young Yale actor William Converse-Roberts was signed to play Dr. Frankenstein. Rehearsals began on October 27, 1980, with a scheduled opening set for December 18th. Previews of <u>Frankenstein</u> began at Broadway's Palace Theatre on December 9th but Ferren's elaborate and intricate special effects demanded more rehearsal time and the opening date was advanced to December 29th. William Converse-Roberts was dropped from the cast on Tuesday, December 16th, due to "a change in the concept of the role" and understudy Mark Winkworth substituted for Converse-Roberts until Friday, December 26th when, whatever the "change in concept" hyperbole meant, an exceptionally talented actor, David Dukes, took over the role of Dr. Frankenstein.

Conceived in spectacular cinematic staging, in which Broadway can not compete with Hollywood, <u>Frankenstein</u> played 29 previews. The Gialanella epic opened on Sunday, January 4, 1981, and closed the same night having accumulated a staggering cost of $2 million, thus becoming the most expensive flop of a straight drama in Broadway history.

Director Tom Moore told Carol Lawson of <u>The New York Times</u>, "I'm leaving the New York theatre. I'm proud of my work, but the critics make it impossible for it to be seen here. This is the greatest disappointment of my life. We did a lot of rewriting. It's not a major piece of American writing, but it was never intended to be. The play was written as a theatrical event. We didn't attempt to say anything with a message in <u>Frankenstein</u>. We attempted to make a grand entertainment--a spectacle--and we did."

<u>Frankenstein</u> (released November 21, 1931) Universal Pictures. Produced by Carl Laemmle, Jr.; Director, James Whale; Screenplay, Garrett Fort, Francis Edwards Faragoh, John Russell, and Robert Florey, based on John L. Balderston's adaptation of the play by Peggy Webling from the novel by Mary Wollstonecraft Shelley; Photography, Arthur Edeson; Special electrical effects, Kenneth Strickfaden; Art director, Charles D. Hall; Makeup devised by Jack P. Pierce; Set designer, Herman Rosse; Scenario editor, Richard Schayer;

Technical assistant, Dr. Cecil Reynolds; Recording supervisor, C.
Roy Hunter; Supervising film editor, Maurice Pivar; Film editor,
Clarence Kolster; Musical editor, David Broekman
  Colin Clive (Dr. Henry Frankenstein); Boris Karloff (The Monster);
Mae Clarke (Elizabeth); John Boles (Victor); Edward Van Sloan
(Dr. Waldman); Dwight Frye (Fritz, the Dwarf); Frederick Kerr
(The Baron); Lionel Belmore (The Burgomaster); Marilyn Harris
(Maria, the child); Michael Mark (Ludwig); Arletta Duncan, Pauline Moore (Bridesmaids); Francis Ford (Wounded Villager)

* * *

GANTRY (George Abbott Theatre, February 14, 1970). Produced
by Joseph Cates and Jerry Schlossberg; A musical based on Sinclair
Lewis's novel Elmer Gantry; Book by Peter Bellwood; Director, Onna
White; Music, Stanley Lebowsky; Lyrics, Fred Tobias; Settings, Robin
Wagner; Lighting, Jules Fisher; Costumes, Ann Roth; Orchestrations,
Jim Tyler; Musical director, Arthur Rubenstein; Dance arrangements,
Dorothea Freitag; Assistant choreographer, Patrick Cummings; Production manager, Ben Janney; Director's assistant, Martin Allen;
Associate producer, Fred Menowitz; Hairstylist, Ernest Adler; Production supervised by Robert Weiner; Vocal arrangements, Stanley
Lebowsky; General managers, Robert Weiner, Nelle Nugent; Stage
managers, Ben Janney, William Letters, Mary Porter Hall
  Robert Shaw (Elmer Gantry); Rita Moreno (Sharon Falconer);
Wayne Tippit (Jim Lefferts); Gloria Hodes (Adelberta Shoup);
David Hooks (Rev. Toomis); Tom Batten (Bill Morgan); Dorothea
Freitag (Sister Doretha); Kenneth Bridges (Rev. Garrison); Bob
Gorman (Trosper); David Sabin (Gunch); Zale Kessler (Prout);
Robert Donahue (Architect); James N. Maher (Photographer); J.
Michael Bloom (Deaf Man); Beth Fowler (His Wife); Ted Thurston
(George F. Babbitt); Chuck Beard, J. Michael Bloom, Kenneth
Bridges, Patrick Cummings, Robert Donahue, Sandy Ellen, Carol
Estey, Beth Fowler, Gloria Hodes, Keith Kaldenberg, Clyde Laurents, Robert Lenn, James N. Maher, Kathleen Robey, Dixie
Stewart, Diane Tarleton, Maralyn Thoma, Terry Violino, Mimi
Wallace (Townspeople, etc.)
SONGS: Wave a Hand; Gantry Gets the Call; Katie Jonas; He Was
There; Play Ball With The Lord; Thanks, Sweet Jesus!; Someone I've
Already Found; We're Sharin' Sharon; He's Never Too Busy; We Can
All Give Love; Foresight; These Four Walls; Show Him the Way; The
Promise of What I Could Be; Gantry's Reaction (Original Cast Album--
RCA Victor Records)

  Conniving, opportunistic Elmer Gantry becomes enamored of
Sister Sharon Falconer, a dedicated evangelist with whom he has an
affair. Hypocritical Gantry views religion as a path to fame and
fortune and his hellfire-and-brimstone oratory quickly establishes
him as a star in the soul-saving arena. Rhetorically regaling congregations with his past glories as a football hero and comparing God
to his blocking back, Gantry's talent for spellbinding spieling is

equalled by his impressive ability to bilk the faithful of their coin of the realm. Cynical newspaperman Jim Lefferts correctly suspects Gantry's sanctimonious charade and attacks him in the press. But the new Right Reverend Gantry overcomes published criticism and public doubt. Pompous real-estate tycoon George F. Babbitt, prospective mayor of Chicago, sponsors Sharon's revival meetings but joins other politicians in opposing her ambitious plan to build a huge tabernacle. Sharon is victorious in getting her Waters of Jordan Tabernacle built in Chicago, but on opening night she loses her life when the tabernacle is destroyed by fire and Gantry is left alone in the ashes.

Thirty-year-old York, England-born Peter L. Bellwood was a writer and performer in English revues who became an associate producer for New York's The Establishment Theatre in 1966 and later played in a touring company of Beyond the Fringe. Bellwood's fragmentary adaptation of Sinclair Lewis's novel Elmer Gantry was considered "flippant and shallow" and his transferrence of the story to Chicago, from Kansas and Atlantic City, covered only the episode of Gantry's involvement with revivalist Sister Sharon Falconer. Beyond rearranging Lewis's novel and referring to the author as "that well known atheist, Sinclair Lewis," Bellwood also injected George F. Babbitt (from Lewis's 1922 novel Babbitt) into the script, and Gantry's old friend and schoolmate Jim Lefferts became a cynical Chicago newspaperman.

Composer Stanley Lebowsky was a former conductor of Broadway musicals (Whoop-Up; Irma La Douce; Tovarich; Half a Sixpence and the beleagured unopened Breakfast at Tiffany's, also known as Holly Golightly), who collaborated with lyricist Fred Tobias on Julius Monk's Plaza 9 revues. Gantry was their first Broadway show, although Tobias had contributed lyrics to Duke Ellington's music for Jerome Weidman's failed adaptation of the classic 1930 film The Blue Angel called Pousse-Cafe, which was a three-performance mishap in 1966.

Robert Shaw, born on Tuesday, August 9, 1927, in Westhoughton, Lancashire, England, made his musical debut in Gantry. A protean performer and gifted author, Robert Shaw died of a heart attack at the age of fifty-one on Tuesday, August 29, 1978, at Tourmakeady, Ireland. Shaw married three times and was the father of ten children. He made his stage debut in England in 1945 and his Broadway stage debut in Harold Pinter's 1951 play The Caretaker. His first book, The Hiding Place, was published in 1959 and his 1967 drama, The Man in the Glass Booth, was successful on the stages of London and New York. Shaw is probably best remembered in America for his excellent performances in the motion pictures The Sting, Jaws, and The Deep. He once told a reporter, "When they write my obituary I would like them to say 'He was an author who wrote one book that will last and he was also a remarkable actor.'"

Robert Shaw starred in Gantry with Rita Moreno, the only performer to have won a "Tony," an "Oscar," a "Grammy," and two "Emmy's." Critics acknowledged the excellence of both performances during the thirty-two previews and one performance of Gantry. The musical lost a total investment of $414,658.58, of which RCA Records contributed $200,000, Joseph Cates, $59,500, and the balance by individual investors. Richard Watts, Jr. (New York Post) found Robert Shaw's "portrayal of a fraudulent American evangelist" the "striking feature of Gantry." In Watts' consideration "the music by Stanley Lebowsky and the lyrics by Fred Tobias add little to the brightness of the proceedings" and Bellwood's libretto failed "in its efforts to capture the essence of the once-famous novel, although, it is by no means a totally disastrous attempt--I believe Gantry misses its aim, but Robert Shaw emphatically doesn't."

Clive Barnes (The New York Times) felt Gantry was worth seeing despite the book and lyrics suffering from a misunderstanding of Sinclair Lewis and the adaptation being "a travesty of Sinclair Lewis' novel," adding, "This is an unusual if musically commonplace, musical. It is not as good as it should have been yet it has enough pure theatrical electricity in its air to make it possibly worth seeing." "Mr. Shaw," Barnes wrote, "gives as good a performance as you will find in this or many other a season." Douglas Watt (Daily News) felt both Robert Shaw and Rita Moreno were miscast and that had a collection been taken during the revival meeting scene, the plates would have remained empty.

Harry Sinclair Lewis, born on Thursday, February 7, 1884, at Sauk Centre, Minnesota, first titled his novel Sounding Brass but, discovering Ethel Mannin had already used that title, changed it to Elmer Bloor. Retaining Elmer, he toyed with the surnames of Skaggs, Flaugh, and even Myron Melish, finally choosing Elmer Gantry. The novel, seen as a devastating satire on the religious sideshow pretentions devised by evangelists Aimee Semple McPherson and Billy Sunday, was published on March 10, 1927, by Harcourt Brace Jovanovich, Inc. with the then-largest first printing on record --140,000 copies. Lewis dedicated Elmer Gantry to H. L. Mencken "with profound admiration."

Alcoholic Lewis, who died at the age of sixty-six on Wednesday, January 10, 1951, of a heart attack outside of Rome, Italy, had refused the Pulitzer Prize for his novel Arrowsmith in 1926. During the research for Elmer Gantry, Lewis held weekly seminars in Kansas City with representatives of several faiths and reaped national notoriety by speaking from a Kansas City pulpit and defying God to strike him down in fifteen minutes. William Allen White, reviewing Elmer Gantry for The New York Times on March 11, 1927, wrote, "Sinclair Lewis stood in the pulpit of a Kansas City church last Spring and defied God to strike him dead. So far as Sinclair Lewis the artist is concerned, in the book Elmer Gantry, God took him at his word. He got so excited making faces at God that he forgot his craftsmanship." Walter Lippmann described Elmer Gantry as "A witch burning to make an atheist holiday" and Lewis's biographer Mark Schorer later wrote that Elmer Gantry was "not so much a literary event as it was a public scandal."

Lewis gave his approval for playwright Bayard Veillers to dramatize his picaresque novel, which Robert Milton agreed to produce. Veillers, author of such plays as The Trial of Mary Dugan and Within the Law, destroyed his completed manuscript of Elmer Gantry in October, 1927, explaining, "My dramatization of the novel was even more bitter than the novel itself. I did not realize how bitter it was until I had completed it. It would have offended a great many people, particularly clergymen. What is the use of making trouble?" Producer Robert Milton had cast Harry Bannister for the leading role in Veillers's dramatization, with Ann Shoemaker and Irene Homer.

Nine months later William A. Brady produced another adaptation of Elmer Gantry on Broadway, which became less of a battle between God, Satan, and Sinners and more of a clash between producer, playwright, and performers.

Elmer Gantry (Playhouse Theatre, opened August 9, 1928--48 performances). Produced by Joseph E. Shea; A drama by Patrick Kearney, based on the novel of the same name by Sinclair Lewis; Director, Lumsden Hare; Settings, Livingston Platt; Costumes, W. H. Matthews
 Edward Pawley (Elmer Gantry); Adele Klaer (replaced Vera Allen) (Sharon Falconer); Gwendolyn Hathaway (Lulu Bains); Ernest Pollock (Deacon Bains); Tom Fadden (Floyd Naylor); Winifred Barry (Hettie Dowling); Lumsden Hare (T. J. Riggs); Frank Johnson (Adelbert Shoop); Rose Burdick (Lily Anderson); Mabel Montgomery (Mrs. Bains); Robert Harrigan (Frank Shallard); Eustace Wyatt (Cecil Ayleston); C. Carlton (replaced Frank Shannon) (Father Harvey); Edward Boralle (Rev. Willis Fortune Tate); Leo Cooper (replaced Arthur Ross) (Rabbi Bernard Amos); Ernest Pollock (Dr. Hickenlooper); Eugene Blake (Josiah Jessup); Henry Sherwood (Oscar Dowling); Patrick Korrigan (Fireman); Eustace Wyatt (Irving Tillish); Jennie Bradley (First Trumpeter); Marion Sargent (Second Trumpeter); Llewella Lloyd (Third Trumpeter); Agnes Geraldi (Fourth Trumpeter); Betty Donn (First Choir Singer); Anna Meares (Second Choir Singer); Mary Anderson (Third Choir Singer); Alma Chase (Fourth Choir Singer); Julia Collier (Fifth Choir Singer); Betty Wald (Sixth Choir Singer); Hazel Clinger (Seventh Choir Singer); Louise Ross (Eighth Choir Singer); Eustace Wyatt (Ninth Choir Singer)

Patrick Kearney, whose play A Man's Man delighted Broadway in 1925 for 120 performances, adapted Theodore Dreiser's 1925 novel An American Tragedy to the stage in 1926, which completed 216 performances on Broadway. Kearney subtitled his adaptation of Sinclair Lewis's controversial novel Elmer Gantry: Three Episodes from the Life of a Modern Crusader. Kearney's format was: 1) Elmer

Gantry Begins the Work of the Lord--Deacon Bains Schoenheim, Kansas home. 2) Elmer Gantry Achieves Salvation through Sharon Falconer--Lincoln, Nebraska, and Atlantic City, New Jersey. 3) Elmer Gantry Undertakes to Purify Zenith--as the Reverend Doctor Gantry of the Wellspring Church.

During the tryout of Elmer Gantry and its subsequent Broadway production, Thompson Buchanan rewrote the third act of Kearney's play. Backstage disagreements resulted in the last-minute replacements of several players and producer William A. Brady declining to be named as producer. Kearney vigorously opposed Buchanan's reconstruction and Elmer Gantry's Broadway opening was postponed from Tuesday, August 7 to Thursday, August 9, 1928.

During the first-act intermission the show's white-robed female trumpeters staged a revival meeting on 48th Street in front of the Playhouse Theatre, loudly trumpeting the old hymn "Throw Out the Life Line," which attracted so many Broadway sinners the police had to intervene. The sacred and profane were disbanded and the ballyhooers reentered the theatre to pass collection plates through the audience, unburdened by contributions from the first-nighters. Robert Edgar Long, press agent for producer William A. Brady, had been stripped of his rank during the backstage battles and got carried away by the trumpeting call to glory. Long joined other "sinners" on-stage during the revival scene by running down the aisle reasonably proclaiming, "I love Jesus more than William A. Brady!"

The New Yorker magazine classified Elmer Gantry as "a real bad play, overcrowded with incidents and certainly acted with a bit more fervor than it deserves." Time magazine reported, "Evangelists are not popular upon Broadway and in the theatre they are monsters of depravity, to be baited and scorned. Sinclair Lewis in his savage history made Elmer Gantry a lewd and naughty figure. But in the play he is so wicked as to be incredible--The crude vigor of the performances and the oily excesses of the actors made Elmer Gantry an exciting, though phony melodrama."

Other theatrical evangelical efforts on Broadway had met with less than religious response. William Hurlbut's play Bride of the Lamb, rated as one of 1926's Ten Best Plays, featured Crane Wilbur as Sanderson Herrick posing as revival evangelist Reverend Albaugh, for whom Alice Brady, as Ina Bowman, poisons her husband to run off with the fraudulent minister only to discover he has a wife. John Meehan and Robert Riskin's Bless You, Sister in 1927 starred Alice Brady as evangelist Mary MacDonald for 24 performances. Bless You, Sister, fashioned on the carnival antics by Aimee Semple McPherson, eventually became Columbia Pictures' 1931 The Miracle Woman, directed by Frank Capra and starring Barbara Stanwyck, which was banned in Great Britain as "irreverent." Sidney Howard and Charles MacArthur's 1928 drama Salvation revealed that evangelist Bethany Jones, played by Pauline Lord, had an easy virtue and feet of clay, through thirty-one performances. Harry Wagstaff Gribble's drama Revolt in 1928 presented an evangelist who fainted at the mere thought of baptism by immersion.

Patrick Kearney's adaptation of Elmer Gantry was first produced by Mannheim and Shea, Inc. at the Little Theatre in Cleveland, Ohio, on May 20, 1928. Director, Joseph Graham; Scenery, Louis Miller Studios; Decor, Paul Radder; General manager, Bert H. Todd; Stage manager, Howard Keegan
 Edward Pawley (Elmer Gantry); Adele Klaer (replaced Regina Wallace) (Sharon Falconer); Margaret Hawkins (Lulu Bains); Peter Doyle (Deacon Bains); Patti Cortez (Mrs. Bains); Howard Keegan (Frank Shallard); Tom Fadden (Floyd Naylor); Frank Johnson (Adelbert Shoop); Herrick Sherman (Cecil Ayleston); Lucile Keating (Lily Anderson); Mannart Kippen (Dr. North); Sallie Sanford (Hettie Dowling); David Cameron (Oscar Dowling); Eustace Wyatt (T. J. Riggs); Alice Hersch, Louis Klein, Beatrice Kane, Jule Stewart, Julia Shelley, Roger Liddell, Sarah Leabold, Ann Charles, Flo Neeley, Walter Beach, Marion Martin, Eleanor Byrne, Jerry Hausner (Choir Singers)

Regina Wallace, playing the part of Sharon Falconer, reacted to various threats of reprisal should Elmer Gantry have the temerity to open and, convinced of immediate arrest, took the first train East from Cleveland to Manhattan, where Actors' Equity forgave her professional sin. Adele Klaer replaced Wallace and when actress Vera Allen left the cast prior to the Broadway opening of Elmer Gantry, Miss Klaer once again went on.

For thirteen years Richard Brooks had tried to get his screen treatment of Elmer Gantry produced in Hollywood. After spending two years making a screen adaptation of Sinclair Lewis's novel (which also included George Babbitt from Lewis's 1922 novel Babbitt), Elmer Gantry was filmed and released by United Artists in 1960. Elmer Gantry garnered three Academy Awards: Burt Lancaster as Best Actor of the Year for his portrayal of the fiery, bombastic, con-man Gantry; Shirley Jones as Best Supporting Actress as the deflowered deacon's daughter, and Richard Brooks for his screenplay.

Elmer Gantry (United Artists). Produced by Bernard Smith; Director and screenplay, Richard Brooks; Camera, John Alton; Art director, Edward Carrere; Set decorator, Frank Tuttle; Costumes, Dorothy Jeakins; Music, Andre Previn; Sound, Harry Mills; Assistant directors, Tom Shaw, Rose Wallerstein, Carl Beringer; Editor, Marge Fowler
 Burt Lancaster (Elmer Gantry); Jean Simmons (Sister Sharon Falconer); Arthur Kennedy (Jim Lefferts); Shirley Jones (Lulu Baines); Dean Jagger (William L. Morgan); Patti Page (Sister Rachel); Edward Andrews (George Babbitt); John McIntire (Reverend Pengily); Michael Whalen (Reverend Phillips); Hugh Marlowe (Reverend Garrison); Philip Ober (Reverend Planck); Rex Ingram (Negro Preacher); Joe Maross (Pete); Everett Glass (Rev-

erend Brown); Wendell Holmes (Reverend Ulrich); Barry Kelley (Captain Holt); John Qualen (Sam)

* * *

THE GARDEN OF SWEETS (ANTA Theatre, October 31, 1961). Produced by Ben Frye and Irving Squires; A drama by Waldemar Hansen; Director, Milton Katselas; Designed by Boris Aronson; Lighting, Tharon Musser; Costumes, Patricia Zipprodt; Music, John Balamos; Production coordinator, Pat Fowler; Stage managers, Richard Blofson, William Woodman

Katina Paxinou (Ana Zachariadis); Lou Antonio (replaced Robert Elston) (Stavro); Madeleine Sherwood (succeeded Martha Greenhouse, who replaced Jo Van Fleet) (Ida); Morgan Sterne (Alex); Martine Bartlett (Helen); Ted Beniades (Nicky); Eleni Kiamos (Sophie); Leslye Hunter (Penny); John Balzac (Costa); Boris Tumarin (Father Athanasios); Alan Howard (A Boy)

Deserted by her husband, Greek-American matriarch Ana "Manna" Zachariadis has succeeded, through thirty years of hard work, in making her Buffalo, New York, ice-cream parlor and candy store, The Garden of Sweets, a profitable business, but she has been unsuccessful in her doting dominance of her three sons and daughter. Ana unites her family to celebrate Easter. Her favorite, youngest son Stavro, returns home after three years and an unconsummated marriage Ana had arranged for him. Alcoholic son Costa works for "Manna," as does his embittered Nordic wife, Ida, who hopes Ana will soon die and they will inherit The Garden of Sweets. Lecherous son Alex, who loathes his mother's Garden of Sweets, has become a successful florist and, like his father, a compulsive gambler and womanizer. Spinster daughter Helen has long since abandoned all hope of love and marriage. Ana dies of a heart attack and even after death tightens the bonds of disunity between her disparate children. Ana leaves The Garden of Sweets to her least favorite son, self-reliant, selfish, and disinterested Alex.

"The Garden of Sweets does not have the sweet smell of success," reported John McClain (Journal American), "there is nothing wrong with a good, grim tragedy, Greek-American style. But the sad fact is, we are never made to care much what happens to these miserable people." John Chapman (Daily News) called the drama, "a work of woe, bum writing and bad acting" while considering Boris Aronson's setting the best he had designed. Howard Taubman (The New York Times) wrote, "In a way Mr. Hansen's play is like an unsparing post-mortem into the afflictions that have turned this family into a grim, unhappy lot--But he fails to communicate his comprehension and compassion so that the audience shares them."

Norman Nadel (New York World-Telegram-Sun) felt that playwright Hansen made a mistake in "substituting misery for tragedy-- The play affords no emotional catharsis, just a persistent queasiness," and the players, "trapped by ridiculous, pompous dialogue and certainly not helped by direction, also are victims of their own excesses." Justin Gilbert (New York Mirror) appraised the play as beginning "on a dark and disspiriting note and closes on one even more depressing. It has gone nowhere, leaving behind a wake of recriminations, ugly and abortive." Richard Watts, Jr. (New York Post) viewed The Garden of Sweets as "Tedious--there hasn't been a gloomier Greek family on the stage since the House of Atreus than the modern clan assembled by Waldemar Hansen--The Garden of Sweets is a play of overwhelming absence of dramatic effectiveness."

The great Greek classical actress Katina Paxinou, who, with her husband Alexis Minotis, was a founder of the Greek National Theatre, made her Broadway stage debut in the title role of Henrik Ibsen's Hedda Gabler on January 29, 1942. Katina Paxinou, who died at the age of seventy-two in her native Athens on February 22, 1973, is best remembered by American audiences for her Academy Award-winning performance as Pilar in Paramount Pictures 1943 screen version of Ernest Hemingway's novel For Whom the Bell Tolls. Howard Taubman observed in The New York Times that "Manna" Ana was "played by the redoubtable Katina Paxinou with a ferocity suitable for Electra."

Guthrie McClintic presented The National Theatre of Greece on Broadway for a limited engagement beginning November 19, 1952. The Greek company, headed by Paxinou and Alexis Minotis, performed Sophocles' Electra and his Oedipus, revised in a modern stage version by Photos Politis called Oedipus Tyrannus. Katina Paxinou had also been seen on Broadway in the title role of Sophie, a dramatization of Rose C. Feld's stories Sophie Halenczik, American, for nine performances beginning December 25, 1944, and in the leading role of Federico García Lorca's The House of Bernardo Alba on January 7, 1951, directed by Boris Tumarin, who played Father Athanasios in The Garden of Sweets.

The Garden of Sweets premiered at Philadelphia's Walnut Street Theatre on October 18, 1961, for two weeks. Henry T. Murdock (The Philadelphia Inquirer) warned that Hansen's attempt at modern Greek tragedy fell "short of that high-estate because of a general lack of purpose and a diffusion of its motives and sympathies," calling it "tortuous and cloudy--It seems to labor unduly in an effort to make cryptic some rather commonplace conclusions" and in The Garden of Sweets "the favorite syrup at the soda bar seems to be gall."

Two years prior to the Broadway production, Tennessee Williams had suggested to Paxinou that she should play the lead in Waldemar Hansen's first play, The Garden of Sweets. Hansen visited the actress in Athens and after reading the script she agreed to play matriarch Ana or "Manna" (Mama in Greek). Unfortunately Katina Paxinou's journey from the glories that were Greece to the faded glory that was Broadway was as futile as The Garden of Sweets.

GOOD NEIGHBOR (Windsor Theatre, October 21, 1941). Produced by Sam Byrd; A drama by Jack Levin; Director, Sinclair Lewis; Settings, Frederick Fox; General manager, Hugo Schaaf; Stage managers, Winfield Smith, Albert Vees

Anna Appel (Hannah Barron); Sam Byrd (Dave Barron); Lewis Charles (Barney Barron); Howard Fischer (Heinrich); Gustav Shackt (Yankel Barron); Albert Vees (Whitey); Edith Shayne (Mrs. Jacobs); Grace Mills (Mrs. Kurtmann); Arthur Anderson (Luther); Edna Mae Harris (Bessie); Helen Carter (Miss Jolly); Marcella Powers (Hildie); Winfield Smith (Leader of the Cavaliers); John A. Sterns (Second Cavalier); Henry Sherwood (Doctor); Susanne Turner (Miss Jaffrey); Leslie Barrett (Western Union Boy); Donald Arbury (Officer Clydesdale)

Dave Barron goes to sea and sends his mother Hannah money to save for his wedding to Hildie. Philanthropic, good-neighbor Hannah uses Dave's money for her oppressed neighbors. Dave returns to be married and finds Hannah has charitably "borrowed" his thousand dollars. Hannah hides Luther Kurtmann, a retarded German boy, wrongly accused of murdering a member of the marauding Cavalier vigilantes. Warned by black prostitute Bessie that the Cavaliers are coming for the boy, Hannah refuses to turn Luther over to them, and when she refuses to accept more money than she has "borrowed" from Dave, the Cavaliers shoot her. But Hannah dies contentedly, knowing Dave will receive her insurance money.

"Good Neighbor is all thumbs as a play and is mixed up with more family crises and neighborhood complications than you can shake a blue pencil at," reported Brooks Atkinson (The New York Times,) adding that the play was acted by what seemed to be "a second-rate stock company." Richard Watts (Herald Tribune) deplored Levin's drama, declaring, "Even tolerance and love of neighbor can become dubious qualities when they result in so terrible a play as the new work at the Windsor Theatre."

Jack Levin's play was tested for a week's engagement beginning September 2, 1941, at the Stony Creek Theatre in Connecticut. Under the title of The Good Neighbor, the play was directed by Sinclair Lewis and produced by Sam Byrd by arrangement with Ronald T. Hammond, with settings by Dagmar Hampf

Anna Appel (Hannah Barron); Jackson Wright (Dave Barron); John Hacker (Barney Barron); Willard Scholz (Heinrich); Gustav Shackt (Yankel Barron); Albert Vees (Whitey); Jane Rose (Mrs. Kurtmann); Arthur Anderson (Luther Kurtmann); Nina Mae McKinney (Bessie); Marcella Powers (Hildie); Donald Arbury (Clydesdale); Walter Plinge (Leader of the Cavaliers); Sidney Sokoloff (First Cavalier); George Forman (Second Cavalier); Harry Borchers III (Boy)

Stage-struck, frustrated-actor, novelist Sinclair Lewis's fascination with the theatre materialized into little more than ambitious dreams and his acceptance as a substantial man of the theatre became a grand illusion. Lewis's first play, The Jayhawker, written with Chicago News drama critic Lloyd Lewis, opened on Broadway on October 15, 1934, starring Fred Stone for twenty-four performances. Lewis, with J. C. Moffet, adapted his best-selling novel It Can't Happen Here to the stage in 1938 but the following year his solo playwright effort, called Queenie and the Japes, could not find a producer.

Mr. Lewis's play Angela Is Twenty-Two, coauthored with King Kong's cinematic love Fay Wray, opened in Columbus, Ohio, on December 30, 1938, with the famed novelist playing the leading role, which he wisely relinquished to actor Philip Merivale on January 24, 1939. Angela aged weekly and closed on April 1, 1939, in Chicago. Undisturbed by his lack of acclaimed thespian talent, Sinclair Lewis returned to the stage in the summer of 1939 at Oquiquit, Maine, as the Stage Manager in Thornton Wilder's classic play Our Town and alternated in the leading roles of Paul Vincent Carroll's drama Shadow and Substance and Eugene O'Neill's Ah, Wilderness!. Later Lewis used the exhaustive 21-city tour of Angela Is Twenty-Two as background for his 1940 novel Bethel Merriday, and Angela was reborn in Universal Pictures 1944 screen version titled This Is the Life.

The celebrated author of Main Street, Babbitt, Arrowsmith, and other best-selling novels persisted in his pursuit of theatrical glory and invested $25,000 of the $30,000 production cost of Baltimore advertising writer Jack Levin's first play, Good Neighbor, which obviously entitled him to direct the sudsy drama. Actor Sam Byrd, who had a remarkable talent for acquiring bad plays, producing them, and playing the leading role, produced Good Neighbor and played the leading male role for an investment of $1,000. Byrd in 1937 produced Samson Raphaelson's 1929 rejected and unproduced play Harlem under the title of White Man and played the leading role for seven performances.

Anna Bercovici Appel, who died at the age of seventy-five on Tuesday, November 19, 1963, in New York's Belleview Hospital, made her first appearance in America with the Yiddish Theatre. Bucharest, Rumania-born Miss Appel played leads for many seasons in the Yiddish Theatre, opposite Maurice Schwartz. During her fifty-year career Anna Appel alternated between the Yiddish- and English-speaking stages and made her last Manhattan stage appearance in The Golem at Off-Broadway's St. Marks Playhouse on February 25, 1959. Brooks Atkinson wrote about her portrayal of Hannah in Good Neighbor, "Anna Appel carries the play on broad and experienced shoulders with generous goodwill. She probably could act the telephone book, if necessary, for she has great strength as an actress and great warmth as a person."

68 / The Goodbye People

* * *

THE GOODBYE PEOPLE (Belasco Theatre, April 30, 1979). Produced by Joseph Kipness and Maurice Rosenfield; A revival of a comedy by Herb Gardner; Director, Jeff Bleckner; Setting, Santo Loquasto; Lighting, Jennifer Tipton; Costumes, Elizabeth Palmer; Associate Producers, Charlotte Dicker, Jamie Rosenfield; General manager, Marvin A. Krauss; Company manager, Gary Gunas; Stage managers, Fritz Holt, Judy Shafran.

Herschel Bernardi (Max Silverman); Melanie Mayron (Nancy Scott); Ron Rifkin (Arthur Korman); Sammy Smith (Marcus Soloway); Michael Tucker (Michael Silverman); Marvin Lichterman (Eddie Bergson)

Aware his recent near fatal heart attack could be terminal, 72-year-old failure Max Silverman pursues his determination to reopen his former less-than-successful Hot Dog-Tropical Drink stand called "Max's Hawaiian Ecstasies," boarded up for eighteen years under the boardwalk at Coney Island. Although it is February, Max returns to Coney Island where he is joined by his daughter, who has abandoned her husband, Eddie Bergson, and changed her name from Shirley Bergson to Nancy Scott; but a new name and her $4,000 nose job has not provided further identity. The new "Nancy" and Max are joined by Arthur Korman, a demoralized young man fleeing from the monotony of writing rhymes at the Jingle Bells Display Company, who comes to Coney Island because "they do a great sunrise." Max's effort to purchase supplies for his wild project is met with astonishment by former suppliers, whose politeness is reserved for the end of the conversation. Max labels them "The Goodbye People." Max declines to recognize his dull son Michael other than as "my lawyer--the son" and resists his former partner Marcus Soloway and Michael's attempt to dissuade him from his suicidal enterprise. Nancy and Arthur fall in love and Max succeeds in his impossible dream and reopens his lavishly garish Coney Island stand before dying of a heart attack.

The revival of The Goodbye People, eleven years after it's original flop on Broadway, met with a quicker demise and bade goodbye after one performance and sixteen previews. Richard Eder (The New York Times) reported, "Not having seen the original, I can't tell whether it has been improved. In any case, the diligence was misspent. It is a play that works so strenuously to be liked that even those things that are likeable in it become distressing. Herschel Bernardi--overplays quite as much as Mr. Gardner has overwritten."

After sixteen previews, the original Broadway production of The Goodbye People opened on December 3, 1968, at the Ethel Barrymore Theatre to play a meagre seven performances. Produced by Cy Feuer and Ernest Martin; A comedy written and directed by Herb Gardner; Setting and Lighting, David Hays; Costumes, Alvin Colt; Production supervisor, Porter Van Zandt; Productions assistants,

Regina Lynn, Patricia Flynn, Joseph E. Miller; Company manager, Milton Pollock, Sound effects, Robert Lifton; Wardrobe supervisor, Lonnie Dann; Stage managers, Ellen Whittman, Andy H. Rasbury

Milton Berle (Max Silverman); Brenda Vaccaro (Nancy Scott); Bob Dishy (Arthur Korman); Tony Lo Bianco (replaced Andy M. Rasbury) (Michael Silverman); Sammy Smith (Marcus Soloway); Jess Osuna (Eddie Bergson)

Brooklyn-born television writer Herb Gardner's previous comedy A Thousand Clowns brightened Broadway from April 5, 1962, to April 13, 1963, for 492 performances. Gardner spent two-and-a-half years writing The Goodbye People and sold the film rights to the play during rehearsals, which were held in the New Amsterdam Theatre Roof, once the setting for Ziegfeld's Midnight Frolics. The Goodbye People brought the irrepressible sixty-year-old (born in New York City on Sunday, July 12, 1908) Milton Berle back to Broadway after an absence of twenty-five years.

Milton Berle's last Broadway appearance was at the Winter Garden Theatre in The Shuberts' production (in association with Alfred Bloomingdale and Lou Walters) of the Ziegfeld Follies, which opened on April 1, 1943, and closed on July 22, 1944, after establishing a record for any Follies of 553 performances. Berle's only previous nonmusical role was in George Abbott's production of Richard Maibaum and Harry Clork's comedy See My Lawyer, directed by Ezra Stone at the Biltmore Theatre on September 25, 1939, which had 224 performances. In The Goodbye People, Berle gave further proof of his ability to play a straight dramatic part, verifying that experienced comedians are capable of portraying tragedy, which is often the catalyst of comedy.

Herb Gardner said of the casting of "Mr. Television" or "Uncle Miltie," "All the energy and humor and wildness that is Milton Berle is valuable to the part of Max. But the thing that attracts me to Milton is his fine skill as an actor and his compassion." Otis L. Guernsay, Jr. (New York Herald-Tribune) wrote, "One of the most poignant experiences of the season was Milton Berle's portrayal of an aged Coney Island concessionaire determined to do or die in making a comeback with a grand opening on the beach--in February--of a hot-dog stand." Clive Barnes (The New York Times) described The Goodbye People as "Characters in search of a play, a play in search of an author, an author in search of funny lines. I feel guilty at not liking it more. The first trouble with the play is that it is not about people but stereotypes for people. The second trouble with the play is that it is not about ideas but cliches for ideas--The next time Mr. Gardner decides to write a play he would do better to wait until he has a play to write." Milton Berle made no apologies for the quick passing of The Goodbye People and on closing night said, "Even if I did this show for only one night I would be very happy about it. If I had to do it again, I would do exactly the same show."

70 / Gorey Stories

* * *

GOREY STORIES (Booth Theatre, October 30, 1978). Produced by Terry Allen Kramer, Harry Rigby, Hale Matthews, and John Wulp; "An entertainment with music" written and designed by Edward Gorey; Director, Tony Tanner; Adaptation, Stephen Currens; Scenery supervision, Lynn Pecktal; Music, David Aldrich; Costumes, David Murin; Lighting, Roger Morgan; Musical director, Martin Silvestri; Production associate, Joanne Schwartz; Assistant conductor, Jeffrey Waxman; Wardrobe, Bill Campbell; Furs, Ben Kahn; Stage managers, Franklin Keysar, Beth Prevor

 Gemze de Lappe (Mona, a Maid); Sel Vitella (Harold, a Butler); Julie Kurnitz (Lady Celie, the Hostess); John Michalski (Hamish, a Beautiful Young Man); Leon Shaw (C. F. Earbrass, an Author); Tobias Haller (Little Henry, a Child); Dennis McGovern (Jasper Ankle, an Opera Freak); Susan Marchand (Ortenzia Caviglia, a Singer); June Squibb (Mary Rosemarch, a Spinster)
STORIES: The Hapless Child; The Wuggly Ump; The Curious Sofa; The Sinking Spell; The Gilded Bat; The Insect God; The Willowdale Handcar; The Doubtful Guest; The Blue Aspic; The Unstrung Harp; The Pious Infant; The Osbick Bird; The Deranged Cousins; The Lost Lions; The Loathsome Couple; The Gashlycrumb Tinies; and limericks from The Listing Attic

 Lady Celia narrates several macabre stories in her drawing room while her guests mime the tales. Middle-aged author C. F. Earbrass narrates his constantly revised novel in Lady Celia's summerhouse gazebo as the guests pantomime Earbrass's bizarre characters.

 Clive Barnes (New York Post) described Gorey Stories as a "unique, odd, perverse, and engaging entertainment--It is theatrical without being theatre. Its impulses are all in the wrong place--If we have any sense at all of Gorey's paraphernalia of Victoriana, we will be briefly enchanted on the page. In the theatre it seems somewhat precious." Barnes considered Gorey's gifts as a designer his only talent for the Broadway stage and that "more skill and distance" was required to "convert a literary cult into a theatrical myth." John Beaufort (The Christian Science Monitor) felt "Gorey Stories does not turn out to be particularly theatrical. What works in miniature drawings somehow doesn't work in make-believe enlargements. Another difficulty stems from the fact that a succession of horror-comic cartoons tends, after a while, to become tedious."

 Edward St. John Gorey was born in Chicago on Sunday, February 22, 1925, and received a B.A. from Harvard University in 1950. The revival of Hamilton Deane and John L. Balderston's 1927 thriller Dracula, which opened on Broadway at the Martin Beck Theatre on October 20, 1977, to ring up 925 performances, won a 1978 Tony Award for the Most Innovative Production of a revival of a play. Edward Gorey also received a "Tony" for his stunning settings and costumes for Dracula. The playbill cover for Dracula was Gorey's illustration from his book Edward Gorey's Dracula, published by E. P. Dutton.

The imposing Mr. Gorey created some forty small volumes of drawings, "with whimsically sadistic texts that read like minuscule versions of Gothic novels, combining the precision of a master nineteenth-century engraver with the macabre wit of an absurdist writer." Edward Gorey's first book was The Unstrung Harp; or, Mr. Earbrass Writes a Novel, a thirty-page account of writing a novel published in 1953. G. P. Putnam's Sons published two collections of Gorey's cartoon-illustrated bizarre stories: Amphigorey in 1972 and Amphigorey Too in 1975.

Amphigorey contains The Unstrung Harp; The Listing Attic; The Doubtful Guest; The Object-Lesson; The Bug Book; The Fatal Lozenge; The Hapless Child; The Curious Sofa; The Sinking Spell; The Willowdale Handcar; The Wiggly Ump; The Gashlycrumb Tinies; The Insect God; The West Wing; and The Remembered Visit.

Amphigorey Too includes twenty more: The Beastly Baby; The Nursery Frieze; The Pious Infant; The Evil Garden; The Inanimate Tragedy; The Gilded Bat; The Iron Tonic; The Osbick Bird; The Chinese Obelisks (bis); The Deranged Cousins; The Eleventh Episode; The Untitled Book; The Lavender Leotard; The Disrespectful Summons; The Abandoned Sock; The Lost Lions; Story for Sara; The Salt Herring; Leaves from a Mislaid Album; and A Limerick.

Stephen Currens' adaptation of Gorey Stories was first produced by the W.P.A. Theatre (Howard Ashman and Stuart White) at their Off-Broadway theatre on December 8, 1977. The setting was created by Edward Gianfrancesco with costumes by Clifford Capone and lighting by Craig Evans. Liz Sheridan portrayed Lady Celia and the rest of the cast in their original parts migrated to Broadway. Mel Gussow (The New York Times) called the Off-Broadway production "a merrily sinister musical collage of Goreyana." Somewhere between lower Fifth Avenue and Broadway's Booth Theatre Gorey Stories must have got lost.

* * *

THE GUYS IN THE TRUCK (New Apollo Theatre, June 19, 1983). Produced by James Conley; A comedy by Howard Reifsnyder; Director, David Black; Scenery and Costumes, John Falabella; Lighting, John Gleason; Sound, T. Richard Fitzgerald; Production supervisor, Jeremiah Harris; General manager, Theatre Now; Associate producer, Paul Levine; Stage managers, Frank Marino, John Actman
    Harris Laskawy (Al Klein); Lloyd Battista (Nick Caruso); Robert Trumbell (Les Hammond); Bobbi Jo Lathan (Billie Fenstermacher); Mike Starr (Doug Frischetti); James Gleason (Harvey Olmstead); Lawrence Guardino (Louie DeFalco); Geoffrey C. Ewing (Charlie Johnson); Gary Klar (Hugo Broonzy)

72 / The Guys in the Truck

From a television remote-control truck parked behind the Cleveland Municipal Stadium, television director Al Klein struggles to orchestrate several on-field cameramen covering the Cleveland-New York football game while threatened with bodily harm from Mafia "hit man" Nick Caruso, for nonpayment of a gambling debt. Klein's efforts to direct various on-field cameras from the truck are further plagued by statistics-mad announcer Les Hammond and his on-going feud with his hulking, stupid broadcasting cohort, former football hero Doug Frischetti, while beset by obtuse demands from Harvey Olmsted, the pompous son-in-law of the studio's top executive. Added to Klein's woes is the arrival of a former girl friend, stripper Billie Fenstermacher, who spices the game and spectators by taking-it-off on the playing field. Despite constant complaints from his TV technician Louie DeFalco, eager to press fractional charges with the union but aided by his efficient assistant director Charlie Johnson, Klein succeeds in balancing his personal problems and frantically monitoring multiple TV screens to give television viewers an exciting coverage of the football game.

"Go, guys, keep on trucking," advised Douglas Watt (Daily News) "Howard Reifsnyder's comedy may be somewhat slapdash, but it's spirited and fun. I'm rooting for it." But observing the expansion of the comedy from its more compact and successful Off-Broadway production, Watt added, "One could wish that Reifsnyder had been able to pull his play together a bit more tightly in the intervening months--But the guys in the truck are good company for a June night--or a July or August one for that matter. I wish them luck."

Mel Gussow (The New York Times) felt that in the transfer of The Guys in the Truck to Broadway, "it seems to have lost most of its rambunctious flavor. The show is like a football player flattened in a goal-line pileup. The effort and the strain of the production are evident on stage--The show was not truly reconceived for Broadway; it was simply made larger."

CBS sports producer Howard Reifsnyder's comedy was first produced by NTC Off-Broadway at the ATA/Sargent Theatre on September 16, 1982. Directed by David Black; Setting and lighting, Kevin Hickson; Sound, George Jacobs; Stage managers, Dawn Eaton and Suzanne Fossett

    Harris Laskawy (Al Klein); Chazz Palminteri (Nick Caruso); Robert Trumbell (Les Hammond); Gail Dahms (Billie); Mike Starr (Doug Frischetti); James Gleason (Harvey Olmsted); Lawrence Guardino (Louie DeFalco); Dan Martin (Charlie Johnson); Gary Klar (Broonzy); Ellen Newman (Emily Klein)

The twenty-two Broadway previews of The Guys in the Truck began on May 27, 1983, starring as TV sports director Al Klein, Elliott Gould, making his first Broadway stage appearance since playing seven performances in Jules Feiffer's 1967 Little Murders. Due to an announced "disagreement" with director David Black and playwright Reifsnyder on how the part of Klein should be played, Gould was dismissed and his understudy, Harris Laskawy, who had originated the part of the harassed TV sports announcer in the Off-Broadway production, replaced Gould on June 11th. The opening date of June 14th was extended to June 19, 1983, for the one and only Broadway performance of The Guys in the Truck.

* * *

HAPPINESS IS JUST A LITTLE THING CALLED A ROLLS ROYCE
(Ethel Barrymore Theatre, May 11, 1968). Produced by Anamark Productions; A comedy by Arthur Alsberg and Robert Fisher; Director, David Alexander; Scenery, Larry Rehling; Lighting, John Harvey; Costumes, Ann Roth; Production assistant, Donna Gray; General managers, Azenberg, Allentuck and Wolsk; Stage managers, Don Doherty, Joe Calvan, Simon Landres

Pat Harrington (Walter Bagley); John McGiver (Andrew McIntire); Lee Bergere (Phil Gorshin); Alexandra Berlin (Andrea Clithero); Hildy Brooks (replaced Louise Sorel) (Myra Bagley); Ray Fulmer (replaced Byron Sanders) (Jerry Ramsey); Phoebe Dorin (Karen Kinsey); Marvin Lichterman (Chuck Kinsey); Shimen Ruskin (Sanford Rutchik)

Walter Bagley is a shy, retiring young lawyer consistently passed over for promotion by his alcoholic boss Andrew McIntire in preference of aggressive Phil Gorshin. Walter's balm for depression is to spend his entire savings on a Rolls Royce for his success-driven, demanding wife, Myra, who promptly leaves him. Walter is rescued from his plight by artistic hippie Andrea who cures his ulcers and unleashes his suppressed passion to heroic eroticism in bed. Impressed with Walter's sudden affluence, as the owner of a Rolls Royce, and his revitalized personality, McIntire makes him a partner in the law firm. Although she is no longer wanted nor needed, Myra returns to her now, unexpectedly, successful husband.

Critic Ernest Schier tersely described Happiness Is,... as "The play with four flat tires." Dan Sullivan (The New York Times) stressed the title's Little Thing, adding, "As one might guess from the inept title, this is as contrived and mechanical a farce as ever sent a summer-circuit crowd to counting the mosquitoes on the ceiling." John Chapman (Daily News) headed his review of the silly proceedings at the Ethel Barrymore Theatre with, "Little Play With Long Title Has Few Laughs," feeling it "couldn't happen, really-- but it did" and was "hopefully labeled a comedy," which "might do for amateur theatricals, or even television, but it isn't robust enough for the commercial stage." Martin Gottfried (Women's Wear Daily) was braver than the other aisle appraisers and left at the intermission.

Richard P. Cooke reported in The Wall Street Journal, "Authors Arthur Alsberg and Robert Fisher have included too many unworkable concepts and show little recognition of the dictum that audiences will accept the impossible but not the improbable." Arthur Alsberg wrote the radio scripts for Our Miss Brooks and co-authored and co-created television's Bachelor Father series. Alsberg's scripts were also credited for the television series I Dream of Jeannie and My Favorite Husband. Robert Fisher co-authored the Broadway hit The Impossible Years in 1965, with Arthur Marx, which completed 670 performances. Fisher and Marx later collaborated on the less-than-successful Minnie's Boys in 1970. The Alsberg-Fisher concoction of Happiness Is... might have succeeded on television but Broadway was not ready for a Rolls Royce masquerading as a comedy.

* * *

HAVE I GOT A GIRL FOR YOU! (Music Box Theatre, December 2, 1963). Produced by Joseph Kipness and Richard W. Krakeur, in association with David Kaufman; A comedy by Irving Cooper, based on a story by Helen Cooper; Director, Don Richardson; Design and lighting, Sam Leve; Costumes, Willa Kim; Wigs and hairstyles, R. Keith; Production assistant, Marge-Toni Hesse; Associate producer, Bernard Howard; General manager, Ben Boyar; Stage managers, Richard B. Shull, Todd King, Donald Mitchell

    Simon Oakland (Joe Garfield); Nancy R. Pollock (Rose Garfield); Paula Lawrence (Sally Jordan); Michael Gorrin (Sam Garfield); Tom Ligon (Steve Kozlek); Karen Thorsell (Helen Baker); Dick Van Patten (Ruby Pulaski); Donald Mitchell (Jonas Wells); Bernard Kates (Ben Garfield); Patricia Benoit (Emily Garfield); Mary Linn Beller (Mitzi Jordan); Hal Riddle (Ted Barker); Joseph Boland (Thad MacKenzie); Tedd King (Western Union Messenger).

    Rose Garfield of the Bronx approves of her abrasive younger married son Ben's successful ownership of two stores but deplores her unwedded thirty-five-year-old son Joe's contentment in being merely a football coach at the East Side's Fremont High School. The father, Sam Garfield, long defeated by Rose's insistent aggressiveness, sympathizes with Joe's dedication to teaching and disinterest in wealth. Rose's dedicated campaign to get Joe married has been unsuccessful despite a succession of prospective brides. Mama Rose really has a girl for Joe in nouveau riche, former Bronx neighbor, overdressed and overelegant Sally Jordan's vapid daughter, Mitzi. Joe rebels at his mother's matchmaking with the Park Avenue Jordans and marries his understanding and sympathetic high school colleague, science teacher Helen Baker.

    "Good it's not" wrote Norman Nadel (New York World Telegram-Sun) and appraised Irving Cooper's characters as not measuring up, as they "give only height and width of characters, but never depth. Not only are these parts poorly written; too much of the time they're not even funny." Howard Taubman (The New York Times) found the "Plotting and characterization are as predictable as the accents and the jokes--Irving Cooper, the author of this labored, clammy effort-- shares the credit with his wife on the ground that he has based it on her story. It would have been more gallant of him not to mention her." John Chapman (Daily News) reported "Have I Got a Girl! is unfunny hokum--almost marvelously unfunny," and Walter Kerr (Herald Tribune) added, "I hesitate to say there's anything funny about Have I Got a Girl for You!. I may be quoted."

* * *

HEATHEN! (Billy Rose Theatre, May 21, 1972). Produced by Leonard J. Goldberg and Ken Gaston in association with E. Paul Woodville; A Hawaiian musical, Book by Robert Helpmann and Eaton Magoon, Jr.; Director, Lucia Victor; Music and lyrics, Eaton Magoon, Jr.; Setting, Jack Brown; Lighting, Paul Sullivan; Costumes, Bruce Harrow; Choreography, Sammy Bayes; Makeup and hairstyles, Ted Azar; Musical director, Clay Fullum; Orchestrations, Larry Fallon; Musical supervision, Vocal, Dance and incidental music, Mel Marvin; Associate choreographer, Dan Siretta; Production assistant, Joan Dietrich; Production associate, Mark Siegel; General manager, Sherman Gross; Stage managers, Alan Hall, Jack B. Craig, Karen Kristin

Russ Thacker (Reverend Jonathan Beacon/Jonathan); Yolande Bavan (Kalialani/Kalia); Edward Rambeau (Mano'Ula/Mano); Dan Merriman (Reverend Hiram Burnham); Ann Hodges (Hepsibah Burnham); Mokihana (Aliki); Tina Santiago (Momona-Nui); Dennis Dennehy (Kaha Kai; The Chanter); Charles Goeddertz (Hawaiian Boy); Honey Sanders (Pueo); Dennis Dennehy, Justis Skae, Sal Pernice (Muggers); Christopher Barrett, Mary Walling, Michael Serrecchia (Church Elders); Ann Hodges, Dan Merriman (Tourists); Charles Goeddertz, Michael Serrecchia, Quitman Fludd (Boys in Jail); Christopher Barrett (Policeman); Nancy Dafgek; Jacklynn Villamil; Mary Walling, Karen Kristin, Dennis Dennehy, Randy DiGrazio, Quitman Fludd, Charles Goeddertz, Sal Pernice, Michael Serrecchia, Justis Skae (Girls and Boys)

SONGS: Paradise; The Word of the Lord; My Sweet Tomorrow; A Man Among Men; Aloha; Kalialani; No Way to Hell; Battle Cry; This Is Someone I Could Love; House of Grass; Spear Games; For You Brother; Kava Ceremony; Christianity; Heathen!; More Better Go Easy; Eighth Day

The Reverend Jonathan Beacon arrives in Hawaii in 1819 to convert to Christianity the unsuspecting, happy "heathen" natives, with particular emphasis on their wearing appropriate if constrictive Anglo-Saxon clothing. Reverend Beacon falls in love with Princess Kalialani, who is beloved by handsome Prince Mano'Ula, while Beacon's puritanical superior, missionary Hiram Burnham and his wife, Hepsibah, succumb to the leisurely life of Hawaii through the friendly, persuasive efforts of jovial, rotund Aliki. By 1972 the descendents of the puritanical Bostonians and the ever-happy natives of the new American State of Hawaii have long since learned to live in complete harmony. Beacon is now a tourist; Mano, the Prince's descendent, has become a beach boy and Kalia, the Princess's kin, sings in a nightclub. Through the juxtaposition of the two eras, mainlanders and natives are revealed as sharing the same basic beliefs, joys, and sorrows as their ancestors.

Heathen! was classified by Douglas Watt (Daily News) as "so bad that it could put a blight on tourist trade throughout the entire Pacific" and he described the production as "Cheap to look at and even worse to listen to." Clive Barnes (The New York Times) wrote, "To say that it is the worst Broadway musical of the season would run the risk of overpraising its virtues. The book by Sir Robert Helpmann and Eaton Magoon, Jr. is both vestigial and ludicrous." Richard Watts (New York Post) found Heathen! "filled with good will, but it is also hopelessly clumsy, inept and amateurish to an extent that is nothing short of complete disaster."

Heathen! was produced by Leonard J. Goldberg and Ken Gaston, who had earlier produced a successful revival of Three Men on a Horse and a one-performance mistake called A Place for Polly, then subjected Broadway to Leon Uris's inept adaptation of his excellent novel Exodus at the Mark Hellinger Theatre on January 15, 1971, which became a 19-performance musical mishap retitled Ari.

James Michener's monumental 1,880-page novel Hawaii, published by Random House in 1959, brilliantly covered the fascinating history of the Pacific paradise, which no latter-day brief tale set to music could possibly equal. Eaton "Bob" Magoon, Jr., born in Hawaii on June 24, 1922, graduated from Yale University in 1945. Magoon's first musical, The 49th Star, was successfully produced in Hawaii, and he was also the writer of several popular songs, including "My Waikiki Girl" and "Fish and Poi." His first Broadway musical comedy, 13 Daughters, was set in nineteenth-century Hawaii and was a reworking, if not an improvement on, the age-old plot of getting the older daughter married before her younger sisters are permitted to take the journey down the aisle. 13 Daughters was a 28-performance blunder which opened on March 2, 1961, at the 54th Street Theatre, starring Don Ameche with Monica Boyar and John Battles.

Heathen! was originally produced in Hawaii during the Spring of 1971 as Thank Heaven for the Heathen. Sixty-three-year-old ballet star, stage and screen actor, choreographer, producer and director, Australia-born Robert Helpmann became a Commander of the Order of the British Empire in 1964 and a Knight Commander of the Order in 1968. Just how Sir Robert became involved in the mishmash of Heathen!, which closed after one performance and six previews was a mystery to all the critics and very possibly to Sir Robert Helpmann.

Brendan Gill (The New Yorker) found the answer, "In the course of the action of Heathen!, the question was asked, 'Why are you teaching my people English? No good will come of it.' That was true."

* * *

HERE'S WHERE I BELONG (Billy Rose Theatre, March 3, 1968). Produced by Mitch Miller; A musical play based on John Steinbeck's novel East of Eden, adapted by Alex Gordon; Music, Robert Waldman; Lyrics, Alfred Uhry; Director, Michael Kahn; Dances and musical staging, Tony Mordente; Scenery, Ming Cho Lee; Lighting, Jules Fisher; Costumes, Ruth Morley; Musical direction and vocal arrangements, Theodore Saidenberg; Dance music, Arnold Goland; Orchestrations, Glenn Osser, Norman Leyden, Jonathan Tunick; Production assistant, Charles Willard; Staff assistants, Paula Lorge, Terry Spierer; Hairstyles, Steve Atha; Company manager, Paul Neufeld; Production stage manager, William Dodds; Stage manager, Don Koehler; Assistant to producer, Joan Leyden; Wardrobe master, Joe Busheme; Assistant conductor, David Saidenberg; Assistant designers, Don Jensen, Leigh Rand, John Braden; Sound engineer, John Tolbott

    Walter McGinn (Caleb Trask); Paul Rogers (Adam Trask); Ken Kercheval (Aron Trask); James Coco (Lee); Heather MacRae (Abra Bacon); Nancy Wickwire (Kate); Dena Dietrich (Mrs. Tripp); Bette Henritze (Mrs. Bacon); Joseph Nelson (Joe); Dorothy Lister (Della); Graciela Daniele (Faith); Patricia Kelly (Mrs. Heink); Casper Roos (Will Hamilton); Barbara Webb (Miss Ida); Scott Jarvis (Rabbit Holman); Aniko Morgan (Eva); Joetta Cherry (Juana); Taylor Reed (Newspaperman); Darrell Askey (British Purchasing Agent); Lee Wilson, Tod Miller (Schoolchildren); Darrell Askey, Joetta Cherry, Graciela Daniele, Elisa De Marco, Larry Devon, John Dickerson, Bud Fleming, John William Gardner, Gene Gavin, John Johann, Ray Kirchner, Jane Laughlin, Dorothy Lister, Andy Love, Richard Marr, David McCorkle, Joyce McDonald, Tod Miller, Aniko Morgan, Joan Nelson, Joseph Nelson, Donald Norris, Taylor Reed, Clifford Scott, Joy Serio, Michele Simmons, David Thomas, Barbara Webb, Lee Wilson (Townspeople, Mexican Field Workers, Denizens of Castroville Street)

SONGS: We Are What We Are; Cal Gets By; Raising Cain; Soft Is the Sparrow; Where Have I Been?; No Time; Progress; Good Boy; Ballet; Act Like a Lady; The Send-Off; Top of the Train; Waking Up the Sun; Pulverize the Kaiser; You're Momma's; Here's Where I Belong; We're a Home (Dropped from production: Sweeping Changes; Perfect; Tell Me About Your Eden) (Original Cast Album--United Artists Records) Musical produced in association with United Artists.

    Austere Salinas Valley farmer Adam Trask raises his twin sons, Caleb and Aron, in the belief their mother died in childbirth but actually Adam's wife deserted him to run a whorehouse in the town of Salinas. Adam prefers his well-behaved, studious son Aron to his ne'er-do-well twin brother Caleb. In 1917 embittered Adam loses his savings, being first to attempt to ship lettuce to the East in refrigerated freight cars, and Caleb discovers his mother Kate's chosen profession. Caleb's intense feeling of rejection and futile efforts to win his father's love is resolved through Abra Bacon, who breaks her engagement to Aron for love of Caleb. The family Chinese servant, Lee, goads Adam into forgiving his wayward son, Caleb, and the entire Trask family, including Kate, is reunited at home on Thanksgiving.

Adapting John Steinbeck's 1952 novel East of Eden would have tested the talents of many composers and librettists, including Rodgers and Hammerstein, Harold Rome, and Aaron Copland--and even given Stephen Sondheim pause. For adapter Alex Gordon, composer Robert Waldman and lyricist Alfred Uhry (whose lyrics were considered "too embarrassing for quotation"), it was a lost cause. Playwright Terrence McNally (represented on- and off-Broadway in 1968 with his plays Tour in Collision Course; Witness; Sweet Eros; Noon; and Cuba Sí) made the original adaptation of Steinbeck's novel set in Salinas, California, in 1915. Terrence McNally was replaced during the road tryout of the show by Alex Gordon.

Dropped from the revised script, along with McNally, were the parts of Ernest Warren (David Thomas); Sam Purcell (Richard Marr); Young Purcell (David McCorkle); Harry Grew (Donald Norris); Humbert Heink (Andy Love); Tyler Tripp (Larry Devon); Schoolteacher (Joyce McDonald); Mexicans (Joy Serio, John Dickerson, Ray Kirchner); Salesgirl (Elisa DeMarco); Farmwoman (Michele Simmons); Delivery Boy (William Gardner); Bank Teller (Gene Gavin); Dr. Edwards (Clifford Scott); and Baker (Bud Fleming). During the usual tryout chaos, Choreographer Hanya Holm was replaced by Tony Mordente, and Dance Music arranged by Genevieve Pitot was reassigned to Arnold Goland.

Fifty-one-year-old Shakespearean actor Paul Rogers of London's Old Vic Company, who had played the title role in Macbeth with the British repertory company and had featured roles in Romeo and Juliet, Richard II, and Troilus and Cressida in 1956, suprised all with a resonant, baritone voice and a fine performance, played with an impeccable American accent. "The star of the show," reported The New Yorker, "was an electrifying young man named Walter McGinn, who managed to make his silly part seem far better than it was." But Steinbeck's sprawling tale was seen as "a sticky melodrama."

Clive Barnes (The New York Times) admired most the scenery of Ming Cho Lee in Here's Where I Belong, calling the adaptation itself "clumsy and leaden-footed" and, considering Steinbeck's story, "unusually somber for a musical. The bland joint efforts of Messrs. Gordon, Waldman and Uhry should probably have ended up not only East of Eden but West of Philadelphia.... The director, Michael Kahn, had the unenviable task of attempting to direct a badly written and weakly plotted play continually being interrupted for a few songs or a little dancing, and he was unable to fuse these two disparate elements."

John Chapman (Daily News) decided that "Somewhere along the line, producer Mitch Miller and his employees have lost the story of Here's Where I Belong." Richard Watts, Jr. (New York Post) agreed that Steinbeck's East of Eden "would make unpromising material for a musical play," and "it provided a desperately dreary evening, despite the presence in a leading role of Paul Rogers, who is one of the most skillful actors on the English speaking stage--Everything appears to have gone wrong with Here's Where I Belong."

Mitchell William "Mitch" Miller, noted impressario of Columbia Records' nineteen "Sing Along" albums, which sold some sixteen million copies, also emceed a popular television show. He produced his first Broadway musical with Here's Where I Belong, backed by $450,000 provided by the Music Corporation of America. Exceptionally talented young actor Walter McGinn gave an "enormously sympathetic" performance as Caleb. McGinn had originated the part of Tom Daley in Jason Miller's 1973 Pulitzer Prize play That Championship Season, which opened on May 2, 1972, at the Public-Newman Theatre and relocated to Broadway's Booth Theatre on September 14, 1972, to complete 844 performances. On March 31, 1977, Walter McGinn was killed at the age of forty in an automobile accident in Los Angeles.

The production cost of Here's Where I Belong amounted to approximately $473,590. Although the show grossed $114,000 during its three-week tryout at Philadelphia's Shubert Theatre in January 1968, losses totaled $56,000. The musical began previews on Broadway at the Billy Rose Theatre on Thursday, February 8th, and producer Mitch Miller contributed well over $100,000 to keep the show on the boards. During the three weeks of twenty previews, there was an additional loss of $116,000. Here's Where I Belong's one-night stand on March 3, 1968, recorded a total loss of approximately $646,000.

Playwright Paul Osborn (The Vinegar Tree, 1930; On Borrowed Time, 1938; Mornings at Seven, 1939; A Bell for Adano, 1944; Point of No Return, 1957; and The World of Susie Wong, 1958) adapted John Steinbeck's 1952 novel East of Eden for Warner Brothers Cinemascope production released in March 1955. The allegorical aspect of the Bible's Cain and Abel tragedy was completely obscured, and Osborn's adaptation comprised only the last ninety pages of the book. For all of Elia Kazan's detailed direction and beautifully mounted production, the cast was fairly flamboyantly theatrical, overburdened with stressing style and excessive "naturalism" until the film became rather portentous and pretentious. Jo Van Fleet, for her superb characterization of Kate, won 1955's Academy Award as the year's Best Supporting Actress.

East of Eden (Warner Brothers). Produced by Warner Brothers; Produced and directed by Elia Kazan; Screenplay, based on John Steinbeck's novel, by Paul Osborn; Photography, Ted McCord; Art directors, James Basevi, Malcolm Bert; Music composed and directed by Leonard Rosenman; Sound, Stanley Jones; Editor, Owen Marks
    James Dean (Caleb Trask); Raymond Massey (Adam Trask); Richard Davales (Aron Trask); Jo Van Fleet (Kate); Julie Harris (Abra Bacon); Albert Dekker (Will Hamilton); Lois Smith (Ann); Burl Ives (Sheriff); Harold Gordon (Albrecht); Nick Dennis (Rantani); Lonny Chapman (Roy); Timothy Carey (Joe); Mario Siletti (Piscora)

John Steinbeck, born at Salinas, California, on February 27,

1902, died on December 20, 1968, in New York City. He was the author of sixteen novels and in 1962 the sixth American writer to win the Nobel Prize. Steinbeck based his novel East of Eden on the biblical quotation, "And the Lord set a mark upon Cain, lest any finding him should kill him. And Cain went out from the presence of the Lord and dwelt in the land of Nod on the East of Eden" [Genesis 4: 15-17]. The famous author kept a diary during the writing of East of Eden, later published as Journal of a Novel: The East of Eden Letters, in which he wrote: "I am choosing to write this book to my sons.... I will tell them ... the story of good and evil, of strength and weakness, of love and hate, of beauty and ugliness. I shall try to demonstrate to them how these doubles are inseparable--how neither can exist without the other and how out of their groupings creativeness is born."

East of Eden was produced as an ABC Novel for Television, shown on February 8, 9, and 11, 1982. Produced by Mace Neufield, Barney Rosenzweig; Director, Harvey Hart; Television adaptation by Richard Shapiro; Photography, Frank Stanley; Associate producer, Ken Wales; Musical score, Lee Haldridge

Jane Seymour (Cathy Ames; later Kate Trask); Timothy Bottoms (Adam Trask); Bruce Boxleitner (Charles Trask); Warren Oates (Cyrus Trask); Sam Bottoms (Cal Trask); Hart Bochner (Aron Trask); Karen Allen (Abra Bacon); Soon-Teck-On (Lee); Lloyd Bridges (Sam Hamilton); Richard Masur (Will Hamilton); Wendell Burton (Tom Hamilton); Anne Baxter (Madame Faye); Howard Duff (Mr. Edwards); Nicholas Pryor (Mr. Grew); Timothy Carey (Preacher); Nellie Bellflower (Mrs. Trask); Vernon Weedle (Mr. Ames); Grace Zabriskie (Mrs. Ames); M. Emmett Walsh (Sheriff George Quinn); Stymie Beard (Cotton Eye Joe); Mike Johnson (Bouncer)

Time magazine reported television's East of Eden as adapted by Richard Shapiro was "Terribly tasteful and tastefully terrible."

* * *

HOME SWEET HOMER (Palace Theatre, January 4, 1976). Produced by The John F. Kennedy Center for the Performing Arts; A musical with book by Roland Kibbee, Albert Marre; Director, Albert Marre; Music, Mitch Leigh; Lyrics, Charles Burr, Forman Brown; Scenery and Lighting, Howard Bay; Costumes, Ray Diffen, Howard Bay; Musical direction, Ross Reimueller; Orchestrations, Buryl Red; Assistant to director, Dwight Frye; Choreographic assistant to Mr. Marre, Michael Mann; Music coordinator, Earl Shendell; Associate conductor, Terrill Jory; Production assistant, Kay Vance; Sound, Lennie Will; Wardrobe supervisor, Angelo Quillici; Hairstylists, Gloria Rivera, Wayne Herndon; Stage managers, Patrick Horrigan, Gregory Allen Hirsch; General managers, Wolsk and Azenberg, Douglas C. Baker

Yul Brynner (Odysseus); Joan Diener (Penelope); Russ Thacker (Telemachus); Penelope's Suitors: Martin Vidnovic (Antinous); Ian Sullivan (Pilokrates); Bill Mackey (Ktesippos); Daniel Brown

(Eurymachus); Brian Destazio (Leokritos); John Aristides (Pimteus); Bill Nabel (Melios); Les Freed (Polybos); Shev Rodgers (King Alkinoos); Diana Davila (Nausikaa); Nausikaa's Handmaidens: Suzanne Sponsler (Therapina); Cecile Santos (Melantho); Christine Uchida (Hippodameia); Darel Glaser (Kerux); P. J. Mann (Dekati Evdomi VII)

SONGS: The Tales; The Future; The Departure; Home Sweet Homer; The Ball; How Could I Dare to Dream; I Never Imagined Goodbye; Love Is the Prize; Penelope's Hand; He Will Come Home Again; Did He Really Think?; I Was Wrong; The Rose; Tomorrow; The Contest; He Sang Songs

After ten years of fighting the Trojan Wars, Odysseus begins his decade-long journey to his home in Ithaca and his faithful wife, Penelope, who, during the long years of her husband's absence, has successfully discouraged an endless line of insistent suitors eager to share her bed. During his ten-year homeward trek Odysseus is distracted by alluring women, including the lovely Nausikaa. Disguised as an infirm old man, Odysseus finally arrives in Ithaca and expels Penelope's amorous suitors with the aid of his devoted son Telemachus. Odysseus is reunited with Penelope and Telemachus finds happiness with hedonistic Nausikaa.

After an American odyssey of thirteen months the much-traveled Home Sweet Homer arrived at its final destination at the Island of Manhattan's Palace Theatre where, following eleven previews, its long journey ended in one performance at a Sunday matinee on January 4, 1976. Martin Gottfried (New York Post) reported "Home Sweet Homer demonstrates the monstrous capacities of the musical theatre when its forces are placed in the hands of the ill-equipped and in the pursuit of the misconceived." Leonard Probst (NBC News) called the musical play "a disaster--You have to see it to believe it, it's that bad." Douglas Watt (Daily News), noting that Home Sweet Homer was played without intermission "For close to two interminable hours" with "uninteresting tunes equipped with equally uninteresting words" with "no dancing and no ensemble singing" dismissed the Homeric hoopla as "a deadly afternoon." Clive Barnes (The New York Times) found "Many of the lines are funny" but "not really supported by either the story itself or Mr. Leigh's score" and he compared Penelope's boorish suitors to "watching a parody called 'Kung Fu Comes to Athens'-- not funny or agreeable to watch."

The musical play that was seen on Broadway as Home Sweet Homer was a misguided metamorphosis of a misconceived manipulation of the epic poem attributed to Homer. Originally titled Odyssey, the musical was adapted by Erich Segal, author of the best-selling novel Love Story, who also supplied the lyrics to Mitch Leigh's music. Odyssey opened on December 10, 1974, at the Hanna Theatre in Cleveland, Ohio, to begin one of the longest (and most profitable) tryout tours in theatre history. During Odyssey's transcontinental tour, the constantly altered musical play grossed approximately $4,260,000.

Originally, the musical play, as produced by Roger L. Stevens, Martin Feinstein and Alexander Morr for The John F. Kennedy Center for the Performing Arts, had the following credits and cast:

Odyssey. Book and lyrics by Erich Segal; Music by Mitch Leigh; Director, Albert Marre; Scenery and Lighting by Howard Bay; Costumes by Ray Diffen and Howard Bay; Choreography by Billy Wilson; Musical director, Ross Reimueller; Orchestrations, Buryl Red; Dance arrangements, Danny Holgate; Company manager, Fred J. Cuneo; Stage managers, Patrick Horrigan, Gregory Allen Hirsch; Associate conductor, Bruce Steeg; Production assistants, Kay Vance, John Hillner; Production manager, Franco Gratale; Assistant choreographer, Jeff Phillips

Yul Brynner (Odysseus); Joan Diener (Penelope); Russ Thacker (Telemachus); Diana Davila (Nausikaa); Penelope's Suitors: Martin Vidnovic (Antinous); Greg Bell (Agelaos); Bill Mackey (Ktesippos); Michael Mann (Eurymachus); Brian Destazio (Leokritos); John Gorrin (Pimteus); Jeff Phillips (Mulios); Derrick Bell (Polybos); Shev Rodgers (King Alkinoos); Ian Sullivan (Polyphemus); Nausikaa's Handmaidens: P. J. Mann (Hippodameia); Christine Uchida (Therapina); Cecile Santos (Melantho); Catherine Lee Smith (Kalypso); Garon Dauglass (Kerux, the Herald)

Reviews on the road were less than ecstatic but Odyssey continued to register healthy gross receipts, largely on the box-office draw of star Yul Brynner. Odyssey was, according to Odysseus/Brynner "85 percent changed from when we opened in Cleveland" and he told Los Angeles critic Bob Thomas that the critics had been unkind to Odyssey; "The fact that Erich Segal wrote the script causes an automatic adverse reaction. Why? Because he made such an ass of himself after Love Story, trying to act like a star." Roland Kibbee and director Albert Marre revised Segal's book, and dances devised by Billy Wilson were discarded.

Yul Brynner left the Homeric homecoming and wisely returned to his most famous role as the King in The King and I, a role he created on Broadway at the St. James Theatre on March 29, 1951, opposite the great, late Gertrude Lawrence as Anna. Rodgers and Hammerstein's excellent musical based on Margaret Landon's best-selling biography Anna and the King of Siam, derived from Anna Leonowen's autobiography, The English Governess at the Siamese Court, completed 1,246 performances.

Twenty-six-year-old Yul Brynner made his Broadway debut at the Plymouth Theatre on February 6, 1946, as Prince Tsai-Yong in Sidney Howard and Will Irwin's adaptation of the Chinese classic Pi-Pa-Ki, called Lute Song, set to music by Raymond Scott with lyrics by Bernard Henighen. Starring Mary Martin, Lute Song closed on June 8, 1946, after 142 performances. It was Mary Martin who recommended Brynner to producers Richard Rodgers and Oscar Hammerstein, II for the role of the King in The King and I. Brynner won two Broadway "Tony" awards (1952 and 1985) and an "Oscar" for his 1956 screen portrayal of the King of Siam.

The King and I was revived many times, with various Kings and Annas, but Yul remained the undisputed musical monarch. After starring with Deborah Kerr in the Twentieth Century-Fox screen version of the musical, in 1956, he returned to Broadway's Uris Theatre on May 2, 1977, to play another 695 performances. For two years Brynner combated lung cancer and, prior to the reopening of The King and I on Broadway in 1985, told the press, "You have to make a choice--being sick in bed, and that's a fearsome thing--or playing in a theatre to standing ovations every night. The choice is obvious. I simply go on playing."

The last revival of The King and I opened at the Broadway Theatre on January 7, 1985, recording astounding weekly gross receipts, in its last week breaking the all-time Broadway box-office record by grossing $605,546. Yul Brynner retired as King Mongket on Sunday, June 30, 1985, after a long and profitable career as the King of Siam, having played the role 4,625 times in New York, London, and on several extensive transcontinental tours over thirty-four years. Frank Rich (The New York Times) wrote about King Brynner in 1984, "Man and role have long since merged into a fixed image that is as much a part of our collective consciousness as the Statue of Liberty."

Yul Brynner died at the age of sixty-five in the New York Hospital, Cornell Medical Center, on Thursday, October 10, 1985. Throughout his career Brynner invented fascinating, exotic fiction regarding his birth, parentage, and real name, which he gave as Taidje Khan. The famous theatrical King of Siam was born off the coast of Siberia, on Sakhalin Island, on Sunday, July 11, 1920, and, according to his sister, Vera Brynner Raymond, their father was a Swiss businessman named Brynner employed in Manchuria and their mother was a Russian actress and singer.

Homer's Odysseus or Ulysses has intrigued writers from Aeschylus to Sophocles to Euripides and was used by Shakespeare as a character in Troilus and Cressida. Dante's The Divine Comedy consigns Odysseus to the Eighth Chasm of the Inferno 26, condemned for spiritual theft and engulfed in flames of his own consciousness. Polish playwright Stanislaw Wyspianski's nineteenth-century play Ulysses' Return and Frank Jewett Mather, Jr.'s Ulysses in Ithaca dramatized Homer's wandering hero.

Stephen Phillip's drama Ulysses starred Herbert Beerbohm Tree at London's Her Majesty's Theatre on February 1, 1902, with Lily Hanburg as Penelope and Gerald Lawrence as Telemachus. Tyrone Power, Sr. starred in the title role of Phillip's Ulysses at New York's Garden Theatre on September 14, 1903, with Rose Coghlan as Penelope and Edgar Selwyn as their son. Christopher Fry's English translation of Jean Giraudoux's play La Guerre de Troie n'Aura pas Lieu (The Trojan War Will Not Take Place), originally produced in Paris by Louis Jouvet in 1935, became Tiger at the Gates in London on June 2, 1955, and on Broadway at the Plymouth Theatre on October 3, 1955, with Walter Fitzgerald as Ulysses.

Ulysses also surfaced in John Erskine's 1925 novel The Private Life of Helen of Troy, which was filmed by Warner Brothers-First National Pictures in 1927 with Tom O'Brien as Ulysses and Gordon Elliott as Telemachus. Kirk Douglas played the title role in Paramount Pictures 1955 release of Dino de Laurentis and Carlo Ponti's Italian-made production of Ulysses, with Silvano Mangano as both Penelope and Circe and Franco Interlanghi as Telemachus.

A parody of the Helen of Troy legend and a spoof of Henri Meilhac and Ludovic Halévy's famous opera bouffe Le Belle Hélène, set to music by Jacques Offenbach in 1864, was the basis for Brendan Gill's book, based on a libretto by Bill Hoffman, called La Belle. John Zacherle played Ulysses, Home Sweet Homer's Joan Diener was Helen of Troy, and Albert Marre directed the rejected La Belle which opened and closed in Philadelphia in 1962.

Had composer Mitch Leigh (Irwin Mitchnick) and director Albert Marre (Albert Moshinski) sought a substitute for Professor Segal's book Odyssey, they might have used Paul Osborn's comedy Maiden Voyage. Featuring Walter Matthau as Odysseus and Colleen Dewhurst as Penelope, Maiden Voyage was "withdrawn for revisions" and closed on the road in Philadelphia on March 9, 1957. Possibly what Sweet Homer needed to get "Home" was a maiden voyage.

* * *

HOOK 'N LADDER (Royale Theatre, April 29, 1952). Produced by Al Moritz; A comedy by Charles Horner and Henry Miles; Director, Al Moritz; Setting and Lighting, Eldon Elder; Costumes, Jerry Boxhorn; General manager, Charles Harris; Stage managers, Edward Strum, Alex Baron
    Vicki Cummings (Christine Rapp); Guy Raymond (Ulysses); Donald McClelland (replaced Walter Kalvun) (George Casey); Charles G. Martin (Doc Cornwall); Judson Pratt (Sam Ross); Loretta Price (Gail Carter); Harry Sothern (Caspar Armbruster); Charles Bang (replaced Allen Nourse) (Steve Barton); Leland Stanford Barris (Mayor Tiddle); Humphrey Davis (Mr. Deaton); Allan Hale (replaced Charles Bang) (Mr. Gilkens); Allen Lee (replaced Maurice Fitzgerald) (J. B. Carpenter)

    Christine Rapp, saleswoman for the Ajax Fire Engine Company, competes with Sam Ross, Steve Barton, and George Casey to sell the small, politically corrupt town of Cloverdale a new fire engine. Ajax's fire engine will not start during a competitive demonstration and J. B. Carpenter, Ajax's president, fires Christine. Fire Chief Ulysses favors Ajax's well-constructed engine while Mayor Tiddle and his grafting political cronies bargain for larger kickbacks on the purchase. Christine manages to start Ajax's engine and is rehired by Carpenter. Meek and honest city clerk Casper Armbruster awards Ajax the contract for their superior fire engine and Christine's competitors, accustomed to political wheeling and dealing, are appalled at such an outrageous display of honest, free enterprise considering it "a hell of a way to do business!"

Charles Horner and Henry Miles were gag writers for television's "Arthur Godfrey Show." Their first play, Hook 'n Ladder, was devised as a slapstick farce which might have succeeded as a High School Senior Play or an early Mack Sennett two-reel comedy. Horner and Miles did include several amusing punch-lines in their script, but the play backfired quicker than Ajax's engine, described by Dudley Jenkins (Philadelphia's Evening Bulletin) as "like a radio or TV script gone berserk." The farce was set in a room in Cloverdale's Majestic Hotel, overpopulated by characters rushing in and out of closets, accompanied by frenetic screaming the like of which even Mack Sennett might not have tolerated.

For twenty years, attractive and talented actress Vicki Cummings had the misfortune of appearing in several incredible flops. Being headlined in Hook 'n Ladder did not alter Miss Cummings' record. Brooks Atkinson (The New York Times) observed, "Miss Cummings has the knack of looking as though everything were tumultuously funny. Sometime a comedy is bound to be as bright as she is." Mr. Atkinson noted with little wonder that critics were surreptitiously leaving the theatre after the second act, led "with considerable elegance and silence" by George Jean Nathan after the first act. J. Brooks Atkinson remained seated during the entire fiasco but considered playwrights Horner and Miles' craftmanship "so sophomoric."

Charles "Chuck" Horner later contributed the book (based on Bernard Waber's tales) for a four-performance musical fiasco called Lyle, which opened on March 20, 1970, at the McAlpin Rooftop Theatre. Producer-director Al Maritz wrote and appeared in The Follies of 1910 at Carnegie Hall Playhouse on January 12, 1960, for a brief run of fourteen performances.

* * *

HUMMIN' SAM (New Yorker Theatre, April 8, 1933). Produced and directed by Allan K. Foster; A Sepia Musical comedy in two gallops by Eileen Nutter, based on Charles T. Dazey's play In Old Kentucky; Music and lyrics, Alexander Hill; Dances and musical staging, Carey and Davis; Orchestrations, Arthur Knowlton; Costumes by Brooks; Musical director, Jimmie Davis
    Gertrude "Baby" Cox (Hummin' Sam); Madeline Belt (Madge Carter); Edith Wilson (Nina May); Lionel Monagas (Yellow George); Speedy Smith (Uncle Ned); Alonzo Bosan (Totem); Lorenzo Tucker

(Edward Holton); Bunny Allen (Hot Cakes); John Lee (Mr. Connors); Robert Underwood (Harlem Dan); Louise Lovelle (Louise); Cecil Rivers (Freddie Marlowe); Flo Brown (Mae Carter); Al Watts (Mr. Carter); Hannah Sylvester (Clara); Louise Cook (Miss Jitters); J. Mardo Brown (Drum Major); Jones and Allen (Caesar and Cicero); Dorothy Embry (Esmaraldae); Catherine Brooks (Emmaraldae); Sandy (Mike); The Two Chesterfields (Jockeys); Mary Mason (Mamaraldae); Jimmie Davis Orchestra

SONGS: How the First Song Was Born; Steppin' Along; Harlem Dan; They're Off; Pinching Yourself; In the Stretch; Jubilee; A Little Bit of Quicksilver; Change Your Mind About Me; If I Didn't Have You; Answer My Heart; Stompin' Em Down; I'll Be True, But I'll Be Blue; Fifteen Minutes a Day; Aint'cha Glad You Got Music?; Dancing, and I Mean Dancing; Jitters.

Hummin' Sam is the protegé of racing tout Harlem Dan and he is the best black jockey in America--he sings to his horses during races instead of whipping them. Sam is tempted with the promise of sudden riches, offered by a gang of racetrack gamblers if he throws his race in the Kentucky Derby. Supported and encouraged by Uncle Ned, Sam declines the gamblers' offer and rides Madge Carter's horse, Boogoo, to victory in the Derby. At a lavish gala celebrating the winning of the Derby, Sam also wins Madge.

Wilella Waldorf (New York Evening Post) called Hummin' Sam "Just a second rate musical comedy of the old school acted with depressing solemnity by a troupe of Harlemites who seemed, on the whole, very ill at ease." Lewis Nichols (The New York Times) reported, "Hummin' Sam was sepia and very, very grim indeed--Someone trained Hummin' Sam so that it lost all its native vitality, and then just didn't bother to set anything up in its place." Burns Mantle (Daily News) appraised the funereal effect of Hummin' Sam and suggested, "You couldn't get even a decent burial for it in Harlem." Robert Garland (World-Telegram) added, "You will have to yawn through a good many pieces of sepia before you find one much sleepia than Hummin' Sam." The Sun's critic just fled from the theatre in total disbelief.

Harvard graduate (1881) Charles Turner Dazey was born at Lima, Illinois, in 1853 and died at the age of eighty-four at Quincy, Illinois, on February 9, 1938. Dazey wrote many plays, including one of the longest-running melodramas in the history of the American theatre. His play In Old Kentucky, written in 1891, was performed for twenty-seven consecutive seasons, in New York or on the road, according to Arthur Hobson Quinn who wrote, "The older melodrama which held the stage by reason of the sincerity of its portraiture of character as well as by the vividness of its situations is exemplified by In Old Kentucky by Charles T. Dazey."

The first production of In Old Kentucky was by Jacob Litt's stock company at St. Paul, Minnesota's Grand Opera House, during

the summer of 1893.
Marion Elmore (Madge Brierly); W. H. Elwood (Frank Layton);
Louis James (Colonel Sandusky Doolittle); Frank Losee (Joe Lorey);
Frederick Bock (Horace Holton); Julia Arthur (Barbara Holton);
George Edeson (Uncle Neb); Mrs. Seldwin Irwin (Aunt Alethea)

The Broadway-bound production of In Old Kentucky premiered at Pittsburgh's Bijou Theatre on August 28, 1893. In Old Kentucky played one week at New York's People's Theatre beginning September 11, 1893, then opened at the Academy of Music on October 23, 1893, for an extensive run.

* * *

IN OLD KENTUCKY. Produced by Jacob Litt; Director, Benjamin Teal, Settings, Joseph Hart; Mechanical effects, Louis Vockel; Incidental music composed and arranged by Percy Gaunt; General manager, A. W. Dingwall
Bettina Gerard (Madge Brierly); William Courtleigh (replaced H. J. Wolfe) (Frank Layton); Burt G. Clark (Colonel Sandusky Doolittle); George W. Deyo (Joe Lorey); William McVay (Horace Holton); Marion Abbott (replaced Ethel Athelstone) (Barbara Holton); Ethel Greybrook (replaced Lottie Winnett) (Alathea Layton); Scott Williams (Brutus); Charles K. French (Neb); J. W. Bristor (Caesar); Burt Grant (Sam); "The Woodlawn Wangdoodles" (Pickininny Band)

Mountain girl Madge Brierly escapes the constant feuding and vendettas of her family and neighbors in Kentucky by swingin' across a chasm where the bridge has been blown away by mountaineers' warfare. Madge meets personable Frank Layton, a wealthy and handsome Kentucky blue grass horse breeder, and saves his thoroughbred horse Queen Bess from a burning stable on Layton's Woodlawn estate. Against the protests of her family and Layton's snobbish friends, Madge horrifies everyone by appearing in riding breeches to ride Frank's horse in the Ashland Oaks race. Madge rides Queen Bess to victory and also wins the love of Frank Layton.

Among the plays which Dazey wrote or co-authored were That American King; Home Folks; The Suburban; One of the Family; War of Wealth; The Higher Law; A Son of the South; Captain Lafitte; Nobody's Girl; and The Little Maverick. Dazey also wrote several screenplays for the silent screen: Wolf Lowry; The Sea Master; The Redemption of Dave D'Arcy; Behind the Mask; Peggy Leads the Way; and New York Luck in 1917, and The Mysterious Client and The Midnight Trail in 1918, among others, occasionally written with his son Frank Dazey.

Despite Dazey's remarkable prolificacy, In Old Kentucky, which brought him fame and fortune, remained his best play.

In Old Kentucky (L. B. Mayer-First National Pictures, released December 15, 1919). Directed by Marshall Neilan; Screenplay, based on the play by Charles T. Dazey, by Thomas J. Geraghty

Anita Stewart (Madge Brierly); Mahlon Hamilton (Frank Layson); Edward Connolly (Colonel Sandusky Doolittle); Adele Farrington (Aunt Aleathia); Edward Coxen (Joe Lorey); Charles Arling (Horace Holten); Marcie Manon (Barbara Holten); Frank Duffy (Eddie Lemhardt); John Currie (Uncle Neb)

In Old Kentucky (Metro-Goldwyn-Mayer Pictures, for release on October 29, 1927). Director, John M. Stahl; Screenplay and adaptation by A. P. Younger, based on Charles T. Dazey's 1893 play; Camera, Maximilian Fabian; Co-Adaptation, Lew Lipton; Assistant director, David Friedman; Settings, Cedric Gibbons, Ernest Fegte; Wardrobe, Gilbert Clark; Editors, Basil Wrangell, Margaret Booth Titles, Marian Ainslee, Ruth Cummings
    Helene Costello (Nancy Holden); James Murray (Jimmy Brierly); Wesley Barry ("Skippy" Lowry); Dorothy Cumming (Mrs. Brierly); Edward Martindel (Mr. Brierly); Nick Cogley (Uncle Bible); Carolynne Snowden (Lily May); Stepin Fechit (Highpockets); Harvey Clark (Dan Lowry)

In Old Kentucky (Fox Films, a talking-screen version released on September 6, 1935). Using the basis of Charles T. Dazey's play in a reconstruction of the story, more humor was injected into the drama tailored to the inestimable talents of Will Rogers. Produced by Edward Butcher; Director, George Marshall; Screenplay, based on Charles T. Dazey's play, by Sam Hellman and Gladys Lehman; Additional dialogue, Henry Johnson; Photography, L. W. O'Connell; Art director, William Darling; Sound, W. D. Flick; Gowns, William Lambert; Musical director, Arthur Lange
    Will Rogers (Steve Tapley); Dorothy Wilson (Nancy Martingale); Russell Hardie (Lee Andrews); Alan Dinehart (Slick Doherty); Etienne Girardot (Pluvius J. Aspinwall); Esther Dale (Dolly Breckenridge); Charles Sellon (Ezra Martingale); Louise Henry (Arlene Shattuck); Charles Richman (Pole Shattuck); John Ince (Sheriff); Bill Robinson (Wash Jackson)

* * *

I WON'T DANCE (Helen Hayes Theatre, May 10, 1981). Produced by David Merrick; A comedy by Oliver Hailey; Director, and incidental music, Tom O'Horgan; Setting, Bill Stabile; Lighting, Craig Miller; Costumes, Marty Pakledinaz; Associate producer, Neal Du Brock; Assistant to director, Nan Penman; Production assistant, Larry Fulton; Stage movement, Wesley Fata; Wardrobe, Clarence Sims; Stage managers, Alan Hall, Ruth E. Rinklin
    David Selby (Dom); Gail Strickland (Lil); Arlene Golonka (Kay)

    Dom has been a paraplegic since childhood and has one leg in a cast after hitching his wheelchair to a car on the Los Angeles Freeway. He could also possibly have murdered his successful lawyer-brother and his sister-in-law, a best-selling novelist, but celebrates their recent unsolved murder with a party. Unsuccessful former actress and part-time prostitute Kay and Lil, his brother's wife's self-centered sister from New Mexico (where she has been having a raging affair with Pueblo Indian Sam Silverhead) join Dom in his Los Angeles home for the revels. Although strongly physically attracted to Dom, Lil declines a sexual relationship and ignores his maudlin bid for sympathy, while Kay encourages him in both. Each probably had a motive for killing Dom's brother and sister-in-law but they are lost in their fantasies and dreams.

David Merrick produced many Broadway hits. He also produced several flamboyant flops. Most of Mr. Merrick's misadventures closed on the road during traumatic tryouts and, although several were superior to many productions exposed to Broadway, savage attacks by the gentlemen of the press and public apathy out-of-town brought foreclosure. Juniper and the Pagans, written by John Patrick and based on James Norman's novel, was a road casualty in 1959, followed by a musical version of William Inge's play Picnic rechristened Hot September in 1965. Truman Capote's Breakfast at Tiffany's, first known on the road as Holly Golightly, schlepped onto Broadway for previewing but never officially opened in 1966. Mata Hari, directed by Vincente Minnelli, was shot more than once in Washington in 1967 and Bill Manhoff's comedy The Unemployed Saint had its final rites in Florida. Bruce Jay Friedman and Jacques Levy's The One-Night Stand (also known as Turtlenecks) should have been true to its title but lasted several weeks on the road before closing shop in 1973. Tennessee Williams' The Red Devil Battery Sign was defused in Boston in 1975. The Baker's Wife, a musical version of Marcel Pagnol and Jean Giono's La Femme du Boulanger, was disputed and deported in 1976. But none of these Merrick out-of-town failures were as dreary as I Won't Dance, which he brought to Broadway.

Frank Rich (The New York Times) had the best recommendation for viewing I Won't Dance; "If you're going to endure Mr. Hailey's preposterous play, to take a handy example, might I suggest that you arrive at the theatre armed with ear plugs and a good book?--This play could not be more incoherent if the scenes were intentionally played out of sequence."

I Won't Dance had its world premiere during the 1979-1980 season at Buffalo's Studio Arena Theatre. The black comedy was produced by Neal Du Brock, directed by Tom O'Horgan with a setting by Bill Stabile, all of whom transferred to Broadway. About David Selby, Frank Rich said "Mr. Hailey overwrites the overwrought Dom to the point of irritation. Then David Selby takes over. With his broad Texas accent and large repertory of goofy grins, this outsize actor wields cuteness like a club" Selby played Dom, Arlene Golonka played Kay, and Shirley Knight originally created Lil.

Douglas Watt (Daily News) reported, "The new Oliver Hailey play--defies rational explanation. The flamboyant director Tom O'Horgan is remarkably restrained here, possibly because the play itself is crazier than anything he might attempt." Clive Barnes (New York Post) expressed surprise that a producer of David Merrick's standards would open a play at a Sunday matinee and found he did not "admire the writing, which, particularly in the first act, took boredom to inordinate lengths, and in the second act jumped around with simplistic ideas as if they were discoveries."

* * *

JOHNNY JOHNSON (Edison Theatre, April 11, 1971). Produced by Timothy Gray and Robert Fletcher, in association with Midge La Guardia; Book and lyrics, Paul Green; Music, Kurt Weill; Director, Jose Quintero; Scenery, Peter Harvey; Lighting, Roger Morgan; Costumes, Robert Fletcher; Musical direction, Joseph Klein; Orchestrations, Kurt Weill; General manager, Norman Maibaum; Production assistant, Anne Kendall; Company manager, John J. Miller; Choreography, Bertram Ross; Stage manager, Jamie Howard
    Ralph Williams (Johnny Johnson); Alice Cannon (Minny Belle Tompkins); Wayne Sherwood (Dr. McBray/Private O'Day/Scottish Colonel/German Priest/Secretary); Paul Michael (Mayor/Private Fairfax/American Commander/Brother Thomas); James Billings (Grandpa Joe/Private Goldberger/Chief/Dr. Mohodan); Norman Chase (Captain Valentine); June Helmers (Miz Smith/French Nurse); Clay Johns (Private Jessell/Private Svenson/Orderly/British Commander/Lieutenant/M.P./Brother George); Alexander Orfaly (Recruiting Sergeant/Corporal George/Belgian Major/Captain/Dr. Frewd); Nadine Lewis (Goddess of Liberty); Norman Riggins (Brother William/English Sergeant/Doctor/French Major General/American Priest); Gordon Minard (Howington/Private Harwood); Bob Lydiard (Photographer/Sniper); Charlotte Jones (Aggie/Sister /Miss Newro); Christopher Klein (Messenger/Howington, Jr.); Wayne Sherwood, Clay Johns, Alexander Orfaly, James Billings, Paul Michael (Wounded French Soldiers); Entire Company (Villagers)
SONGS: Over in Europe; Democracy's Call; Up Chickamauga Hill; Johnny's Melody; Aggie's Song; Oh, Heart of Love; Farewell, Goodbye; The Sergeant's Chant; Valentine's Tango; You're in the Army Now; Johnny's Oath; Song of the Goddess; Song of the Wounded Frenchmen; Tea Song; Cowboy Song; Johnny's Dream; Song of the Guns; Music of the Stricken Redeemer; Army Song; Mon Ami, My Friend; Allied High Command; The Laughing Generals; The Battle; Prayer: In Times of War and Tumults; No Man's Land; The Psychiatry Song; Hymn to Peace; Johnny Johnson's Song; How Sweetly Friendship Binds; Finale

    Gentle, honest and peace-loving twenty-five-year-old rural tombstone cutter Johnny Johnson has carved a huge monument to Peace being unveiled in his village when President Woodrow Wilson declares War on Germany in April 1917. Johnny reluctantly volun-

teers in the belief this is the war to end all wars and becomes a
soldier in the A.E.F., to the great delight of his excessively patriotic sweetheart, Minerva (Minny Belle) Tompkins. Johnny's native
practicality and honesty befuddles an Army psychiatrist and his
various efforts to end wholesale killing culminate in spraying a tank
of laughing gas on the Allied High Command when they refuse his request to stop the war. Johnny's pacifist actions get him sent back to
the U.S.A. where he completely confounds psychiatrist Dr. Mahodan
by being sane. The doctor, however, sends Johnny to an insane
asylum for ten years to recover from his advanced and dangerous
"peace monomania." Johnny and his asylum inmates assume the stature of statesmen and form their own peaceful League of World Republics. Finally defeated by the insanity outside the asylum Johnny
is released. Minny Belle has married a wealthy wartime laxative profiteer and Johnny, still retaining his faith in the basic goodness of
mankind, becomes a street peddler selling toys to good little girls
and boys.

Thirty-five years and several wars after the first production
of Paul Green's "fantastic drama" with a musical score by Kurt Weill,
Johnny Johnson returned to Broadway. Clive Barnes (The New York
Times) appraised the revival as "a period piece--interesting because
of the role it played in the American musical, and most of all, for
Weill's music," while determining "Jose Quintero's staging lacked pace
and conviction" and the author's book and lyrics were "not only a
little irrelevant but also enormously obvious," adding, "Moreover,
the book and lyrics by Paul Green take the parable and unimaginatively grind it into political dust. Weill's music--acts as a transfusion.
It creates a melodic world of its own" in "a bloodless show."

Richard Watts (New York Post) described Kurt Weill's music as
"as fresh and beautiful as ever" but Paul Green's book, as in 1936,
was found to be "unequal to the rigorous demands made on it."
Watts praised Ralph Williams in the title role of Johnny Johnson but
advised, "What we are left with is the Weill score, and it is one of
his most enchanting achievements." Douglas Watt (Daily News) recommended that the public "Go to Johnny for the music. It's marvelous" and "one of Weill's best. It is both sardonic and lyrical and
employs a small orchestra brilliantly. The work emerges more as
opera theater than a play with incidental music and the effect is
striking."

Johnny Johnson (44th Street Theatre, November 19, 1936--68 performances). Produced by The Group Theatre; A "Fantastic Drama"
by Paul Green with music by Kurt Weill; Director, Lee Strasberg;
Settings, Donald Oenslager; Costumes, Paul DuPont; Musical direction,
Lehman Engel; Technical director, Isaac Benesch; Production coordinator, Cheryl Crawford; Stage manager, Michael Gordon; Assistant
stage managers, Alfred Saxe, Bess Eitingon, Judson Hall
    Russell Collins (Johnny Johnson); Lee J. Cobb (Dr. McBray/
    Brother George/French Major-General); Morris Carnovsky (Dr.

Mahodan/Chief of the Allied High Command); Phoebe Brand (Minny Belle Tompkins); Roman Bohnen (Grandpa Joe/American Commander-in-Chief/Brother Claude); Art Smith (Sergeant Jackson/Doctor/Brother Thomas); Albert Van Dekker (Corporal George/Brother Hiram); Luther Adler (English Sergeant/Belgian Major-General/Brother Henry); Bob Lewis (The Mayor/French Premier); Sanford Meisner (Captain Valentine); Elia Kazan (Private Kearns/Dr. Frewd); Jules Garfield (Johann Lang); Curt Conway (A Boy/Private Patrick O'Day/Brother William); Joseph Pevney (West Point Lieutenant); Tony Kraber (The Editor/Private Harwood/Brother Theodore); William Challee (Private Fairfax/A Doctor); Will Lee (Photographer/Private Goldberger); Grover Burgess (Anguish Howington); Suzanna Senior (Aggie Tompkins); Eunice Stoddard (A Camp Dolly); Alfred Saxe (American Priest); Herbert Ratner (Private Svenson/Military Policeman/Attendant); Judson Hall (British Soldier/A Soldier); Paula Miller (French Nurse); Paul Mann (Orderly); Ruth Nelson (A Sister from the O.D.S.D.L.D.); Orrin Jannings (His Majesty, A King); Eddie Ryan (Anguish Howington, Jr.); John Most (British Commander-in-Chief); Thomas C. Kennedy (Scottish Colonel); Jack Saltzman (Liaison Officer); Paul Mann (German Priest); Kate Allen (Dr. Mahodan's Secretary); Robert Joseph (Brother Jim); Peter Ainsley, James Blake (Soldiers); Jean Burton (Song)

SONGS: Over in Europe; Democracy's Call; Up Chickamauga Hill; Aggie's Sewing Machine; Oh, Heart of Love*; Oh, the Rio Grande*; Mon Ami, My Friend*; Johnny's Melody; Captain Valentine's Tango; Song of the Goddess; Song of the Wounded Frenchman; Song of the Guns; The Allied High Command; In Times of Tumult and War; Johnny's Arrest and Homecoming; How Sweetly Friendship Binds; The Psychiatry Song; Hymn to Peace; Johnny's Song (Listen to My Song)* [*Published by Chappell & Company. "Johnny's Song" was published with lyrics by Edward Heyman as "To Love You and to Lose You"]

The newly formed Group Theatre, Inc., an offspring of the Theatre Guild, presented Paul Green's drama The House of Connelly as their first production at the Martin Beck Theatre on September 28, 1931, which relocated in the Mansfield Theatre on November 16, 1931, to complete 91 performances. Five years later the leftist-leaning Group Theatre produced Paul Green's fantasy play, augmented by the first American score written by German refugee composer Kurt Weill. Cheryl Crawford, one of the Group Theatre founders and directors, took Weill to Chapel Hill, North Carolina, to meet Green and during the summer of 1936 the German composer and the American playwright created "A Fable of Ancient and Modern Times" they called Johnny Johnson.

Paul Green, who won the Pulitzer Prize for his first full-length play, In Abraham's Bosom, in 1926, later told Newsweek magazine, "The character is named Johnny Johnson because war records show that there were 30,000 Johnsons in the American Army. Three thousand of these were John Johnsons." He described his play as a "musical biography of a common soldier whose natural common sense runs counter to a sophisticated civilization" told within the framework of comedy, tragedy and satire.

Kurt Weill and his wife, Lotta Lenya, fled Hitler's mad fatherland in 1933 and in 1935 settled in New York. Weill and Bertolt Brecht's classic treatment of John Gay's eighteenth-century work The Beggar's Opera called Die Dreigroschenoper (The Threepenny Opera) had initially failed at Broadway's Empire Theatre on April 13, 1933, in twelve performances. Not until 1954, at the Theatre de Lys in Greenwich Village, did The Threepenny Opera deservedly become an outstanding success in a new translation by Marc Blitzstein with Lotta Lenya recreating her original role of Jenny. The Threepenny Opera's revival completed 2,611 performances.

Weill composed a musical score for Max Reinhardt's production of Franz Werfel's biblical drama The Eternal Road, which was postponed due to financial problems and later opened at the Manhattan Opera House on January 7, 1937, for 153 performances. Johnny Johnson was financially saved by investments from John Hay Whitney and Mrs. Motty Eitingon and others and opened at the 44th Street Theatre on November 19, 1936. Historian George Freedley described Johnny Johnson as "One of the best anti-war plays of the present century."

Robert Benchley (The New Yorker) felt that, with Johnny Johnson, "The Group Theatre bit off quite a chunk of dramaturgy-- The fact that it sometimes proves more than they can handle is unfortunate, but when you consider what they are trying to do, their occasional failure is almost endearing. And in the light of what they do accomplish, which is to make you laugh, cry and boil, I would be inclined to overlook the weak spots and be very grateful for the whole thing." Mr. Benchley admired Kurt Weill's music which became "an integral part of the whole crazy quilt through its very irrelevance."

Burns Mantle (Daily News) found there was a "divergence of opinion centered about the effectiveness of the play's statement rather than the quality of its writing" in a "legend that was a little fantastic but very earnest." Brooks Atkinson (The New York Times) wrote, "Under the buffoonery of this fugacious satiric legend Mr. Green knows that Johnny is the most tragic figure in the world. The world has slapped him with its ultimate indignity. It can no longer find room for a completely honest man, for it has surrendered to the charlatans, opportunists and rogues who are the captains and kings of destruction." Time magazine found the Group Theatre to "have fashioned a show which does not hesitate to exploit any form of theatrical procedure necessary to attain its end." Green's play was called "a profound and witty evangelical address to a world he at one point concedes to be 'bass ackwards'" and praised Kurt Weill "for the weird, haunting little ballads and Europeanized fox trots which immensely help to articulate the play."

94 / Johnny No-Trump

<u>Johnny Johnson</u> was a natural choice of production for Hallie Flanagan's Federal Theatre, created during the Great Depression by the WPA Work Program. The Paul Green-Kurt Weill fantasy was produced by the Federal theatres in Boston and Los Angeles during the 1936-1937 season. The Boston production, directed by Gerald Cornell with scenery by Paul Cadorette and Charles Frank as musical director, featured Arthur Barry (Johnny); Patricia McMackin (Minny Belle Tompkins); John Taylor (Grandpa Joe); Frank Thomas (Dr. Mahodan/British Commander-in-Chief); Paul Sheehan (Sergeant Jackson/American Commander-in-Chief); Ramon Greenleaf (Captain Valentine); Louise Kirtland (French Nurse) in a cast of eighty.

The Green-Weill "fantastic drama" was revived at the Carnegie Hall Playhouse on October 21, 1956. Produced and directed by a former Group Theatre alumnus, Stella Adler, designed and lighted by Wolfgang Roth, with costumes by Betty Coe Armstrong and choreography by Robert Joffrey, and with Samuel Matlowsky as musical director, the revival of <u>Johnny Johnson</u> featured twenty-five performers creating the sixty-two characters in the play.

The principal roles were performed by James Broderick (Johnny Johnson); Rosemary O'Reilly (Minny Belle); Maurice Edwards (Grandpa Joe); Gene Saks (Dr. Mahodan); Joanne Linville (A Sister from the O.D.S.D.L.D.; or Organization for the Delight of Soldiers Disabled in the Line of Duty); Charles Tyner (Dr. McBray); Logan Ramsey (Captain Valentine); Virginia McMahon (Minny Belle's Friend); Jonathan Bush (Anguish Howington); Elizabeth Parrish (French Nurse); Jack Waltzer (Orderly); Robert Minford (English Sargeant); Edward Printz (Johann); Alice Winston (Aggie Tompkins); Sidney Armus (Mayor) with other characters played by Frances Lane, Betty Kent, Art Alisi, James Vazules, Bruce Williamson; Edmund Gaynes, Joseph Kahan, James Moran, Gerald Garrison, James MacDonald.

* * *

<u>JOHNNY NO-TRUMP</u> (Cort Theatre, October 8, 1967). Produced by Theatre 1968 (Richard Barr, Clinton Wilder, Charles Woodward, Jr.); A comedy-drama by Mary Mercier; Director, Joseph Hardy; Setting, Lighting and Costumes, William Ritman; Production assistant, James Prideaux; Executive assistant, Seth Dansky; General manager, Michael Goldreyer; Stage managers, D. W. Koehler, Charles Kindl
    Pat Hingle (Harry Armstrong); Sada Thompson (Florence Edwards); James Broderick (Alexander Edwards); Don Scardino (John Edwards); Bernadette Peters (Bettina); Barbara Lester (Mrs. Franklin)

Sixteen-year-old John Edwards and his well-educated, divorced schoolteacher mother, Florence, share a Suffolk County, Long Island, home with Johnny's cantankerous uneducated sixty-year-old Uncle Harold, a taxi-driver. Uncle Harry considers Johnny a kook and homely and warns Florence that Johnny is fated to face life with a

stacked deck and no trumps. Rebelling against his Uncle Harry's
constant reprimands, Johnny decides to leave school to become a poet.
During Johnny's birthday party his alcoholic, unsuccessful artist
father, Alexander, suppresses Johnny's rebellion with the knowledge
that Uncle Harry once aspired to become a great singer but his impossible dream never materialized and in his advancing age the dream
has turned to bitterness. After Johnny's party, his mother is killed
in an automobile accident and Johnny instinctively turns to surrogate
father Uncle Harry for solace and support. Harry tells Johnny that
writing poetry is really a respectable vocation and to pursue his
dream.

Richard Watts, Jr. (New York Post) discovered "many likeable
things" in Mary Mercier's first play, Johnny No-Trump, noting it
"has believable and understandable characters and it deals with a
recognizable family situation in a sympathetic and sensible way, but,
despite an unexpected touch at the conclusion, it never succeeds in
creating more than the mildest kind of dramatic stimulation" and was
"a worthy try but a disappointment." George Oppenheimer (Newsday)
praised the play with "It has honesty, humor and infinite compassion,
rare commodities in our theatre today."

The Village Voice considered Johnny No-Trump "possibly the
most honest and unpretentious dramatization of the conflict between
young and old Broadway will see this season." Clive Barnes (The
New York Times) classified the play as "schizophrenic" (although
beautifully acted) and suggested that the playwright "has taken a
cliche, and now and again, embroidered it with truth" in which
characters' dialogue shifted quickly from "absolute truthfulness" to
"slick gibberish." Richard P. Cooke (The Wall Street Journal) wrote,
"The play has much to recommend it. There are stimulating insights
in Miss Mercier's play and although not especially original, they are
convincingly presented." Two weeks after the opening of Mary
Mercier's play, Walter Kerr wrote in the Sunday New York Times
that enormous damage was done by the sudden closing of Johnny
No-Trump, "Beyond doubt, author Mary Mercier's confidence has
been damaged. She is at this moment a failure rather than a discovery. Yet she is--or should have been--a discovery. Her struc-
tural gaucheries were almost unimportant; she has a voice."

Producer Richard Barr blasted the New York critics in The
New York Times for the quick demise of Johnny No-Trump: "The
fact that the critics did not appreciate that this play was so far above
the level, both in writing and production of almost any American play
for the past several seasons indicates to me that there is a great
struggle ahead for sensitive, intelligent, talented playwrights. We
can't fight this lethargy on the part of the critics." Barr's impulsive
closing of the show was based solely on the review written by The
New York Times's former dance critic, recently elevated to drama
critic, Clive Barnes.

Thirteen days after the closing of Johnny No-Trump Clive Barnes reviewed his appraisals: "This season, even this early, has regrets as well as its triumphs. Personally, I regret that Johnny No-Trump, not a brilliant but a promising play, superbly acted with a lovely cast, led by Pat Hingle, was abruptly taken off by its producer before it had a chance to get word-of-mouth resuscitation. This was Broadway at its most savage. Some plays need nursing, and Johnny No-Trump was a perfect example." The show cost $84,000 to produce but the cost was actually $67,000 as of opening (and closing) night. Former actress Mary Mercier was seeking employment.

A Midwestern writer of children's books, Susan Jacobs, in 1972 wrote an entire book documenting the history of Johnny No-Trump, called On Stage: The Making of a Broadway Play published by Alfred A. Knopf. The same year Marilyn Stasio, drama critic for Cue and later drama critic for the New York Post, and the only female member of the New York Drama Critics Circle, wrote a fascinating and informative book called Broadway's Beautiful Losers, published by Delacorte Press.

The Losers consisted of five plays shunned on Broadway which deserved better fate: Hugh Wheeler's 1961, five-performance comedy, Look, We've Come Through; S. J. Perelman's 1962, 85-performance The Beauty Part, starring the irrepressible and incomparable Bert Lahr; Saul Bellow's 1964, twenty-eight performance farce The Last Analysis; Jack Richardson's 1965, quick four-performance Xmas in Las Vegas, with Tom Ewell; and Mary Mercier's play Johnny No-Trump. Marilyn Stasio wrote, "Johnny No-Trump has become a generic term for the flop célèbre" and "In his acerbic best-selling book of 1969, The Season, William Goldman used Johnny No-Trump, which he called 'the best new American play of the season,' to launch the book's most controversial chapter." Goldman also felt Johnny No-Trump compared favorably, and was better written, than Frank Gilroy's 1965 Pulitzer Prize play The Subject Was Roses.

Marilyn Stasio's appraisal of Johnny No-Trump is probably more accurate than the assessments made on October 9, 1967: "Johnny No-Trump is a fine, honest, family drama. Its dramatic goals are modest--the character of their interrelationships--but it attains them admirably, with a good deal of emotional power and a superb depth of sensitivity. Its dramatic structure is a wobbly affair, but the sheer force of its compassion, the superior quality of its writing and the flesh-and-blood dimensions of its characters easily compensate for its sketchy plot mechanics."

Clive Barnes's closing statement in his October 9, 1967, review in The New York Times found the play "with good enough passages and strong enough (if rickety) architecture to support a sextet of good players. I personally would have preferred to have written it than, say Cactus Flower, but that does not mean it will run as long."

* * *

JULIA, JAKE AND UNCLE JOE (Booth Theatre, January 28, 1961). Produced by Roger L. Stevens and John Shubert, in association with Sherman S. Krellberg; A comedy by Howard M. Teichmann, based on Oriana Atkinson's novel Over at Uncle Joe's; Director, Richard Whorf; Settings, lighting and costumes, Frederick Fox; Miss Colbert's clothes by Sophie of Saks Fifth Avenue; Company manager, Roy Jones; Production stage manager, Joseph Olney; Stage managers, Kelly McCormick, John Garner

    Claudette Colbert (Julia Ryan); Myles Eason (Jake Ryan); Boris Marshalov (Uncle Joe); Ludmilla Tchor (Elena); Lynne Charnay (Anya Petrovna); Grant Gordon (Oliver Pendergast); Alexander Clark (replaced John D. Seymour) (Dickinson Wadsworth); Michael Sivy (Major Kolnikov); Don Briggs (A. J. Webb); F. Samuel Fisher (Gregor); Joseph Leon (Boris); Miles Baker (Constantin Trigorin); Eigil Silju (Sergei Prosorov); Kelly McCormick (Marine Sergeant); John Garner (Knox); Tony Cichoke (General Lopakhin); Maurice Brenner (Professor Rasenik); Laryssa Lauret (Natalya Stephanovna); Herbert Jones (Dr. Von Meinholz); R. K. Lowry, Jim Holder (Russian Soldiers)

Drama critic and inveterate bird-watcher Jacob J. Ryan is assigned to Russia in July, 1945, as Moscow correspondent for his New York newspaper. Leaving his wife, Julia, in Moscow's Hotel Metropole, Jake pursues his fascination with ornithology in Luchinsky Park, bounded by the Kremlin, the Soviet War College, NKVD Headquarters, and the Ministry of Defense, where his bird-watching is interpreted by the Soviets as spying and he is quickly sent to Lubyanka Prison. Charming, resourceful, and vivacious Julia, despairing of the ineffectual Washington bureaucrats and double-talking diplomats of Moscow's American Embassy to obtain her husband's release from prison, arranges an audience with Uncle Joe Stalin in the Kremlin, using the subterfuge she is privy to details of the atomic bomb recently dropped on Japan. Julia fails to convince Uncle Joe she is privy to much more than being a devoted wife and Jake is released from prison in the Spring of 1946.

The tocsin tolled by out-of-town critics should have indicated Julia, Jake and Uncle Joe required a good deal more than charming performances by an enthusiastic cast. Ernie Schier (Philadelphia Evening Bulletin) reported Teichmann's play was "a comedy which might be described as suffering from malnutrition of the typewriter" which, "filled the evening with sketchy situations and vagrant gags-- the playwright, the director and the producer had better put their heads together in a hurry and come up with something better. Like a miracle." Jerry Gaghan (Daily News) felt the cast was "betrayed by the script. The curtain lines fall more silently than the curtain."

S. S. Irving (Jewish Exponent) wrote, "You see this play about Brooks Atkinson's adventures behind that certain curtain is billed as a new play. That is like saying <u>See Here, Private Hargrove</u> was a new book instead of a reissue of all the jokes we elders read in <u>Dere Mabel</u>. Mr. Teichmann drags out all the standard anti-Soviet gags. Bad plumbing. Crowded rooms. Espionage, counter-espionage, and counter-counter espionage. Even the one about calling perfume 'October Revolution.'"

Despite its multiple out-of-town problems, <u>Julia, Jake and Uncle Joe</u> bravely made a one-night stand at Broadway's Booth Theatre on January 28, 1961. Howard Taubman (<u>The New York Times</u>) confirmed out-of-town appraisals with "Howard M. Teichmann has come up with an embarrassing, unfunny comedy" which "starts with identifiable people in a realistic situation, shifts into farce and becomes a concoction that is neither fresh comment nor lively invention." Supremely talented Claudette Colbert was applauded by all critics for her "engaging and deftly comic performance" capsulized by Robert Coleman (<u>New York Mirror</u>) as "Colbert a gem. But play isn't."

Since 1923 Claudette Colbert had been in many plays and, after an extensive and impressive film career, she returned to the theatre in 1958 to co-star with Charles Boyer on Broadway for 433 performances in Leslie Stevens' comedy <u>The Marriage-Go-Round</u>. Miss Colbert's long experience in plays and motion pictures brought the realization that <u>Julia, Jake and Uncle Joe</u> would not work in Moscow, New York, or even Hollywood. Whitney Bolton (<u>Morning Telegraph</u>) underscored her theory with "She frowns, laughs, giggles, comforts, embraces, joshes, uses all the skills of an expert timer, does everything at an actress' command to pump reality, fun, and magic into the play. Seldom has a distinguished actress worked harder to achieve not much."

Teichmann's comedy premiered in Wilmington, Delaware, and there, said actress Colbert, "the closing should have come. I asked them to close it then and do extensive rewriting, either that or let me out. One of the producers just turned to me and said, 'I didn't know you were a quitter!' When you get up in front of an audience and try to be funny you know pretty quickly how well you're doing. I knew the first day in Wilmington. That was the time to do something drastic. It taught me a lesson. Now I'll wait for the rewrites. It's always sad when this much effort is put into something. People ask, 'How do intelligent people get mixed up in something like this?' It's never that simple. Anyway, in the entertainment field, everyone falls on his face regularly."

Oriana Atkinson's book <u>Over at Uncle Joe's: Moscow and Me</u> was published by Bobbs Merrill in 1947. That same year her husband Brooks was awarded the Pulitzer Prize for Journalism for his articles on the Soviet Union, based on his ten-month assignment in Moscow as foreign correspondent for <u>The New York Times</u>, and one of his nine books, a collection of essays gleaned from his thirty-one years as drama critic for <u>The New York Times</u>, <u>Broadway Scrapbook</u>, was published. Mrs. Atkinson's recall of life in Moscow during her husband's assignment had mixed reviews from "There is nothing very profound about this book. It is light and enjoyable" (<u>Chicago Sun Book Week</u>) to Henry Sowerby's report in <u>The Christian Science Monitor</u>, "Oriana Atkinson has abundance of clever comment and vivid portrayal; but her propensity for translating most of her observations into the language of ridicule, not of the subtlest variety, can only appeal to those who crave light amusement regardless of what offense is being occasioned in the process."

Chicago-born (1916) playwright Howard M. Teichmann, an English professor at Barnard College and Columbia University, had written the successful Broadway comedy <u>The Solid Gold Cadillac</u> in 1953 with George S. Kaufman, and he became his late collaborator's biographer in 1972 with <u>George S. Kaufman: An Intimate Portrait</u>. Teichmann's plays <u>Miss Lonelyhearts</u>, adapted from Nathanael West's novel, and <u>The Girls in 509</u> were not glowing successes and his 1963 comedy, <u>A Rainy Day in Newark</u>, lasted only six performances. Mr. Teichmann's wife Evelyn's suggestion that he read Mrs. Atkinson's book reminded him of Charlotte Shaw's dogged insistence that her husband Bernard should write a play based on the life of Joan of Arc.

Teichmann observed, "I saw in the book two things: rich material that could make a humorous and amusing show; satiric comment on what had happened to two former comrades--the USSR and the U.S.--who overnight had become strangers." But Howard M. waited ten years, until Brooks Atkinson had retired as drama critic from <u>The New York Times</u>, to adapt the book to the stage, feeling "It would be unethical to put him on the spot of reviewing a play based on his wife's book." Mrs. Atkinson recommended Claudette Colbert to play her counterpart, Julia Ryan.

The gentle-mannered Harvard graduate Dean of American Drama Critics was born Justin Brooks Atkinson on November 28, 1894, in Melrose, Massachusetts. Mr. Atkinson's thirty-one years of perceptive and literate reviewing of plays was well described by playwright Arthur Miller: "There cannot have been another critic as trusted as Brooks Atkinson was by so large a proportion of the theatregoing public. He is the only one who can be said to have presided over Broadway. Above all, he made the reader see what he had seen and this left some room for dissent. His presence lent the theatre a dignity and importance it did not usually merit, but his influence served to raise the sights of everyone it touched."

Indicative of Brooks Atkinson's dedicated reviewing for the theatre was an unusual celebration of March 2, 1958, when he was coerced into attending an anniversary party for Mr. and Mrs. Lee Strasberg at Sardi's Restaurant, open that Sunday for the first time since 1929. The "Strasberg Anniversary" was a surprise tribute to <u>The New York Times</u> drama critic, organized by Helen Hayes and

Mrs. Strasberg and attended by the elite of the theatre. Hosted by Oscar Hammerstein, II, who read a letter from Sean O'Casey praising Atkinson's "artistic perception and common sense." Kitty Carlisle Hart read a letter from her husband, Moss, expressing astonishment that such a gala would be given by "theatrefolk for a dramatic critic!" Helen Hayes and Paula Miller Strasberg presented the astonished critic with a silver tray autographed by each guest, among them Sir Laurence Olivier, Lillian and Dorothy Gish, Thornton Wilder, Lillian Hellman, and all the distinguished assembled celebrants. Mary Martin, accompanied by Richard Rodgers on the piano, sang "I'm in Love with a Wonderful Guy" and Actors Equity president Ralph Bellamy extolled Atkinson's standards of reviewing.

Two years later Brooks Atkinson became the first critic to have a theatre named for him. Michael Myerberg, owner of the Mansfield Theatre on West 47th Street, deploring the retirement of Brooks Atkinson from The New York Times, renamed his theatre the Brooks Atkinson saying, "The stage is set for a revival of the arts and we are suddenly faced with the loss of a great force at the peak of his effectiveness." A bronze plaque renaming the theatre read "Brooks Atkinson, Author-Critic-Humanist. To Whom This Theatre Is Dedicated, September 7, 1960, In Honor of Thirty-Five Years of Selfless Devotion to the Theatre."

Brooks Atkinson, who married Mrs. Oriana Torrey MacIlveen in 1926, died at the age of eighty-nine on Friday, January 13, 1984, in Huntsville, Alabama. Ten years before his death Atkinson said, "I was glad to quit in 1960. The last two years I didn't think were worth the trouble. I used to rush back to write reviews of plays that weren't very interesting."

* * *

KELLY (Broadhurst Theatre, February 6, 1965). Produced by David Susskind and Daniel Melnick, in association with Joseph E. Levine; A musical with Book and Lyrics by Eddie Lawrence; Music, Moose Charlap; Directed and Choreographed by Herbert Ross; Scenic production by Oliver Smith; Costumes, Freddy Wittop; Lighting, Tharon Muser; Musical director, Samuel Matlovsky; Orchestrations, Hershy Kay; Dance music, Betty Walberg; Associate producer, Robert L. Livingston; General manager, Philip Adler; Company manager, Edward Blatt; Production stage manager, Randall Brooks; Production assistant, Janet O'Morrison; Sound, Jack Mann; Hairstylist, Ronald De Mann; Stage managers, Tom Porter, Kathleen O'Sullivan, Louis Kosman
    Don Francks (Hop Kelly); Wilfrid Brambell (Dan Kelly); Anita Gillette (Angela Crane); Jesse White (Stickpin Sidney Crane); Mickey Shaughnessy (Jack Mulligan); Eileen Rodgers (Fay Cherry); Leon Janney (Augie Masters); Josip Elic (Charlie); Steve Elmore (Frank James); Brandon Maggart (Carruthers); Hamilton Camp (Mayor Tully); Jack Creley (Major Broome); Leslie Franzos (Daphne Smythe); Bill Richards (Sparkenbroke, the butler); Barbara Monte

(Tough Kid); J. Vernon Oaks (Police Chief); Robert L. Hultman (Policeman); Bette Jenkins (Lollypop Girl); Lynn Fields (The Redhead); Louis Kosman, Anthony De Vecchi, Michael Nestor (Three Tough Guys); Sterling Clark (The Rube); Ron Stratton (The Drunk); Larry Roquemore, Paul Charles (Young Man); Leslie Franzos, Eleanor Treiber, Kathleen Doherty (Three Ladies); Bill Richards (Beggar); Stanley Simmonds (Chief Dignitary); James Moore, Larry Roquemore, Bill Richards (Bums); Thomas Rezarf (Englishman); James Moore (Sailor); Hanne-Marie Reiner (Young Girl); Kathleen Doherty, Lynn Fields, Leslie Franzos, Bette Jenkins, Barbara Monte, Hanne-Marie Reiner, Eleanor Treiber, Sterling Clark, Paul Charles, Anthony De Vecchi, Michael Nestor, Bill Richards, Larry Roquemore, Ron Stratton (Dancing Ensemble); Georgia Creighton, Ceil Delli, Carol Joplin, Larene Latine, Donna Monroe, Maggie Task, Walter P. Brown, Steve Elmore, Howard Hartman, Robert L. Hultman, J. Vernon Oaks, William Wendt (Singing Ensemble)

Dropped during tryout: Ella Logan (Ma Kelly); Carol Joplin (Phyllis Smythe); Walter P. Brown (Raffles); Richard Schaal (Jesse James); Leon Janney replaced Marty Ingels during rehearsals. Steve Elmore replaced Avery Schreiber as Frank James after the out-of-town opening. Hanne Marie Reiner's part as Sarah Bernhardt was written out of the script.

SONGS: Ode to the Bridge; Six Blocks from the Bridge; Simple Ain't Easy; That Old Time Crowd; I'm Gonna Walk Right Up to Her; A Moment Ago; This Is a Tough Neighborhood; Life Can be Beautiful; Everyone Here Loves Kelly; Ballad to a Brute; Heavyweight Champ of the World; Me and the Elements; Never Go There Anymore
Dropped during tryout: We Got a Deal; Soliloguy; The Times that Linger; He'll Get It; A Man is a Man; The Big Town; Saturday Night at Augies; Home Again (Original Cast Album--Columbia Records)

On the Bowery, boxing champion Jack Mulligan, Stickpin Sidney Crane and Augie Masters make sizeable bets that uneducated Irish immigrant busboy Hop Kelly will come out of the East River alive after his repeatedly proposed but not yet performed leap from the Brooklyn Bridge. The gamblers attempt to assure their bets by encouraging braggart Kelly to substitute a dummy instead of making the actual jump. Sarcastic, swaggering Kelly refuses the gambler's deception and hopes his bizarre exploit will elevate his low status on the Bowery and impress his girl friend, Angela, and his impoverished father, Dan. Kelly finally leaps from the Brooklyn Bridge and emerges from the East River to sudden fame.

The critics unanimously deplored Kelly. "Rarely have so many labored so diligently over such a small idea, and it is therefore a tribute of some kind that the proceedings are not a total debacle-- but it is at best a middling musical," reported John McClain (Journal American). Richard Watts, Jr. (New York Post) wrote, "The new musical comedy isn't the worst you can imagine, though you might have to pause and think for a while before coming up with its peer in that respect--Kelly is surrounded by an aura of hopeless ineffectuality." Walter Kerr (Herald Tribune) capsulized Kelly as "a bad idea gone wrong."

Norman Nadel (New York World Telegram-Sun) recognized that "There is a good musical in the colorful story of Brooklyn Bridge. Kelly certainly isn't it. Somehow, almost everything about the show seems to have turned out wrong. Lawrence's writing--at least as it has reached the stage--is unbelievably fatuous." Howard Taubman (The New York Times) congratulated Ella Logan for being written out of Kelly and noted that Eddie Lawrence and Moose Charlap had asked the court to enjoin the opening of the show because of the drastic rewriting and changes made during the traumatic tryout of the musical. Taubman added, "I don't know about the merits of what has been eliminated from Kelly. But to judge by what is left, there are ample critical, if not legal, grounds for an injunction."

Producer David Susskind told the Herald Tribune, "I have never been so shocked, so surprised in my life. I believed in Kelly. I believed in the cast. I believed in the staging--the songs. Then I saw the reviews. They raised a huge unanswered question mark in my brain. What happened to my taste? Did I put on something crass? Could I be this wrong?" The Herald Tribune's one-liner should have answered Mr. Susskind's questions: "Hitler got better notices in World War II."

Producers Susskind and Melnick, partners in Talent Associates-Paramount, Ltd., raised $350,000, Joseph E. Levine invested $250,000, and Columbia Records contributed $50,000 toward the recreation of the saga of the Brooklyn Bridge's legendary highdiver Steve Brodie, which drowned in its rechristening as Kelly. The $650,000 disappeared, as quickly as Kelly's leap, from the Broadhurst Theatre bridge.

Toronto, Canada's television and nightclub performer Don Francks made his American stage debut in the title role of Kelly, and pert, talented Anita Gillette, who had been seen on Broadway in the musical comedies All-American and Mr. President in 1962, played his sweetheart, Angela Crane. Ella Logan, who had not appeared on Broadway for seventeen years since brightening the musical comedy Finian's Rainbow, singing the glories of "Glocca Morra," first heard of Kelly when producer Edward Padula optioned the property. Logan was recommended to Susskind and associates by Richard Burton's foster father, Philip, to play "Ma" Kelly and English actor Wilfrid Brambell was cast as "Pa" Dan Kelly. Then a grandmother of substantial girth, Ella Logan was assigned two songs, "The Times That Linger" and "Life Can be Beautiful."

Comedian Jesse White, in Hollywood for seventeen years since his last Broadway appearance as Marochek in Jean-Paul Sartre's drama Red Gloves, in 1948, returned to the stage in Kelly as Stickpin Sidney Crane, the prototype of "Diamond Jim" Brady. Brooklyn-born Mickey Shaughnessy, who had appeared in many Hollywood films, was making his Broadway debut in Kelly as John L. Mulligan (changed to "Jack") patterned after boxing champion John L. Sullivan. Former child star Leon Janney had been in numerous Broadway shows and was cast in Kelly as Bowery cafe owner Augie. The cast was excellent. Kelly was not.

Eddie Lawrence was born Lawrence Eisler in Brooklyn, New York, on March 2, 1919. He graduated from Brooklyn College and attended the Académie de la Grande Chaumière in Paris, where he also studied painting at the Atelier Leger under Fernand Leger. He became involved in French film production with his scenario The Ladies and the Men, based on four stories of Guy de Maupassant. Lawrence began his career in vaudeville and later created an outrageous comic character, "The Old Philosopher," which he played successfully on radio and television. He was seen as an actor on Broadway in Bells Are Ringing and Sherry! and on the screen in Quelque Part dans la Monde (Act of Love) and as Scratch in The Night They Raided Minsky's.

Morris I. "Moose" Charlap, born in Philadelphia on December 19, 1928, died of a heart attack at the age of forty-five in Lennox Hill Hospital in New York on July 8, 1974. As "Mark" Charlap he wrote the score for Mary Martin's 1954 Peter Pan and composed the scores for the Broadway musicals Whoop-Up (December 22, 1958--56 performances) and The Conquering Hero (January 16, 1961--8 performances).

Kelly premiered at Philadelphia's Shubert Theatre with a special public preview on December 26, 1964, and opened a three-week engagement on December 28th. Out-of-town reviews were dirges, lamenting the first full-length play by Eddie Lawrence as "straight, hot, cold and Freud." The Evening Bulletin's critic Ernest Schier found the show "distressingly out of focus. At present, it is wandering around lost with a one-dimensional oaf for a hero and an exceedingly minor historical footnote to support its shaky structure."

The frenetic atmosphere during the tryout included cutting a scene involving the robbery of the Bowery Savings and Loan Bank by the James Brothers, Jesse and Frank, which eliminated actors Avery Schrieber and Richard Schaal from the cast. Hanne-Marie Reiner's part as Sarah Bernhardt also disappeared. Songs were discarded and new numbers were added, amid a good deal of sabre rattling.

Jack Perlis, press agent for producer David Susskind, invited The Saturday Evening Post to cover Kelly from its first rehearsal, on November 8, 1964, on the seventh floor of the New Amsterdam Theatre, to its unexpected quick demise several months later at the Broadhurst Theatre. "Nobody on Broadway could remember such a spectacular disaster within the recent history of the theatre," noted Lewis H. Latham as prologue to his postmortem account in The Saturday Evening Post of the backstage histrionics of Kelly, aptly titled Has Anybody Here Seen Kelly? Latham's detailed and amusing documentation of the hotly contested and chaotic backstage drama of Kelly would have made a more interesting book for the musical than the one presented on Broadway.

The producers' constant demands for new scenes to be written met with resistance from author Lawrence, who had appeared as Crookfinger Jake in 1955's revival of The Threepenny Opera. Lawrence had visualized Kelly in a Bertolt Brecht anti-hero concept and not as a stereotyped All-Americanized lovable hero parading through yet another overproduced, duplicated, glamorized Broadway musical. Backstage warfare erupted between the producers, author, composer, director, and several cast members. Kelly escaped to Boston where Susskind and Melnick won from the New York Supreme Court a temporary stay of injunction to close the show which had been filed by Lawrence and composer Charlap, who both left the show on January 16, 1965, in Philadelphia.

Boston critics roughed up Kelly more than the constantly revised script. Elliot Norton (Record American) called Kelly, "the noisiest musical of the season, a rattling cover for emptiness." David Susskind admitted he had backed "a bad show" and, dismissing Lawrence and Charlap as thinking they had written the Holy Scripture, imported television writers Mel Brooks and Leonard Stern from California to doctor and rewrite Lawrence's script. Ella Logan, the one box-office drawing card the show really had, was summarily fired. Logan's part of "Ma" Kelly was considered to be irrelevant.

Back in New York the new script by Brooks and Stern was paced with Catskill nightclub humor and placed in rehearsal on January 25, 1965, while Justice Samuel Gold of the New York Supreme Court heard the case of Lawrence & Charlap vs. Susskind and Associates. Justice Gold took under consideration the authors' charge of the producers' willful destruction of their work against the producers' loss to date of $500,000, but he denied Lawrence and Charlap's attorney's demand for an injunction to stop the opening of Kelly on Broadway.

After five previews, Don Francks as Kelly was launched on wires from the "Brooklyn Bridge" at the Broadhurst Theatre. Francks' one jump, on February 6, 1965, drowned in the show's excesses and the obituaries of the press. NBC perceptively saw Kelly as "a musical by committee" and the Associated Press dismissed the fiasco as "a monumental bore." Four days later, following Kelly's one-night stand, stage manager Randy Brooks accompanied Oliver Smith's setting for the doomed musical to McKay's Secaucus Dump, where it disappeared under a bulldozer quicker than the memory and fleeting fame of Brodie's jump from the Brooklyn Bridge. But that's show-biz, or, as critic Burne Reiff later phrased it, "But then, Kelly had no business being a show."

* * *

LET ME HEAR YOU SMILE (Biltmore Theatre, January 16, 1973). Produced by Michael and Barclay MacRae; A comedy by Leonora Thuna and Harry Cauley; Director, Harry Cauley; Setting, Peter Larkin; Lighting, Neil Peter Janpolis; Costumes, Carrie F. Robbins; Producer's assistant, Christi Hatcher; Hairstylist, Hector Garcia; General manager, Richard Seader; Company manager, Malcolm Allen; Stage managers, Ben Janney, Philip Cusack
    Sandy Dennis (Hannah Heywood); James Broderick (Neil Heywood)
    Paul B. Price (Willy Farmer)
SONG: Slap That Bass, by George and Ira Gershwin

    Nervously confronting her thirty-ninth birthday on Christmas Eve 1940 in a small New Jersey village, Hannah Heywood decides to leave her loving husband, Neil. Hannah's brother Willy, beset with bladder problems and deserted by his wife, encourages them to recall their childhood and the joys of kindergarten in 1905. Their marriage survives and at the age of seventy Neil has sold his hardware business and ponders resettling in New Zealand. Hannah ridicules his daydream as a sure sign of senility and Neil reluctantly agrees to postpone his leaving--for a while.

    During Let Me Hear You Smile, "One had a certain difficulty in even hearing a laugh," reported Clive Barnes (The New York Times), calling the play "pointless, sad and totally unmemorable"; calling the performances "valiant failures" and viewing the comedy's uncertainty due to the author's indecision on "what kind of play they were writing." Richard Watts (New York Post) felt the playwrights had a sense of humor despite the play's meaningless title, with "some of it quite funny--but emphatically not stimulating. One can wish Let Me Hear You Smile well, but it is harder to find reasons for expressing enthusiasm over its mildness." Douglas Watt (Daily News) asked "What is this static, foolish play written by Leonora Thuna and Harry Cauley and staged by the latter supposed to be and how did it get here?"

    The first producing venture of Michael and Barclay MacRae had seven previews and one performance. Johnny Green's recording of George and Ira Gershwin's song "Slap That Bass" (from Fred Astaire's 1937 film Shall We Dance) was nostalgic, but Let Me Hear You Smile remained unmemorable.

* * *

LITTLE JOHNNY JONES (Alvin Theatre, March 21, 1982). Produced by James M. Nederlander, Steven Leber, David Krebs and the JFK Center; A musical comedy with Book, Music and Lyrics by George M.

106 / Little Johnny Jones

Cohan, adapted by Alfred Uhry; Director, Gerald Gutierrez; Settings, Robert Randolph; Lighting, Thomas Skelton; Costumes, David Toser; Choreography and Musical staging by Dan Siretta; Musical director, Lynn Crigler; Dance arrangements, Russell Werner; Additional orchestrations, Eddie Sauter, Mack Schlefer; Vocal arrangements and additional dance arrangements, Robert Fisher; Production supervisor, Robert V. Strauss; Production associate, Warren Pincus; Musical consultant, Alfred Simon; Management assistants, Barbara Softcheck, Beth Fremgen; Props, Paul Mazurek, Charles Zuckerman; Wardrobe, Colleen Gieryn; Hairstylist, Howard Leonard; Assistant to director, Jennifer McCray; Casting, Warren Pincus; Assistant conductor, Don Rebic; Production assistant, Charles Suisman; Sound, Abe Jacobs; Stage managers, Robert V. Strauss, John Actman, Earl Aaron Levine; General management, Marvin A. Krauss Associates
  Donny Osmond (Johnny Jones, American Jockey); Maureen Brennan (Goldie Gates, Copper Heiress); Peter Van Norden (Anthony Anstey); Jane Galloway (Florabelle Fly, Society Editor); Tom Rolfing (Timothy D. McGee); Ernie Sabella (Whitney Wilson); Anna McNeely (Mrs. Kenworth, Goldie's Aunt); Al Micacchion (Bellboy); Bruce Chew (Sing-Song, Sports Editor); Jack Bittner (Captain Squirvy/Announcer); David Fredericks (Newsboy); Jack Bittner (Starter at Hotel Cecil); Richard Dodd, David Fredericks, James Homan, Gary Kirsch, Bobby Longbottom, Al Miacacchion, David Monzione, Keith Savage (American Boys, Porters, Sailors); Colleen Ashton, Teri Corcoran, Susie Fenner, Linda Gradl, Debra Grimm, Lori Lynott, Annette Michelle, Mayme Paul (American Girls)
SONGS: The Cecil in London; Then I'd Be Satisfied with Life; Yankee Doodle Boy; Oh, You Wonderful Boy; The Voice in My Heart; Captain of a Ten Day Boat; Goodbye Flo; Life's a Funny Proposition; Let's You and I Just Say Goodbye; Give My Regards to Broadway; Extra! Extra!; American Ragtime

Donny Osmond, the seventh son of nine children of the vastly talented Mormon Osmond family was born in Ogden, Utah, on December 9, 1957. He had been preceded by brothers Virl, Tommy, Alan, Wayne, Merrill, and Jay and followed by their lone sister, Marie, and youngest brother, Jimmy. The versatile Osmonds play a variety of musical instruments, sing and dance and have become part of American folklore. Twenty-four-year-old Donny's debut on the Broadway legitimate stage was to recreate the first starring role of George M. Cohan, then twenty six years old, in the feisty, flag-waving song-and-dance man's own musical play Little Johnny Jones. A tough act to follow even after seventy-eight years.

The revival of Little Johnny Jones was heralded by a very loud band in front of the Alvin Theatre on corded-off 52nd Street. Prior to the opening chorus, the audience was requested to rise and sing "The National Anthem." At the final curtain an immense American flag was unfurled, covering the proscenium. But all the constant unfurling of Old Glory and audience participation in "The Star Spangled Banner" could not reincarnate Little Johnny Jones, which had not occasioned a national holiday nor dancing in the streets when it was first produced in 1904 with the original Yankee Doodle Dandy.

"This musical is a listless, not to mention listing, farrago," reported Frank Rich (The New York Times) "--the show's staging gives it the aura of a wax museum with sets (mainly drops), costumes and at times sepulchral lighting to match." While conceding Donny, "known to television's fans everywhere for his flashing white teeth, clean-cut graces and Hawaiian Punch commercials," would not intrude on anyone's memory of George M. Cohan nor his impersonators, James Cagney and Joel Grey, Rich added, "The young Mr. Osmond is as yet a limited performer whose dancing is more like prancing and whose expressions range from a mild pout to a broad grin (with few gradations in between). But he is sincere and does know how to sing."

The affable, talented Donny Osmond had opened in Little Johnny Jones at a Sunday matinee on January 10, 1982, in Washington, D.C.'s Kennedy Center Opera House for a four-week engagement, during which the show grossed over $800,000. David Richards (The Washington Post) reported Donny "Takes a Small Step in George M. Cohan's Shoes--he is not yet galvanizing Little Johnny Jones, and that, I fear, is the obligation of whatever actor decides to step into Cohan's shoes. Right now, Osmond appears to be pulled along by the show; he doesn't propel it--with great good will, Osmond joins in. But joining in may not be enough." Richards also added, "It is a fairly silly show--the story is a dithering mishmash. Little Johnny Jones consists of lots of pretty decorations looking for something to hang themselves on."

Douglas Watt (Daily News) considered Osmond "a colorless performer, however likeable." Clive Barnes (New York Post) believed "miscasting could have gone no further" and appraised Osmond as "modestly talented but positively obnoxious" while describing his dancing as "like a toothpaste advertisement with terpsechorean delusions" and dismissed Donny as being "the silliest thing in an old-fashioned show."

Director Gerald Gutierrez wrote an open letter to the New York critics, disclaiming any responsibility for the show.

Six of the seventeen songs Cohan composed for the original production of Little Johnny Jones were retained in the 1982 revival. The six other songs in the '82 production were interpolated from other Cohan shows or compositions. "Then I'd Be Satisfied With Life" was a Cohan song published in 1902; "Oh, You Wonderful Boy" had been "Oh, You Wonderful Girl" in 1911's The Little Millionaire; "The Voice in My Heart" originated in 1922's Little Nelly Kelly; "Let's You and I Just Say Goodbye" came from the score of 1923's The Rise of Rosie O'Reilly and "American Ragtime" was originally heard in 1908's The American Idea. "Extra, Extra" was composed by

Alfred Uhry, the adaptor of the Goodspeed 1982 revival, and interpolated as a short filler performed before the curtain while the final large set was being set.

The Goodspeed Opera House at East Haddam, Connecticut, revived Little Johnny Jones from July 18, 1980, through September 13, to the general rejoicing of the press and public.

Produced for the Goodspeed Opera House by Michael P. Price; Director, Gerald Gutierrez; Book, Music and Lyrics by George M. Cohan; Adaptation by Alfred Uhry; Scenery, John Lee Beatty; Lighting, Peter M. Ehrhardt; Costumes, David Toser; Choreography and musical staging, Dan Siretta; Musical supervision, Lynn Crigler; Musical direction, Robert Fisher; Dance arrangements and additional orchestrations, Russell Warner; Music research consultant, Alfred Simon; Technical director, Jim Crossley; Production assistant, Warren Pincus; Assistant choreographer, Bronna Lipton; Production stage manager, Peter Weicker; Production assistant, William S. Nagel; Assistant technical director, Dan Dour; Assistant to director, Mitchell Rizzo, Kathy Urmson, Lynda Wormell; Hairstylist, Karol Coeyman

Thomas Hulce (succeeded by Eric Weitz) (Johnny Jones, An American Jockey); Maureen Brennan (Goldie Gates, An American Copper Heiress); Peter Van Norden (Anthony Anstey); Jane Galloway (Florabelle Fly); Lenny Wolpe (Timothy D. McGee); Ernie Sabella (Whitney Wilson, The Great Unknown); Anna McNeeley (Mrs. Kenworth); Bruce Chew (Sing Song); Jack Bittner (Captain Squirvy/English Derby Announcer/Hotel Cecil Starter); Al Micacchion (A Bellboy); David Fredericks (A Newsboy); Keith Savage (A Waiter); Bobby Longbottom (A Policeman); Stephen Gorin (English Jockey/Elevator Operator); David Fredericks, Gary Kirsch, Bobby Longbottom, Al Micacchion, David Monzione, Keith Savage (American Boys, Porters, Cabbies, Sailors); Colleen Ashton, Susie Fenner, Linda Gradl, Lori Lynott, Bronna Lipton, Mayme Paul (American Girls)

SONGS: The Cecil in London; Oh, You Wonderful Boy; Then I'd Be Satisfied With Life; Yankee Doodle Boy; 'Op in Me 'Ansom; The Voice in My Heart; Blue Skies, Gray Skies; Captain of a Ten-Day Boat; Goodbye Flo and the Boys; Life's A Funny Proposition; Let's You and I Just Say Goodbye; Give My Regards to Broadway; Extra! Extra!; American Ragtime ("Blue Skies, Gray Skies" was from Cohan's score for 1927's musical The Merry Malones)

Malcolm L. Johnson (The Hartford Courant) enthused about Goodspeed's revival, "The songs and the book have been charged with new life by Goodspeed's loving revival, which has been directed with honesty and theatrical flair by Gerald Gutierrez." Thomas Hulce, playing the title role, was described as "a nimble, cocksure, dandyish figure who is at once a younger embodiment of our engrained image of Cohan--James Cagney in Yankee Doodle Dandy." Johnson found Hulce more secure as a singer than a dancer and quoted The Hartford Courant's appraisal of Cohan's performance when Little Johnny Jones premiered in Hartford in 1904; "He has no voice at all and he knows it, contenting himself with speaking, very plainly, the words of his songs; he dances with every muscle of his body and assumes remarkable shapes as he flies about the stage to music."

"Cohan would have loved it," wrote Rex Reed (Daily News), "it's a great tragedy that he didn't live to see the current star-spangled production of Little Johnny Jones." Reed raved over the settings designed by John Lee Beatty and David Toser's costumes and greatly admired the performance of talented Thomas Hulce, "He tap-dances like a dervish and sings with a heartfelt vibrato that warms the cockles of the soul, and when he sails through "Yankee Doodle Dandy," combining musical skills and marvelous acting techniques no hoofer can learn, the ghost of Cohan and the still fresh memory of Cagney both sail along with him."

John Corry (The New York Times) wrote, "John Lee Beatty's sets are gorgeous and inventive," and he admired the choreography devised by Dan Siretta, feeling that the revival had been staged "with a wonderful sense of fun." Reservations were made about the performing of Thomas Hulce who was considered "winsome enough, but not weighty enough. You hunger for James Cagney--You would be pleased to see a little of the younger Joel Grey," but he added, "George M. Cohan would have been pleased."

Thomas Hulce, born December 6, 1953, at Plymouth, Michigan, made his Broadway stage debut in 1975, replacing Peter Firth as Alan Strang in Peter Shaffer's memorable drama Equus, then starring Anthony Perkins. Hulce had played the horse-blinding Alan in Los Angeles and he made his musical-comedy debut in Goodspeed's production of Little Johnny Jones. Tom Hulce's compelling performance as Mozart in the 1984 film version of Peter Shaffer's brilliant play Amadeus received an Academy Award nomination for Best Actor of the Year, but the award was won by F. Murray Abraham for his equally excellent performance in the same film, as Antonio Salieri. For Goodspeed's first national tour, Eric Weitz replaced Thomas Hulce in Little Johnny Jones and was found appealing in the part but, according to critic William B. Collins, "the star quality that could suggest a Cohan performance is missing."

Twenty-eight-year-old Eric Weitz was replaced by thirty-one-year-old David Cassidy, son of the late Jack Cassidy and Evelyn Ward, for several months of the long road tour of Little Johnny Jones, which included among other profitable engagements Detroit (6 weeks); Chicago (4 weeks); Dallas (3 weeks); Seattle (5 weeks); and Los Angeles (7 weeks). Cassidy had appeared on Broadway at the Broadhurst Theatre on January 2, 1969, as Billy Stone in Allan Sherman and Albert Hague's four-performance musical flop The Fig Leaves Are Falling. He became a teenage idol after appearing as Keith Partridge in ABC's long-running television series The Partridge Family, which starred his stepmother, Shirley Jones.

110 / Little Johnny Jones

Twenty-four-year-old Donny Osmond was considered a more potent box-office draw for Broadway and he began rehearsals in the title role of Cohan's old musical in December 1981. Following the Washington, D.C., break-in, Little Johnny Jones gave twenty-nine previews at New York's Alvin Theatre before it opened and closed on Sunday, March 21, 1982.

George M. Cohan made his debut as a Broadway star, billed as "The Yankee Doodle Comedian," in his first successful musical play, which was also the initial production of the celebrated theatrical firm of Cohan and Harris. George Michael Cohan (né Keohane) and Samuel Henry Harris's production of Little Johnny Jones opened in Hartford, Connecticut, on October 10, 1904. George's father, Jerry, and mother, Helen, were featured in the cast, but sister Josephine, with her husband, Fred Niblo, had defected from the famous Four Cohans to join Klaw and Erlanger's vaudeville farce The Rogers Brothers in Paris.

Little Johnny Jones's leading lady was the first Mrs. George M. Cohan, the versatile and talented Ethel Levey (née Ethelia Fowler), and rotund former minstrel man Tom Lewis was the show-stealing detective. Cohan and Harris engaged a young dancer and singer named Donald Brian, then appearing in the Irish musical Myles Aroon, for the juvenile lead. Donald Brian would attain stardom three years later, after he replaced John Saville during rehearsals in Henry W. Savage's hugely successful production of Franz Lehar's perennially joyous operetta The Merry Widow. In the chorus of Little Johnny Jones were Lola, Agnes, and Alice Nolan. Cohan would later marry Agnes and Sam Harris would wed Alice.

Billed as "A Musical Play," Little Johnny Jones (The American Jockey) opened on Broadway at the Liberty Theatre on November 7, 1904. Produced by Cohan and Harris; Book, music and lyrics by George M. Cohan; Director, George M. Cohan, assisted by James Gorman; Settings by W. F. Hamilton; Musical director, Charles Gebest; Stage manager, John Kauffman
    George M. Cohan (Johnny Jones); Ethel Levey (Goldie Gates, Rosario Fauchette, Earl of Bloomsbury); Jerry Cohan (Anthony Anstey); Donald Brian (Henry Hapgood); Sam J. Ryan (Timothy D. McGee); Tom Lewis (The Unknown); Helen F. Cohan (Mrs. Andrew Kenworth); Truly Shattuck (Florabelle Fly); Edith Tyler (Bessie); Joseph Leslie (Stevens); Charles Bachmann (Inspector Perkins); C. J. Harrington (Jenkins/Captain Squirvy); Charles Stevens (Chung Fow); J. Bernard Dylln (Sing Song); Fred Williams (Hung Chung); William Seymour (Bellboy)
SONGS: The Cecil in London Town; They're All My Friends; Mam'selle Fauchette; 'Op in the 'Ansom; Nesting in a New York Tree; Yankee Doodle Boy; Off to the Derby; Girls from the U.S.A.; Sailors of St. Hurrah; Captain of the Ten-Day Boat; Good-by, Flo; So Long, Sing Song; Good Old California; A Girl I Know; Give My Regards to Broadway; March of the 'Frisco Chinks; Life's A Funny Proposition After All

Self-assured, brash and slangy American jockey Johnny Jones arrives in London to ride the Earl of Bloomsbury's horse, Yankee Doodle, in the English Derby. Johnny refuses gambler Anthony Anstey's bribe to throw the race, but when Yankee Doodle loses, Anstey accuses Johnny of deliberately losing the race. Denounced as a fraud and a crook, Johnny decides to remain in England to clear his name and stays on the Southampton pier as the ship Hurrah sails for New York. Johnny's good friend, a detective, sails on the ship, assuring Johnny that if he finds evidence of the frame-up he will have a rocket fired from the ship. As Johnny regretfully sings his regards to Broadway, a rocket is fired from the ship. Anstey kidnaps Johnny's girl friend, heiress Goldie Gates, taking her to his San Francisco gambling house run by Sing Song. Johnny leaves for San Francisco, where he overcomes Anstey and rescues Goldie. Having cleared his name and won his girl, Johnny philosophically soliloquizes that life is a funny proposition after all.

"In Little Johnny Jones Mr. Cohan has written a melodrama with musical trimmings, as it were," reported The New York Dramatic Mirror, "It seems a pity that he has decided to take such a serious view of his abilities and has elected to play a part that gives him no opportunity to show himself at his best--The play was well mounted, the scenery, costumes and accessories being pretty and in good taste. The electrical effects were excellent, and the performance showed clearly that it had been carefully supervised by the author, who has few superiors as a musical comedy stage manager."

The critical carping that Little Johnny Jones was less "musical comedy" than "musical melodrama," despite Cohan's advertising and program heading stressing the show as a "musical play," contributed to a brief Broadway run of 52 performances. During an extensive and highly successful road tour Cohan constantly rewrote his play and on May 8, 1905, returned to Broadway with Little Johnny Jones, at the New York Theatre, where its success lasted until August 26th. After a brief road tour Cohan returned once again to the Liberty Theatre on November 13, 1905. Little Johnny Jones closed on December 9th, having accumulated over 200 performances. Cast changes included William E. Meehan (Henry Hapgood); Adele Rafter (Florabelle Fly); Charles Bachmann (Sing Song) Fred Walcott (Inspector Perkins); Harry Kittridge (Chung Fow), and Frank McNish, Jr. (Nung Chung).

Stanley Green (The World of Musical Comedy) succinctly described Little Johnny Jones in 1960, "The naive, patriotic sentimentality of Little Johnny Jones, combined with its headlong pace, caught the spirit of a country just beginning to emerge as a world power." Gerald Bordman (American Musical Theatre) noted, "Little Johnny Jones was as fine and progressive a musical as 1904 New York had ever seen--Cohan's melodramatic yarn was carefully wrought and never lost sight of. Its dimensions were human: the characters had blood that rushed to their cheeks and their dialogue was vibrant. And all the excellent Cohan songs--not just the classics--were a telling adjunct to the story line. Most critics were unkind."

Cohan and Harris sent a road company of Little Johnny Jones on tour during the 1907-1908 season with the following cast:
Bobby Barry (Johnny Jones); Stella Tracey (Goldie Gates, Rosario Fauchette, Earl of Bloomsbury); Jack Raffael (Anthony Anstey); William E. Meehan (Henry Hapgood); Sam J. Ryan (Timothy D. McGee); Tom Lewis (The Unknown); Lottie Medley (Mrs. Andrew Kenworth); Adele Rafter (Florabelle Fly); Hazel Lowry (Bessie); Harry Pearson (Stevens); Tom Penfold (Inspector Perkins); C. J. Harrington (Jenkins/Captain Squirby); Ed Sheehan (Chung Fow); Frank Montgomery (Sing Song); Harry Kittredge (Hung Chung); William Seymour (Bellboy).

George M. Cohan, fascinated with the flamboyant career of American jockey Tod Sloan, reputedly based Little Johnny Jones on the diminutive rider. James Todhunter Sloan, born on August 10, 1873, at Kokomo, Indiana, became the toast of the English racing world, admired by Edward, Prince of Wales, and the wealthy English riding set. His innovative riding, known as "monkey-on-the-seat-style," changed the more erect and rigid jockey's style, especially in England, which led him to many racing victories. He rode William C. Whitney's horse Ballyhoo Bey, to win the 1900 Futurity stakes. Sloan, slightly under five feet tall and weighing in at approximately ninety-five pounds, was extravagant, profligate, pretentious and sartorially elegant, at one time possessing thirty-eight trunks of clothing and supporting a valet and a secretary.

Self-confident and overbearing Tod, who had won three races riding under the colors of the royal stables in 1897, made the mistake in England of bidding against Royalty on the purchase of a yearling, and he was also accused of smashing a champagne bottle over the head of an Ascot waiter. The English Jockey Club refused to renew his license, which also banned him from racing in the United States. Two years later, in Paris, the Stewards of the French Jockey Club banned him for creating trouble at the track, but Sloan appealed the decision and in 1904, he was reinstated.

The irrepressible Sloan was married to musical comedy star Julia Sanderson, from 1907 to 1913, and from 1920 to 1927 he was the husband of actress Elizabeth Saxon Malone. On December 11, 1905, Sloan appeared in vaudeville on Broadway, at Hammerstein's Victoria Theatre, doing a monologue on his racing career. Tod also appeared in several silent motion pictures in Hollywood, including The Killer (1921), When Romance Rides (1922), and Hot Heels in 1928. James Todhunter "Tod" Sloan died at Los Angeles on December 21, 1933.

Hollywood sang a song of silence by producing many Broadway musical comedies for the silent screen. In 1920 Warner Brothers filmed George M. Cohan's 1906 musical comedy 45 Minutes From Broadway, and in 1923, George Washington, Jr., which had included the Yankee Doodle Dandy's song "You're a Grand Old Flag," originally titled "You're a Grand Old Rag," until public outcry convinced Cohan to change "Rag" to "Flag." The Warners also produced for the silent screen Sally (1925), Irene, Mlle. Modiste, and Twinkletoes (1926), and Oh, Kay (1928). On August 19, 1923, Warner Brothers released their silent-film version of Little Johnny Jones:

Produced by Warner Brothers Pictures; Directors, Arthur Rosson and Johnny Hines; Adaptation and screenplay by Raymond L. Schrock; Camera, Charles E. Gilson; Assistant director, Charles Hines; Editor, Clarence Kolster
    Johnny Hines (Johnny Jones); Molly Malone (Edith Smythe); Wyndham Standing (The Earl of Bloomsbury); Margaret Seddon (Mrs. Jones); Herbert Prior (Sir James Smythe); Mervyn Le Roy (George Nelson, jockey); Pauline French (Lady Smythe); George Webb (Robert Anstead); Fatty Carr (Chauffeur); Brownie (Johnny's Dog)

    Warners' First National Pictures remade Little Johnny Jones using the Vitaphone process. Mervyn Le Roy, who had played Jockey Nelson in the silent-screen version, directed the sound version which was released on November 17, 1929:

Director, Mervyn Le Roy; Adaptation and screenplay, Adelaide Heilbron and Eddie Buzzell; Dialogue and titles, Adelaide Heilbron; Camera, Faxon Dean; Editor, Frank Ware
    Eddie Buzzell (Johnny Jones); Alice Day (Mary Baker); Edna Murphy (Vivian Dale); Robert Edeson (Ed Baker); Wheeler Oakman (Wyman); Raymond Turner (Carbon); Donald Reed (Ramon)
SONGS: Yankee Doodle Boy; Give My Regards to Broadway (George M. Cohan); Painting the Clouds with Sunshine (Al Dubin, Joe Burke); Straight, Place and Show (Herman Ruby, M. K. Jerome); Go Find Somebody to Love (Herb Magidson, Michael Cleary); My Paradise (Herb Magidson, James Cavanaugh)

    Warner Brothers paid George M. Cohan $50,000 for the screen rights to his remarkably flamboyant life story, including approval of casting and screenplay which would exclude any reference to his first wife, the talented Ethel Levey. Cohan heartily approved of the casting of dynamic James Cagney in the title role. Both Cohan and Cagney were five-feet-six-inches tall and both were song-and-dance men. "Psychologically I needed no preparation for Yankee Doodle Dandy or professionally either. I didn't have to pretend to be a song-and-dance man. I was one," Cagney later wrote in his 1976 autobiography Cagney by Cagney.

    Cagney hired former Cohan performer John Boyle to coach him in Cohan's inimitable dancing style, from clog-taps and stiff-legged strut to scaling the side of the proscenium arch. William Collier, Sr., who was a partner with Cohan in several shows, was engaged as the

114 / Marilyn's Affairs

film's technical advisor. Walter Huston and Rosemary De Camp played George's parents, and Cagney's sister Jeanne played Josephine Cohan. The film's finest production number was a reproduction of the second act finale from Little Johnny Jones.

Warner's one-and-a-half-million-dollar production of Yankee Doodle Dandy, expertly directed by Michael Curtiz, opened on Broadway in May, 1942, to become a screen classic, indisputably James Cagney's finest screen performance, for which he received a justifiable Academy Award as Best Actor of the Year. Cohan wired Cagney, "Thanks for a wonderful job" and saw his life unreel in Yankee Doodle Dandy several times before his death at the age of sixty-five on Thursday, November 5, 1942. Through the efforts of Oscar Hammerstein, II, the only statue of an actor on Broadway is appropriately that of George Michael Cohan, America's "Yankee Doodle Boy" standing at 46th and Broadway.

One block north, at the Palace Theatre, on April 10, 1968, Broadway's musical tribute to the shamelessly flag-waving Cohan opened. George M., written by Michael Stewart, John and Fran Pascal, with Cohan's music and lyrics, directed by Joe Layton, completed 435 performances before closing on April 26, 1969. Diminutive Joel Grey gave a sterling performance in the title role, and the first-act finale of George M. was a reproduction of the second finale of Little Johnny Jones.

* * *

MARILYN'S AFFAIRS (Mansfield Theatre, March 15, 1933). Produced by John Paffrath, Inc.; A comedy by Arthur Ebenhack; Directed by the author; Settings, Vail Scenic Construction Company; General manager, Joseph A. Daly; Company manager, J. A. Hutcheon; Stage manager, Thomas F. Brown, Jr.

Loretto Shea (Marilyn Royden); Santos Ortega (Cortez); Stanley Marlowe (Tony Martino); Lynn Edwards (Dan Callahan); Linda Eder (Dora Paden); George Junior (Robert Culver); Viola Kane (Marie); George Taylor (Commissioner Hammond); William Bonelli (Adolph Blerkmeyer); Gertrude Mudge (Mrs. Royden)

High-living, hard-drinking Marilyn Royden bets her friend Dora Paden she can get any man to propose marriage to her within twenty-four hours. Marilyn tests her theory on Tony Martino, a shoe-repair man, young Irish policeman Dan Callahan, and handsome taxi-driver Cortez. Marilyn wins her bet but falls in love with taxi-driver Cortez only to discover he is the son of Commissioner Hammond.

Marilyn's Affairs had been produced under the title of Cinderella's Brothers on January 29, 1933, at the Sutton Theatre, where the Times critic recommended it should be dropped into the East River. Produced by restauranteur John Paffrath, Cinderella's

Brothers surfaced on Broadway as Marilyn's Affairs. Brooks Atkinson (The New York Times) approving of his colleague's appraisal of Cinderella's Brothers, suggested, "It is not a play that would float very long." Arthur Ruhl (Herald Tribune) found the retitled farce "remained incredibly vapid and ridiculous in spite of what may have been done to it in the meantime and its change of name." The World-Telegram critic was terse: "Let this obituary be brief. There need be no excitement about Marilyn's Affairs. Requiescat in pace."

* * *

MASKS AND FACES (Liberty Theatre, March 18, 1933). Produced and directed by Paul E. Martin; A comedy by A. J. Minor; Setting by Mensching Studies
    Ann Deighton (Geraldine Keith); William Roselle (DeWitt Keith); Donald Foster (Elliot Williams); Gordon Richards (Schuyler Ewing); Enid Romany (Frances Ballou); Edgar Nelson (Herbert Baxter); Kathleen Lowry (Gloria Sprague); Allen B. Nourse (Kenneth Ritchie); Edward Broadley (Potter)

    Geraldine Keith is convinced she has a phantom lover who replaces her husband, DeWitt, whenever he makes love to her. Psychiatrist Frances Ballou suggests their close friends Elliot Williams and Schuyler Ewing as likely candidates. DeWitt leaves Geraldine to Elliot and Schuyler, but her erotic hallucination quickly disappears and she waits impatiently for DeWitt's return.

    Masks and Faces turned in several different directions and The New York Times declared "it was nigh impossible to determine in which direction it was headed--The entire affair was disheartening."

* * *

MASQUERADE (John Golden Theatre, March 16, 1959). Produced by Richard W. Krakeur, in association with Louis d'Almeida; A comedy by Sigmund Miller; Director, Jed Horner (succeeded Warren Enters); Setting and Lighting, Paul Morrison; Costumes, Robert Mackintosh; Music, Sol Kaplan; General manager, Herman Bernstein; Stage managers, Herman Shapiro, William Callan
    Cloris Leachman (succeeded Marjorie Steele) (Amy Grenville); Donald Cook (Oliver Casey); Glenda Farrell (Isabel Chamberlain); Mark Richman (Dr. Ralph Grenville); Gene Lyons (Jess Grenville); Jack Cannon (Charles Morrell); Anne Ives (Mrs. Emily Hilburt)

    Amy Grenville's devoted marriage to Dr. Ralph Grenville is traumatized by her unsatisfactory performance in and repellent attitude toward sex. Receiving no help nor guidance from her prudish, if frequently divorced, independent mother, Isabel, Amy attempts an unsuccessful affair with her husband's brother Jess, but succeeds in her sexual encounter with her French teacher, Charles Morrell.

Sage advice and encouragement from her sophisticated and sympathizing ex-stepfather, playboy Oliver Casey, further restores her self-confidence. Dr. Grenville reacts violently to Amy's sexual experimentation but returns to their Connecticut home to prevent her suicide, with the resolve to help his frustrated wife toward a more mature and happier marriage.

Brooks Atkinson (The New York Times) expressed the plight of actors in a doomed play who "must know the value of the lines they have to speak and the silliness of the situations they have to make and unmake" especially in Sigmund Miller's Masquerade, where "The social chatter in the first half of the play is unendurable; the dramatized psychoanalysis of the second half is crushing." Mr. Atkinson conceded the players' professionalism had them all acting "as faithfully as though they were unfolding a masterpiece."

John McClain (Journal-American) wrote, "There isn't much to be said about Masquerade-except that it isn't good; waste of talent, too. It is difficult to imagine how so many talented people could have been engulfed in such a banal typhoon," concluding the play was "a hopeless theatrical fiasco." Robert Coleman (Daily Mirror) found "Infidelity dull in Masquerade" whose "major virtue is its brevity." Richard Watts, Jr. (New York Post) felt the failure of Masquerade was "a respectable one," but "There are no signs that Mr. Miller has a gift for writing comedy." John Chapman (Daily News) noted that Masquerade's "heroine is frigid--and so is one drama reviewer," and "Instead of being a theatrical discussion of feminine frigidity it may strike a member of the audience--me, for example--as a piece of Krafft-Ebing cheese."

Huntington Hartford had purchased the film rights to Masquerade prior to production of the play and his wife, Marjorie Steele, was cast in the leading role of Amy Grenville. Mrs. Hartford was replaced during rehearsals by Cloris Leachman, of whom Walter Kerr wrote, "Miss Leachman is an accomplished and most attractive actress; she is simply unlucky to have been available when they were casting Masquerade." Expert actor Donald Cook, who could wring laughs from the most innocuous lines, was defeated by Sigmund Miller's rhetoric.

Sigmund Miller's first play was produced on Broadway by Howard Lindsay and Russel Crouse. Called One Bright Day, it opened on March 19, 1952, and, despite excellent performances by Walter Matthau, Howard Lindsay, and Glenn Anders, the play faded after twenty-nine performances.

* * *

MATING DANCE (Eugene O'Neill Theatre, November 3, 1965). Produced by Eliot Martin; A comedy by Eleanor Harris Howard and Helen McAvity; Director, Ronny Graham; Setting, Eldon Elder; Lighting,

John Harvey; Costumes, Florence Klotz/ Title song, Albert A. Beach and Lawrence Grossman; General manager, C. Edwin Knill; Company manager, Helen Richards; Stage managers, Wally Peterson, Nelle Nugent
    Van Johnson (Bruce Barrett); Marian Hailey (Kelly Lewis); Marian Winters (Senator Lucia Barrett); J. D. Cannon (Oscar Davenport); Richard Mulligan (Roger MacDougall); Judith Barcroft (Deedee Dinehart); Rick Lenz (Jeff); Paul Sorvino (Officer Lynch); Don Calfa (Ramesh Ramru); Esther Jane Coryell (Lyn Hoyt); Robert H. Wiensko (Junior); Ruth Newton (Mrs. Grindell)

    Fearing an election-year scandal, U.S. Senator Lucia Barrett, the estranged wife of publisher Bruce Barrett, refuses to consent to a divorce permitting her husband to marry much younger etiquette columnist Kelly Lewis until after the election. The senator's lawyer, Oscar Davenport, suggests his junior colleague Roger MacDougall become a "beard" accompanying Bruce and Kelly in public, posing as Kelly's lover to ward off suspicion and gossip. Roger, a rabid amateur ornithologist, however, sympathizes with the lovers and gives them a frenetic demonstration of the mating dance of the whooping crane, with Kelly as his mate, as the senator's political opponents surreptitiously photograph the sensuous choreography. The senator demands that Kelly and Bruce end their affair, but Kelly has found true love with lawyer Davenport.

    Howard Taubman (The New York Times) classified Mating Dance as an "unfunny comedy" plus "It isn't much of a mating dance, but then Eleanor Harris Howard and Helen McAvity haven't written much of a play." Norman Nadel (New York World Telegram) felt Mating Dance might amuse ornithologists, "But there's a question as to how many of them would sit through so prosaic a comedy for the sake of one funny actor in a bird-like role, and one briefly exciting scene." Adding to the generally poor reception of Mating Dance, despite its rather lilting title song played on a flute before the opening curtain, was a first-act fiasco when star Van Johnson was left alone on stage at the end of the scene: Unflappable Johnson explained to the audience, "curtain was supposed to come down here" and strode off-stage.

    Mating Dance opened its tryout tour in New Haven, Connecticut, on September 29, 1965, at the Shubert Theatre. The comedy was then under the direction of Henry Kaplan with the following cast:
    Van Johnson (Bruce Barrett); Marian Hailey (Kelly Lewis); Marian Winters (Senator Lucia Barrett); J. D. Cannon (Oscar Davenport); Richard Mulligan (Roger MacDougall); Fleury D'Antonakis (Alikki Papannkos); Paul Sorvino (Fred Porter); Rick Lenz (Bob); Esther Jane Coryell (Lyn Hoyt); Don Calfa (Ramesh); Rose Roffman (Peggy Nichols); Toby Mickes (Devra); Remere Rochon (Koemba); Fulice Asakawas (Mioshi); Robert H. Wiensko (Charlie Nichols)

    Out-of-town reviews for Mating Dance would have sent the

Ballet Russe de Monte Carlo into shock. Engagements of two weeks in Wilmington and Boston were cancelled after one week because of the poor critical and public reception. Undisturbed by these harbingers of impending oblivion, Mating Dance jetéd into Broadway.

Forty-nine-year-old Van Johnson, who began his Broadway career as a chorus boy in New Faces of 1936, 1939's Too Many Girls and Pal Joey in 1940, headed the London production of The Music Man in 1961, after a long career as Metro-Goldwyn-Mayer's perpetual boy-next-door. Johnson returned to Broadway for 36 performances in Garson Kanin's comedy Come On Strong in 1962. Mating Dance did not advance his Broadway odyssey. Twenty years later Van Johnson returned to Broadway to replace Keith Michell in Jerry Herman's glowing musical La Cage aux Folles.

* * *

ME AND THEE (John Golden Theatre, December 7, 1965). Produced by Delancey Productions; A comedy by Charles Horine; Director, Perry Bruskin; Setting and costumes, Charles Evans; Lighting, V. C. Fuqua; Music, George Fischoff; Lyrics, Charles Horine, Hank Miles; Fashion coordinator, A. Christina Giannini; Stage managers, Ben Janney, David Eliscu

    Barbara Britton (Alice Carter); Durward Kirby (Paul Carter); Randy Kirby (Roger Carter); Charles Braswell (Dr. Grant Reeves); Carolan Daniels (Lela)

Psychiatrist Dr. Grant Reeves advises his middle-aged friends and neighbors, architect Paul Carter and his wife, Alice, to get more out of life and "let the psychic pendulum swing." Paul eagerly pursues the suggestion and brings home a Greenwich Village oddball named Lela. Sexy, aggressive Lela only "plays" when cold sober. After a few drinks Lela becomes as puritanical as a newly arrived Pilgrim. Alice investigates a fling with Dr. Reeves. The Carters' son, Roger, arrives home from Harvard and finds Lela sufficiently strange to marry her. Paul and Alice continue their happily married life without swinging on a psychic pendulum.

Philadelphia producers Ethelyn Thrasher and Paul Stoudt opened Me and Thee in Wilmington, Delaware, and booked the insipid affair for two weeks in Philadelphia, where the reviews clearly indicated a ninety-mile journey to New York could endanger its health to say nothing of Broadway. Ernest Schier (The Evening Bulletin) dismissed Me and Thee as "a witless piece." Henry T. Murdock (The Philadelphia Inquirer) felt the play would survive as a television series called "Life with the Kirbys"--Durward being the father of Randy Kirby-- and described the piece as a "quick cartoon sketch of the modern American family."

Howard Taubman (The New York Times) reported "no one in his right mind would call it a comedy--its heart is as pure as its mind is simple--How did they--and we--get into this?" Norman Nadel (New York World-Telegram) advised "Me and Thee Not for Thou. Me and Thee emerges as a brave defeat, not that I expect that adjective to particularly cheer playwright Horine." Walter Kerr (Herald Tribune) found Me and Thee "full of shaped jokes which are without discernible cause. There is never any reason for setting the whole not-so-merry-go-round in motion and the perpetual motion of the principal actors cannot conceal the fact." John Chapman (Daily News) called Me and Thee "A nice but awful little play. It really is a terrible little comedy" and John McClain (Journal American) described the comedy as "a sort of antiquated and well-intentioned foozle, hung on a freakish premise and proceeding through five scenes to an implausible finish."

* * *

A MEETING BY THE RIVER (Palace Theatre, March 28, 1979). Produced by Terry Allen Kramer and Harry Rigby; A drama by Christopher Isherwood and Don Bachardy; Director, Albert Marre; Scenery, Robert Mitchell; Lighting, Clarke W. Thornton; Costumes, Marianne Custer; Incidental music, Glen Roven; Associate producer, Jack Schlissel; Assistant to director, Ed Kerrigan; Production assistants, Adam Marre, Cathy Caster; Wardrobe, Patricia Lang; Hairstylist, Wayne Herndon; Stage managers, Susie Cordon, Andy Bew, Ron Durbian

    Siobhan McKenna (Margaret); Simon Ward (Oliver); Keith Baxter (Patrick); Sam Jaffe (Tarun Maharaj); Meg Wynn-Owen (Penelope); Keith McDermott (Tom); Paul Collins (Rafferty); Gilbert Cole (Asin); Ronald Bishop (Head Swami); Faizul Khan (Second Swami); Arjun Sajnani (Third Swami); Leslie Goldstein (Fourth Swami); Ed Kerrigan (Swami Vegananda); Harsh Nayyar (Photographer); Jonathan Epstein (Passport Official)

    The ambivalence between two British brothers has been constant throughout their lives. Charming, sensuous, bisexual Patrick, a former publisher, has become a Hollywood film producer maintaining a wife and a young male lover, Tom, in Los Angeles. Oliver deserted a career in banking to become a Quaker and a Red Cross worker in Africa, then migrated to India to study Buddhism under the tutelege of guru Tarun Maharaj. After an unsatisfactory exchange of letters between the brothers and their mother, Margaret, Patrick arrives at the Buddhist monastery outside Calcutta on the Ganges River to dissuade Oliver from taking his final vows. Patrick tempts Oliver with an offer of an influential position with the United Nations but Oliver remains adamant and continues his study of Sanskrit mantras. Tom drunkenly mistakes Oliver for Patrick on an overseas telephone call and openly declares his love. Oliver accepts Patrick's confession of his bisexuality and on the night of the Sannyas he becomes ordained. Patrick, defeated in his efforts, embraces his Buddhist priest brother and resolves to abandon his male lover and return to his wife and two daughters.

A Meeting by the River was called by Richard Eder (The New York Times), "an exercise in High Twaddle by Christopher Isherwood and Don Bachardy--Even if the characters were more palatable--the play would be sunk by its speeches which are, almost literally--unspeakable," adding that it became "a tedious failure because its personages have no believable character but only a series of ascribed emotions and beliefs, conveyed in speeches that can hardly get through an actor's mouth." Douglas Watt (Daily News) described the play as "An exercise in transcendental obfuscation--Albert Marre has staged this stately, discursive nonsense with as much care and respect as if he were directing a revival of The King and I with Richard Rodgers looking over his shoulder." Clive Barnes (New York Post) found "The acting is impeccable and exemplary," but "The seriousness of the novel has gone." Glenne Currie (United Press International) added, "The dialogue at times is surprisingly poor for someone of Isherwood's reputation, and a rather boring time is had by all. The treatment of the theme is unconvincing; the exposition is clumsy, the drama non-existent."

At least the producers added an acknowledgment to "The Swamis of the monastery at Belue Math, Calcutta for their gracious hospitality to Mr. Marre, Mr. Mitchell and Mr. Ward for allowing them to observe various services and ritual and to record the accompanying music and chants. All the music and ritual used in the play derives from these specific sources." Christopher Isherwood added, "The author wishes to thank James Bridges without whose encouragement and help this play would not exist."

James Bridges directed the world premiere of *A Meeting by the River* at the Mark Taper Forum in Los Angeles in April 1972. Produced by the Center Theatre Group of the Forum, with scenery and costumes by Jeremy Railton and lighting by Donald Harris, the play was performed by the following cast:
   Florida Friebus (Mother); Sam Waterston (Oliver); Laurence Luckinbill (Patrick); Susan Brown (Penelope); Gordon Hoban (Tom); and Sirri Murad, John Ritter, Jason Wingreen, Jack Bender and Logan Ramsey.

The New Phoenix Repertory Company's (Harold Prince, Stephen Porter, Michael Montel--Artistic Directors) "Sideshow" series of five new plays to be given one or two performances, produced by Managing Director T. Edward Hambleton, mounted *A Meeting by the River* for one performance at Manhattan's Edison Theatre on December 18, 1972. The play was directed by Michael Montel with lighting by Ken Billington. The play's involvement with letter reading and cross-continental telephone conversations required little more than effective lighting. The two brothers were exceptionally well acted by Sam Waterston and Laurence Luckinbill who had created the roles in Los Angeles. The New Phoenix Repertory Company cast included:
   Jacqueline Brookes (Mother); Sam Waterston (Oliver); Laurence Luckinbill (Patrick); Robin Strasser (Penelope); Gordon Hoban

(Tom); Stephan Macht (Rafferty); Tom Tarpey (First Swami); Anthony Mainionis (Second Swami/Passport Official); Charles Turner (Third Swami/Passport Official)

Seven years later the Broadway bound production of A Meeting by the River played a successful engagement at the Clarence Brown Theatre of the University of Tennessee in Knoxville, from February 24th to March 10th in 1979. Encouraged by the response in Knoxville, the producers canceled a two-week tryout in Boston and brought the drama directly to Broadway for ten previews and its one and only official performance, on March 28, 1979.

Christopher Isherwood's short novel A Meeting by the River was published by Simon and Schuster in 1967. The New York Times Book Review on June 25, 1967 noted "Hinduism and homosexuality have long been favorite themes of Christopher Isherwood. Here he combines them in a short novel, composed entirely of letters and diaries, that is rather old-fashioned in form...." Stanley Kauffmann (New Republic) wrote, "Isherwood has made a novel that is credible, moving and ultimately ironic," while E. J. Gaines in Library Journal found the novel "rather artificial and precious. Isherwood does not achieve the necessary distance between himself and his material."

Several decades prior to A Meeting by the River, Christopher Isherwood co-authored two plays with W. H. Auden, The Dog Beneath the Skin in 1935 and The Ascent of F 6 in 1936, which attained artistic success among the intelligentsia in England. Playwright John Van Druten adapted and directed Isherwood's The Berlin Stories under the title of I Am a Camera, produced by Gertrude Macy with Walter Starcke on November 28, 1951, at New York's Empire Theatre for a run of 262 performances. Fashioned after Kurt Weill's Die Dreigroschenoper (The Threepenny Opera), Joe Masteroff's adaptation of I Am a Camera, called Cabaret, was set to music by John Kander with lyrics by Fred Ebb. This expertly contemporaneous musical opened at the Broadhurst Theatre on November 20, 1966, and the magical Cabaret remained for 1,165 performances.

* * *

MONEY MAD (49th Street Theatre, May 24, 1937). Produced by Edwin A. Relkin; A comedy by Fritz Blocki; Director, Rowland G. Edwards; Settings, Stagecraft Studios; Lighting, Duwico; Costumes, Mildred Manning; Company manager, Joseph M. Grossman; Stage manager, Charles Ashley, John Foster
    Ludwig Satz (Lou Chance); David Milton (Milton Chance); Bernice Caryl (Bernice Chance); Doris Underwood (Ma Chance); John Clarke (Bruce Humberston); Gladys Shelley (Gladys); Lane Allan (Lane); William Valentine (Wiggins); Juliette Howell (Juliette); Walter Fenner (Baxter); Scott Moore (McCauley); Leslie King (Cyrus P. Watts); John Foster (Telegraph Boy)

122 / Money Mad

Lou Chance wins $150,000 on a horse named Slow Poke in the Irish Sweepstakes. His nouveau riche family quickly and extravagantly spend their unaccustomed wealth and just as quickly revert to their more accustomed poverty. Lou's son Milton's contribution to the family's reversion to poverty was an investment in a Texas oil well. The oil well suddenly erupts and the Chance family is once again on easy street.

Money Mad had originally appeared on Broadway for eight performances in the previous month at the John Golden Theatre, under the title of Bet Your Life. Bet Your Life had not received noticeable blessings from the critics nor public yet the comedy was rewritten and recast and braved Broadway again as Money Mad. Douglas Gilbert (World Telegram) called it "a lamentable attempt at rehabilitation" and Richard Watts, Jr. (Herald Tribune) who considered Bet Your Life "the worst play of the year" said of the refurbished Money Mad: "It isn't any funnier in the current incarnations--It is merely longer." Brooks Atkinson (New York Times) headed his commentary with "Two Bites of a Turkey," adding, "One more version of Bet Your Life would make nervous prostration a contagious disease--There will be danger of a public uprising if Bet Your Life turns up wearing a third title!"

The slight variation on the theme of get-rich-quick between Money Mad and Bet Your Life was that pater familias Chance won a second sweepstakes ticket which Burns Mantle noted, "Might have gone on indefinitely, but fortunately didn't." Comedian Willie Howard originally collaborated with Fritz Blocki on this moribund farce and vaudevillian and former musical comedy star Lew Hearn played Papa Chance in Bet Your Life. Veteran commedienne Lulu McConnell struggled in vain to inject laughter into her role of Ma Chance.

Bet Your Life (John Golden Theatre, April 5, 1937--8 performances). Produced by Ben Stein; A farce comedy by Fritz Blocki and Willie Howard; Director, A. H. Van Buren; Settings, Stagecraft Studios; Lighting, Duwico; Costumes, Mildred Manning; Stage managers, Charles Ashley, John Foster
   Lew Hearn (Willie Chance); Lulu McConnell (Ma Chance); John Call (Luke Chance); Claire Carleton (Ima Chance); John Clarke (Bruce Humberston); Jean McCool (Clarice); William Valentine (Wiggins); Blanche Haring (Marjorie); Scott Moore (McCauley); Edgar Charles (Chauffeur); J. Robert Haag (Mark Burton); John Foster (Telegraph Boy)

The recasting of Papa Chance, played by Lew Hearn in Bet Your Life, caused Willie to become Lou in Money Mad, played by Ludwig Satz, who was born in Lemberg, Poland, in 1894 and was one of the Yiddish Theatre's leading actors. Satz spent his childhood acting with the Polish Municipal Theatre and, after migrating to America, was engaged by Jacob P. Adler at Philadelphia's Arch Street Theatre in a series of Yiddish plays. While in Philadelphia,

Satz made his screen debut in Sigmund Lubin's motion pictures and later became the principal comedian at Adler's Grand Street Theatre in New York.

Ludwig Satz was one of the founders of New York's Garden Theatre Yiddish Acting Company and made his English-speaking Broadway debut as Abe Potash in Potash and Perlmutter, Detectives, with Robert Leonard as Mawruss Perlmutter, on August 31, 1926, at the Ritz Theatre. Montague Glass and Charles Klein's comedy Potash and Perlmutter, based on Glass's Saturday Evening Post stories, was produced by A. H. Woods at the Cohan Theatre on August 16, 1913, starring Barney Bernard as Abe Potash and Alexander Carr as Mawruss Perlmutter for a run of 441 performances. Potash and Perlmutter, Detectives survived only 47 performances. Ludwig Satz, who died at the age of fifty in 1944, returned to the Yiddish Theatre after the Money Mad madness.

* * *

THE MOON BESIEGED (Lyceum Theatre, December 5, 1962). Produced by Lorin E. Price, in association with Louise Arnold; A drama by Seyril Schochen; Director, Lloyd Richards; Settings and Lighting, Ming Cho Lee; Costumes, Robert Fletcher; Musical direction, Fred Hellerman; Dances, Myrna Shedlin; Production coordinator, Marilyn Shapiro; Production assistant, Lynn Epsteen; General manager, Walter Fried; Company manager, James Awe; Stage managers, Mortimer Halpern, Jeff Chambers
    Charles Tyner (John Brown); Ted Van Griethuysen (Oliver Brown); Kathryn Hays (Martha Brewster); Helen Shields (Mary Brown); James Congdon (Watson Brown); Ken Jenkins (Dauph Thompson); Elizabeth Lawrence (Abby Brown); Vincent Beck (Salmon Brown); Penelope Allen (Bella Thompson Brown); Jamie Ross (Will Thompson); Ellen Madison (Annie Brown); Valentine Pringle (Daingerfield Newby); Mark Gordon (Billy Leeman); Robert Earl Jones (Shields Green); Anthony Zerbe (Lieutenant Kogl); George Bartenieff (Stewart Taylor); Walter Mason (Lewis Leary); William Kinsolving ("Quaker Boy" Coppoc); Bob Saidenberg (Charley Tidd); Barry Kornfeld (Anderson); Penny Fuller, Helen Jean Arthur (Wedding Guests)

    Oliver, the youngest son of firebrand abolitionist John Brown, marries peace-loving, non-violent Quaker Martha Brewster. Opposed to his father's rabid radicalism, Oliver attempts to placate Martha's conviction that his mercilessly fanatical father is a bloodthirsty tyrant obsessed with hatred and a thirst for vengeance rather than a piously self-proclaimed and ardent abolitionist, directed by God in his cause of liberating Negro slaves. Oliver's efforts to dissuade his father from his proposed capture of the U.S. Arsenal at Harper's Ferry and the holding of personnel hostage for the exchange of Negro slaves, in anticipation of a general rebellion and uprising of slaves in the South rallying to his support, are ignored by "Old Osawatomie" Brown. Oliver, Martha, and the family await the outcome of John Brown's raid on Harper's Ferry on October 16, 1859, which culminates in a catastrophe. Two of Brown's sons are killed and old John is captured and indicted by the U.S. Government for conspiracy, treason, and murder. Although John Brown's truth of the ultimate freedom of slaves went marching on, his death by hanging on December 2, 1859, did not end the agony and suffering he inflicted upon his family during his lifetime.

The community of critics composed no paeans of praise for The Moon Besieged. "Seyril Schochen, obviously an earnest woman and possessing some gift for poetic expression, has made a rather undramatic folk drama out of the history of John Brown," reported John Chapman (Daily News). Richard Watts, Jr. (New York Post) recognized that John Brown's martyrdom never ended but continued "mercilessly in bad plays that are written about him from time to time. His latest persecution is Seyril Schochen's The Moon Besieged --written in such pretentious, oratorical and ponderous style that it loses its value as a dramatic narrative--it seems strangely bloodless, flat and ineffectual." Walter Kerr (Herald Tribune) called the play "mighty windy and dull" and Howard Taubman (The New York Times) added, "If there is a way to keep a fanatic like John Brown from becoming tiresome on a stage, Seyril Schochen has not discovered it."

The famous puritanical abolitionist firebrand John Brown, born at Torrington, Connecticut, on May 9, 1800, was married twice and sired twenty children. Brown became a national, if controversial, hero after battling superior pro-slavery forces in Osawatomie, Kansas. Despite his fanatical fight for freedom and the abolition of slavery, Brown was hanged as a criminal on December 2, 1859, but his cause and death kept marching on.

William Steffe, who is credited with composing the music to Julia Ward Howe's poem "Battle Hymn of the Republic," written on November 19, 1861, supposedly adapted the music for the song "John Brown's Body," based on the ancient air "Glory Hallelujah!" and a Methodist hymn, "Brothers, Will You Meet Us?" which became popular at Southern Camp Meetings in 1858. After Brown's Harper's Ferry raid and death, Charles S. Hall, or Henry Howard Bramwell, or Thomas Brigham Bishop, or Frank E. Jerome, added new lyrics to Steffe's song, under the title of "John Brown's Body," which was first played on May 12, 1861, at Fort Warren, Massachusetts. The contested authorship of the new lyrics to Philadelphian William Steffe's equally contested music was copyrighted by several others and was also known as "Glory Hallelujah!" The lyrics were as follows:

> John Brown's body lies a-mould'ring in the grave,
> Glory, Glory, Glory Hallelujah! His soul is marching on!
> The stars of heaven are looking kindly down on the grave
>   of old

John Brown!
Glory, Glory, Glory Hallelujah! His soul is marching on!

Steffe's, or whoever, "John Brown's Body" became as famous in the North during the Civil War as Dan Emmett's minstrel song "Dixie" in the South where it unintentionally became the battle hymn of the Southern Confederacy.

The overture to America's Civil War began seventeen months after John Brown was buried on December 8, 1859, at North Elba, New York, when the first shots were fired at Fort Sumter, verifying Brown's final words before hanging, "I, John Brown, am now quite certain that the crimes of this guilty land will never be purged away but with blood!"

Brown's exploits first reached the American stage in Mrs. J. C. Swayze's 1859 drama Ossawattomie [sic] Brown which opened at the Bowery Theatre on December 17, 1859, as The Insurrection; or, Kansas and Harper's Ferry, with George C. Boniface as John Brown. The pious fanatic became the subject of several books and plays. Ronald Gow's drama Gallows Glorious [in which Wilfrid Lawson portrayed John Brown], produced in London in April, 1933, appeared at Broadway's Ethel Barrymore Theatre on January 22, 1934, as John Brown. George Abbott produced, directed, and starred in the title role of John Brown but the critical grapes of wrath were stored against Mr. Abbott and the play. "John Brown's body is to be found in Ronald Gow's drama entitled John Brown. But his soul goes marching on somewhere outside the theatre," wrote Brooks Atkinson (The New York Times). Mr. Abbott and John Brown left the Ethel Barrymore Theatre after two performances.

Beset with "torpid direction" and poor acting, Theodore Ward's play, called John Brown, produced in arena-staging by The People's Drama Company Off-Broadway on May 3, 1950, was pronounced "wholly inadequate" by Brooks Atkinson (The New York Times), claiming Ward "has reduced the John Brown legend to the level of an enigmatic family squabble." Irving Pakewitz portrayed John Brown and Rod Steiger was his son Jason. The most famous theatrical presentation of the Brown legend was Charles Laughton's excellent adaptation to the stage of Stephen Vincent Benét's one-volume, 377-page epic poem John Brown's Body, published by Doubleday, Doran Company in 1928 and awarded the 1929 Pulitzer Prize for poetry.

Charles Laughton adapted and directed Benét's John Brown's Body as a concert-platform reading which was produced in 1952 by Paul Gregory. The Walter Schumann Chorale of eighteen voices, directed on-stage by Richard White, acted as a Greek Chorus and supplied an integral musical background to the reading, with effective dancing by Donna Jeanne McDaniel and Robert F. Jensen. The acclaimed Laughton version of John Brown's Body starred Tyrone Power, Judith Anderson (succeeded by Anne Baxter), and Raymond

126 / The Moon Besieged

Massey. The three players in formal dress recited and acted the two-hour presentation of Benét's epic Civil War poem against a balustrade, or a three-foot-high "acting bar" on an otherwise bare stage.

The Laughton-Benét John Brown's Body made an extensive tour of sixty cities in twenty-eight states and opened on Broadway at the New Century Theatre on February 14, 1953, to play 65 performances. Brooks Atkinson (The New York Times) lauded Laughton's adaptation and direction and the depth and range of Power, Anderson, and Massey, calling John Brown's Body "a stage performance of fire and beauty--a work of art, not only in print, but in the theatre--the production of John Brown's Body refreshes the whole conception of theatre." Stephen Vincent Benét's poem was adapted for television by Harold Flender and directed by Joseph K. Chomyn as a CBS Special on January 14, 1962. The video version was narrated by Richard Boone with Douglas Campbell as John Brown.

Barrie Stavis's play Harper's Ferry based on the Bible-thumping abolitionist was produced by Tyrone Guthrie at Minneapolis's Tyrone Guthrie Theatre on June 4, 1967. Edward Binns portrayed John Brown and Michael Moriarty, J. Robert Pierce, and James Wallace played his sons, with Len Cariou as Lieutenant John Kagl. Walter Kerr (The New York Times) called Harper's Ferry "transparently primitive stuff, loose and loquacious, filled with more foolishness than fury, content to describe in standard rhetoric what is almost never taking place on the stage--a school-book outline for a play. Mr. Guthrie was surely napping when this one came by." An extended version of Benét's John Brown's Body, comprising thirty-seven speaking parts, was devised and directed by Jack Sydow for the National Repertory Theatre at Ford's Theatre in Washington, D.C., in 1968 with G. Wood as John Brown. A scheduled tour of the podium reading of Laughton-Benét's John Brown's Body, as part of the failed Bicentennial, starring Rock Hudson, Claire Trevor, and Leif Erickson, closed in Denver, Colorado, in June, 1976.

Warner Brothers' Sante Fe Trail opened on Broadway at the Strand Theatre on December 20, 1940, starring Errol Flynn as J. E. B. Stuart with Ronald Reagan as General George Armstrong Custer. The Hal B. Wallis Production of Sante Fe Trail, directed by Michael Curtiz, was an entertaining, exciting motion picture and as historically inaccurate as most of the Brothers Warners' gratuitous corruptions of history. The title was a misnomer, as the screenplay by Robert Buckner related the opposition to and pursuit of John Brown, through his raid on Harper's Ferry, his trial, presided over by General Robert E. Lee, and his eventual hanging. Raymond Massey portrayed John Brown and Alan Baxter and Gene Reynolds were his sons Oliver and Jason.

Toronto, Canada-born Raymond Massey spent a portion of his long career as Abraham Lincoln, through 472 performances freeing the slaves on Broadway in Robert E. Sherwood's 1939 Pulitzer Prize play, <u>Abe Lincoln in Illinois</u>, which he reprised in RKO's 1940 screen version of the play and repeated on television in 1950 and 1951. Massey also appeared on-stage in <u>John Brown's Body</u> and again impersonated John Brown in Allied Artists 1955 film production of <u>Seven Angry Men</u>, retelling Brown's Osawatomie, Kansas, victory, the raid on Harper's Ferry, and Brown's trial for treason and his death by hanging.

* * *

THE MOONY SHAPIRO SONGBOOK (Morosco Theatre, May 3, 1981). Produced by Stuart Ostrow in association with T.A.T. Communications Company; A musical with Book, Music, and Lyrics by Monty Norman and Julian More; Director, Jonathan Lynn; Musical numbers staged by George Faison; Setting, Saul Radomsky; Lighting, Tharon Muser; Costumes, Franne Lee; Musical direction, Elman Anderson; Technical supervisor, Jeremiah Harris; Dance arrangements, Timothy Graphenreid; Vocal arrangements, Ray Cook; Associate conductor, Irving Joseph; Musical supervisor, Stanley Lebowsky; Assistant to director, Nina Lightstone; Projections, Wendall K. Harrington; Sound, Otts Muderloh; Production assistant, Howard P. Lev; Wardrobe, Bill Campbell; Hairstylist, Lyn Quiyou; Stage managers, Phil Friedman, Perry Cline, Philip Hoffman
 Jeff Goldblum; Judy Kaye; Timothy Jerome; Annie McGreevey; Gary Beach
SONGS: Songbook; East River Rhapsody; Talking Picture Show; Meg; Mister Destiny; Your Time Is Different to Mine; Pretty Face; Je Vous Aime; Les Halles; Olympics '36; Nazi Party Pooper; I'm Gonna Take Her Home to Momma; Bumpity-Bump; The Girl in the Window; Victory; April in Wisconsin; It's Only a Show; Bring Back Tomorrow; Happy Hickory; When a Brother Is a Mother to His Sister; Climbin'; Don't Play That Lovesong Anymore; Lovely Sunday Mornin'; Rusty's Dream Ballet; A Storm in My Heart; The Pokenhatchit Public Protest Committee; I Accuse; Messages; I Found Love; Golden Oldie; Nostalgia

 Illegitimate, Liverpool-born, Irish Catholic Michael Moony emigrates to America where he is adopted by a Jewish New York East Side couple named Shapiro. Moony becomes a songwriter, finding fleeting fame in Hollywood and marrying and divorcing a Swedish actress. Throughout his predominantly failed career Moony's songs reflect the constantly changing course of popular music from World War I to Disco. His death at the age of sixty-nine during a power failure on the West Coast of Ireland inspires his friends to assemble many of his less-than-notable songs in a show, as a posthumous tribute to the ambitious, prolific, if not especially talented songwriter.

 Clive Barnes had seen <u>Songbook</u> in London during the summer of 1979, when he called it "The best British musical of recent years." Referring to Broadway's retitled <u>The Moony Shapiro Songbook</u>, he reiterated in the <u>New York Post</u>, "I liked its sleazy charm even more." Other critics did not share Mr. Barnes's enthusiasm for the English import performed by an American cast. Frank Rich (The New York Times) wrote "There's the germ of a funny, spiffy satirical revue in The Moony Shapiro Songbook" but he classified the musical pastiche as a "forlorn little musical" which "has been given a sloppy production on Broadway. Even on those rare occasions when the material clicks, the evening has the scrappy, amateurish air of a collegiate jape." Douglas Watt (Daily News) disliked the English musical, calling it "Moony to be sure. And loony, too--a monumentally silly minimusical burlesque--steadfastly devoted to lousy songs. By the dozen --They are not funny-dumb songs, just dumb ones--The show itself is inane."

Monty Norman and Julian More were the creators of "The James Bond Theme." Their first success in the theatre was the musical Expresso Bongo, which opened at London's Saville Theatre on April 23, 1958, headlining Paul Scofield and Victor Spinetti, to complete 315 performances. Norman and More also made the successful English book and lyrics adaptation of Alexandre Breffort's French hit Irma La Douce in 1958. Their later British musicals were Make Me an Offer; The Art of Living; Belle, or the Ballad of Dr. Crippen; and Quick Quick Slow. The duo's revue Songbook opened at London's Globe Theatre on July 25, 1979, to generally good reviews. While resisting producing Broadway's version of Songbook, producer Hal Prince recorded a voice-over for the English production, which was also included in Broadway's The Moony Shapiro Songbook.

Songbook (Globe Theatre, London, opened July 25, 1979--315 performances). Produced by Jack Gill, by arrangement with Stoll Productions, Ltd. and The Cambridge Theatre Company, Ltd.; A Musical Revue with Book, Music, and Lyrics by Monty Norman and Julian More; Director, Jonathan Lynn; Designed by Saul Radomsky; Musical numbers staged by Gillian Lynne; Lighting by Joe Davis; Production musical director and vocal arrangements, Ray Cook; Musical director, Grant Hossack; Production executive, Robert Burns; Company and stage manager, Rosemary Cutt; Assistant stage managers, Andrew Empson, Christine Crow, Peter Evelyn
  Anton Rodgers; Gemma Craven; Diane Langton; Andrew C. Wadsworth; David Healy and the voice of Hal Prince
SONGS: Songbook; East River Rhapsody; Talking Picture Show; Such Sweet Poison; Mister Destiny; Your Time Is Different to Mine; Pretty Face; Je Vous Aime, Milady; Les Halles; Olympics Song; Nazi Party Pooper; I'm Gonna Take Him Home to Momma; Bumpity-Bump; The Girl in the Window (Das Madchen Am Fenster); Victory V; April in Wisconsin; Happy Hickory; Lovely Sunday Mornin; Rusty's Dream Ballet; A Storm in My Heart; The Pokenhatchit Public Protest Committee; I Accuse; Messages I; Messages II; I Found Love; Don't Play That Lovesong Any More; Golden Oldie; Nostalgia

* * *

MOOSE MURDERS (Eugene O'Neill Theatre, February 22, 1983). Produced by Force Ten Productions; A comedy by Arthur Bicknell; Director, John Roach; Setting, Marjorie Bradley Kellogg; Lighting, Pat Collins; Costumes, John Carver Sullivan; Dance coordinator, Mary Jane Houdina; Stage violence, Kent Shelton; Technical supervisor, Jeremiah Harris; Sound, Chuck London; Associate producer, Ricka Kanter Fisher; Wardrobe, Kathleen Gallagher; Production assistant, Pierce Bihm; Hairstylist, Ronald DeMann; General management, Theatre Now: William Court Cohen, Edward H. David, Norman E. Rothstein, Dorothy Finn, Ralph Roseman; Props, Laura Koch; Stage managers, Clifford Schwartz, Jerry Bihm; Song "Jeepers Creepers," Music, Harry Warren; Lyrics, Johnny Mercer

    Holland Taylor (Hedda Holloway); Don Potter (Howie Keene); June Gable (Snooks Keene); Jack Dabdoub (Joe Buffalo Dance); Mara Hobel (Gay Holloway); Scott Evans (Stinky Holloway); Dennis Florzak (Sidney Holloway); Lisa McMilland (Nurse Dagmar); Lillie Robertson (Lauraine Holloway Fay); Nicholas Hormann (Nelson Fay)

During an autumn thunderstorm, wealthy Hedda Holloway, accompanied by her heavily bandaged, wheelchair-confined husband, Sidney, his dictatorial nurse, Dagmar, her young daughter, Gay, and drug-addicted son, Stinky, arrives to take possession of their recently purchased Wild Moose Lodge in the Adirondacks. Hedda's married daughter, Lauraine, and her husband, Nelson Fay, accompany them. They are met by former residents Snooks and her blind husband, Howie, "the Singing Keenes," and a middle-aged Irishman wearing war paint who calls himself Joe Buffalo Dance and has a fetish for wearing a moosehead. Son Stinky passionately lusts for his mother, and daughter Gay compulsively breaks into tap-dancing routines while several characters are mysteriously murdered. Everyone appears to want to kill Hedda. Sidney remarkably rises from his wheelchair to kick a mysterious intruder, dressed as a Moose, while giddy Hedda provides her daughter with a vodka laced with poison. Hedda laughs hysterically and applauds Gay's final frenetic tap dance as her daughter collapses and dies.

"Moose Murders should not have been mounted," reported Douglas Watt (Daily News), "Moose Murders shouldn't happen to a moose," and he called this unbelievable disaster an "incredibly sappy murder mystery farce." Brendan Gill (The New Yorker) concluded that Moose Murders "would insult the intelligence of amoebas--it happened to be trash--In a play that manifested not a scintilla of talent, what could be expected of its cast and director?" Commenting on the elaborate program credit to Kent Shelton for "Stage Violence" Gill added, "Whatever such violence may be, it isn't a patch on the violence I felt in my heart as this rubbishy work fumbled and stumbled its way to a sorry close."

Frank Rich (The New York Times) relieved theatregoers scarred by past Broadway disasters with "A visit to Moose Murders is what will separate the connoisseurs of Broadway disaster from mere dilettantes for many moons to come," appraising the inane dialogue as being "only improved by its inaudibility." Clive Barnes (New York Post) felt Moose Murders "had the ineffable effrontery to open--This murderously uncomic murder comedy was so indescribably bad that I do not intend to waste anyone's time by describing it--what it needs is a mercy killing." Barnes also noted "Eve Arden had all the luck," referring to the wise departure from the Wild Moose Lodge by the sophisticated comedienne Eve "Our Miss Brooks" Arden.

Moose Murders began previews with Eve Arden playing the Hedda Holloway lead with the play scheduled to open on February 7th. Miss Arden left the fiasco on February 5th and previews were cancelled for additional rehearsals with Holland Taylor as Hedda. The opening was again announced for February 14th but postponed yet again until February 22, 1983. The hunting season arrived early in 1983 and the well-armed mainstem marksmen had a fine target in Arthur Bicknell and his out-of-any-season Moose Murders.

Harry Warren and Johnny Mercer's song "Jeepers Creepers" was introduced by Louis Armstrong in 1938's film Going Places and was nominated for an Academy Award. Moose Murders was nominated for the season's, and the decades's, worst play.

* * *

THE MOTHER LOVER (Booth Theatre, February 1, 1969). Produced by Leland Hayward in association with Joseph E. Levine and AVCO Embassy Pictures Corporation; A comedy by Jerome Weidman; Director, Larry Blyden; Setting and Lighting, Ben Edwards; Costumes, Jane Greenwood; Production supervisor, Joe Calvan; Production assistant, Paula Lorge
    Larry Blyden (Seymour); Eileen Heckart (Mrs. Haber); Valerie French (Griselda)

Accountant Seymour Haber interrupts his insatiable passion for call girls to dutifully visit and vigorously harass his mother in her Queens apartment every Sunday morning desperately hoping she will soon die. Mrs. Haber rents one of her rooms to English prostitute Griselda, whose wardrobe excludes underwear. Seymour quickly beds Griselda, who in turn quickly and happily helps him dispose of his mother in a convenient trunk.

Leland Hayward had produced several of Broadway's more notable hits, including A Bell for Adano (1944); State of the Union (1945); Mister Roberts (1948); Call Me Madam (1950); and he co-produced Gypsy (1959) and The Sound of Music (1959). Ten years later he rashly produced The Mother Lover. Jerome Weidman had supplied the book (with George Abbott) for the outstanding musical Fiorello, which won 1960's Pulitzer Prize. Based on a novel by Samuel Hopkins Adams, Wiedman co-authored with George Abbott the libretto for 1960's musical Tenderloin and in 1962 adapted for the stage his own novel I Can Get It for You Wholesale, with music and lyrics by Harold

Rome. Weidman's 1966 book for Duke Ellington's music, produced on Broadway as <u>Pousse-Cafe</u>, lasted three performances. <u>The Mother Lover</u> was Weidman's sole effort requiring no music and obviously no production.

Clive Barnes (<u>The New York Times</u>) wrote "The kindest thing I can say about this repulsively titled comedy is that it is brief-- The humor was of monumental banality--Larry Blyden, whose first directing assignment this was, would have stood a better chance directing traffic." Richard Watts, Jr. (<u>New York Post</u>) properly buried <u>The Mother Lover</u> stating, it "may not be the worst play I've ever seen, but it is surely the most deplorable to come from an author of established reputation--the sheer witlessness of his latest work is virtually breathtaking."

* * *

MOURNING PICTURES (Lyceum Theatre, November 10, 1974). Produced by Samuel H. Schwartz; The Lennox Arts Center/Music Theatre Performing Group Production; A drama by Honor Moore; Director, Kay Carney; Setting, John Jacobsen; Lighting, Spencer Mosse; Costumes, Whitney Blausen; Music, Susan Ain; Lyrics, Honor Moore; Producers, Lyn Austin, Mary Silverman; Directorial assistant, Ellyn Marshall; Music supervisor, Larry Abel; Wardrobe supervisor, Florence Aubert; Company manager, Robert P. Cohen; Stage managers, Frank Marino, Duane Mazey
    Leora Dana (Maggie); Kathryn Walker (Margaret); Donald Symington (Philip); Leslie Ackerman (Abigail); Daniel Landon (David); Philip Carlson (Doctors: Rumbach, Cassidy, Berryman and Potter); Dorothea Joyce (Singer); Musicians: Amy Rubin (Electric and Accoustic Pianos); John Carbonne (Accoustic and Fender Base); Sue Ann Kohn (Flute); Joe Passaro (Percussion)
SONGS: What Will She Leave Me?; It's Such a Beautiful Day; What Are You Saying About Me Now?; Sweet Clear Sun; The Garden; Wait Until the Sun; I Want to Go Home; Paul Arrives; There Is a Birthday

Fifty-year-old Maggie is dying of cancer. Maggie's oldest of nine children, twenty-seven-year-old poet Margaret, tries to define, explain, and accept her mother's death. For seven months Maggie's minister husband and other children visit her, giving each other united support in their unwelcome and inexperienced confrontation with death and sorrow. They fathom their own mortality and recall their once happy life as a family. Maggie, who resisted chemotherapy but submitted to faith-healing and ineffective diets from several doctors, finally dies.

<u>Mourning Pictures</u> was seen accurately by the critics as obviously autobiographical, which it was. "Despite much lovely writing, it is not memorable as poetry and it is certainly not theatrical--The presence of songs does not make theatre musical. Moore has created neither story, characters nor mood. Even a play about death must

have life," reported Martin Gottfried (<u>New York Post</u>). Clive Barnes (<u>The New York Times</u>) wrote, "I suspect that <u>Mourning Pictures</u> proved to be essential therapy for the playwright and perhaps her family. But for the rest of the world I would presume that only those who wish to identify with its situation, both closely and immediately, will get a great deal out of it." Douglas Watt (<u>Daily News</u>) described the play as "more threnody than play--it deliberately avoids the pulse of drama. <u>Mourning Pictures</u>--in its present form, at least--does not belong on a stage." The Associated Press noted, "<u>Mourning Pictures</u> was a terribly sincere, simply terrible play about private grief." Brendan Gill, however, observed in <u>The New Yorker</u>; "Miss Moore is a very good writer, and there is scarcely a word too many in her text. She has pruned it and left room within it for silences that put me in mind of passages in Eliot's <u>Four Quartets</u>."

Honor Moore in a program note for her play explained the title of the play, "Grief was given visible form in the mourning picture, popular in the early nineteenth-century, especially in New England. Mourning pictures were stitched or painted by young women as gifts for the bereaved family."

Boston-born Jenny McKean Moore, the wife of the Right Reverend Paul Moore, Jr., the prominent if controversial Episcopal Bishop of New York, whom she married in 1944, died at the Washington Hospital Center on October 3, 1973, at the age of fifty, from inoperable cancer of the liver which had been diagnosed in March, 1973. Mrs. Moore had graduated from Barnard College in 1946, enrolled in writing courses at George Washington University in 1971, and was the author of <u>The People on Second Street</u>, published in 1968, which recounted her active, frustrating social work among the poor during her husband's ministry in Jersey City. Jenny Moore was the mother of nine children: Paul III, Adelia, Rosemary, George, Marian, Daniel, Susanna, Patience, and playwright-poet Honor.

Jenny Moore continually wrote of her emotions in confronting death and she composed a funeral service in which she requested that Senator Eugene J. McCarthy, for whom she had actively campaigned during the 1968 presidential election, read William Butler Yeats's <u>The Pilgrim Soul</u> and that music be played by a string quartet. Instructions were for the inscription on her gravestone to read: "The loneliness and hilarity of survival." Jenny McKean Moore's funeral was held at the Washington Cathedral on Friday, October 5, 1973, and ten days later a memorial service was scheduled in New York at the Cathedral Church of St. John the Divine.

Honor Moore's play <u>Mourning Pictures</u> in 1974 was another memorial.

* * *

A MURDERER AMONG US (Morosco Theatre, March 25, 1964). Produced by Jeff Britton; A comedy by Yves Jamiaque, adapted from the French by George White; Director, Sam Wanamaker; Settings and lighting, David Hays; Costumes, Fred Voelpel; Music, Paul Reif; Production assistant, Thomas H. Diringer; General manager, Irving Cooper; Company manager, Warren O'Hara; Stage managers, Joseph Brownstone, Michael Flanagan

    Pierre Olaf (Jerome Lahutte); Tom Bosley (Cabouche); Severn Darden (Birgasse); Loring Smith (Mayor); George S. Irving (Marolles); Lauri Peters (Louisette); Dana Elcar (Pertuiset); Edith King (Madame Maille); Jane Hoffman (Mlle. Suisson); Michael Flanagan (Policeman)

    Meek librarian Jerome Lahutte is given a gala reception when he returns to his Provence village of Belle Fontaine, in France, after spending ten years in prison for a murder he did not commit. Lahutte astounds the small community by announcing he is entitled to one murder in justification of his unjust imprisonment. Intent to "take the bread for which I have already paid," Lahutte buys a pistol and seeks the most sinful village citizen for his victim. None of the villagers are without sin and they feel they could reasonably be killed for many of their indiscretions and casual corruptions. Police chief Marolles, baker Pertuiset, and cafe owner Cabouche conspire with the pompous mayor to kill the village's despised usurer, Birgasse the banker, who holds money more precious than his life, intending once again to frame Lahutte for the crime. Sympathetic young Louisette, aware that guileless Lahutte's threats of revenge are empty, tries to protect him, but the cartel of cowards succeed and innocent Lahutte is again charged with a murder he did not commit.

    A Murderer Among Us was seen as a reflection of Jean Giraudoux and Maurice Valency's 1948 The Madwoman of Chaillot, with overtones of Friedrich Duerrenmatt's 1958 drama The Visit, without the delightful comedy or seering tragedy of either. "A Murderer Among Us," wrote Walter Kerr (Herald Tribune), "which rather unreliably calls itself a comedy, is really a parable about man's inhumanity to man. At the end of the play we are told that everyone is guilty. I do hope that includes the playwright and the director." John Chapman (Daily News), however, considered Jamiaque's play "a delightfully whimsical comedy which is given bite by a cool, Gallic cynicism."

    John Mitchell (Journal-American) compared A Murderer Among Us to a French souffle fallen flat which laid an egg on 45th Street. It was "Made to look appetizing by a peppery cast, the play is palatable, but without distinction--There are rare moments of contagious comedy, bright bubbles on the surface of a dull play." Richard Watts, Jr. (New York Post) found "something stubbornly perverse about A Murderer Among Us" as, despite its many advantages, "the effect is one of almost incredible flatness." Howard Taubman (The New York Times) detected in the English translation of Jamiaque's

French text "a Gallic relish for verbal fencing" in "a gibberish of styles and a noisy distortion of content" which "behaves like a zany farce, degenerates into burlesque, then recovers itself and attempts a dry, stylized approach." Norman Nadel (New York World-Telegram and Sun) wrote, "Characters are merely sketched; there's little depth in them. So A Murderer Among Us is not so much a play in the desirable sense, as it is the facade of a play."

Yves Jamiaque's A Murderer Among Us had been successful in Paris in 1962 and preproduction announcements for the Broadway presentation included Art Carney for the role of the innocent librarian Lahutte, with Burgess Meredith as director. Following fourteen previews, A Murderer Among Us was convicted after one performance.

* * *

MYSTERY MOON (Royale Theatre, June 23, 1930). Produced by James M. Graf in association with Paul M. Trebitsch; A musical comedy with Book by Fred Herendeen; Music and lyrics by Carlo and Sanders; Director, Victor Morley; Dances and ensembles arranged by Bunny Weldon; Costumes by Brooks; Musical director, Ernie Valle; Orchestrations, Hilding Anderson, Maurice DePackh, Hans Spialek, Joe Weiss; Settings, Theatrical Art Studios

Frank Shannon (Joe Hendricks); Frances Shelley (Lola Harriott); Charles Lawrence (Sam Martin); Kitty Kelly (Mildred Middleton); Marjorie Gaines (Pearl Lindy); Arthur Uttry ("Flash" Darrell); Winifred Barry (Queenie North); Harry Short (Smith Banks); Arthur Campbell (Don Bradley); Maude Brooks (May Delight); Pauline Dee (Goldie Del Monte); Curtis Karpe (Lee Foo); Frank J. Marshall, Jr. (James Boyd); Virginia Watts (Gladys St. James); Virginia Dawe (Bessie Van Neer); Harrison Brockbank (Ben Flint); Jane Taylor (Doris Flint); Larry Woods (Constable Smedley Baker); Juliana (Premiere Danseuse); Ernie Vallee (Ernie Vallee); Ernie Vallee's Orchestra

SONGS: One Night in the Rain; Clean Out the Corner; Mystery Moon; If You and I Incorporate; Milkmaids from Broadway; You Always Talk of Friendship; It's All OK

Joe Hendricks, stage manager of Portal, North Dakota's Palace Theatre, in league with the impressario of a musical-comedy touring company, terrorizes the show's performers. Hendricks and his partner, "Flash" Darrell, try to convince the cast that the old Opera House is haunted in order to hide their lucrative opium-smuggling business. The dope-dealing culprits are caught and the show goes on.

Percy Hammond (Herald Tribune) called Mystery Moon "a cordial fumbler, groping unsteadily between a flimsy ghost story and a suburban revue." Wilella Waldorf (New York Post) disliked the musical mystery which she claimed was "punctuated at intervals with some of the most uninspired songs we've ever heard." Stephen Rathbun

(The Sun) saw Mystery Moon as "a fair-to-middling musical comedy that has several serious defects. Its comedy is not funny enough" and "the chills and terror remained on the wrong side of the footlights--a lengthy but slim entertainment." Alexander Woollcott (The New York Times) described the musical as "a hodge-podge combining some not very effective mystery drama and some not very distinctive musical comedy specialties--the newcomer is certainly nothing to call for dancing in the streets nor red fire in Times Square."

Mystery Moon was based on Fred Herendeen's 1929 melodrama One Night Only, which he adapted to the musical stage with a score by Monte Carlo and Alma Sanders. Carlo and Sanders' only success on Broadway was 1921's musical comedy Tangerine, which was followed by a succession of flops aided by their dismal, tinkling musical scores: Elsie (1923); The Chiffon Girl, Bye, Bye, Barbara, Princess April (1924); and Oh! Oh! Oh! Nurse (1925). The songwriters also furnished the musical score for 1928's The Houseboat on the Styx, which opened at Broadway's Liberty Theatre on December 25, 1928, and managed 103 performances. After the debacle of Mystery Moon, Carlo and Sanders waited seventeen years before attempting another Broadway musical but the wait was futile. Their score for Louisiana Lady submerged in four performances in 1947.

Following the break-in of Mystery Moon at Brighton Beach on June 9, 1930, Franker Woods was replaced by Charles Lawrence and a reshuffling of cast members postponed the scheduled Broadway opening from June 16th to Monday, June 23, 1930. An audience arrived at the Royale Theatre on Tuesday, June 24th, but the musicians refused to enter the orchestra pit because the producers failed to post a surety bond guaranteeing their wages. There was no second performance of the musical as the curtain did not rise and the audience left the theatre. Mystery Moon closed at a $35,000 loss.

Three years later Earl Carroll produced, directed, and wrote (with Rufus King) a more successful musical comedy whodunit. Carroll's Murder at the Vanities opened at the New Amsterdam Theatre on September 8, 1933, to run 207 performances. Bela Lugosi, James Rennie, Olga Baclanova, Jean Adair, Billy House, and Robert Cummings were the players involved in the backstage murder of a Vanities showgirl, committed by the wardrobe mistress hoping to further the career of her chorus-girl daughter.

Herendeen's original title, One Night Only, would have been a more appropriate title for Mystery Moon.

* * *

THE NATURAL LOOK (Longacre Theatre, March 11, 1967). Produced by David Black and Loren E. Price, in association with Susan Slade. A Helen Harvey production; A comedy by Lee Thuna; Director, Martin Fried; Settings, Ed Wittstein; Lighting, Jules Fisher; Costumes,

Patton Campbell; Production manager, Jose Vega; Production assistant, Joel Cook; Hairstyles, Kenneth Salon; General manager, Eugene V. Wolsk; Stage managers, Gene Perlowin, Gene Williams
  Gene Hackman (Dr. Barney Harris); Brenda Vaccaro (Reedy Harris); Jerry Orbach (Malcolm); Ethel Griffies (Countess); Dolph Sweet (Steven Kenny); Doris Roberts (Edna); Zohra Lampert (Jane Fenice); Patrick Baldauff (Norman Carmichael); Andreas Voutsinas (Addison Demas)

Reedy Harris's position as advertising director of Contessa Cosmetics, Inc. is threatened by her aggressive assistant Malcolm, hired by the firm's eccentric founder, The Countess. Reedy's marriage is also threatened, by her husband's former girlfriend, Jane Fenice, a dedicated homemaker still in anxious pursuit of Barney. To save her marriage, Reedy resigns from Contessa Cosmetics to become a full-time housewife in their Park Avenue apartment, but Barney refuses to have her become a house-slave like his mother. The Countess discovers that Malcolm is a spy for a competing cosmetic company and fires him. Reedy joyously returns to Contessa Cosmetics, Inc. feeling secure as Barney's wife and occasional housekeeper.

Walter Kerr (The New York Times) reported, "If The Natural Look were about anything, it might be quite a pleasant casual entertainment" but he found "Miss Thuna does not so much coax comedy into existence as hoax it along...." John McCarten (The New Yorker) wrote, "Under the heavy handicaps of the script, most of the players seemed resigned to walking through their weary assignments."

Twenty-eight-year-old Brenda Vaccaro left her featured role of Toni in the long-running comedy hit Cactus Flower to take her first starring role, as Reedy Harris in The Natural Look. Eighty-seven-year-old British actress Ethel Griffies, who died in London at the age of ninety-seven on September 7, 1975, made her stage debut at the age of two, on February 26, 1881, and was the oldest working actress on the English-speaking stage. For ten years Gene Hackman had appeared on Broadway in a series of forgotten plays. Returning to his native California, Hackman made several films of passing interest and reached stardom with his vivid performance as Jimmy "Popeye" Doyle in William Friedkin's 1971 screen thriller The French Connection. Lee (Leonora) Thuna, a former Madison Avenue ad-copyist, attempted playwriting, but The Natural Look wasn't it, nor was another one-performance calamity in 1973, written with Harry Cauley, called Let Me Hear You Smile. The Natural Look cost $123,000.

Aside from the general tone of most of the reviews, Norman Nadel (World Journal Tribune) added, "Even after the cast learns its lines and the director decides on a style, The Natural Look still will face problems that defy any solution short of total re-writing."

* * *

NED AND JACK (Little Theatre, November 8, 1981). Produced by Ken Marsolais, Martin Markinson, All Starr Productions and Axbell Productions; A drama by Sheldon Rosen; Director, Colleen Dewhurst; Scenery, James Leonard Joy; Lighting, Robby Monk; Costumes, David Murin; Technical supervisor, Jeremiah H. Harris; Sound, Tony Meola; Wardrobe, Tony Karniewich; Production assistant, Tom Bundrick; Props, Merlyn Davis; Casting, Bonnie G. Timmermann; General management, Joseph P. Harris, Peter T. Kulock, Steven E. Goldstein, Nancy Simmons; Stage managers, Richard Elkow, Buzz Cohen

  John Vickery (Edward "Ned" Sheldon); Peter Michael Goetz (John "Jack" Barrymore); Barbara Sohmers (Ethel Barrymore); Sean Griffin (Danny); Charlie (Barton, a Cockatoo)

   After his enormously successful opening in Hamlet at Broadway's Sam H. Harris Theatre on November 17, 1922, actor John Barrymore visits his close friend and confidant, successful, innovative playwright Edward "Ned" Sheldon, who brought realism to the theatre with his plays. Barrymore seduces a teenaged supernumerary backstage following his acclaimed performance and eighteen curtain calls and, in his Prince of Denmark costume, complete with sword, climbs fourteen flights of a fire escape, toting three bottles of bootleg Mumm's champagne to Sheldon's sumptuous upper East Side Manhattan apartment. The two old friends carouse, consuming champagne while reflecting on their past escapades and glories and pondering their foreboding futures, pausing only to urinate from the balcony. Flamboyant, alcoholic, quixotic Jack has decided he has professionally peaked as an actor as "a star always burns brightest just before it fizzles out" and he plans to forsake the stage for less work and more money in Hollywood. Suave, sophisticated, poised Ned reveals to Jack that he is slowly succumbing to the insidious, debilitating arthritis which will eventually paralyze his entire body and blind him--but never thwart his keen, active, witty, and brilliant mind. Both Ned and Jack realize they are helpless to avoid their fate. Jack's future inexorably leads to willful self-destruction and parody of his theatrical genius and Ned becomes a living corpse.

   Sheldon Rosen's play Ned and Jack was first produced in New York by David Kerry Heefner and Judson Barteaux at their Off-Broadway Hudson Guild Theatre on May 13, 1981, where it played forty performances. "Ned and Jack is a modest, circumscribed drama that aims only to give us a passing glimpse into its tragically self-destructive hero. At this it succeeds--especially in Miss Dewhurst's forceful and generally well-cast production," was Frank Rich's appraisal of Rosen's play. The Off-Broadway production included scenery by James Leonard Joy, costumes by David Murin, and lighting by Robby Monk, featuring Dwight Schultz as Ned, Peter Michael Goetz as Jack, and Barbara Caruso as Ethel Barrymore.

   Remounting Ned and Jack for Broadway, the play was "improved" but the "improvements" clouded its original zest, compounded and weakened by the casting of John Vickery in the role of Ned

Sheldon. Vickery's Ned was described as "artificial" and a "caricature" in an "opaque, actorish performance." Additionally, Rosen had enlarged his script since its tightly written Canadian premiere in 1977, to include Ethel Barrymore in a first-act contrived exposition scene. Comparing the Off-Broadway Ned and Jack with Broadway's version, Frank Rich perceptively noted, "Perhaps it's because they've worked too hard that last spring's labor of theatrical love now seems like a chore."

Edwin Wilson (The Wall Street Journal) wrote, "The play spends so much time on the celebrity of the two men--the people they know, the things they've done--that they become cut-out figures from a fan magazine, not real people." Douglas Watt (Daily News) called Ned and Jack "a wholly synthetic evening, a lifeless charade--I couldn't believe a word of it." Clive Barnes (New York Post) added, "The play is inevitably wordy--not a play for people who do not wish to listen intently, but it is fascinating in the contrast of characters, and for that matter, the contrast of destinies." The Christian Science Monitor, as did all the other appraisers, praised the impressive Broadway directorial debut of actress Colleen Dewhurst, but the play itself "seldom penetrates much deeper than an effective but showy emotionalism. Rosen clearly respects and values the two men and the talents they represent."

Playwright Sheldon Rosen, born in the Bronx, New York, on August 26, 1943, graduated from the University of Rochester with a B.A. in Psychology. Prior to Ned and Jack, he had written the plays Meyer's Room, Stag King, and Love Mouse. Rosen, a resident of Toronto, Canada, received several Canadian playwright awards and his drama Ned and Jack was first produced at the Vancouver East Cultural Center on November 11, 1977. The play was directed then by Pamela Hawthorn, designed by Richard Cook, with lighting by Marsha Sibthorpe and costumes by Christina McQuarrie. Tom Wood played Ned, Jan Muszynski was Jack, and Guy Bannerman played Sheldon's butler, Danny.

The Stratford, Canada, Festival Theatre produced Ned and Jack on June 30, 1978, directed by Peter Moss, with a setting by Shawn Kerwin and lighting by Harry Frehner. Jack Wetherall was cast as Ned and Alan Scarfe played the part of Jack Barrymore. Stratford's Avon Stage revived Ned and Jack on June 5, 1979, with Dean Hawes as Ned, Jim McQueen as Danny, and Alan Scarfe given a remarkable performance as Jack. "For true bravura playing there's nothing else at this year's Stratford Festival to match the incredible performance of Alan Scarfe in Sheldon Rosen's fine new play" wrote critic Jamie Portman.

* * *

NO HARD FEELINGS (Martin Beck Theatre, April 8, 1973). Produced by Orin Lehman, Joseph Kipness and Lawrence Kasha; A comedy by

Sam Bobrick and Ron Clark; Director, Abe Burrows; Setting and Lighting, Robert Randolph; Costumes, Theoni V. Aldridge; Production assistant, Gary Keeper; Production associate, Charlotte Dicker; Company manager, David Wyler; Stage managers, Lanier Davis, David Marlow, Philip Price

Eddie Albert (George Bartlett); Nanette Fabray (Roberta Bartlett); Conrad Janis (Jimmy Skouras); Stockard Channing (Joanna Wilkins); A. Larry Haines (Alex Springer); Beverly Dixon (Bunny Sutton); David Marlow (Fred); Dino Narizzano (Policeman); Alan Manson (Voice of Judge)

Middle-aged George and Roberta Bartlett have just seen their only daughter, Joanna, married. Returning to their suburban home, Roberta packs her bags and informs smug and irascible George that she is leaving him to live with her younger lover, Jimmy Skouras, a Greek waiter with whom she has been having an extended affair and whose child she is carrying. Abrasive, successful, lighting-fixture businessman George rejects the consoling advances of predatory divorcée Bunny Sutton but receives no sympathy from his business partner, Alex Springer, nor from his unexpectedly pregnant daughter, who supports her mother's decision. George attempts to buy off Jimmy the Greek, then accidentally shoots him in the foot. George is packed off to a psychiatrist and a judge gives him a suspended sentence of one year, contingent on his not seeing Roberta. After the legal year George visits Roberta and Jimmy in their West Side flat and finding them, with their baby Dimitrius, still perfectly happy, resorts to his normal explosive, chauvinistic nature.

No Hard Feelings was a type of comedy Broadway enjoyed for several decades but after television spewed out endless similar situation comedies over the years, Bobrick and Clark's comedy faced a bleak reception. Douglas Watt (Daily News) called it "a pathetic little farce--The air is so thick with gags that the players were occasionally stumbling over them--a mean and clumsy contrivance that sends one into the street with low spirits."

Clive Barnes (The New York Times) saw No Hard Feelings as "an essentially undemanding, modestly effective light comedy. Nothing is at all credible, and the characters are TV-style stereotypes. Yet some of the jokes have a well-ironed effectiveness, and there is a certain trim charm to the play." Brendan Gill (The New Yorker) viewed Abe Burrows' staging as succeeding in its goal of "an almost unbroken sequence of funny lines spoken by funny people." Richard Watts (New York Post) considered No Hard Feelings "no blockbuster, but it is an unpretentiously amusing piece of fooling, frequently funny, and it is vastly aided by the expert performances of a cast headed by Eddie Albert, Nanette Fabray and Conrad Janis and the unfailingly knowing direction of Abe Burrows."

Abe Burrows was born in New York City on December 18, 1910 and he died at the age of seventy-four on Friday, May 17, 1985.

During rehearsals of No Hard Feelings at the Martin Beck Theatre, while enthusiastically directing Nanette Fabray, he fell into the over twelve-foot-deep orchestra pit. After two weeks in the hospital, during which his son James Edward Burrows assumed the directorial chair, Abe returned to direct the play in Boston from a wheelchair, and he watched the New York dress rehearsal from a stretcher. Eddie Albert returned to Broadway in No Hard Feelings, for the first time since 1949 when he had appeared in Irving Berlin's musical comedy Miss Liberty. Nanette Fabray made her first Broadway appearance in No Hard Feelings since starring in Irving Berlin's 1962 musical comedy Mr. President.

Playwrights Sam Bobrick and Ron Clark were born one day and one year apart; Bobrick in Chicago on July 24, 1932, and Clark in Montreal, Canada, on July 25, 1933. Their first Broadway comedy, Norman, Is That You?, opened on February 19, 1970, and, although better written than No Hard Feelings, it disappeared after twelve performances.

* * *

THE NOVEMBER PEOPLE (Billy Rose Theatre, January 14, 1978). Produced by Shelly Bechok and Jim D'Spain; A drama by Gus Weill; Director, Arthur Sherman; Setting, Kert Lundell; Lighting, Thomas Shelton; Costumes, Joseph G. Aulisi; Production assistant, Shauna Vey; Wardrobe supervisor, Virginia Sylvain; Management associate, Thelma Cooper; Company manager, Gail Bell; Stage managers, Alan Hall, Richard Elkow
    Cameron Mitchell (Mitch); Jan Sterling (Mary); James Sutorius (Brian, their older son); Pamela Reed (Kathleen, Brian's Wife); John Uecker (Donny, their younger son)

Former state comptroller, Irish-American Mitch returns to his home on a November Sunday after serving only eighteen months of a possible twenty-year sentence in prison for embezzlement, the sentence magnanimously reduced by a paid-off judge. Mitch's wife, Mary, has invited several of her husband's political friends to a homecoming party, but it is two days before the gubernatorial election and Mitch's one-time bureaucratic cronies resist further reflected tarnishing. The party becomes a family affair, attended by their older son Brian, assistant press secretary to the governor, with whose wife he is having an affair; the mentally disturbed, pill-popping and presumptuous poet, their younger son Donny, and Brian's estranged wife, Kathleen, who is revolted by politics and her husband's family. Aware that Kathleen will divorce him for further political shenanigans, Brian nevertheless succeeds in bribing federal attorney Coogan to save the governor from indictment, also discovering he is the illegitimate son of the governor.

Douglas Watt (Daily News) called The November People "as convoluted and turgid as the politics it describes." Clive Barnes

(New York Post) condemned the drama as "a 24-carat Broadway flop, the kind of play so obviously inept that you wonder idly how anyone could have imagined it to have a breathing chance on Broadway." Mel Gussow (The New York Times) reported, "Just as the losing head of a political ticket can damage his running mates, everyone connected with this effort shares in the defeat, including such professionals as Arthur Sherman, the director, and Kert Lundell, the designer--Faced with the emptiness of The November People, one can only wonder how the play ever reached Broadway."

Gus Weill, one-time executive secretary to the governor of Louisiana, had his drama, To Bury a Cousin, produced at Off-Broadway's Bowerie Lane Theatre in 1967 for 5 performances. Weill's two one-act plays, Parents and Children and Geese, produced under the title Geese, was one of the first productions to display total nudity at Off-Broadway's Players Theatre on January 12, 1969.

* * *

ON AN OPEN ROOF (Booth Theatre, January 28, 1963). Produced by Ridgely Bullock, Milton Katselas and Current Productions, in association with W. Clement Stone; A drama by Avraham Inlender; Director, Milton Katselas; Setting and Lighting, Jean Rosenthal; Costumes, Florence Klotz; Hairstylist, Tivice; Company manager, James Awe; Stage managers, Lo Hardin, Robert Keegan
    Don Gordon (Miguel Escobar); Diana Van Der Vils (Jane Escobar); Josephine Nichols (Mrs. Rawlins); Ted D'Arms (Bill Shannon); Alfred Sandor (Otto Vidor); Ellen Siccama (Vera Vidor); Pamela Fraser (Suzy Escobar)

Puerto Rican lawyer Miguel Escobar refuses to compromise his rigid principles and dedication to social injustice in New York's Spanish Harlem which reduces his family to living in a cold-water rooftop Manhattan apartment. Depressed and contemplating suicide, Miguel reluctantly accepts financial assistance from his mother-in-law, Mrs. Rawlins, while revolting against defending a Spanish client, the defense of whom he finds objectionable and against his restrictive code of morality and justice. His wife, Jane, decides to use the money contributed by her mother to have an abortion.

Thirty-year-old Avraham Inlender's first two playwriting efforts were produced by Ridgely Bullock and Milton Katselas for $85,000 and were to be presented in repertory. Rehearsals for On an Open Roof began on November 26, 1962, and rehearsals for the second play, called Kadish, started on December 3, 1962. On an Open Roof gave eight previews and one performance. Kadish, scheduled to open on February 5, 1963, never appeared.

Kadish, subtitled Dialogues for a Dramatic Vaudeville, had the same production credits as On an Open Roof, with the addition of music arranged by "Colonel" Tiger Haynes and the following cast:

Louis Guss (Kadish); Eli Mintz (Sam); Sasha Von Scherler (Miriam); Hollis Irving (Christine); Ted D'Arms (Jones); Tiger Haynes, Frank Brown, Frank Humphries, Eddie Williams (Musicians)

Critical estimates of the merits of On an Open Roof were extremely low. Howard Taubman (The New York Times) wrote, "Its dramatic structure is inept, its characterizations mediocre, its humor flat and its irony wide of the mark--the play is so ponderously written that it also makes the audience miserable."

* * *

ONCE FOR THE ASKING (Booth Theatre, November 20, 1963). Produced by Jon Burgin and Bruno di Cosmi; A comedy by Owen G. Arno; Director, Reginald Denham; Designed and lighted by Feder; Costumes, Audre; Company manager, Leonard Mulhern; General manager, Elias Goldin; Stage managers, Mortimer Halpern, Norman Shelly
    Scott McKay (Ashley Robbins); Jan Sterling (Madelaine Robbins); Russell Nype (Alex Krumbull); Janet Fox (Gretchen); Dorothy Sands (Mrs. Goolsby); Leona Powers (Grace Hollingshead); Donna Scott (Michele Robbins); Bonnie Jones (Sondi); Martin Ross (Bradford); Ralph Dunn (Martin Hollingshead); Fayne Blackburn (Doreen Krumbull): Richard Poston (Eddie); Jeanne Tanzy (A Little Girl); Humphrey Davis (George Richardson); Maurice Brenner (A Taxi Driver); Walter Flanagan (A Stranger)

Advertising copywriter Ashley Robbins has exhausted ideas for new advertising campaigns but his Long Island North Shore neighbor, the eccentric and strange elderly Mrs. Goolsby, rescues him from certain unemployment. Mrs. Goolsby, her pocketbook filled with magic powder and crumb cake, assures Ashley she is a genuine fairy capable of providing anyone with his or her most cherished desire for twenty-four hours. Ashley submits to Mrs. Goolsby's magic powder and, within twenty-four hours, writes new and inspired copy for all of his firm's advertising accounts. Celebrating his success at a victory dinner, Mrs. Goolsby, bolstered by bourbon, magnanimously dispenses her magic powder to all the guests with lunatic un-magical results reincarnating them into other forms and voices. They all eventually readjust to their normal, frenetic existence.

Having elaborated on the magical shenanigans of good fairy Mrs. Goolsby, Lewis Funke (The New York Times) reported, "What that good fairy did not do was to turn Owen G. Arno's Once for the Asking into a good comedy," for the play "got pretty tiresome and the lines were not very funny." John McClain (Journal American) found "the plot wears thin, and in an attempt to keep it alive the author wanders wildly afield--But I'm afraid Once for the Asking is not long for this troubled world." Richard Watts, Jr. (New York Post) wrote, "There is only heavy and inept clumsiness in its apparently promising tale--But Once for the Asking expends its energy on achieving an evening of hopelessness."

Rehearsal for the $125,000 production of Once for the Asking began on October 7, 1963, and the show was tested in Boston at the Wilbur Theatre, beginning October 31st. Nydia Westman, playing "good fairy" Mrs. Goolsby, was replaced on November 11th by Dorothy Sands, "because of extensive rewrites in the characterization of the role." The comedy received five negative reviews in Boston. Elinor Hughes (Boston Herald) saw the play as "One quite funny idea which doesn't add up to a full evening's entertainment." Frederick H. Guidry (The Christian Science Monitor) predicted, "Once for the Asking might fare well in a summer tent; whether the homey magic will beguile Broadway, however, is quite another matter."

Owen G. Arno, an evaluator and script-appraiser for Twentieth Century-Fox studios in Hollywood, originally titled his fey comedy Along Came a Blackbird, which Shepard Traube planned to produce and direct in May, 1961, with a cast hopefully headed by Tony Randall and Dorothy Stickney. Traube's rehearsals for Along Came a Blackbird were announced to begin on October 15, 1961, with a cast including Loring Smith, Ruth McDevitt, Mindy Carson, and Orson Bean. Blackbird never came along.

Despite Mrs. Goolsby's self-acclaimed, doubtful assertion of being "the only good fairy ever to live on Long Island," sprites, fairies, genies, leprechauns, witches, nymphs and such ilk have inhabited the world's stages from the beginning of the theatre, even prior to Ovid's Metamorphoses. Shakespeare introduced a kingdom of fairies in A Midsummer Night's Dream where, under orders from Oberon, King of the Fairies, mischievous Puck sprinkled a love potion on Lysander instead of on Demetrius and placed a donkey's head on weaver Nick Bottom. Sir James Barrie's hardy perennial Peter Pan pleaded with world audiences to believe in fairies and the cockeyed Cinderella charade of an addled good fairy entered the theatre in various disguises in many comedies prior and superior to Once for the Asking.

Closely related to Mrs. Goolsby was Noel Coward's hilariously meddling, inept medium Madame Arcati in 1941's Blithe Spirit. Jerome Chodorov's play Barnaby and Mr. O'Malley, based on Crockett Johnson's comic strip, featured a devilish fairy godfather but expired in Baltimore before reaching Broadway in 1946. Ryan O'Neal's father, Charles, and Abe Burrows adapted O'Neal's novel to the musical comedy stage in 1952 in which three miraculous wishes were granted to Jamie McRuin in Three Wishes for Jamie.

Reginald Denham was more successful as the director of heavier fare than Once for the Asking. Denham was the noted director of such plays laden with suspense or mystery as his own 1940 drama Ladies in Retirement, and his expert guidance extended to Guest in the House (1942); The Two Mrs. Carrolls (1943); Portrait in Black (1947); Dial "M" for Murder (1952) and The Bad Seed (1954).

New York Times's Lewis Funke praised the heroic efforts of the exceptionally talented cast, "But that was not enough for Once for the Asking. It was simply asking the impossible. And that, unhappily, was beyond even Mrs. Goolsby."

* * *

ONCE THERE WAS A RUSSIAN (Music Box Theatre, February 18, 1961). Produced by Leonard Key, Morton Segal, Kenneth Schwartz, Mel Howard and Dick Randall in association with Justin Sturm; A comedy by Sam Spewack; Director, Gene Frankel (replaced Douglas Seale); Scenery and costumes, Tony Walton; Lighting, Klaus Holm; Company manager, Ben Boyar; General manager, Walter Fried; Stage managers, Walter Neal, Leon Gursten
    Walter Matthau (Potemkin); Francoise Rosay (Catherine, the Great); Albert Salmi (John Paul Jones); Julie Newmar (Sura); Sig Ruman (Polgunov); Eric Christmas (Admiral Radbury); Marvin Silbersher (Kolbas); Carol Grace (Vera); Michael Lewis (Prince Nassau Von Siegen); Tom Brannum (Muralov); Louis Guss (Baron Razumni); Roger C. Carmel (Pasha); Steven Frey (Soldier); Ryan MacDonald (Officer); Alberta Nelson (Servant); Tom Rummier (Soldier); Kennard Melton (Eunuch); Laen Retlaw (Barber)

    Catherine the Great, Empress of Russia, makes a grand tour of the Crimea in 1787, arranged by her once-favorite lover, Field Marshal Governor General Potemkin. Catherine engages American Revolutionary War naval hero Captain John Paul Jones to lead the Russian fleet against the Turks. Potemkin uses his considerable wiles, wits, and intrigue to discredit the former American hero, aware that Catherine is attracted to Scotsman Jones. Nymphomaniac Sura, one of Potemkin's "nieces," gets John Paul drunk and into her boudoir. But staunch Presbyterian Jones's Calvinistic lecturing momentarily reforms sexpot Sura. Potemkin's fear of becoming merely another discarded lover of Empress Catherine is calmed when he is, temporarily, reinstated in Catherine's promiscuous favor.

Samuel Spewack with his wife, Bella Cohen Spewack, wrote several successful plays, including Clear All Wires! (original title, Swing High Sweeney) in 1932, which they adapted to the musical stage six years later as Leave It to Me. Produced and directed by George Abbott, their comedy Boy Meets Girl opened at the Cort Theatre on November 27, 1935, to accumulate 669 performances. Cole Porter set to music the Spewack's delightful and stylish libretto Kiss Me, Kate in 1952, and in 1953 Sam and Bella adapted to the English-speaking stage Albert Husson's bizarre and comedic French play La Cuisine des Anges, as My Three Angels. On his own, Sam had written less notable plays, including The War Song (1928); Two Blind Mice (1949); and Under the Sycamore Tree (1952).

    Russian-born (Ukraine, Saturday, September 16, 1899) six-foot-one Spewack, who died at the age of seventy-two on Thursday,

October 14, 1971, migrated to America as a child. He left Columbia University after three years to become a reporter for the New York World. During his nine years with the World, Spewack became their correspondent in Russia in the mid-1920's and in 1922 married Bucharest-born Bella Cohen. Without Bella, Samuel took on Catherine the Great in his less-than-great comedy Once There Was a Russian.

Richard Watts, Jr. (New York Post) categorized Once There Was a Russian as a "minor satire--there is nothing particularly wrong with the play save that it never quite comes to life or succeeds in being more than intermittently amusing." Robert Coleman (New York Mirror) said "Nyet to Spewack's Russian," finding "It is difficult to believe that the same Sam Spewack who collaborated on the book of that delightful musical Kiss Me, Kate, could have penned such a dullie as Once There Was a Russian.--The jokes are labored, and a stellar cast labors valiantly to sell them--It just doesn't come off." John Chapman (Daily News) admired the play and was aware that Spewack had blithely combined fact with fiction but "used it intelligently and entertainingly."

Four years later Samuel Spewack rewrote Once There Was a Russian, in collaboration with Frank Loesser, who also composed the music and lyrics to the retitled play, Pleasures and Palaces. Author-Composer-Lyricist Frank Loesser's glowing Broadway successes had been Where's Charley? (1948); Guys and Dolls (1950); The Most Happy Fella (1956); and How to Succeed in Business Without Even Trying (1961). Loesser's delightful musical Greenwillow was only slightly successful in 1960 with 95 performances. All of Loesser's great musicals were based on past successful plays or novels. Setting Once There Was a Russian to music did not improve the play.

Pleasures and Palaces (Opened March 11, 1965, Detroit, Michigan; Closed there on April 10, 1965). Produced by Allen B. Whitehead in association with Frank Productions, Inc.; Book, based on Sam Spewack's play Once There Was a Russian by Frank Loesser and Sam Spewack. Music and Lyrics, Frank Loesser; Director and choreographer, Bob Fosse; Settings and lighting, Robert Randolph; Costumes, Freddy Wittop; Musical director, Fred Werner; Orchestrations, Philip J. Lang

  Alfred Marks (succeeded by Jack Cassidy) (Potemkin); Hy Hazell (Catherine); John McMartin (John Paul Jones); Phyllis Newman (Sura); Leon Janney (Bureyev); Mort Marshall (Kollenovitch); Eric Brotherson (Radbury); Burt Bier (Suslovski); Sammy Smith (Von Siegen); Darrell Notara (Minister); Woody Romoff (Polgunov); Stan Page (Policeman); John Anania (Captain Pasha); Henrietta Valor (Nun); Michael Quinn (Father Feddor); David Gold (Guard); John Anania, Michael Davis, Howard Kahl, Walter Hook (Prisoners); Michael Quinn, Burt Bier (Villagers); John Anania, Ken Avers, Burt Bier, Michael Davis, Alice Evans, Laurie Franks, Walter Hook, Howard Kahl, Zona Kennedy, Stan Page, Michael Quinn, Dana Simmons, Henrietta Valor, Carole Woodruff (Singers); Pat

146 / Once Upon a Time

Cummings, Kathryn Doby, Don Emmons, Eddie Gasper, Gene Gavin, David Gold, Dick Korthaze, Darrell Notara, Leland Palmer, Renata Powers, Brooke Roma, Betty Rosebrock, Barbara Sharma, Ron L. Steinbeck (Dancers)
SONGS: Salute; I Hear Bells; My Lover Is a Scoundrel; To Marry; Hail Majesty; Thunder and Lightning; To Your Health; Turkish Delight; Neither the Time Nor the Place; In Your Eyes; Truly Loved; The Sins of Sura; Hoorah for Jones; Propaganda; Barabanchik; What Is Life; Ah, to be Home Again; Pleasures and Palaces; Tears of Joy; Far, Far, Far Away.

* * *

ONCE UPON A TIME (Labor Stage, December 20, 1939). Produced by Harold Aaron Salzman; A "satirical fantasy" by Lawrence Joseph Dugan; Director, Richard Z. Segal; Settings by Cirker and Robbins; Lighting, Bolton Wilder; Company manager, Irving Cooper; Stage managers, Leonard Zurit, Charles Brodsky

Alan Fleming (Olaf); Robert Busch (Miles); Charles Powers (Wolf); Miriam Stone (Rose); A. Courtney White (Mr. Moon); Jewel Hart (Ditty); Leslie Gorall (General A); Charles Brodsky (General B); Perry Burton (General C); Johnny Lynn (General D); Walter Ward (General E); John Foster (General F)

Militaristic Wolf threatens the lives and loves of two couples. While the boys climb mountains seeking their dreams, the girls relate their troubles to the Moon. Mr. Moon tells them military dictatorship and war will end forever if provoked by laughter. The girls heartily laugh at Wolf and his pretentious Generals and the war lords die.

Written by the past summer's drama school graduate Lawrence Joseph Dugan and originally produced at Yale University, Once Upon a Time would have embarrassed the Brothers Grimm. Dugan's fantastic fantasy had none of the hysterical wit of George S. Kaufman and Morrie Ryskind's 1930 libretto for Gershwin's Strike Up the Band nor the progression of the delights and horrors of war reached in England's imported 1964 musical, Oh, What a Lovely War. It did have one performance, and John Mason Brown (The Evening Post) wrote, "Once upon a time there was a satirical fantasy the name of which was Once Upon a Time--And, it was bad, very, very bad--Its badness was almost pathetic" resulting in a "series of maudlin scenes; a hodgepodge of poor Maeterlinck and worse Ruskin."

Richard Lockridge (The Evening Sun) found the fable lacking in either fantasy or poetry but "full of twittering robins, and twittering actors and aspirations, which twitter, too--Mr. Dugan rather singularly lacks these attributes, with the result that Once Upon a Time is precisely as silly as it sounds. And the acting is extremely elfin." Brooks Atkinson (The New York Times) felt Mr. Dugan's fantasy might have enchanted Yale but "On Broadway it seems precocious."

Jasper Deeter produced and directed Once Upon a Time at his renowned Hedgerow Theatre in Moylan, Rose Valley, Pa. on September 23, 1940. The twittering continued with this cast:
Richard Basehart (Olaf); David Metcalf (Miles); Davis Page (Wolf); Dolores Tanner (Rose); Maurice Minnick (Mr. Moon); Rosalind Metcalf (Ditty); Morgan Smedley, Michael De Beauset, John Develin, Sam Banham, Ray Franklyn (The Generals)

* * *

ONWARD VICTORIA (Martin Beck Theatre, December 14, 1980). Produced by John N. Hart, Jr. in association with Hugh J. Hubbard and Robert M. Browne; Director, Julianne Boyd; Book and lyrics by Charlotte Anker, Irene Rosenberg; Music by Keith Herrmann; Musical staging, Michael Shawn; Scenery, William Ritman; Lighting, Richard Nelson; Costumes, Theoni V. Aldridge; Music direction, Larry Blank; Orchestrations, Michael Gibson; Dance Arrangements, Donald Johnstone; Vocal arrangements, Keith Herrmann and Larry Blank; Sound, Lewis Mead; Assistant conductor, Donald Rebic; Hairstylist, Robert DeNiro; Wardrobe, William Campbell; Production assistant, Howard P. Lev; Technical advisor, Jeremiah J. Harris; Stage managers, Ed Aldridge, Joseph Corby, Renee F. Lutz
Jill Eikenberry (Victoria Woodhull); Edmond Genest (Theodore Tilton); Martha Jean Sterner (Beth Tilton); Michael Zaslow (Henry Ward Beecher); Ted Thurston (Cornelius Vanderbilt); Dorothy Holland (Susan B. Anthony); Beth Austin (Tennie Claflin); Ian Michael Towers (Perkins); Dan Cronin (Jim); Laura Waterbury (Elizabeth Cady Stanton); Scott Fless (Johnson); Rex Hays (William Evarts); Linda Poser (Eunice Beecher); Jim Jansen (Anthony Comstock); Gordon Stanley (Fleming); Carrie Wilder (Mrs. Fleming); Karen Gibson (Mrs. Baxter); John Kildahl (Baxter); Lora Jeanne Martens (Mrs. Randolph/Little Girl); Marty McDonough (Randolph/Telegraph Boy); Carol Lurie (Woman Investor #1); Dru Alexandrine (Woman Investor #2); Kenneth H. Waller (Congressman Butler/Grant Speaker/Maginnes/Judge); Lenny Wolpe (Charlie Delmonico/Fullerton); Lauren Goler (Jim's Girlfriend)
SONGS: The Age of Brass; Curiosity; Magnetic Healing; Beecher's Processional; I Depend on You; Victoria's Banner; Changes; A Taste of Forever; Unescorted Women; Love and Joy; Everyday I Do a Little Something for the Lord; It's Easy for her; Respectable; You Cannot Drown the Dreamer; Another Life; Read It in the Weekly; A Valentine for Beecher; Beecher's Defense.

Philadelphia-born playwrights Charlotte Anker and Irene Rosenberg's first play was titled Victoria for President and given a reading at the Manhattan Theatre Club in 1977. Keith Herrmann, a Broadway musical-comedy orchestra conductor, composed his first musical score for what became Onward Victoria, which the Joseph Jefferson Theatre Company produced at Off-Broadway's Greenwich Mews Theater from February 22 through March 11, 1979. The musical play was produced by Cathy Roskam and directed by Julianne Boyd with settings by

148 / Onward Victoria

Raymond C. Recht; Lighting by Boyd Maston; Costumes by Kenneth M. Yount; Choreography by Judith Haskell; Musical director, John Mahoney; Technical director, Philip Lippel; Stage managers, David Rosenberg, Mary Lockhart, and Renne F. Lutz.

Susan Bigelow played Victoria Woodhull, Louisa Flaningam was Tennie, and Michael Zaslow portrayed Henry Ward Beecher, supported by Allan Carlsen, Karl Heist, Natalie Helms, Jim Jansen, Christina Putnam, Tom Rolfing, Sheldon Silver, Martha Jean Sterner, Evan Thomson, and Lenny Wolpe. The playwrights fictionalized Victoria's stranger-than-fiction life to include an improbable torrid love affair with the Reverend Henry Ward Beecher, with whom she was at odds throughout their relationship, and she testified against him during his sensational trial for adultery.

Rehearsals for the $1.1-million-dollar Broadway production of Onward Victoria started on September 29, 1980. After twenty-three previews the elegiac critiques on December 15th halted Victoria's progress with one performance on December 14, 1980. Frank Rich (The New York Times) saw Onward Victoria marching "very peaceably to oblivion" and compared the musical to "a dinner theatre home-grown answer to Hello, Dolly!," noting that even of "incidents--based on historical fact and speculation, not one of them is credible in Onward Victoria. The book and lyrics battle to a standoff as they attempt to top each other in witlessness."

Douglas Watt (Daily News) reported, "Onward Victoria loses ground so steadily that after awhile it seems to be going backward--though a handsomely costumed period piece, elevates sluggishness to a form of art--The song lyrics are bad enough in themselves, but Keith Herrmann's score, though deftly orchestrated by Michael Gibson, is of absolutely no help." Marilyn Stasio (New York Post) wrote that Onward Victoria was "Defeated by its dull score, leaden book and miscast star, the show pays dearly for distorting its heroine into a love goddess and reducing her career to a few sappy romances."

There should be sufficient fascination, humor, and dramatic impact in any play or musical based on the life of Victoria Woodhull to assure success. Uniquely inconoclastic Victoria predated Nora Helmer's declaration of women's independence by slamming the door in Ibsen's 1879 play A Doll's House; she was cut from the same cloth as Dolly Bloomer, the inspiration for the delightful Harold Arlen 1944 musical comedy Bloomer Girl. Victoria also had the zest and chutzpah of Thornton Wilder's Mrs. Levi of The Merchant of Yonkers which became The Matchmaker and later gained immortality as Hello, Dolly!.

Beautiful Victoria Claflin Woodhull was an original, vociferous suffragette and became the first woman in the United States to address a Congressional Committee. She was also the first woman to run for president of the United States, not once but four times! Known as "The Bewitching Brokers," Victoria and her sister Tennessee became "The Queens of Finance" as the first women to open a brokerage house on Wall Street. Between these activities Victoria married three times, bore two children, and was arrested with remarkable frequency for her outspoken beliefs and inflammatory publications.

As a teenager, Victoria Claflin married much older, alcoholic Dr. Canning Woodhull, by whom she had a son, Byron, and a daughter, Zulu Maud. Following her divorce from Woodhull, Victoria married James H. Blood and in between the dissolution of those marriages had affairs with several prominent males while sister Tennessee became the lover of Commodore Cornelius Vanderbilt.

Thomas Nast's <u>Harper's Weekly</u> cartoon on February 17, 1872, portrayed Victoria as "Mrs. Satan" advocating "Be Saved by Free Love." Victoria's speech at Steinway Hall shook Manhattan and startled most of the nation. "Yes!" Victoria exclaimed, "I am a Free Lover! I have an inalienable, constitutional, and natural right to love whom I may, to love as long or as short a period as I can, to change that love every day if I please. I have the further right to demand a free and unrestricted exercise of that right, and it is your duty not only to accord it, but as a community, to see that I am protected in it. I trust that I am fully understood, for I mean just that and nothing less." Right on, Victoria!

The newly formed Equal rights Political Party meeting at Apollo Hall on May 10, 1872, nominated Victoria for president of the United States and, unknown to him, the black orator for human rights and abolition of slavery, Frederick Douglass (Bailey) was nominated for vice-president. Victoria accepted the nomination as "the most prominent representative of the only unrepresented class in the Republic. While others argued the equality of women with men, I proved it by successfully engaging in business; while others sought to show that there was no valid reason why women should be treated, socially and politically, as being inferior to men, I boldly entered the arena."

Victoria's campaign for the presidency was not supported by suffrage pioneers Susan B. Anthony and Elizabeth Cady Stanton. She received no votes and Republican Ulysses S. Grant won over Democrat Horace Greeley to become president of the Republic. Eight years later, Victoria ran for president again but was defeated without a vote by James A. Garfield. Four years later she again recorded no votes and Stephen Grover Cleveland won the presidential election. After Victoria again received no votes in 1888, in her fourth bid for the White House, she retired from politics.

Through her suffragette compatriots, women's rights leaders Susan B. Anthony and Elizabeth Cady Stanton, Victoria was well informed of the full scope and scandal of the Reverend Henry Ward Beecher's four-year affair with Elizabeth Richards Tilton. The gentlemen of the New York press declined to publish the well-known story about the great and beloved minister and orator, and Elizabeth's husband, Theodore Tilton, persuaded Victoria to withhold publication. Handsome Theodore was so persuasive Victoria took him for her lover. Only after being verbally abused and attacked in print by Beecher's sisters Harriet and Catherine did Victoria retaliate and release the full, lurid account of the pious Reverend Beecher's fall from grace with his adulterous mistress, Mrs. Tilton. The story appeared in her November 2, 1872, issue of Woodhull and Claflin's Weekly, for which she and her sister Tennie were summarily tossed into the Ludlow Street Prison for thirty-one days, charged with sending inflammatory publications through the United States mail.

Theodore Tilton later charged Brooklyn's highly respected and beloved minister of Plymouth Church, and orator of national fame, with libel, adultery, and alienation of his wife's affections. Victoria, naturally, testified on behalf of Tilton. The six-month, steamy, headlined trial ultimately ended in a hung jury which was seen as an exoneration of Beecher, who was strongly supported by the majority of the public and the press throughout the ordeal. Ironically, eight years later, the trial judge of the Beecher-Tilton court case presided over the throng of celebrants and supporters of Beecher at the gala celebration of his 70th birthday.

Sister Tennessee married England's Sir Francis Cook and Victoria's third husband was Englishman John Biddulph Martin. John and Victoria discovered the biography of Henry Ward Beecher, containing "The Beecher-Tilton Scandal--with Mrs. Woodhull's statement" in the holdings of The British Museum, which related Harriet Beecher Stowe's famous brother's luridly publicized affair with Mrs. Tilton and its ensuing sensational trial and also labeled Victoria as "a blackmailer." Victoria again accomplished another "first" by suing The British Museum for libel--and won!

After eighteen years of marriage, John B. Martin died at the age of fifty-six in 1899 and left Victoria over eight hundred thousand dollars. Called "The United States Mother of Women's Suffrage," sui generis Victoria Woodhull, born at Homer, Ohio, on September 23, 1838, died at the age of eighty-eight on Thursday, June 9, 1927, in England, where she had continued her lectures and compiled her publication The Humanitarian. In one of her last press interviews Victoria said, "The truth is that I am too many years ahead of this age and the exalted views and objects of humanitarianism can scarcely be grasped as yet in the unenlightened mind of the average men."

Longevity had finally brought respectability to the infamous but fascinating Victoria Woodhull.

* * *

A PIN TO SEE THE PEEPSHOW (The Playhouse Theatre, September 17, 1953). Produced by Nancy Davids; A drama by F. Tennyson

A Pin to See the Peepshow / 151

Jesse and H. M. Harwood; Director, Peter Cotes; Setting, Ariel
Ballif; Lighting, Feder; Costumes, Ruth Morley; General Manager,
Al Goldin; Company manager, Charles Strakosch; Production assistant,
Janet Frankl; Stage managers, Len Bedsow, Betty Ann Metz

    Joan Miller (Julia Almond); Roger Moore (Leo Carr); Claude Horton
(Herbert Starling); Eva Leonard-Boyne (Mrs. Almond); Bill Griffis (George Almond); Marie Paxton (Marian Lestrange); Basil
Howes (Dr. Ackroyd); Martha Farrar (Anne Ackroyd); Jerome
Kilty (Mr. Ringwood); Winifred Cushing (Gipsy Danvers); Frederic
Warriner (Captain Embury/Dr. Ogilvie); Valerie Cardew (Lilly
Kitt); Margaretta Warwick (Bertha Starling); Joy Saunders (Elsa);
Ronald Long (Police Inspector); James Morley (Police Constable);
Shirley Gale (A Wardress); Nell Clarke (Matron); Richard Towers,
Crandall Diehl, Richard Lederer, Charles Shelvey, Winnifred
Cushing, Pat Malone, Len Bensow (Prison Officials and Others)

    During World War I young London shopgirl Julia Almond impulsively marries much older Herbert Starling. Julia later falls in
love with a much younger man, Leo Carr, but Starling refuses to
consent to a divorce. Julia aborts Herbert's child and remains his
wife in name only while her passionate letters to Carr express hope
for Starling's death and her early widowhood. While walking with
Julia at midnight in St. Clement's Square, Starling is attacked and
killed by Leo with a wrench. Julia and Leo are arrested and charged
with Starling's murder. Julia's inflammatory letters to Leo repeatedly
wishing for her husband's death are read at the trial. Leo and Julia
are condemned for murder and both led to the gallows to be hanged.

    Playwright H. M. Harwood's most successful plays were in
1930: The Man in Possession, a brittle comedy starring Raymond
Massey in London, and Leslie Banks on Broadway; and a drama,
Cynara, written with R. Gore Browne, based on Browne's novel The
Imperfect Lover. Gerald du Maurier and Gladys Cooper successfully
played the leads in London's Cynara, and Philip Merivale and Phoebe
Foster recreated the roles on Broadway. Harwood, with his wife,
Friniwyd Tennyson Jesse, adapted her 1934 novel A Pin to See the
Peepshow (first published in the United States in 1974 by St. Martin's
Press) to the stage in 1951. A Pin to See the Peepshow was the
eighth of eleven novels written by the late F. Tennyson Jesse, who
died in 1958.

    Roger Moore, the son of a London policeman, born on Friday,
October 14, 1927, at Adelbert Terrace, Stockwell, South London,
had been on the stage nearly a decade prior to being cast as the
amorous murderer in A Pin to See the Peepshow. Moore arrived in
America in March 1953 and the following month appeared on the
Robert Montgomery Presents telecast of The World by the Tail, with
Diana Lynn and Phyllis Kirk, followed by television appearances on
Hallmark's Hall of Fame productions of Black Chiffon and Julius
Caesar. He would later gain fame as television's Simon Templar on
The Saint series and as Beau Maverick on Maverick. Moore appeared

in several American and English films before succeeding Sean Connery as Agent 007 as the screen's James Bond.

Actor, producer, director Peter Cotes (born Sydney Boulting), the director of London's longest-running play, Agatha Christie's The Mousetrap, originally planned to produce A Pin to See the Peepshow in Manchester in 1948, but England's Lord Chamberlain refused a license for public performance of the play. Two years later, in October, 1950, Cotes became manager, producer, and director of the subscription-sponsored New Boltons Club Theatre in Drayton Gardens, South Kensington, London, where the Lord Chamberlain's official ban of the play was ineffective. Peter Cotes produced and directed a successful production of A Pin to See the Peepshow at New Boltons on May 8, 1951, with settings by Richard Lake and the following cast: Joan Miller (Julia Almond); Maurice Kaufmann (Leo Carr); John Stuart (Herbert Starling); Vi Stevens (Mrs. Almond); Richard Coke (George Almond); Pearl Dadswell (Marian Lestrange); Alan Gordon (Dr. Ackroyd); Hazel Douglas (Anne Ackroyd); Brian Haines (Mr. Ringwood); Doreen Richards (Bertha Starling); Althea Parker (Gipsy Danvers/Wardress); John Westbrook (Embury); Robert Sewell (Dr. Ogilvie); Tamara Owen (Elsa); Bettie Dickson (Lily); Aubrey Dexter (Police Inspector); Joseph Chelton (Prison Governor); Alan T. Aldridge (Police Constable); Donovan Winter (Police Officer)

Canadian-born (Vancouver, British Columbia) Joan Miller (Mrs. Peter Cotes) won high praise for her characterization of Julia Almond, but London's Theatre World found the play "unhappily sordid and squalid" and considered Frank Vosper's 1927 drama People Like Us, based on the Thompson-Bywaters case, "better constructed" with "deeper character studies." Vosper's play ran over a year in Paris but England's Lord Chamberlain refused to license People Like Us after members of the Thompson and Bywaters families claimed it would create renewed anguish and publicity for them. The Lord Chamberlain's ban, based on a general rule to refuse a license for at least three generations if a near relative objects, was lifted, and People Like Us was produced in London in 1929.

It was during the successful engagement of Henry Sherek's production of People Like Us at London's Wyndham's Theatre that Peter Cotes attempted to stage A Pin to See the Peepshow at Manchester's Library Theatre in 1948. H. R. Thompson, the brother of the murdered Percy, wrote to the Lord Chamberlain requesting that both plays be banned immediately. Thompson acknowledged that he had neither seen Vosper's play nor read F. Tennyson Jesse's novel but strongly objected to the subject matter and pleaded for peace for himself and his family. Producer Henry Sherek was summoned to a meeting with Sir Terence Nugent, the Comptroller, and H. R. Thompson in St. James's Palace in September, 1948, and was told Cotes had been denied a license and that rehearsals had stopped on the Manchester production of A Pin to See the Peepshow. Producer

Sherek was also told, "it would be madly complicated unless you take your play off--and at once."

The Lord Chamberlain's office issued a statement, published by London's Daily Express, regarding the hotly contested Thompson-Bywaters dramatizations: "It is a rule to withhold a license from a play dealing with people who lived if a near relative objects. The play People Like Us was licensed only after it had been submitted many times. The Lord Chamberlain consented in the end because more than twenty years had elapsed without any relative coming forward. This play had been running for some time when Thompson's brother objected to the play by Mr. Harwood and Miss Jesse. There could be little point in interfering with the earlier play." But there was.

Henry Sherek was required to relinquish his license and close the profitable People Like Us at Wyndham's Theatre. H. M. Harwood told the press "The censor, having read the book, expressed the opinion that there was nothing in the circumstances dealt with unsuitable for stage production" but angrily observed, "no indication is given as to what degree of consanguinity is necessary in such a case, and what it amounts to is that the Lord Chamberlain makes up his own rules as he goes along." Only after the death of the last of Percy Thompson's relatives, his sister, was the ban on People Like Us and A Pin to See the Peepshow lifted in 1964. The controversy had raged for forty-one years after the hanging of Edith Thompson and her lover, Frederick Bywaters.

Harold Marsh Harwood and F. Tennyson Jesse's drama A Pin to See the Peepshow's one performance on Broadway was deplored by critic John Chapman in his The Best Plays and the Year Book of the Drama in America, which he edited after the death of Burns Mantle, at the age of seventy-four at Forest Hills, New York, on February 9, 1948. Chapman in his compilation Theatre '54 wrote, "Not in several seasons had a Broadway play closed after one performance. A Pin to See the Peepshow was not as bad as this hopeless record indicates. It was professionally written, professionally acted and professionally directed." Chapman praised the performance of Joan Miller as "highly emotional and physically remarkable," adding, "The general critical complaint was that the drama was little more than a documentary, offering little excitement to the audience as Julia's life developed until the final twenty minutes in a police station and in the death cell."

Brooks Atkinson (The New York Times) lauded the performances given by the entire cast and the meticulous staging by Peter Cotes through the intricate thirteen scenes, noting, "Joan Miller gives a flawless performance that becomes powerful in the last two or three scenes." Atkinson, however, felt "A Pin to See the Peepshow never comes to life on the stage until the last fifteen or twenty minutes of a genteel evening," despite acknowledging that the authors "have written a murder drama scrupulously. That speaks well for their ethics but it leaves the theatregoer with a tepid play. The authors have gone to endless trouble to write a character study instead of a melodrama."

People Like Us (Opened November 3, 1929, Strand Theatre, London). Produced by The Repertory Players; A drama written and directed by Frank Vosper
   Marie Ney (Ethel Carter); Henry Oscar (Harold Carter); Atholl Fleming (Rowlie Bateson); Hugh E. Wright (Mr. Underwood); Muriel Asked (Mrs. Underwood); Louise Hampton (Mrs. Bateson); Margery Binner (Ivy); Reginald Gardiner (Dickie Miles); Marion Fawcett (Wardress); H. G. Stoker (The Governor); John Clifford (A Neighbor); Constance Anderson, Josephine Middleton (Two Wardresses)

The play was reopened on December 10, 1929, at London's Art Theatre with the following cast:
   Marie Ney (Ethel Carter); Henry Oscar (Harold Carter); Owen Reynolds (Rowlie Bateson); Alfred Clark (Mr. Underwood); Barbara Gott (Mrs. Underwood); Louise Hampton (Mrs. Bateson); Margery Binner (Ivy Underwood); Kim Peacock (Dickie Miles); Marion Fawcett (Wardress); C. Jervis Walter (The Governor); John Clifford (A Neighbor); Cecily Corbett-Wilson, Daisie Alexander (Two Wardresses)

People Like Us was revived by Henry Sherek at London's Wyndham Theatre on July 6, 1948, directed by Murray MacDonald, with a setting by Anthony Holland, and the following cast:
   Kathleen Michael (Ethel Carter); Clive Morton (Harold Carter); Robert Flemyng (Rowlie Bateson); Miles Malleson (Mr. Underwood); Alison Leggatt (Mrs. Underwood); Olga Lindo (Mrs. Bateson); Anna Turner (Ivy Underwood); George Rose (Dickie Miles); Molly Lumley (Wardress); Derek Anderson (The Governor); Charles Whiteley (A Neighbor);

The following year an American production of People Like Us was mounted, bound for Broadway, but the play collapsed on the road. People Like Us (Opened October 4, 1949, Toronto, Canada; Closed, October 15, 1949, Detroit, Michigan). Produced by William L. Taub, by arrangement with Henry Sherek in association with Brian Doherty; A drama by Frank Vosper; Director, Clarence Derwent; Settings, Raymond Sovey; Costumes, Alice Gibson
   Ann Dvorak (Ethel); Sidney Blackmer (Harold Carter); Hugh Reilly (Rowlie Bateson); Ernest Cossart (Mr. Underwood); Viola Roache (Mrs. Underwood); Mary Young (Mrs. Bateson); Brook Byron (Ivy Miles); Stephen Gray (Dickie Miles); Elfrida Derwent (Wardress); Edward Cooper (The Governor); Arthur Koulias (A Neighbor); Helen Baron (Second Wardress); George Spelvin (Prison Guard)

Frank Vosper acknowledged his play People Like Us was based on the Thompson-Bywaters case, but F. Tennyson Jesse, once a reporter for London's Times and Daily Mail, carefully prefaced her novel A Pin to See the Peepshow with "Every character in this book is entirely fictitious, and no reference whatsoever is intended to any living person." Both plays and novel were based on one of England's most notorious and highly publicized scandals, the Thompson-Bywaters murder case.

Edith Thompson, manager of a London millinery shop, married shipping clerk Percy Thompson in 1916. While on holiday on the Isle of Wight in the summer of 1921, the Thompsons met a twenty-year-old ship's writer employed by the P & O Line personnel office, named Frederick Bywaters. Bywaters moved into the Thompsons' Ilford, Essex, home before sailing to the Far East for P & O in September, 1921. Frederick and Edith had become lovers.

Twenty-eight-year-old Edith wrote passionate and revealing letters to Frederick. Proclamations of her love for him were interspersed with macabre plans for assuring her early widowhood, which she actively pursued by mixing a ground-up light bulb ("big pieces too--not powdered") into Percy's dinner. She encouraged Frederick's ardor and expressed hope that his gnawing jealousy would excite him into "doing something desperate" when he returned to England, assuring him, "I want you to be jealous--he has the right by law, to all that you have the right to by nature and love."

Bywaters returned to England and Edith a year later, and on October 3, 1922, as Edith and Percy were returning from the theatre, Bywaters fatally stabbed Thompson. Remorseful Edith accused her lover of her husband's murder the following day. Frederick and Edith were both charged with the murder of Percy Thompson. Edith's steamy and condemning letters, intent on inciting Frederick to murder, were read to the jury during an emotional and sensational trial at London's Old Bailey in December 1922. The lovers were found guilty. Bywaters was hanged at Pentonville Prison on January 9, 1923, at the exact hour Edith Thompson was hanged at Holloway Prison. Edith Thompson became the last woman to be hanged in England, until the hanging of Ruth Ellis in 1955 and the abolishment of capital punishment in the United Kingdom.

Twenty-eight-year-old Mrs. Ruth Ellis's passionately violent two-year affair with twenty-five-year-old David Blakely, an upper-class, possessive, and arrogant race-car driver, culminated in a miscarriage, depression, and insane jealousy of David's continuing promiscuity. Ruth fatally shot David for his constant attentions to other women, and on June 21, 1955, she was convicted of murder. Ruth Ellis was hanged at Holloway Prison in London on July 13, 1955, amidst great public clamor for criminal reform. Home Minister Gwilym Lloyd George refused to commute Ruth's death sentence despite vociferous indignation and angry outcries for abolishment of capital punishment. The House of Commons on February 16, 1956, voted 293 to 262 to abolish capital punishment in the United Kingdom, and on March 21, 1957, the law was signed by Queen Elizabeth II.

Ruth Ellis was the last woman to be hanged in Great Britain. Her sordid story was loosely fictionalized in the 1956 film Yield to the Night, with Diana Dors and Michael Craig as the ill-fated lovers. In March 1985, Twentieth Century-Fox released Dance with a Stranger, written by Shelagh Delaney, which minutely documented the Ellis-Blakely case. Miranda Richardson portrayed Ruth Ellis and Rupert Everett was cast as David Blakely.

The British Broadcasting Corporation produced A Pin to See the Peepshow for television during the 1973-1974 season. The four fifty-minute episodes were televised by America's Public Broadcasting System as one feature on March 8, 1975. Produced in England by Rex Tucker, F. Tennyson Jesse's novel was adapted for television by Elaine Morgan and was directed by Raymond Menmuir, with the following cast:

Francesca Annis (Julia Starling); John Duttine (Leo Carr); Bernard Hepton (Herbert Starling); Mary Chester (Mrs. Almond); John Nettleton (George); Marian Melford (Marian Lestrange); Ron Pember (Almond); Petronella Barker (Anne Ackroyd); Anthony Rowe (Julia's Counsel); Georgine Anderson (Bertha Starling); Queenie Watts (Mrs. Humble); Keith Drinkel (Alfie); Kenneth Breda (Crown's Counsel); Rosemary Blake (Elsa); Maggie Flint (Mildred); Victor Brooks (Police Inspector); Frank Jarvis (Policeman)

* * *

A PLACE FOR POLLY (Ethel Barrymore Theatre, April 18, 1970). Produced by Ken Gaston and Leonard Goldberg with David G. Meyers; A comedy by Lonnie Coleman; Director, Ronny Graham; Setting and lighting; Clarke Dunham; Costumes, Frank Thompson; Incidental music, William Fisher; Hairstylist, R. Rusty Bonacorso; Associate producer, Henry Stern; Production coordinator, Joel Dein; Production assistant, Brian Richmond; General Manager, Helen Richards; Company manager, Jesse Long; Stage managers, D. W. Koehler, Didi Francis
Marian Mercer (Polly); Cathryn Damon (Angela); Konrad Matthaei (Otis); Alan Manson (Tony); Evelyn Russell (Joyce); Robert Moberly (Dan Da Vinci); Daniel Keyes (Mr. Bigelow); Dortha Duckworth (Mrs. Bigelow); William Mooney (George)

Bitchy, globe-trotting Pulitzer Prize-winning foreign correspondent Angela arrives at her placidly liberal sister Polly's Greenwich Village home with her new book, based on South Africa's apartheid dilemma. Polly's ruthlessly ambitious publisher husband, Otis, senses an immediate best-seller in Angela's first novel, which would assure him the vice-presidency of his company. Polly sponsors and encourages young South African writer Dan Da Vinci and discovers

Angela has used Da Vinci's unpublished, nonfiction manuscript for her first novel. Rebelling at the constant domination of her glamorous sister, Polly exposes Angela's plagiarism. Equally revolted at her husband's lack of integrity and frivolous flirtations, Polly leaves her home, seeking a place for herself in the world, returning to her former job as Broadway producer Tony's secretary.

John J. O'Connor (The Wall Street Journal) wrote about A Place for Polly, "There are a few funny lines, some hints of a promising plot and one or two capable performances." Richard Watts (New York Post) described Coleman's play as "a tepid comedy--which is not disastrous but is far from stimulating." Douglas Watt (Daily News) reported, "The author has come up with two or three fair gag lines, but most of the writing ranges from lackluster to tasteless." Clive Barnes (The New York Times) found "Nothing terribly wrong with A Place for Polly, yet there is also nothing too much right about it--Everything is fundamentally false, and the producers should have recognized this at a first reading--you will see nothing that is as poor a value for your money as A Place for Polly."

Lonnie Coleman, born William Lawrence Coleman in Bartow, Georgia, on August 2, 1920, had his first play, Jolly's Progress, based on his 1953 novel Adam's Way, produced on Broadway by the Theatre Guild and Arthur Loew on December 5, 1959. Featuring Eartha Kitt, Wendell Corey, and Anne Revere, Jolly's Progress ceased at nine performances. A Place for Polly was a new play only to Broadway. The play had been produced in 1963 for the summer theatre circuit by Harold Prince and Howard Erskine, under the title of She Didn't Say Yes. Directed by Harold Prince, with a setting designed by Curtiss Cowan, lighting by V. C. Fuqua, and costumes by Christina Giannini, She Didn't Say Yes starred Joan Caulfield and Peggy Cass.

She Didn't Say Yes (Summer, 1963).
  Joan Hackett (Polly); Joan Caulfield (Angela); Peggy Cass (Joyce); William Redfield (Otis); Jordan C. Harney (Dan); Alan Manson (Tony); Grace Carney (Thelma); Edwin Cooper (Alfred); Joe Ponazecki (George); Pearl Singer (Lorraine)

She Didn't Say Yes was revived six years later for another tryout tour on summer theatre stages, with Joan Hackett as Polly, Betsy Von Furstenberg as Angela, Darryl Hickman as Otis, and with Michael Hadge as Dan, and Evelyn Russell as Joyce. The 1969 production was directed by Arthur A. Seidelman and was reviewed as getting older but not wiser.

After seven years of tryouts and a change of title, to A Place for Polly, there was little improvement on the comedy. Leonard Harris (WCBS) recognized Coleman's fluctuation from Ibsen's drama to Neil Simon's comedy but with A Place for Polly "neither choice seems open to him--A Place for Polly is a hokey place. In it there is little humor, less truth and almost no sign of life."

PLAY ME A COUNTRY SONG (Virginia Theatre, June 27, 1982). Produced by Frederick R. Selch; A musical with book by Jay Broad; Music and lyrics, John R. Briggs and Harry Manfredini; Director, Jerry Adler; Settings, David Chapman; Lighting, Marc B. Weiss; Costumes, Carol Oditz; Choreography, Margo Sappington; Musical direction and vocal arrangements, Phil Hall; Sound, Robert Kerzman; Associate producer and casting director, Cheryl Raab; Wardrobe, Josephine Zampedri; Production assistants, Andrea Selch, Jeannie Banker; General manager, Robert S. Fishko; Stage managers, Alisa Adler, Jonathan Weiss; Development supervision, Milton Moss
   Louisa Flaningam (Lizzie); Kenneth Ames (Buster); Rene Clements (Jerome); Reed Jones (Norm); Mary Gordon Murray (Ellen); Stephen Crain (Tony); Jay Huguely (Fred); Ronn Carroll (Howard); Katen Mason (Frances); Mary Jo Catlett (Penny); Candace Tovar (Meg); Rick Thomas (Hank)
SONGS: Sail Away; Why Does a Woman Leave Her Man; Rodeo Dreams; Waitin' Tables; Eighteen-Wheelin' Baby; Playing for Position; Just Thought I'd Call; Sing-a-Long; If You Don't Mind; Play Me a Country Song; Coffee, Beer and Whiskey; Only a Fool; Big City; You Can't Get Ahead; My Sweet Woman; You Have to Get It Out to Get Away; All of My Dreams; Rodeo Rider

   Eight regular customers gather to commemorate the closing night of Woody's Rocky Mountain Colorado Truck Stop due to its isolation by a new interstate highway. Proprietor Fred and waitress Lizzie encourage their faithful customers to have one last fling and enliven the closing of Woody's with an all-night impromptu song-and-dance celebration, while exposing their personal lives to everyone.

   Clive Barnes (New York Post) dismissed Play Me a Country Song as "depressingly jolly and jolly depressing." Frank Rich (The New York Times) reported, "It's a series of ersatz country-and-western songs, linked together by a book that is rife with maudlin down-home anecdotes and sub-Grand Ole Opry gags." While acknowledging that "country-flavored music has its place on Broadway--as Carol Hall proved in her fine score for The Best Little Whorehouse in Texas," Frank Rich felt that "Play Me a Country Song could set this cause back 10 years" and "Jerry Adler's direction of this show could set the musical theater back further than that." Douglas Watt (Daily News) noted, "In order to make what is essentially a staged song-and-dance recital qualify as a full-fledged show, a silly, half-hearted book has been provided by Jay Broad."

   Brendan Gill (The New Yorker) described Play Me a Country Song located in "Nowheresville--somewhere between Denver and Phoenix this sorry little nonentity of a musical might have found a natural home; certainly it didn't belong on or near, Broadway."

RAINBOW JONES (Music Box Theatre, February 13, 1974). Produced by Rubykate, Inc., in association with Phil Gillin and Gene Bambic; A musical fantasy with Book, Music and Lyrics by Jill Williams; Director, Gene Persson; Setting, Richard Ferrer; Lighting, Spencer Mosse; Costumes, James Berton Harris; Assistant to producers, Warren Knowlton; Musical direction and orchestrations, Danny Holgate; Musical staging, Sammy Bayes; Company manager, Ken Meyers; Stage managers, Kate Pollock; Ferne Bork

   Ruby Persson (Rainbow Jones); Peter Kastner (Joey Miller); Gil Robbins (C. A. Fox); Peggy Hagen Lamprey (Leona); Andy Rohrer (Bones) Stephanie Silver (Cardigan); Kay St. Germain (Aunt Felicity); Daniel Keyes (Uncle Ithaca)

SONGS: A Little Bit of Me in You; Free and Easy; Do Unto Others; It's So Nice; Bad Breath; I'd Like to Know You Better; Alone, At Last, Alone; Her Name Is Leona; We All Need Love; The Only Man for the Job; What a Little While; One Big Happy Family; Who Needs the Love of a Woman?

   Orphan Beatrice "Rainbow" Jones loses her job at Bloomingdales and, to escape the wrath of her television-addicted Aunt Felicity, escapes to Central Park to daydream with a book of Aesop's Fables. In her fantasy, Rainbow becomes friends with an imaginary lamb, Cardigan, C. A. Fox, Bones, a dog, and a friendly lioness named Leona. Rainbow falls in love with Central Park jogger Joey Miller, a Madison Avenue copywriter. Suspicious of Rainbow's animated conversations with imaginary animals, Joey doubts her sanity. Rainbow runs away to her Uncle Ithaca's Ohio farm but then returns to discover that Joey, by opening Aesop's Fables, has learned to talk with her animal friends, and that he is in love with her.

   Richard Watts (New York Post) found Rainbow Jones "always pleasant but nevertheless disappointing," describing it as "far from being a disaster--but it isn't the brilliant show it might have been with greater skill." Clive Barnes (The New York Times) classified the show as a "coy and simpering little musical--the kind of a show that gives people proclaiming the death of Broadway something to point to. The book is as bad as the music, and the lyrics are as bad as either." Douglas Watt (Daily News) suggested that "for the common good," Miss Williams should be "denied access either to a typewriter or a musical instrument of any kind."

* * *

RAW MEAT (Provincetown Playhouse, March 22, 1933). Produced by the Provincetown Playhouse Guild; A comedy by Myla Jo Closser and Homer Little; Director, William A. Williams; Settings, Hugh Mason; Lighting, Kirk Glover; Costumes, Clara Hannington; Directorial assistant, John Turner; Animal heads, Frederick Fox; Stage manager, Lawrence Menkin; Production executive, Loyd Gough

   Thomas Beck (Junior); Jean Clarendon (Peter Drake); Margaret Hatfield (Jo Drake); Alfred Jenkin (Fergus); Betty Upthegrove

(Babs Walker); John Clymer (Lenny O'Neill); Hal Don (Hiram Hall); James Dunmore (Birbal); Lawrence Menkin (Earl Bonaparte); May Marshall (Ann)

Junior Drake is considered a coward by his famous and retired explorer parents because of his quiet nature and preference for photographing butterflies in the Connecticut fields. A lion named Hero escapes from a visiting circus and the Drakes and their intrepid explorer guests find frantic if flimsy excuses for not prowling the landscape at night in search of the beast. Junior astounds everyone when he singlehandedly captures the escaped, if relatively tame, circus lion.

John Mason Brown (New York Post) reported Raw Meat had "its scattered moments of comic invention, but suffers from being a one-act idea that is stretched to the breaking point in three thin and forced acts," and he described the writing as "far-fetched to the point of silliness." Lewis Nichols (The New York Times) wrote "Raw Meat has a good many expert lines and a good many fine situations," but he felt better plays might eventually be written about the "exploring racket--There also can be written much worse ones."

* * *

REPRISE (Vanderbilt Theatre, May 1, 1935). Produced by Frederick E. Mailey; A drama by W. Daingerfield Bristol; Director, George Sommes; Setting, John Biddle Whitelaw
    Donald Randolph (Roy Carter); George Blackwood (Peter); Barbara O'Neill (Julie) Zamah Cunningham (Madame Carter)

Peter's suicide by leaping from the fifteenth-floor Carter penthouse is prevented by Roy Carter, who resolves to enrich the handsome young man's restored life. Roy falls in love with Peter, who lusts after Roy's unhappily married sister Julie. Needing money to run off with Julie, Peter sells Roy's gift of stock in his lucrative automotive-accessories business to Roy's competitor Collins, who gains control of the company. Julie, enraged at Peter's treachery, declines his proposal and deserts him. Madame, Roy and Julie's brandy-swigging grandmother, urges Peter to reprise his previously planned leap from life. Over the playing of "Claire de Lune," Roy, Julie, and Madame quietly discuss the invasion of the perfidious Peter, unaware he has followed Madame's advice and committed suicide.

The reviews for Reprise might have driven Kentucky-bred playwright Bristol, who claimed he could write only on the subway, to reprise the final act of his protagonist, Peter. John Mason Brown (The Evening Post) called Reprise "one of the most tiresome offerings of the year--the curtain follows Peter's example and falls. The real truth is it ought never to have gone up." Robert Garland (New York World-Telegram) dismissed the play, saying "Sophomoric is probably the word which should be hurled as an epithet at Mr. Bristol's play-

writing head." Brooks Atkinson (The New York Times) called
Reprise "The season's bitterest pill--Badly written, it is also badly
acted, which prevented it from being as unsavory as had been hoped
for."

Bernard Sobel (New York Mirror) added, "A monstrous usurpation of other people's time--And I, for one, hereby fervently hope that there will be no reprise." Gilbert W. Gabriel (The American) denounced the play as "a cheerful little swatch of funeral crepe." Richard Lockridge (The Evening Sun) reported, "There can be little doubt that there is, somewhere, a message in it all, but I fear I missed it. I did not miss the fact that it is a pretty bad play, which is, after all, something." Whitney Bolton (New York Telegraph) summarized the consensus with "Reprise is a play about which the least said the better."

Reprise had been tested in January 1934 by the Mayfair Players at Dobbs Ferry. Produced by Vera Murray in association with Brock Pemberton, Reprise was directed by William MacFadden with a setting by John Biddle Whitelaw; General manager, C. B. Maddock and Production manager, LeRoy Bailey. The cast included, James Bell (Roy Carter); Raymond Hackett (Peter); Blanche Sweet (Julie), and Marie Kenney as Madame. Later the play was again tested on the straw-hat circuit, with Guido Nadzo as Roy, George Blackwood as Peter, Betty Starbuck as Julie, and Zamah Cunningham as Madame.

* * *

REUNION (Nora Bayes Theatre, April 11, 1938). Produced by Kenneth W. Robinson and Norman H. White, Jr.; A drama by Ambrose Elwell, Jr.; Director, Freeman Hammond; Settings, George Pearson; Production assistant, Winifred Cameron; Stage manager, Blanche Haring
    Andrew J. Fox, Jr. (John Edwards); Robert J. Lance (Von Machen); Dodee Wick (Ruth Wilton); Cleda Hallett (Helen Newton); Arthur Holland (Bill Newton); Blanche Haring (Mary Carlin); Gilbert King (Drake Carlin); Haakon Ogle (Ebel); Ted E. Peckham (McEwen); Dearon Darney (Brules); Donald MacDonald (Landlord); Wilbur Valsch (Ahrend); Raymond Nelson (Ambulance Driver); James Young (Guard)

John Edwards graduates from Harvard in 1927 and is employed by the Von Machen Chemical Company in Berlin, Germany, to perfect a poison gas for the Nazis. John rebels against the Nazi doctrines and rejects the love of fellow American chemist Ruth Wilton. Edwards returns to America for the decennial reunion of his college class at Harvard and weds Helen Newton, the widow of one of his former classmates.

Harvard University's 1920-graduate Norman H. White, Jr.'s lone Broadway play, Reunion, was written under the pseudonym of

162 / Ring Round the Bathtub

Ambrose Elwell, Jr. and was originally tested at Brighton Beach, with twenty supers as undergraduates caroling "Fair Harvard." Wolcott Gibbs (New Yorker) described Reunion as marking "the year's apex in critical suffering" and Robert Coleman (Daily Mirror) called White's drama "a deuce of a dull evening."

Richard Watts, Jr. (New York Post) reported, "It is announced that the actors are not members of Actors' Equity, which should make Equity pretty happy." Brooks Atkinson's (The New York Times) tongue-in-cheek review noted, "The show was picketed before curtain time. 'It is not cricket to picket.' This was the only vulgar note in the evening--Several cultivated actors play Mr. White's Class Day charade with the poise and earnestness of educated people--It deserves a regular Harvard cheer and a dive into the class day fountains after the yard has been cleared of the women folks."

Benjamin P. Schulberg purchased the film rights to Reunion as a starring vehicle for Sylvia Sidney and Herbert Marshall, who had been teamed in the screen version of Samson Raphaelson's play Accent on Youth in 1935. White's Reunion did not reach the screen.

* * *

RING ROUND THE BATHTUB (Martin Beck Theatre, April 29, 1972). Produced by Jacqueline Babbin and Jay Wolf; A comedy by Jane Trahey; Director, Harold Stone; Setting, Ed Wittstein; Lighting, Roger Morgan; Costumes, Joseph G. Aulisi; Sound, Gary Harris; Hairstylist, Joe Tubens; Production assistant, Ellen Siegel Perkiss; General Manager, Victor Samrock; Company manager, Morry Efron; Stage managers, Steven Zwegbaum, Joel Wolfe
    Elizabeth Ashley (Maggie Train); Richard Mulligan (Dan Train); Carol Kane (Esme Train); Eileen Kearney (Darcy Train); Carmen Mathews (replaced Ruth McDevitt) (Gran); Louis Turenne (Louis Rockosy); Margaret Linn (Cousin Esther); Alek Primrose (Mr. Enright); James Greene (Captain Harfeather); Kate Wilkinson (Nurse Samson); John Gannon (Radio Commentator)

Turmoil erupts in the Irish-American, Catholic Train family during the Great Depression in Chicago when liberated and liberal Maggie's campaigning for a Democratic Reform political candidate results in her blustering Republican husband, Dan, losing his job as a city fireman. Teenaged daughter Esme enjoys her excessively morose hypochondria, while the Train's younger daughter, Darcy, becomes proficient in writing innumerable twenty-five-words-or-less contest letters and acquiring unclaimed birthday cakes at half-price, after ordering them under fictitious names. The bleak prospects of the Train family are ameliorated when Darcy's letter to the Chicago Tribune, detailing the family's justifiable accreditation as the City's Neediest Case, wins first prize on Christmas Eve.

Ring Round the Bathtub had its world premiere at Nina Vance's

Alley Theatre in Houston, Texas, on December 3, 1970, with a cast including James Broderick, Jeannette Clift, Mary K. Isaacs, Gertrude Flynn, and others. The Jacqueline Babbin-Jay Wolf production of Jane Trahey's comedy opened in Boston on April 8, 1972, to one mildly good review. After three previews at New York's Martin Beck Theatre, Ring Round the Bathtub exposed itself to the cleansing of the critics.

During the 1930's and 1940's, Broadway abounded in successful family plays exposing, among others, the whacky households of Gertrude Tonkonogy's Three-Cornered Moon, Kaufman and Hart's perennially hilarious Pulitzer Prize comedy, You Can't Take It With You, and Mary Chase's account of the addled Dowd family and their invisible pet, Harvey. Howard Lindsay and Russel Crouse's endearing, long-running hit Life With Father and Eugene O'Neill's Ah, Wilderness!, which later also succeeded as the musical comedy Take Me Along, joined a series of remembrances-of-things-past with John Van Druten's I Remember Mama and George S. Kaufman and John P. Marquand's The Late George Apley. It was also an era for showcasing precocious youth in such fare as F. Hugh Herbert's Kiss and Tell and Jerome Chodorov and Joseph Fields's comedies Junior Miss and My Sister Eileen. Over nearly a half-century, nostalgia had paled and Jane Trahey's comedy Ring Round the Bathtub did not recapture it.

Brendan Gill (The New Yorker) found neither the title nor the play amusing, claiming, "Jane Trahey is without the slightest trace of talent as a writer, and she also lacks invention." Successful advertising writer Jane Trahey's play was obviously a memoir of the same fond recall but far inferior to Kathryn Forbes's Mama's Bank Account, which John Van Druten adapted to the stage as I Remember Mama. Mel Gussow (The New York Times) found Ring Round the Bathtub, "the kind of unfashionable nostalgic piece that few would write today--at least with any hope of getting as far as Broadway. If better written, the play might be considered warm and affectionate. Instead it is, at its best, modestly appealing."

Ring Round the Bathtub," wrote Richard Watts (New York Post) "is not my conception of an attractive title for a play, but then it isn't my idea of an attractive play." Douglas Watt (Daily News) called it "a play of small consequence" which "tries hard to be a family comedy, but its heart isn't in it."

* * *

THE RITZ (Henry Miller Theatre, May 2, 1983). Produced by Bavar/Culver Productions in association with James R. Cunningham; A comedy by Terrence McNally; Director Michael Bavar; Setting, Gordon Micunis; Lighting, Todd Lichtenstein; Costumes, George Potts; Choreographer, Robert Speller; Men's Wardrobe, Egon von Furstenberg; Music, Man Parrish; Production and directorial assistant, Donald

Roberts; Production assistants, Dan Zittel, Pierce Bihm; Casting,
Larry Goossen; Sound, David Kobernuss; Wardrobe, Terry Snyder;
General management, Kingwill Office; Company manager, Leonard
A. Mulhern; Stage managers, T. L. Boston, Arlene Wege
> Holly Woodlawn (Googie Gomez); Joey Faye (Abe); Don Potter
> (Claude); Michael Greer (Chris); Taylor Reed (Gaetano Proclo);
> Casey Donovan (Michael Brick); Pi Douglass (Tiger); Roland Rodriguez (Duff); Jan Meredith (Maurine); Danny Dennis (Carmine
> Vespucci); Dolores Wilson (Vivian Proclo); Peter Radon (Crisco);
> Paige Edwards (Sheldon Farenthold); John Koons (Chacha); John
> Burke (Butch); George Sardi (Patron in Chaps); Tom Terwilliger
> (Patron from Sheridan Square)

    Honoring his Mafioso father's dying request to "get" despised
son-in-law Proclo, Carmine Vespucci trails his middle-aged Cleveland
garbage-collecting brother-in-law, Gaetano Proclo, to a gay Manhattan
bath called "The Ritz" where obese Proclo seeks uneasy protection
and shaky sanctuary. There, Proclo meets former army buddy Claude
Perkins and is actively pursued by homosexual patrons. Singularly
untalented Puerto Rican singer Googie Gomez, engaged to perform
by the pool on talent night, mistakes Proclo for a Broadway producer,
and young, falsetto-voiced detective Michael Brick, hired by Carmine
by telephone, mistakes Carmine for Proclo. Proclo's beefy wife,
Vivian, is quickly divested of her mink coat by Claude, who cons
Proclo and oversexed, promiscuous Chris into entering the Ritz's
talent contest, which they win with a parody of the Andrews Sisters.
Carmine halts the performance with a pistol, but he is prevented
from killing Proclo by the Ritz's clerk Maurine, who informs Carmine
that "The Ritz" is one of the Vespucci family's lucrative properties.
Vivian rescues her terrified husband and Carmine is arrested in a
raid.

    The original production of The Ritz opened at the Longacre
Theatre on January 20, 1975, and had completed 398 performances
when it closed on January 4, 1976.

The Ritz. Produced by Adela Holzer; A comedy by Terrence McNally;
Director, Robert Drivas; Settings and Costumes, Lawrence King,
Michael H. Yeargan; Lighting, Martin Aronstein; Assistant to director,
Tony de Santis; Production assistant, Gary Keeper; Wardrobe supervisor, Mariane Torres; Production supervisor, Mitch Miller; Sound,
Lenny Will; Company manager, Leo K. Cohen; Stage managers, Larry
Forde, Steve Beckler; Hairstylist, Vidal Sassoon; General managements, Theatre, Now, Inc, Edward H. Davis, William Court Cohen
> Rita Moreno (succeeded briefly by Chi Chi Navarro) (Googie
> Gomez); Jack Weston (succeeded for two weeks by George Dzundza) (Gaetano Proclo); Jerry Stiller (succeeded by Mike Kellin)
> (Carmine Vespucci); F. Murray Abraham (succeeded for two weeks
> by Robert Drivas) (Chris); Stephen Collins (Michael Brick); Paul
> B. Price (Claude Perkins); John Everson (succeeded by Larry
> Gilman) (Tiger); Christopher J. Brown (Duff); George Dzundza

(Abe); Hortensia Colorado (Maurine); Ruth Jaroslow (succeeded by Antonia Rey) (Vivian Proclo); Tony de Santis (Sheldon Farenthold); Ron Abel (Pianist); Bruce Bauer (succeeded by Thomas Leopold) (Policeman); John Remme (succeeded by John Minton) (Patron in Chaps); Richard Boccelli (Crisco); Steve Scott (Patron from Sheridan Square)
SONGS: Everything's Coming Up Roses (Styne-Sondheim); Life Is Just a Bowl of Cherries (Brown-Henderson); The Three Caballeros (Esperon-Cortazar-Gilbert); Laugh Funny Funny (Mark-Hudson)

PROGRAM NOTE: "Mr. Drivas wishes to express his gratitude to Messrs. Rossini, Verdi, Leoncavallo, Puccini, Brown, Henderson, Hudson, Styne and Sondheim."

The Ritz's producer, Adela Holzer, was convicted of seven counts of grand larceny after a six-week trial and in March 1981 was sentenced to prison for a period of two to six years.

Born in St. Petersburg, Florida, November 3, 1939, playwright Terrence McNally's plays And Things That Go Bump in the Night (1965) and Noon (1968) were not notable theatrical milestones on Broadway. His Off-Broadway short plays Tour (one of eleven brief plays included under the general title Collision Course), Sweet Eros, Witness, and Cuba Si (1968) were also not notable. His short play Next, performed with Elaine May's play Adaptation, was an Off-Broadway success for 707 performances and Where Has Tommy Flowers Gone?, produced Off-Broadway in 1971, had 78 performances. Produced by Adela Holzer and directed by Robert Drivas, with scenery and costumes by Michael H. Yeargan and Lawrence King (all of whom would be represented in the same assignments for 1975's production of The Ritz), McNally's comedy Bad Habits played 64 performances at the Astor Place Theatre before moving to Broadway's Booth Theatre on May 5, 1974, to complete 176 performances. Broadway, Broadway, McNally's 1978 comedy expired during a tryout at Philadelphia's Shubert Theatre but was revived for fifteen performances at Manhattan's Actors and Directors Theatre beginning November 18, 1982, under the title of It's Only a Play.

The Ritz was originally tested at Yale's Repertory Theatre under the title of The Tubs. The farce delighted Broadway for almost a year although the film version of The Ritz failed to capture the fast-paced lunacy under the proscenium. Why, seven years later, a Broadway revival of the farce seemed appropriate or vital is questionable. The revival lacked the vitality given the comedy by the original cast and the 1983 players were unequal to the farce.

Mel Gussow (The New York Times) correctly observed, "The Ritz should have been given a longer rest" and found the revival's "problem is not so much in any single performance as in the insistence of Michael Bavar's production, which is about as subtle as a wet towel," and, he added, "Of the three versions of the show I have

seen, this is easily the least amusing and the most overbearing."
Cast in Rita Moreno's hilarious role of Googie Gomez was Holly Woodlawn (born Harold Danhakl in Puerto Rico) a transvestite who had appeared in Andy Warhol's appropriately named film Trash which, like all of Warhol's cinematic nonsense, came under Pauline Kael's keen description of "time killers on the way to the grave." Gussow classified Holly Woodlawn's performance as the inept Puerto Rican singer as "not bad, but he is not Googie."

When The Ritz closed on Broadway after nearly a year's run, eight members of the cast [*see cast list below] left for England's Twickenham Studio to film McNally's merry romp. Produced by Warner Brothers and Courtyard Films; Producer, Denis O'Dell; Director, Richard Lester; Screenplay, based on his play of the same name, by Terrence McNally; Photography, Paul Wilson; Production designer, Phillip Harrison; Assistant director, Dusty Symonds; Costumes, Vangie Harrison; Special effects, Colin Chilvers; Music director and arranger, Ken Thorne; Makeup, Paul Rabiger; Stunt arranger, Paul Weston; Production manager, Barrie Melrose; Sound editor, Don Sharpe; Sound recorders, Roy Charman, Gerry Humphreys; Songs recorded by C. T. Wilkinson
   *Rita Moreno (Googie Gomez); *Jack Weston (Gaetano Proclo); *Jerry Stiller (Carmine Vespucci); *F. Murray Abraham (Chris); *Paul B. Price (Claude); *John Everson (Tiger); *Christopher J. Brown (Duff); *Tony De Santis (Sheldon Farenthold); Kaye Ballard (Vivian Proclo); Treat Williams (Michael Brick); Dave King (Abe); Bessie Love (Maurine); Ben Aris (Patron with Bicycle); Peter Butterworth (Patron in Chaps); Ronnie Brody (Small Patron); Hal Gallili (Patron with Cigar); George Coulouris (Old Man Vespucci); Leon Greene (Muscle-Bound Patron); Freddie Earle (Disgruntled Patron); John Ratzenberger, Chris Harris (Patrons); Hugh Fraser (Disc Jockey); Bart Allison (Old Priest); Samantha Weyson (Gilda Proclo); Richard Holmes (Pianist)

The Ritz, like many previous Broadway comedies transferred to the screen, lost a good deal of its zest and impact. British critic John Pym reported, "Richard Lester's Ritz--seems a badly stage-managed farce (for most of the running time, it simply doesn't work fast enough)" but it "still retains the outline of a well-made farce. The Ritz is above all redolent with waspish self-parody--Lester's heavy hand cannot, however, completely dispel the gutsy exuberance of McNally's script. Rita Moreno, in particular, is a consistent gum-chewing pleasure." Critic Desmond Ryan, while admiring the skill and expertise of Lester's films A Hard Day's Night and The Three Musketeers, felt in The Ritz the director had permitted his actors to "proceed unbridled" with Rita Moreno "the film's one engaging element," but, he added, "The emphasis which this kind of farce requires in the theatre is magnified into the absurd by the camera. In every way, this sorry film has turned The Ritz into a flophouse."

The Ritz was similar to but more hilarious than Avery Hopwood and Charlton Andrews' half-a-century-old comedy Ladies' Night (In a Turkish Bath) which opened on August 9, 1920, at Broadway's Eltinge Theatre, for 375 performances. Adapted to the London stage by Austin Melford and Douglas Furber, Ladies' Night completed 165 performances. Ladies' Night in a Turkish Bath was successfully filmed by First National Pictures in 1928, and in 1942 the play was adapted by Cyrus Wood as Good Night, Ladies. Good Night, Ladies ran nearly two years in Chicago and opened at Broadway's Royale Theatre on January 17, 1945, to play 78 performances.

Terrence McNally's farce, originally titled The Tubs, premiered in New Haven early in January 1974, at the Yale Repertory Theatre. Directed by Anthony Holland; Setting and costumes by Michael H. Yeargan; Lighting by Barb Harris; Sound by Fred Goldsmith; Production stage manager, Frank S. Torok
  Michael Vale (Gaetano Proclo); Stephanie Cotsirilos (Rita "Googie" Gomez); Jerome Dempsey (Carmine Vespucci); Ted Tally (Michael Brick); Joseph Costa (Abe); Kurt Kasznar (Sheldon Farenthold, M.D.); Charles Levis (Tiger); Eric McFarland (Chris); Marion Paone (Vivian Proclo); Frederic Warriner (Claude Perkins); John J. Brown (Duff); Jeremy Geidt (Arthur Steelwood Poe)

Mel Gussow (The New York Times) admired The Tubs, describing the play as "a free-wheeling entertainment--Terrence McNally has written a spirited Feydeauvian farce...."

* * *

THE ROAD TOGETHER (Frazee Theatre, January 17, 1924). Produced by A. H. Woods; A drama by George Middleton; Scenery, Dickson Morgan; Stage Manager, Willard Jensen
  Marjorie Rambeau (Dora Kent); A. E. Anson (Wallace Kent); H. Reeves-Smith (Tom Porter); Ivy Troutman (Julia Deering); John Dwyer (Warren); Harry Minturn (Fred Safford); Charles W. Guthrie (George Gilmore); William Balfour (Fred Taintor); Robert Adams (Armour Deering); Ethel Tucker (Mary)

Dora Kent rejects the man she loves to marry ambitious lawyer Wallace Kent. Over the years she makes many sacrifices to assure Wallace's success but reveals the truth of their marriage-of-convenience when he plans to throw away his career as district attorney by embracing political corruption. Wallace confesses he, too, has always loved another woman and proposes a separation. Without love, Dora and Wallace have clawed their way to the top and have become accustomed to and dependent on one another and they decide to remain on the road together.

"Matrimony has never seemed quite as tedious as this Road Together," reported John Corbin (The New York Times). Time magazine called the drama "a rather depressing chapter in the dramatic adventures of Marjorie Rambeau. She was forced to fight her way through the tangling verbal underbrush of a three-act jungle planted by George Middleton and nourished to a state of public display by A. H. Woods."

Producer Al H. Woods announced the one-performance closing of The Road Together "at the request of George Middleton, the author, who was dissatisfied with the performance given on opening night." Veteran actress Marjorie Rambeau went up in her lines, mispronounced words and gave what was termed an "indifferent" performance. Rambeau's performance appeared to be more than simply first-night jitters and her erratic performance affected the rest of the cast. The following day A. H. Woods canceled Rambeau's $1,500-a-week salary. The actress's physician, Dr. Max Wolf, claimed she had suffered a nervous breakdown. At the time of The Road Together, Marjorie Rambeau was involved in a divorce from Hugh Dilman after four years of marriage which had followed a tempestuous five-year marriage to Charles Willard McLaughlin, better known as Willard Mack, author-actor-playwright.

San Francisco-born (July 15, 1889) Marjorie Rambeau was a fine actress who had attained stardom on Broadway in several plays, Sadie Love (1915); Cheating Cheaters (1916); Eyes of Youth (1917); Daddy's Gone A-Hunting (1921); The Goldfish (1922) and others. She became a star of the silent screen in 1917 and in 1930 returned to Hollywood to appear in more than fifty films, including Academy Award nominations as Best Supporting Actress in 1940's Primrose Path and 1953's Torch Song. Marjorie Rambeau's acting career had spanned seventy years when she died on July 7, 1970, at the age of eighty, in Palm Springs, California.

George Middleton, in his 1947 autobiography These Things Are Mine, recalled about his nervous star of The Road Together, "Though she lacked soul, she could assume its trappings. Beautiful, too, and eye-arresting, she impressed by the commanding way she moved about. Mistress of stage strategy, gained from hard years in stock, she could handle resourcefully almost any demand of emotion or comedy. With vitality and a perfectly controlled voice she had become so popular that her presence in a play guaranteed it a public." The Road Together was not symbolic of continued compatible traveling by Mr. Middleton and Miss Rambeau. A great calamity (besides The Road Together) was Marjorie Rambeau's unbelievable refusal in 1922 to play the role of Sadie Thompson in John Colton and Clemence Randolph's dramatization of W. Somerset Maugham's short story Miss Thompson, called Rain.

Playwright George Middleton was a founder of the Dramatist Guild whose plays, among others, included Polly with a Past (1917); Adam and Eva (1919); and The Cave Girl (1920), co-authored with Guy Bolton. Middleton and Bolton also adapted Pierre Saisson's French play The Light of the World in 1920. With A. E. Thomas, Middleton wrote The Big Pond in 1928 and, ten years later, Paterson,

New Jersey-born Middleton adapted Marcelle Maurette's French play Madame Capet to the English-speaking stage. George Middleton died at the age of eighty-seven on December 23, 1967.

The Road Together was originally produced by Thomas Wilkes at Los Angeles's Majestic Theatre on September 23, 1923, directed by George Middleton, with scenery by Dickson Morgan
  Marjorie Rambeau (Dora Kent); Richard Tucker (Wallace Kent); H. Reeves-Smith (Tom Porter); Maude Leone (Julia Deering); Robert Adams (Armour Deering); Arthur Rutledge (Warren); Albert Roscoe (Fred Safford); Ferdinand Munier (George Gilmore); Willard Jensen (Fred Taintor); Marie Baker (Mary)

* * *

SATELLITE (Bijou Theatre, November 20, 1935). Produced by Edward Davidow and John Cameron; A farce by Kerry Shaw and Joseph Mitchell; Director, John Cameron; Settings, A. W. Street; Songs by Samuel Pokrass; Lyrics, Manny Kurz, Mitchell Parrish, Kerry Shaw
  Noel Francis (May Manning); Stanley Smith (Bruce Taylor); Barbara Weeks (Margaret Manning); Carlyle Bennett (Jack Palmer); Joyce White (Leona Manning Wilson); George Sherwood (Gene Wilson); Joseph Striker (Emil Bierkraut); Bernard Gorcey (Max Goldblatz); Rose Tapley (Mrs. Miller); Jack Soanes (Mr. Miller); Samuel Pokrass (Himself); Diane Tempest (Sunny Lane); Gerald Vaughn (Liquor Man); Charlotte Reynolds (Rose Cheerful); Christola Williams (Lily); Madame Poo (Ben Bernie)
SONGS: Honestly; Satellite; The Girl was Beautiful

Bruce Taylor arrives in Manhattan from Iowa with $20,000 to open a florist shop but meets gold-digging, baby-talking blonde May Manning, a chorus girl more famous for headlining notorious scandals in the tabloids than for theatrical talent. May quickly seduces Bruce and reduces his bankroll to a deficit. Bruce is saved from further disgrace by the love of May's ambitious, hardworking chorine sister, Margaret.

Many members of the audience left the theatre before Satellite disintegrated and the remaining critics hoped it might disappear into orbit. John Mason Brown (The Evening Post) wrote, "If ever there was a satellite in the proud firmament of the drama, Mr. Shaw's and Mr. Mitchell's farce-comedy is it. There seems to be no need to dwell upon the inexpertness of the playwriting. One can only say "Booh to it, pooh, pooh to it." Gilbert W. Gabriel (The American) dismissed the fiasco as "one of the wholly dim things of the year."

Noel Francis and Barbara Weeks returned to Broadway from lackluster film careers. Stanley Smith left Hollywood where he had attained fleeting success as the leading man in several early screen musicals, Sweetie; Follow the Leader; Good News; Honey; Queen

High; and The King of Jazz. Satellite was not worth the journey from the West Coast.

* * *

SOMETHING OLD, SOMETHING NEW (Morosco Theatre, January 1, 1977). Produced by Adela Holzer; A comedy by Henry Denker; Director, Robert H. Livingston; Setting and costumes, Lawrence King and Michael H. Yeargan; Lighting, Clarke Dunham; Assistant set designer, B. Ursula Belden; Assistant costume designer, Donna Tomas; Wardrobe supervisor, Warren Morrill; Stages managers, Martha Knight, Ken Sherber; Company manager, James Mennen; General manager, Leonard A. Mulhern
 Molly Picon (Laura Curtis); Hans Conried (Samuel Jonas); Dick Patterson (Mike Curtis); Lois Markle (Eleanor Curtis); Matthew Tobin (Dr. Arthur Morse); Holland Taylor (succeeded Beryl Towbin) (Cynthia Morse); Ahvi Spindell (Bruce Morse); Cynthia Bostick (Angela)

 Aware that Social Security endorses living in sin, widow Laura Curtis and widower Samuel Jonas decide to spend what remains of their geriatric life together, without benefit of marriage or upsetting the social security system which would reduce their monthly allowance if they became legally united. Their respective children are horrified and bitterly opposed to their parents' arrangement. Samuel's daughter's hysterical husband, psychiatrist Dr. Arthur Morse, finds deep Freudian motives in the oldsters' commitment, while Laura's wife-dominated son worries about appearances and ultimate gossip. Laura and Samuel conclude they will be a very respectable, loving, married couple or even a better unmarried couple.

 Following a tryout on the road and fourteen previews on Broadway, Something Old, Something New bravely opened on the night of the New Year 1977. The prior New Year's Eve compulsive revels and prescribed hysteria for an old year's passing was not reprised at the opening of the New Year's first play, despite warm and charming performances from Molly Picon and Hans Conried. Clive Barnes (The New York Times) deplored the play was "the worst comedy--so far--of 1977. Had it been a day earlier it would have done the same favor for 1976." Barnes compared the direction to a surgeon operating with a sledgehammer and described the acting as "uncomfortably awful"; the costumes "absolutely hideous"; and the lighting "made the mistake of being turned on."

 Martin Gottfried (The New York Post) found "There isn't a thing right with Something Old, Something New" while William Glover (Associated Press) dismissed the comedy as "a frail little turkey" and Martin Gottfried questioned how such plays could be written and produced; "It is difficult to comprehend how one of them could be attempted on Broadway today." Several critics singled out one of Denker's comedic gems to exemplify the overall dialogue of the comedy: "How long has your mother been a widow?" Reply: "Ever since my father died!"

Sixty-three-year-old former lawyer Henry Denker, born in New York City on November 25, 1912, produced, wrote, and directed ABC's award-winning radio series (1947-1959) The Greatest Story Ever Told. Denker's first Broadway success was his play Time Limit!, written with Ralph Berkey in 1956. Henry Denker's play based on Sigmund Freud, A Far Country, ran 274 performances in 1961, but the following year his Venus at Large disappeared after four performances. His adaptation of Louis Nizer's book My Life in Court as A Case of Libel in 1963 starred the late Van Heflin for 242 performances, while his 1967 comedy What Did We Do Wrong? struggled through 48 performances.

Something Old, Something New originally opened, under the title of Second Time Around, for a month's tryout at Atlanta's Midnight Sun Dinner Theatre on April 27, 1976. Second Time Around was produced and directed by Robert Ennes Turoff, with a setting by Ray Perry, lighting by David Ferguson, and costumes by Paige Southward.
Molly Picon (Laura Curtis); Hans Conried (Samuel Jonas); Richard Armbruster (Mike Curtis); Kathleen Klein (Eleanor Curtis); Philip Le Strange (Dr. Arthur Morse); Jane Bergere (Cynthia Morse); David W. Milford (Bruce Morse); Sharon Ferguson (Cindy)

Adela Holzer, producer of the 1975 Broadway hit The Ritz, acquired Henry Denker's comedy for a Broadway production. Rehearsals of Second Time Around began on October 12, 1976, with stars Picon and Conried but with an otherwise entirely new cast and a new director, Robert H. Livingston. Producer Holzer convinced playwright Denker his title would be confused with Sammy Cahn and James Van Heusen's 1960 popular song "The Second Time Around" and with Twentieth Century-Fox's 1961 film of the same name. Danker changed the play's title to Something Old, Something New. Out-of-town reviews of the rechristened comedy indicated Something Old, Something New would face critical damnation and rapid eviction from Broadway.

After the savage Boston reviews of the comedy, Conried and Picon pleaded with playwright Denker and producer Holzer to close the show and not attempt a Broadway opening. Adela Holzer brought in a gag writer to enliven Denker's script, which had been cut, pasted, overaltered and overrehearsed by director Livingston. Producer Holzer did not bother to attend the Broadway opening of Something Old, Something New on New Year's Day, 1977. Sixty-year-old Baltimore-born Hans Conried, who made his Broadway stage debut in Cole Porter's 1953 hit musical Can-Can and subsequently was seen on Broadway in Tall Story, 70 Girls 70, and Irene, and who died at the age of sixty-six on January 5, 1982, at Burbank, California, gave the cast a party at Sardi's Restaurant after the opening, but Something Old, Something New was not the start of a Happy New Year.

Seventy-eight-year-old Molly Picon, born on Broome Street in New York City on February 28, 1898, relocated with her family to Philadelphia in 1903 and made her stage debut the following year as Baby Margaret. Petite Molly became a star of the Yiddish Theatre in America and in Europe and made her Broadway stage debut on April 16, 1940, in Sylvia Regan's play Morning Star, which completed 63 performances. Her second English-speaking Broadway role was as Mrs. Rubin in Julie Bern's failed seven-performance comedy For Heaven's Sake, Mother, which starred Nancy Carroll at the Belasco Theatre on November 16, 1948. Molly co-starred with Robert Morley on March 9, 1960, in the London stage production of Leonard Spigelgass's comedy A Majority of One.

Pert, talented, four foot, five-inch Molly Picon's best Broadway assignment was in the role of Clara Weiss, the "yenta" of Jerry Herman's tuneful and pleasant musical comedy Milk and Honey, at the Martin Beck Theatre on October 10, 1961, which she played 543 times. Seymour Vail's two-character musical revue How to Be a Jewish Mother teamed Molly with black comedian Godfrey Cambridge for 21 performances on Broadway in 1967. Between her sparse Broadway engagements, Molly had closed on the road in George Baxt's comedy Make Momma Happy in 1953 and wisely left the cast prior to the disastrous Philadelphia opening of the musical Chu Chem in 1966. She co-starred for 96 performances with Sam Levene in Richard Seff's comedy Paris is Out! in 1970 and in 1979 she took to the road heading a cast of eleven in her autobiographical revue Those Were the Days!, preamble to her autobiography, Molly, published by Simon and Schuster the following year.

Ironically, Henry Denker's comedy found a measure of success in regional theatres under its original title, Second Time Around, which Pat O'Brien and his wife Eloise Taylor O'Brien took on the road in 1978. Molly Picon reprised her role of Laura Curtis in Second Time Around for four weeks beginning January 17, 1978, at Sarasota, Florida's Golden Apple Dinner Theatre, with Frank Bara, Philip Le Strange, Lydia Franklin, Kathleen Klein, J. Robert Dietz, and Peter Ivanov.

* * *

SPECIAL OCCASIONS (Music Box Theatre, February 7, 1982). Produced by Morton Gottlieb, Ben Rosenberg, Warren Crane; A comedy by Bernard Slade; Director, Gene Saks; Setting, David Jenkins; Lighting, Tharon Muser; Costumes, Jennifer von Mayrhauser; Associate producers, Martin Cohne, Milly Schoenbaum; Produced in association with Thornhill Productions, Inc.; Production assistant, Thomas Santopietro; Props, Joseph P. Harris, Jr., Laura Koch; Wardrobe, Rosie Wells; Hairstylist, Dale Brownell; General manager,

Ben Rosenberg; Company manager, Martin Cohen; Stage managers,
Warren Crane, Kate Pollock
 Suzanne Pleshette (Amy Ruskin); Richard Mulligan (Michael Ruskin)

Aggressive ex-alcoholic Amy Ruskin and her introverted television-writer-turned-playwright husband, Michael, celebrate their fifteenth wedding anniversary by planning their divorce. Amy and Michael are frequently reunited after their divorce, over the next ten years. They meet for such mutual special occasions as problems besetting their three children; Amy's short-lived marriage to Michael's best friend, and weddings, baptisms, and burials. Amy and Michael develop a closer relationship during the passing decade but realize they are better equipped to handle a friendly divorce than an unhappy, stormy marriage.

The critics rejoiced in Suzanne Pleshette's return to the Broadway stage after years of toil in Hollywood and on television, but Bernard Slade's two-character comedy was described as "an attenuated television play that uneasily mixes the conventions of the situation comedy and soap opera. It's not nearly as amusing as 'The Bob Newhart Show,'" reported Frank Rich (The New York Times). Clive Barnes (New York Post) suggested "for anyone wanting more weight with their wit and more depth to their comedy, Special Occasions will probably seem a case of too much fluff surrounding too little stuff-- Special Occasions is not a bad evening in the boulevard theater-- But it is not, by any stretch, a special occasion." Douglas Watt (Daily News) added, "Suzanne Pleshette and Richard Mulligan are such amiable and deft performers that one aches for them in the ordeal Slade has put them through," calling the play a "labored hodgepodge" where "The laughs are few and far between."

Former actor Bernard Slade's first plays, Simon Says Get Married and A Very Close Family, were produced in Canada, where he was born at St. Catherines in 1930. After writing some 100 television scripts in Hollywood, Slade's first Broadway-produced play was a runaway success. Same Time, Next Year opened on Broadway on March 13, 1975, and remained for 1,453 performances. The two-character play examined the constancy of one couple's annual adultery each year in February, while through the years they remained married and unwilling to divorce their spouses. Ellen Burstyn and Charles Brodin were Same Time, Next Year's original adulterers, succeeded by Joyce Van Patten, Loretta Swit, Sandy Dennis, Hope Lange, and Betsy Palmer; and Conrad Janis, Ted Bessell, Don Murray, Monte Markham, and Charles Kimbrough. Bernard Slade and his wife Jill played the annual February lovers at Edmonton, Canada's Citadel Theatre.

Slade's second Broadway success was Tribute, an eight-character comedy that was heightened by a sterling performance by Jack Lemmon as ambitious screenwriter Scottie Templeton, terminally ill with cancer, being given a tribute by his peers but, more importantly, reaching a closer relationship with his neglected son. It opened on June 1, 1978, to play 212 performances. On November 8, 1979, Bernard Slade's six-character <u>Romantic Comedy</u> opened on Broadway, starring Anthony Perkins and Mia Farrow, telling of playwright Jason Carmichael's requirement of several years to realize he is in love with his collaborator, Phoebe Craddock.

Two-character plays have had a measure of success on Broadway. Eugene Walters's adaptation of Louis Verneuil's French drama <u>Jealousy</u> in 1928 had 136 performances with Fay Bainter and John Halliday, and Jan de Hartog's charming 1950 comedy <u>The Fourposter</u> with Hume Cronyn and Jessica Tandy accumulated 632 performances. William Gibson's two-character 1958 play, <u>Two for the Seesaw</u>, starring Henry Fonda and Anne Bancroft, was a successful duo-drama for 750 performances, and Bill Manhoff's <u>The Owl and the Pussycat</u>, with Alan Alda and Diana Sands in 1964 remained for 427 performances. D. L. Coburn's two-character play <u>The Gin Game</u>, given an acting tour-de-force by Jessica Tandy and Hume Cronyn, won the 1978 Pulitzer Prize. <u>Special Occasions</u> disappeared after twenty-six previews and one performance, stressing that man's best friend is no longer the dog but his ex-wife.

* * *

STAGES (Belasco Theatre, March 19, 1978). Produced by Edgar Bronfman and Stuart Ostrow; A play by Stuart Ostrow; Director, Richard Foreman; Scenery, Douglas W. Schmidt; Lighting, Pat Collins; Costumes, Patricia Zipprodt; Music, Stanley Silverman; Sound, Roger Jay; Wardrobe supervisor, Clarence Sims; Production assistants, Jane Rottenbach, Victoria Merrill; Hairstylist, Patrik D. Moreton; Stage managers, D. W. Koehler, Frank DiFilia; Company manager, Nancy Simmons; General managers, Ira Bernstein, Joseph Harris
    Jack Warden; Diana Davila; Tom Aldredge; Philip Bosco; Ralph Drischell; William Duell; Roy Brocksmith; Howland Chamberlin; Gretel Cummings; Brenda Currin; Caroline Kava; Manuel Martinez; Lois Smith; Max Wright
    <u>STAGE I--DENIAL</u>: Jack Warden (Jason Kahn, The Actor); Lois Smith (Silvia); Philip Bosco (Frank Faye); William Duell (Colin Dickinson); Caroline Kava (Jill Kahn) Diana Davila (Chic Lady); Max Wright (Arnold Glickman); Gretel Cummings (Dundeen Dickinson); Brenda Currin (Joeie); Ralph Drischell (Mr. Harris); Howland (Chamberlin (Theatre Owner); Roy Brocksmith (Pianist); Tom Aldredge (Bill Blue)
    <u>STAGE II--ANGER</u>: Jack Warden (The Witness, the Actor); Tom Aldredge (Chairman); William Duell (Attorney for the Witness); Ralph Drischell (Counsel); Philip Bosco (New Member); Howland Chamberlin (2nd Member); Roy Brocksmith (3rd Member)
    <u>STAGE III--BARGAINING</u>: Jack Warden (Constantine, the Actor); Diana Davila (Butterfly); Lois Smith (Blonde Sister); Greta Cummings (Redheaded Sister); Ralph Drischell (Blonde Husband);

Tom Aldredge (Redheaded Husband); Max Wright (Father)
  STAGE IV--<u>DEPRESSION</u>: Max Wright (Jack); William Duell (Stanley); Tom Aldredge (Harold); Caroline Kava (Linda); Roy Brocksmith (Doctor); Jack Warden (Danny Steinman, the Actor); Lois Smith (Justine/Nurse); Philip Bosco (Garage Command)
  FINAL STAGE--<u>ACCEPTANCE</u>: Jack Warden (Abe Thibault, the Actor); Manuel Martinez (Gonzalo Bolivar); Philip Bosco (Jesse Thibault); Howland Chamberlin (Trench Coat Customer); Roy Brocksmith (Fat Customer); Tom Aldredge (Mrs. Steven); Lois Smith (Lady Customer); Max Wright (Trooper); William Duell (The Banker)

  Each of the five segments of <u>Stages</u> is a metaphor for one actor's confrontation with life's frustrations and failures and his unwilling progression into old age. <u>Denial</u> is the shocking mediocre reception and failure of his play. <u>Anger</u> erupts as he ineptly defends himself against being blacklisted before a 1950's Congressional House Un-American Activities witch-hunting committee. <u>Bargaining</u> betrays his lost pursuit of bedding his beautiful young bride, despite his great wealth and position, because of his physical ugliness. <u>Depression</u> is underscored by his aging fragility and inability to deal with dictatorial, flamboyant medical personnel but enriched by being seduced by an attractive hostess. The actor in his final stage of <u>Acceptance</u> has become the aged proprietor of a declining haberdashery, finally prepared to accept death, which comes instead to his unwilling partner.

  "The play was so bad that even Richard Foreman's direction, which consists of applying certain antiquated and tiresome avant-garde devices arbitrarily to any material that comes to hand, was a welcome relief," reported John Simon (<u>New York</u>). Edwin Wilson (<u>Wall Street Journal</u>) commented: "Though sometimes amusing and arresting, the world of <u>Stages</u> remained inchoate" and "attempted to be both more serious and more to be avant-garde." Clive Barnes (<u>New York Post</u>) described <u>Stages</u> finest moment was "its final curtain. The arcane pretentiousness of <u>Stages</u>, its blockheaded pomposity, and unlikeable sense of self-satisfaction, are difficult to explain. It was indeed totally absurd." Richard Eder (<u>The New York Times</u>) called <u>Stages</u>, "Lugubrious vaudeville, a sedate and portentous effort of fusing the theatre of the absurd with the theatre of the sentimental--It is an unlikely marriage of talents, and like some other unlikely marriages, unconsummated," claiming it was a work "that never manages to be more than a gathering of distantly acquainted metaphors."

  Stuart Ostrow was better known as the producer-director of the hit musical <u>Here's Love</u>, which opened on October 3, 1963, to complete 334 performances, and also as the producer of two of Broadway's greatest musical successes, <u>1776</u> (March 16, 1969--1,217 performances) and <u>Pippin</u> (October 23, 1972--1,944 performances).

176 / The Starcross Story

* * *

THE STARCROSS STORY (Royale Theatre, January 13, 1954). Produced by John C. Wilson, S. S. Krellberg, and Messrs. Shubert; A drama by Diana Morgan; Director, John C. Wilson; Setting, Watson Barrett; Costumes supervised by Audre; Company manager, Edward Woods; Stage managers, Ward Bishop, Charles Campbell
 Eva Le Gallienne (Lady Starcross); Mary Astor (Anne Meredith); Anthony Ross (James Trenchard); Christopher Plummer (George Phillips); Una O'Connor (Ellen); Marta Linden (Chloe Gwynn); Margaret Bannerman (Alice Venning); Phillipa Bevans (Laura Shipman); Lynn Bailey (Christine Starcross); Doris Patston (Jean Benson [Halliday]

 Motion picture producer James Trenchard, director George Phillips, and screenwriter Chloe Gwynn arrive at Lady Mary Starcross's London home, Chicwick Hall, to finalize plans to film the inspirational life story of her husband, heroic explorer Christian Starcross, who, fifteen years ago, died with six companions on an expedition to Tibet's Khublai Desert. Research for the film, to be titled "The Magnificent Attempt" (or "The Magnificent Failure") has revealed Starcross as much less than the legendary heroic paragon that Lady Starcross has promoted and kept evergreen. Starcross is exposed as a self-glorifying coward and a fraud, responsible for his death and the deaths of his companions, in pursuit of a mythical Shangri-La in the Himalayas he knew did not exist. The truth is bitterly confirmed by Anne Meredith, Starcross's mistress, who insists the film must never be made. Lady Starcross succeeds in persuading the filmmakers to produce the story, thereby preserving the myth and protecting the illusion of millions of people who believe her husband's legend and to whom it has provided inspiration. Mary defiantly produces her husband's "last" letter, proclaiming his dedicated quest and eternal love for her, but she does not reveal the passionate last letter found after her husband's death, written to his mistress, Anne Meredith.

 The Starcross Story received excellent reviews in its out-of-town tryout and gave an "invitation only" preview on Tuesday, January 12, closing after one performance on January 13, 1954, due to a plagiarism suit filed in New York's District Court on January 13, 1954, by Stanley Kauffmann. Kauffmann claimed the play was an unauthorized dramatization of his 1949 novel The Hidden Hero. Kauffmann, actor, author, essayist, and drama critic for The New York Times twelve years later, set his novel in Mexico and Connecticut, described by critic E. S. Brown as "A novel about a man and a woman who each must make a kind of atonement and reassertion of past cowardice."

 Beyond Stanley Kauffmann's plagiarism claim, The Starcross Story was yet another recounting of the dismantling of an idol. Ida Alexa Ross Wylie's 1942 novel, Keeper of the Flame, was a variation on the same theme, in which a legendary national hero is finally exposed as an avowed fascist by his wife who has earlier perpetuated the heroic legend. Metro-Goldwyn-Mayer filmed Keeper of the Flame in 1943 with Katharine Hepburn and Spencer Tracy. Neither Wylie nor M-G-M screamed plagiarism. The "fallen idol" theme has been recurrent in literature and on the stage, including Daphne Du Maurier's classic Rebecca and Quentin Reynolds's documentation as fact of the life of George Dupree's hoax in The Man Who Wouldn't Talk.

A. A. Milne's 1922 play The Truth About Blayds dramatized the deception of a famous Victorian poet, Oliver Blayds, who, at the age of ninety confesses his acclaimed poetry was actually written by a deceased twenty-year-old poet named Jenkins. After Blayds' death his family decided to continue the deception and they perpetuated his fame. The exposé of candidates for sainthood detoured to purgatory had been used from the early Greek Theatre to Dante to Citizen Kane, and Dore Schary pursued the same theme in his failed 1970 play Brightower, whose fallen Pulitzer Prize-winning author fell to oblivion--after one performance.

Robert Coleman (Daily Mirror) recognized the similarity between The Starcross Story and Milne's The Truth About Blayds but found "The Starcross Story has intriguing plot--the type of play that catches our fancy. We like scripts that have something to say," but "Miss Morgan hasn't done full justice to an arresting idea. It's a case of almost, but not quite." Walter Kerr (Herald Tribune) praised the superlative performing by the cast but found the play "all very British, very noble, very old-fashioned, and very empty." Richard Watts, Jr. (New York Post) felt Diana Morgan had "written one of the most cynical plays since the Restoration--a rather ineffectual drama, rambling, long-winded, muddled and shallow--a sardonic and even convincing drama could have been written on the subject, but Miss Morgan hasn't provided it."

Praise was lavished on the cast of The Starcross Story, William Hawkins (New York World-Telegram and Sun) wrote "This drawing-room melodrama offers Eva Le Gallienne the chance for an unexpected coup that is stirring theatre," which she played with "flashes of grandeur and authority that are rare and exciting. The play has a magazine serial flavor but virtue enough in providing the stars with roles they can really perform." Mary Astor, co-starred with Eva Le Gallienne, drew the greatest accolades. "Take a Bow, Mary Astor," exclaimed John McClain (Journal American), "I think she was magnificent. We all know she is decorative, but she has authority and aplomb, and she stood up to Eva Le Gallienne, the other star, traded punches toe-to-toe, and certainly came away with no less than a draw. She is a fine actress. Something slightly less laudatory can be said of the play itself."

The lovely and talented Mary Astor, after three decades in innumerable Hollywood motion pictures, had appeared on-stage on the West Coast in Noel Coward's Tonight at 8:30 and opposite Elliott Nugent in the first tryout of his and James Thurber's delightful comedy The Male Animal. Mary Astor made her Broadway stage debut in Clare Kummer's comedy Many Happy Returns in January, 1945, which did not return after three performances. Prior to Starcross she had toured in S. N. Behrman's play Biography and Arthur Laurents's Time of the Cuckoo.

Diana Morgan's play had been successful in London in 1952, where it played 107 performances under the title of After My Fashion.

After My Fashion (Ambassadors Theatre, London, opened May 8, 1952). A play by Diana Morgan; Director, Reginald Tate; Settings and Costumes, Tina Horniman and Martin Beckwith.
  Sonia Dresdel (Lady Starcross); Valerie White (Sybil Emerson); Jean Stuart (Ellen); Michael Sepley (succeeded by Reginald Tate) (James Trenchard); Richard Johnson (George Phillips); Diana Morgan (Chloe Gwynn); Beatrice Kane (Mrs. Vanning); Gladys Tudor (Mrs. Shipman); Eileen Moore (Christine Starcross); Cicely Walper (Mrs. Benson)

Theatre World favorably appraised After My Fashion; "Diana Morgan's play has a theme which grips the imagination and holds the attention."

The Starcross Story was produced by Richard Aldrich at his Dennis, Massachusetts, Cape Playhouse on August 24, 1953, in association with Charles Mooney. The play was directed by Luther Kennett and the setting designed by Paul Bertelsen
  Eva Le Gallienne (Lady Starcross); Faye Emerson (Anne Meredith); Glenn Anders (James Trenchard); Scott Forbes (George Phillips); Ona Munson (Jean Benson); Elizabeth Dillon (Chloe Gwynn); Una O'Connor (Ellen); Phillipa Bevans (Laura Shipman); Leslie Penhallow (Christine Starcross); Cherry Hardy (Alice Venning)

* * *

STATUS QUO VADIS (Brooks Atkinson Theatre, February 18, 1973). Produced by George Keathley and Jack Lenny; A comedy written and directed by Donald Driver; Setting, Edward Burbridge; Lighting, Thomas Skelton; Costumes, David Toser; Hairstylist, Randy Coronato; Production associate, Joy Welfeld; Co-producers, Richard Jansen, Aaron Gold
  Gail Strickland (Irene Phillips); Bruce Boxleitner (Horace Elgin); Ted Danson (Paul Regents III); Rebecca Taylor (Joyce Grishaw); John C. Becher (Mr. Grammerky); Geraldine Kay (Mrs. Elgin); Roberts Blossom (Mr. Elgin); Charles Welch (Laporski); Ralph Strait (Reinke); Lee Zara (Barbara); Don Marston (Don Walgren); Kenneth Kimmins (Professor Russel); William Francis (Rev. John Purdy); Robert E. Thomson (Father Mathias); James S. Lucas,

Jr. (Coffman); Katherine Korla (Sarah); John C. Becher (Detective); Sue Renee, Diana Corto (Choir Boys).

The class conscious, rigidly structured and stratified American society is exemplified by designating everyone's status by numbers worn conspicuously on their clothing, from lowly five to number one. Horace Elgin, a high-school dropout, is a lowly # 5 working as a hard-hat hole-maker who advances his social position through an affair with a # 3 secretary, Joyce Grishaw, and he is persuaded to finish high-school at night. Returning to school, Horace has an affair with his teacher, # 1 Irene Phillips, a wealthy girl bent on helping the lowly. Irene encourages Horace to publish his explicitly erotic poetry, which his slatternly mother refuses to believe is dirty since it is in print. Horace feels he has arrived in the upper status by impregnating Irene. But Horace's blatantly pornographic poetry is reviled by the Catholic Church and he overreaches himself. He returns to Joyce, who has become pregnant by # 1 Harvard man Don Marston. Horace has quickly returned to his status quo of # 5.

Douglas Watt (Daily News) reported, "Status Quo Vadis misfires. Donald Driver, who both wrote and directed it, has seized on a trite theme and enthusiastically presented it in a dated theatrical style," achieving a play on which a great deal of care has been expended for no visible reason at all." Clive Barnes (The New York Times) described Status Quo Vadis as "a modern morality play" in which the author "is much obsessed with class in American society. In this way he may be making a valid sociological point, but it does not necessarily leave him with a valid play--Yet it is amazing how much humor Mr. Driver can extract from his own script. He is much helped by an agreeably talented cast." Richard Watts (New York Post) expressed admiration for Donald Driver's 1968 adroit transformation of Shakespeare's Twelfth Night into the hit musical Your Own Thing and felt that in Status Quo Vadis, Driver "has taken on all America as his target, and I think his most remarkable achievement is that he has managed the task as successfully as he has. Status Quo Vadis often irritated but more frequently impressed me."

Playwright Driver said he based Status Quo Vadis on the premise that "the gap between classes is ever widening and it is more difficult to move freely from one to another because of birth, education, organizations and the personality of the machine. Thus the play is a social satire about a young man, a victim of the system, whose reach falls short of his grasp--a present-day Horatio Alger in reverse." Driver also included a program note: "Equality has become an inalienable right to be equal with the people above so we need not be equal with the people below."

Status Quo Vadis had been a great success in Chicago and in Washington, D.C. Richard Coe (The Washington Post) called the play "an amusingly different essay in theatre. Driver's entire cast is first-rate and we owe Chicago a thank you for discovering this

180 / Status Quo Vadis

funny, sometimes provocative mix of writing and staging." Mel Gussow, reporting to The New York Times on the Washington production wrote, "Like its unlucky hero, the comedy sinks to its own level. The class finally is situation comedy, not satire. As a writer Driver is more marked by cleverness than wit, but as a director he has a brisk sense of how to make the most of his comic characters."

Donald Driver had been a dancer with the Ballet Russe de Monte Carlo and in several Broadway musicals. He directed the first American-produced version of Peter Weiss's The Persecution and Assasination of Jean-Paul Marat as Performed by the Inmates of the Asylum of Charenton Under the Direction of the Marquis De Sade which opened on Broadway at the Majestic Theatre on January 3, 1967, two years after The Royal Shakespeare Company's original Broadway limited-run production in 1965. Driver also directed Murray Schisgal's play Jimmy Shine in 1968, which starred Dustin Hoffman.

The World Premiere of Donald Driver's Status Quo Vadis was at the Ivanhoe Theatre in Chicago on August 26, 1971. Originally scheduled for a two-week engagement, the play became an instant success and completed a twenty-eight week run. The Chicago reviews reflected the popularity of the comedy. Hugh Dickinson (Chicago New World) wrote, "Driver has craftily devised an intricate structure of action, a sure-fire plot that generates suspense as well as action." William Leonard (Chicago Tribune) described the play as "a sparkling, galloping, highly entertaining combination of satire and farce" and the Chicago Herald enthused, "It's hilarious, entertaining and very truthful--a rollicking comedy that makes a lot of sense."

Produced by Richard D. Jansen and George Keathley; directed by Donald Driver; Setting Rick Paul; Costumes, David Toser; Technical director, Ivan Carlson; Production stage manager, Thomas M. Guerra; Assistant stage manager, Philip A. Scorza
    Gail Strickland (Irene Phillips); David Wilson (Horace Elgin); Joel Stedman (Paul Regents III); Rebecca Taylor (Joyce Grishaw); Doug Alleman (Mr. Grammerky); Geraldine Kay (Mrs. Elgin); Otto L. Schlesinger (Mr. Elgin); Joe Shea (Laporski); Neil Crane (Reinke); Lee Zara (Barbara); Don Marston (Don Walgren); J. S. (Joe) Young (Professor Russel); George Womack (Rev. John Purdy); Bob Thompson (Father Mathias); William Vines (Coffman); Kathy Korla (Sarah); Doug Alleman (Detective); Mark Blasingame, Robert Ford, Thomas King, David Montgomery (Choir Boys)

The Ivanhoe Theatre production of Status Quo Vadis opened at Washington, D.C.'s Arena Stage on April 7, 1972. Produced by George Keathley; Directed by Donald Driver; Setting by Rick Paul and Hugh Lester; Lighting by Vance Sorrells; Costumes by Georgiana Jordan; Production manager, Hugh Lester; Technical director, Henry R. Gorfein. Cast changes from the Chicago production were:
    Bruce Boxleitner (Horace Elgin); Judd Reilly (Paul Regents); Max Howard (Professor Russel); Edgar Meyer (Father Mathias); Martin

Zagon (First Man); Neil Crane (Second Man); Jeffrey Farron, Eddie Ormond, William Owens, Earl Wilkes (Altar Boys)

On June 29, 1972, the comedy returned to Chicago with the Arena Stage cast and Jose Ramos, Steven Rupp, Nathaniel Hendrix, and Teofillo Bruno as Altar Boys.

* * *

STEP ON A CRACK (Ethel Barrymore Theatre, October 17, 1962). Produced by Roger L. Stevens and Herbert Swope, Jr.; A drama by Bernard Evslin; Director, Herbert Swope, Jr.; Setting and Lighting, George Jenkins; Costumes, Patricia Zipprodt; Original music, Bobby Scott; Incidental Choreography, Buddy Schwab; Hairstyles, Michael Falo; Company manager, Robert Kamlet; Stage managers, Frank Hamilton, Frank Gero, Dan Ferrone

Gary Merrill (Dr. Bill Hurlbird); Donald Madden (Mark Hurlbird); Pauline Flanagan (replaced Nancy Kelly who replaced Rita Hayworth) (Ellen Hurlbird); Maggie McNamara (Naomi Mazer); Margaret Hayes (Maggie McCoy); Barbara Mattes (Cathy Hurlbird); William Hickey (Bagdad); Richard Durham (Carl Hinser); Dan Ferrone (Peter Culhane); William H. Bassett (Mike); Ronnie Haran (replaced Joey Heatherton) (Little Margaret)

Alcoholic ex-vaudevillian Ellen Hurlbird is insanely jealous of her philandering husband's new receptionist, Naomi Mazer, and consoles herself with self-pity and vodka. The Hurlbirds' neurotic son, Mark, is incestuously devoted to his mother and aware of his father's promiscuous, amorous adventures. Naomi is invited to Hurlbird's Margate, New Jersey, home to celebrate the Fourth of July. Mark celebrates Independence Day by tying Naomi to a post in the tool shed and lighting a large supply of fireworks around her feet. Naomi is saved from death but Mark has lost his mind.

"There is no reason for losing any time in getting down to telling you that Step on a Crack is terrible--it is a play of transcendent and embarrassing badness" reported Richard Watts, Jr. (New York Post). Howard Taubman (The New York Times) called Evslin's drama an "overblown, pretentious effort--mired in the suffering cliches of modern drama." Robert Coleman (New York Mirror) wrote, "Remember the old children's rhyme, 'Step on a crack and break your mother's back.' Well, that explains the title. Okay, so this entry almost broke our back; for its humor is heavy-handed and its psychological probing ponderous." Norman Nadel (New York World Telegram-Sun) decided the play was "ridiculous, over-blown and downright embarrasing" and that playwright Evslin had "written an impossible play, a stupid play, and by posturing as some kind of poet of the peat bogs, he has outraged the beauty of language."

The New York Times's Howard Taubman had written "Of all the helpless, writhing actors ensnared in the disastrous Step on a Crack, pity Donald Madden most. Not long ago he played Hamlet." Twenty-eight-year-old Donald Madden, born in Manhattan on November 5, 1933, was an excellent classical actor who was acclaimed the previous season in the title role of the Phoenix Theatre's March 16, 1961, production of Hamlet. Madden, who died on January 22, 1983, at the age of forty-nine, had matched John Barrymore's 101 performances as the Prince of Denmark and appeared to be an excellent choice for the role of soliloquizing Mark in Step on a Crack.

Gary Merrill became the fourth husband of Bette Davis on July 28, 1950, and appeared on stage with her through a long road tour during the 1959-60 season in a concert reading of The World of Carl Sandburg, adapted by Norman Corwin. Merrill was last seen on Broadway in James B. Allardice's 1949 farce At War with the Army. After his divorce from Bette Davis on July 6, 1960, Merrill became romantically involved with Rita Hayworth, who had shed her fifth husband, James Hill, in September 1961. The fading screen career of Hollywood's once-famous sex goddess convinced Hayworth she should make a stab at Broadway and accept the part of Ellen Hurlbird in Step on a Crack. Glamorous Rita, then forty-four years old, studied voice control with Alfred Dixon and arrived at the Ethel Barrymore Theatre on August 14, 1962, to begin rehearsals of Step on a Crack. After one week's rehearsal Rita entered the Flower Fifth Avenue Hospital on Tuesday, August 21st, felled by "nervous exhaustion."

Nancy Kelly was paged to replace Hayworth and Step on a Crack bravely opened at the Royal Alexandra Theatre in Toronto, Canada, on September 10, 1962, where it inspired slashing reviews. Ronald Evans (Toronto Telegram) reported, "The play reveals a sturdy, incipient talent, misguided and mainly unrealized--it should not be allowed to go near Broadway for it will be destroyed there." Wendy Michner (Toronto Star) added, "It's not just a weak, inconsequential or dull play, but a spectacularly inept and pretentious piece of poppycock."

Undaunted by the predictions of the Toronto scribes, Step on a Crack moved south to Cleveland, Ohio, where E. J. Whitney's (Cleveland Plain Dealer) lamentation of praise for the cast concluded with "If William Shakespeare had gotten wilfully drunk and tried to write Picnic, it is expected that he might have come up with something like the preposterous and hysterical hodge-podge that is Step on a Crack." Nancy Kelly, citing "misgivings about the direction" of Herbert Swope, Jr., left the company in Cleveland and on September 24, 1962, her understudy, Pauline Flanagan, was assigned the part of Ellen. Joey Heatherton was replaced in Detroit by Ronnie Haran as Little Margaret and the besieged players, including Mrs. Herbert Swope, Jr. (Margaret Hayes), headed for Broadway where Step on a Crack broke its back in one performance.

Philadelphia-born playwright Bernard Evslin's first play was an adaptation of Henry James's novel The Bostonians, which was produced in 1948 by the Provincetown Playhouse. Evslin also adapted Mark Twain's story The Man That Corrupted Hadleyburg, which opened and closed in Philadelphia in April 1951. His play The Geranium Hat survived thirty-two performances at Off-Broadway's Orpheum Theatre in 1959. But, as Richard Watts, Jr. observed, Step on a Crack was "An unhappy evening for everybody."

* * *

STOP PRESS (Vanderbilt Theatre, March 19, 1939). Produced by the Acting Company, Inc.; A drama by John Stradley; Director, Charles de Sheim; Production supervisor, Alan Peters

Ralph Bell (John Snell); Houseley Stevens (Alfred Snell); Frank Maxwell (Hereford); Norman Porter (William Gore); Archie King (Larry); Gilbert Fates (Wilson); Bernard Kaydison (White); Phillipa Bevans (Ann Thomas); Carl Johnson (Jerry); Charles Mendick (Johnson); Clancy Cooper (Webber); Lewis Gilbert (The Gent); Edith Tachna (Mary Kendall); Tony Kraber (Mulrooney); Al Jenkins (Kendall); Juan Root (Harkinski); Frederick Olmstead (Smyth); Marguerite Walker (Kitty Blake); Russ Conway (Deputy); John Marlieb (Matty); Lou Turkil (A Man)

Small-town newspaper owner Alfred Snell prints editorials opposing strike breakers and supporting the owners of a steel mill during a strike by the mill workers. Snell's son John rallies the reporters on his father's newspaper to write the truth about the strike. The governor of the state enters the conflict and the reporters, backed by John Snell, resolve to organize their own newspaper and print only the truth.

John Stradley's first play sacrificed itself on the altar of propaganda until his overblown message destroyed the play. The New York Times appraiser noted "Good theatre can seldom be non-partisan, but Mr. Stradley's love of the liberal view runs away with his play." The Acting Company, Inc.'s purpose was to produce new plays on Sunday evenings. Stop Press was an unhappy choice.

The Acting Company was formed by Art Smith of the Group Theatre to present plays on Sunday evenings with players currently appearing on Broadway in other plays. It was a losing experiment.

* * *

LA STRADA (Lunt-Fontanne Theatre, December 14, 1969). Produced by Charles K. Peck, Jr. and Canyon Productions, Inc.; A musical drama based on the film of the same name by Federico Fellini; Director, Alan Schneider; Book by Charles K. Peck, Jr.; Music and Lyrics, Lionel Bart; Dances and musical numbers staged by Alvin Ailey; Settings, Ming Cho Lee; Lighting, Martin Aronstein; Costumes, Nancy Potts; Musical director, Hal Hastings; Orchestrations, Eddie Sauter;

184 / La Strada

Dance music arrangements, Peter Howard; Hairstylist, Steve Atha; General managers, Joseph Harris, Ira Bernstein; Company manager, Sam Pagliaro; Stage managers, Terence Little, William Callan, Stan Page, Lola Shumlin

    Stephen Pearlman (succeeded Vincent Beck) (Zampano); Bernadette Peters (Gelsomina); Larry Kert (Mario, the Fool); Peggy Cooper (Mama Lambrini); John Coe (Alberti); Anne Hegira (succeeded Miriam Phillips) (Mother); Lisa Belleran (Little Elsa); Mary Ann Robbins (succeeded Lee Wilson) (Eva); Susan Goeppinger (Sophia); John Coe (The Old Man); Susan Goeppinger (replaced Lee Wilson) (Sister Claudia); Lucille Patton (Castra); Paul Charles, Harry Endicott (Acrobats); Loretta Abbott, Glen Brooks, Henry Brunjes, Connie Burnett, Robert Carle, Paul Charles, Barbara Christopher, Peggy Cooper, Betsy Dickerson, Harry Endicott, Anna Maria Fanizzi, Jack Fletcher, Nino Galanti, Susan Goeppinger, Rodney Griffin, Mickey Gunnersen, Kenneth Kreel, Don Lopez, Joyce Maret, Stan Page, Odette Panaccione, Mary Ann Robbins, Steven Ross, Larry Small, Eileen Taylor (The Company)

SONGS: Seagull, Starfish, Pebble; The Great Zampano; What's Going on Inside?; I Don't Like You; Belonging; Wedding Dance; Encounters; There's a Circus in Town; You're Musical; Only More!; What a Man; Everything Needs Something; Sooner or Later; The End of the Road

<u>Dropped from Production</u>: The Seashell Game; To Be a Performer; Ciao; I Can Wait; My Turn to Fall; Where Will We Be Tomorrow?; Zampano's Farewell; What's Left?

<u>Dropped from Script</u>: Lynn Lipton (Anna); Mary Ann Robbins (Bride); Jack Fletcher (Groom); Patricia Marand (Marita); Stan Page, Nino Galanti (Roustabouts); Mickey Gunnersen (Taza); Connie Burnett (Nina); Henry Brunjes, Nino Galanti (Policemen); Miriam Phillips (Nun)

<u>Dropped from Company</u>: Don Bonnell, Stephen Pearlman, Olive Thompson, Jackie Villamil; Lee Wilson

    Brutish and stupid strongman Zampano buys dim-witted peasant girl Gelsomina from her mother, to become part of his carnival act in which he breaks chains by expanding his chest. The two strange, disparate misfits travel around rural Southern Italy in a caravan mounted on a three-wheeled motorcycle while Zampano unsuccessfully tries to teach childlike Gelsomina to play the trumpet. Gelsomina falls in love with the ferocious Zampano despite his mistreatment of her and his stealing of a crucifix from some nuns. They join a circus where Gelsomina is flattered by the attention of a depressed clown, Mario, the Fool. Insanely jealous, Zampano kills Mario, and Gelsomina's tenuous hold on reality gives way to insanity. Zampano deserts the insane waif but after hearing of her death he realizes how dependent he had become on her.

    Richard Watts, Jr. (<u>New York Post</u>) praised the musical staging and choreography devised by Alvin Ailey in his first Broadway assignment and called Alan Schneider's debut as a director of a musical "inventive," also finding Lionel Bart's score, "unfailingly attractive."

Watts called La Strada "a superior musical--Its virtues are many and distinguished." John Chapman (Daily News), however, categorized La Strada as "a generally lugubrious show" with "a sappy libretto by Charles K. Peck, Jr." Conceding that it was "most beautifully staged, with bewitching sets by Ming Cho Lee" he concluded he would "rather see a good revival of Carnival."

Clive Barnes acknowledged in The New York Times that, ironically, La Strada was "often so very good" but "Unfortunately, the book is weak, and the music and lyrics by Lionel Bart are undistinguished to the point of Muzak-like oblivion." Additional music and lyrics had been added to the show by Martin Charnin and Elliott Lawrence. Charles K. Peck, Jr. defended his libretto as a play with music with Brechtian overtones: "I always saw in La Strada a way to do a musical with the kind of epic theatre quality that Mother Courage has. That was the concept I sold Fellini on. I have musicalized La Strada. I have not rewritten it."

The first of Federico Fellini's films to be transferred to the musical stage was his 1957 Italian comedy Nights of Cabiria, which Neil Simon adapted as Sweet Charity, with Cy Coleman and Dorothy Fields contributing the music and lyrics. Expertly directed by Bob Fosse and starring the inimitable Gwen Verdon, Sweet Charity inaugurated Broadway's famous vaudeville Palace as a legitimate theatre on January 29, 1966, to play 608 performances.

La Strada (The Road) won Fellini the 1954 Venice Film Festival Award and several other continental awards. The Academy of Motion Picture Arts and Sciences in Hollywood awarded their "Oscar" for the Best Foreign Language Film of the Year to La Strada in 1956 and The New York Times selected it as one of five Best Foreign Films of the Year.

La Strada. Produced by Dino de Laurentiis and Carlo Ponti; Director, Federico Fellini; Screenplay, based on a story by Federico Fellini and Tullio Pinelli, by Federico Fellini, Ennio Flaiano and Tullio Pinelli; Photography, Otello Martelli; Art director, Mario Ravasco; Music, Nino Roto, conducted by Franco Ferrara; Editor, Leo Catozzo
    Anthony Quinn (Zampano); Giulietta Masina (Gelsomina); Richard Basehart (Il Matto); Aldo Silvani (Colombaioni); Marcella Rovere (La Vedora); Livi Venturine (Mother)

Broadway's 1969 presentation of La Strada closed after twelve previews and one performance, at a loss of some $650,000. William Glover (Associated Press) heralded the end of the road as "a murky, musical mistake."

* * *

STRANGE ORCHESTRA (Playhouse Theatre, November 23, 1933). Produced by Charles Hopkins and Raymond Moore; A comedy by

186 / Strange Orchestra

Rodney Ackland; Director, Charles Hopkins; Setting, Robert Redington Sharpe; Company manager, Jesse Long; Stage manager, Charles Kradoska; Production manager, Ada Ellison
  Cecilia Loftus (Vera Lyndon); Edith Barrett (Jenny Lyndon); Ian Emery (Peter); Valerie Cossart (Laura); Robert C. Conway (Jimmie); Gerald Oliver-Smith (George); Helen Trenholme (Esther Lyndon); Leslie Denison (Gordon Lyndon); Harry Ellerbe (Val); Mary Newham-Davis (Freda); Patricia Calvert (Sylvia)

Frowsy Vera Lyndon, the slovenly chatelaine of a Bohemian Chelsea boarding house in London, sleeps in her hallway and copes with her idealistic children and her equally desperate, pretentious boarders. Aware that she is losing her eyesight, elder daughter Jenny has an affair with Peter, a hustler posing as an artist, who steals her savings of twenty pounds and jewelry. Peter disappears when Jenny goes blind at Jimmie and Laura's wedding party. The newlyweds, despairing of the fear of parting, attempt suicide by opening the gas jets in their room but are saved from death by Vera and her residents. Vera stresses her philosophy that life is suffering but surviving prevents further suffering. Jenny is told Peter has been killed in an accident but when he reappears she learns the truth. Vera retires to her hallway couch.

Richard Lockridge (The Evening Sun) labeled Ackland's play "An ooze of sentimental morbidity" which "manages to combine in rather overwhelming measure the whimsy of A. A. Milne at his worst and the false pathos of a Dickens sobbing over the death of Little Nell--treated by the author in a vein of light sentiment, which makes it that much worse." Brooks Atkinson (The New York Times) dismissed the charade and suggested it should be retitled Potty Band rather than Strange Orchestra. Critic and historian George Freedley claimed Ackland "chose Chekhov as his literary inspiration."

Rodney Ackland's comedy was first produced in London at the Embassy Theatre on June 30, 1931, directed by A. R. Whatmore.
  Gwladys Evan Morris (Vera Lyndon); Muriel Randall (Jenny Lyndon); Francis James (Peter); Peggy Carter (Laura); Arnold Riches (Jimmie); Hugh Dempster (George); Gabrielle Casartelli (Esther Lyndon); T. G. Saville (Gordon Lyndon); Andre Van Gyseghem (Val); Merle Tottenham (Freda); Leonora Corbett (Sylvia)

Strange Orchestra was reproduced at London's St. Martin's Theatre by Charles Buckmaster and H. Trevor Jones on September 27, 1932, for a run of 135 performances. Directed by John Gielgud, the comedy went into rehearsal with the temperamental and difficult actress Mrs. Patrick Campbell, for whom George Bernard Shaw in 1913 had written the role of Eliza Doolittle in Pgymalion. Shaw recalled his "Eliza" after her death in Paris on April 9, 1940, as "Not a great actress but she was a great enchantress" adding, "Unfortunately, she was professionally such a devilish nuisance that nobody who had been through a production with her ever repeated the experience if it were possible to avoid it." Gielgud in 1928 had played Oswald opposite Mrs. Campbell's Mrs. Alving in Ibsen's Ghosts and he was aware of her professional peccadillos but he still felt she was right for the role of Vera.

Beatrice Stella Tanner, better known as Mrs. Patrick Campbell, imperiously told the press the name of the play was Jazz and strongly suggested to playwright Ackland that he change the title of his play to Jazz, since it was simply a "whoopee sort of thing, but not funny-- untidy." She also feigned bewilderment of the play and its characters, driving Gielgud and Ackland to despair with caustic comment and asking "Who are all these extraordinary characters? Where do they live? Does Gladys Cooper know them?" Mrs. "Pat" arrived late for every rehearsal and, although brilliantly interpreting the slatternly proprietor of the Chelsea Bohemian menage with full knowledge of the play, she persisted in her contentious manner, quarrelling with playwright Ackland and director Gielgud and threatening them with "I am leaving in a fortnight; you must get someone else to play this part." Mrs. Campbell finally left the company and was replaced by Laura Cowie.

Strangely, London's Sphere, while admiring Laura Cowie's virtuoso performance, saw the character of Vera Lyndon as "the sort of character Charles Dickens might have created for Mrs. Patrick Campbell had that been possible." Trinculo in The Bystander (October 12, 1932) wrote, "Laura Cowie's translation of herself into this frowsy, orchidaceous goddess of Bohemia is immense," but he found the play "vague and thin, having neither beginning nor end" and compared it to "Chekhov in Chelsea." Charles Morgan in an October 5, 1932 dispatch to The New York Times considered Rodney Ackland "a dramatist to watch" although the misled Chekhovian overtones were formless and "the lesser threads of narrative, though each of them is ingeniously woven, do not in this play make a rope--Mr. Ackland has failed to establish a relation between the Lyndon household and the world."

The Buckmaster-Jones production of Strange Orchestra, directed by John Gielgud had a setting by Motley; Costumes by Lilian Lawlor; Company manager, Charlton Mann; Stage manager, Gerald Cross and the following cast:
Laura Cowie (Vera Lyndon); Jean Forbes-Robertson (Jenny Lyndon); Hugh Williams (Peter); Carol Rees (Laura); Leslie French (Jimmie); David Hutcheson (George); Mary Casson (Esther Lyndon); Clifford Bartlett (Gordon Lyndon); Robert Harris (Val); Nadine March (Freda); Elizabeth Astor (Sylvia)

Barry Jackson produced Strange Orchestra at his Birmingham, England, Repertory Theatre on April 7, 1934. Directed by Herbert M. Prentice; setting and costumes, Jean Campbell; Stage manager, Charles Victor; Assistant stage managers, Gordon Crier, Mary Mills.

Margaret Halstan (Vera Lyndon); Margaret Hood (Jenny Lyndon); Godfrey Kenton (Peter); Mary Mills (Laura); Gordon Crier (Jimmie); James Hayter (George); Helena Siddons (Esther Lyndon); Vernon Harris (Gordon Lyndon); Stephen Murray (Val); Faith Bennett (Freda); Eva Mulville (Sylvia)

John Gielgud later recalled, in his memoir Early Stages (Macmillan & Company, Ltd. 1939), "Rodney Ackland's plays have a distinctive rhythm; the moods and subtleties of his characters are delicately woven together in a pattern. His vision is apt to be limited to his own particular type of atmosphere, but at least he deals with real people, struggling with the circumstances under which they live, unlike the creatures of so many playwrights' imaginations, who wander about the stage, well clothed and fed with no visible means of practical support. I was proud to be associated with Strange Orchestra. The play was only a moderate commercial success, but it had great quality 'as much superior to the ordinary stuff of the theatre as tattered silk is to unbleached calico'--as James Agate so aptly put it."

Rodney Ackland's career as an actor began in 1924 and his first play, Improper People, appeared in 1929. Ackland would later adapt Hugh Walpole's novel The Old Ladies to the stage in 1935, which was produced by John Gielgud and Richard Clowes, directed by Gielgud and starring Edith Evans, Jean Cadell, and Mary Jerrold. Ackland's successful adaptation of Fyodor Dostoievski's famous 1865 novel Crime and Punishment, directed by Anthony Quayle, was acclaimed in London in 1946. James Agate wrote, "I cannot imagine a better reduction to stage terms of a masterpiece conceived away from the theatre" while Theatre World added, "Rodney Ackland's dramatization of Dostoievsky's famous novel has made a deep impression and provided a real dramatic feast for London theatregoers." John Gielgud's performance as Raskolnikoff was highly praised. Theodore Komisarievsky, Russian director, designer, and successor to Meyerhold, revised and directed the Broadway production of Crime and Punishment, which failed to repeat its London's success, even with Gielgud in his original role.

Strange Orchestra was produced and directed by Gilmor Brown at Los Angeles Playbox Theatre in 1940.
Virginia Lykins (Vera Lyndon); Ellanora Needles (Jenny Lyndon); William Pullen (Peter); Barbara Lee or Louise Allbritton (Laura); Harry Lewis (Jimmie); Harry Bloom (George); Vallory Stevens (Esther Lyndon); John Blackburn (Gordon Lyndon); Robert Claborne (Val); Maxine Chevalier (Freda); Louise Allbritton or Teddi Sherman (Sylvia)

* * *

THE SUNDAY MAN (Morosco Theatre, May 13, 1964). Produced by Cornelius Productions, Inc.; A comedy by Louis S. Bardoly, adapted

from Ferenc Dunai's Hungarian play A Nadrag (The Trousers); Director, Alexander Dore; Designed by Donald F. Jensen; Production assistant, Judy Insel; General manager, Paul Vroom; Company manager, Richard Osorio; Stage managers, Joseph Olney, John Garner
David Brooks (Jim); Vivienne Martin (Penny); Stephen Strimpell (Peter); Jen Nelson (Georgia); Dean Dittmann (Harry); Paula Trueman (Miss Mulligan)

Industrial executive Jim Davenport is unable to attend a Sunday dinner given by his firm to celebrate his promotion because his pregnant mistress, Penny, has spilled butter on his trousers and, after washing them, burns the pants in ironing. A pair of pants for Jim is forcefully taken from Penny's unsuspecting suitor, Peter, who retrieves them. Jim then acquires an oversized pair of trousers from his envious, obese assistant, Harry. Jim's wife, Georgia, invades his every-other-Sunday, Sutton Place love nest to find him in a purloined pair of bright red pants and promises him a very expensive divorce.

"Plays such as The Sunday Man could give infidelity a bad name" reported Norman Nadel (New York World Telegram-Sun). Howard Taubman (The New York Times) found that The Sunday Man "proves that an illicit love affair can be more banal and obnoxious than an unhappy marriage" and "makes the most primitive bedroom comedies of 40 years ago seem like inspired masterpieces." Richard Watts, Jr. (New York Post) called the play "a work of singular flatness and tedium--stupefying in its dullness." Walter Kerr (Herald Tribune) wrote, "The Sunday Man is a play in which three of the male actors lose their pants. I leave you to guess what is going to happen to the producers' shirts."

John McClain (Journal American) judged The Sunday Man as easily running high "in any listing of the Worst of Broadway 1963-4." John Chapman (Daily News) extolled the virtues and charm of Muriel Resnik's delightful comedy in which an executive visited his mistress on Wednesday. Resnik's Any Wednesday was playing to capacity business at the Music Box Theatre, where it had opened on February 18, 1964, but Chapman observed, "Any similarity between The Sunday Man and Any Wednesday isn't just coincidental; it's a major accident."

The Sunday Man had been produced in England as The Importance of Being Dressed, in which Vivienne Martin also played the part of Penny. Dr. Louis Bardoly, who perpetrated this Hungarian goulash, had his own hospital on Long Island and produced The Sunday Man through his own Cornelius Productions, Inc. Forty-seven-year-old David Brooks had been the leading man in such musicals as Bloomer Girl and Brigadoon and fared better with his pants.

* * *

A TEASPOON EVERY FOUR HOURS (ANTA Theatre, June 14, 1969).

190 / A Teaspoon Every Four Hours

Produced by Bernard M. Weber; A comedy by Jackie Mason and Mike Mortman; Director, Jeremy Stevens; Setting, Robert Randolph; Lighting, John Jay Moore; Costumes, Winn Morton; Incidental music, Joseph Raposo; General Manager, Norman Maibaum; Company manager, Michael Goldreyer; Stage managers, Mortimer Halpern, Leonard Auerbach

    Jackie Mason (Nat Weiss); Lee Meredith (Trixie); Billie Allen (Virginia); Barry Pearl (Bruce Weiss); Vera Moore (Patty); Marilyn Cooper (Sylvia Rubin); Roger Morgan (David Weiss); Lee Wallace (Mike); Bernie West (Lou Abrams)

    The friends of middle-aged Nat Weiss, a Jewish widower with two sons, forcefully encourage him to remarry. Several panting, prospective female candidates actively pursue him, intent on smashing the glass, including a dismally dumb but anatomically explosive blonde named Trixie. His son Bruce falls in love with black Patty Collins and believes she is pregnant with his child. Nat finds solace, understanding, and a breath of romance with Patty's mother, Virginia.

    A Teaspoon Every Four Hours established a Broadway record, with 97 previews--then made the irreversible mistake of opening. Among other things, the play was called "totally tasteless" and "overlaid with offensive situations and dialogue." Clive Barnes (The New York Times) politely classified the comedy as "not a particularly distinguished play" but added, "May I say about Mr. Mason himself-- with his eyebrows auditioning for Tevye and his voice so kosher that I am surprised they dare serve it at Saturday matinees--is a rather attractive performer." However Mr. Barnes, observing the evidence at hand, concluded Mr. Mason's talents did not extend to playwriting.

    Mason told writer Joe Adcock, nearly a decade later, "I did a couple of ego trips. I wanted to be a superstar. So I said to myself 'What could be better than writing a Broadway play and starring in it?" Adcock responded "What could be better? Any Broadway play other than A Teaspoon Every Four Hours would probably have been better. Mason lost a good deal of money on that venture, as did his backers." Maralyn Lois Polak headed her interview with Mason the same year (1978): "Jackie Mason: Master of the Sleazy Bleep" and she recorded his contempt for audiences, "I think the average person's taste stinks--ridiculous--retarded--they don't even know how simple they are." Mason then modestly rated himself as "One of the good, great comics that ever lived. I think I'm the most brilliant man that ever lived--I'm trying to be the world's biggest star." Mr. Mason claimed original authorship of A Teaspoon Every Four Hours, with assistance from Mike Mortman and Bernard Weber. He invested $48,000 in the $125,000 production.

    Yacob Moshe Maza, later known as Jackie Mason, was born on June 9, 1930, at Sheboygan, Wisconsin, and descended from a long line of rabbis originating in Minsk, Russia. His father and three brothers were rabbis, and Jackie traditionally entered the temple but deserted rabbinical rites for ribald rhetoric as a stand-up comedian. Mason gained questionable national fame on Sunday, October 18, 1964, on television's <u>Ed Sullivan Show</u> when he thumbed his nose at and gave "the finger" to host Sullivan. Sullivan, producer Bob Precht, and staff were shocked at Mason's "obscene gesture." They summarily fired him and canceled his contract for five more appearances at $7,500 per show.

The thumbed nose and "the finger" should have been reserved for <u>A Teaspoon Every Four Hours</u>.

* * *

<u>TELL MY STORY</u> (Mercury Theatre, March 15, 1939). Produced by the Freeman Theatre Group; A drama by Richard Rohman; Director, Marcel Strauss; Scenery not credited

Gordon Nelson (Mateo, a Socialist Deputy); Robert H. Harris (The Duke); Harry Bellaver (Domino, an American Gunman); George Beban, Jr. (Violette, an Assassin); David Turk (Mendola, a Liberal Deputy); Lee Hillery (Thiero, a Spy); Richard Bengali (De Bello, Director of Police); William H. Chambers (Silvestra, a Journalist); Sydney Andrews (Vulpri, an Assassin); George Moss (Ricoremo, an Assasin); Franklin Klein (Malacro, an Assassin); William Toubin (Filippo, Government Editor); William Webb Saunders (Finzio, Secretary of Interior); Arthur Spencer (Marino, Government Secretary); Edwin Rand (Rosoo, Chief of Government Press); Frederic Giuliano (Police Clerk); Richard Benedict (A Boy); Beth Cantreau (A Girl); Joseph Olney (Clerk)

Conservative Socialist Deputy Mateo contests the fascist Duke's bid for power, hoping to establish reforms and greater liberty and prosperity for his countrymen in a European state. The ruthless and unprincipled Duke, aware that Mateo could win his cause, has American gangster Domino kill him. The Duke then establishes his unopposed dictatorship, eliminating the henchmen who plotted against and killed Mateo for him.

Playwright Richard Rohman assigned Italian names to all of his characters in <u>Tell My Story</u> but substituted "European state" for Italy. The program carried a declaration that all characters in <u>Tell My Story</u> were fictitious but the play was clearly based on fascist Benito Mussolini's murder of Deputy Giacomo Matteotti, secretary-general of Italy's Unitarian Socialist Party. Matteotti had attacked the legality of the Fascisti elections and was kidnapped on the banks of the Tiber River in Rome on June 10, 1924, and killed. A Requiem Mass for Matteotti was held on June 17, 1924, in Rome, attended by his family and friends. The Fascisti were noticeably absent and Fascist Premier Mussolini professed horror at the murder of Matteotti, well aware that his brownshirt Fascists had killed the deputy.

Brooks Atkinson (<u>The New York Times</u>) felt "Fascism invariably seems to be too dramatic for the stage--The story is drama with only a little editing. But like most of the attempts to cut fascism to stage dimensions, Tell My Story is hardly more than a succession of explosive speeches in the theatre." Billboard reported, "It was, of course, a tremendously dramatic story even when it was told about Matteotti rather than Mateo, but Mr. Rohman achieves the amazing feat of making it seem both dull and unbelievable--The characters are all cartoons, the events are strange combinations of bare synopses and useless cumbersome details, and the dialog is almost--if not entirely--beyond description--The consensus seems to be that the acting was as bad as the writing--which would make it very bad acting indeed."

* * *

TIMBER HOUSE (Longacre Theatre, September 19, 1936). Produced by Clinton E. Fiske and Paul Hammond; A melodrama by John Boruff; Director, J. Edward Shugrue; Setting, Donald Oenslager; Stage managers, Frank Gabrielson, Austin King

Donald Cameron (Edward Brinold); Lenita Lane (Miriam Brinold); Robert Shayne (Ralph Miller); Frieda Altman (Alvina Glouster); Thomas Louden (Markam Walling); Ann Dere (Mohena); Melvin Benstock (Al Roberts); Edward Marr (Martin Winnow); Paul Hammond (Allen Garver)

Aware his life will soon be terminated by brain cancer, author Edward Brinold arranges his suicide so that it will appear as murder committed by his unfaithful wife, Miriam, and her lover, Ralph Miller. Insanely jealous Brinold establishes a motive for his false murder by taking out a large life-insurance policy. He retrieves and disposes of the cartridge from a bullet fired into a sack of flour and plants the revolver on Ralph, then shoots and kills himself. Ballistic reports indicate the gun found in Ralph's possession is the murder weapon, but insurance investigator Alvina Glouster proves Brinold committed suicide.

The opening of Timber House was scheduled for Wednesday, September 16, 1936, but Eda Heineman was replaced by Frieda Altman in the role of Alvina Glouster and the melodrama braved judgment on Saturday, September 19th. There were no defenders nor margin for reasonable doubt among the jury of the press. The New York Times dismissed Timber House as "just another melodrama--in itself undistinguished," and the World-Telegram found "Its pace is ambling, its incidents perplexing, its manners obvious and its characters out of the play shop rather than life." Richard Watts, Jr. (Herald Tribune) added, "Some fancy writing that is of no more help to the drama than it is to belles lettres."

Timber House was originally produced on August 4, 1936, at the Deal Conservatoire Theatre in Deal, New Jersey. Produced by the Fiske-Hammond Players, the play was directed by J. Edward

Shugrue, with a setting by Austin King; Stage manager, Regina Kahn; Assistant stage managers, Arno Tanny, Lucille Meredith.
Donald Cameron (Edward Brinold); Yvonne Castle (Miriam Brinold); Bruce MacFarlane (Ralph Miller); Frieda Altman (Alvina Glouster); Robert Harris (Markham Walling); Lucille Meredith (Mohena); Melvin Benstock (Al Roberts); Herbert Vigran (Martin Winnow); Paul Hammond (Allen Garver).

Timber House was reminiscent of an elaborately mounted "thriller that does not thrill" called A Room in Red and White, written by actor Roy Hargrave with assistance from Laura Adair and Thomas Scofield, which opened for 25 performances beginning January 18, 1936, at the 46th Street Theatre. The story of A Room in Red and White was not dissimilar to Timber House: Beatrice Crandall (Chrystal Herne) with help from her devoted son Lawrence (Richard Kendrick) poisons her sadistic, despicable husband, Philip (Leslie Adams), aware he is going insane, arranging his death to appear to be suicide--all to no avail, since Philip was soon to die of terminal cancer.

Actor John Perry Boruff returned to Broadway as a playwright in 1938 when the Theatre Guild produced his adaptation, with Walter Hart, of Dalton Trumbo's novel Washington Jitters for twenty-five performances. Arthur Beckhard and David Merrick produced Boruff's play Bright Boy, which completed sixteen performances in 1944. Boruff adapted Ruth McKenney's novel The Loud Red Patrick to the stage, opening on Broadway on October 3, 1956, for a run of ninety-three performances. Boruff made his acting debut in 1929 and on September 24, 1963, had another one-performance casualty when he appeared in the role of Bentley in Bicycle Ride to Nevada.

* * *

'TIS OF THEE (Maxine Elliott's Theatre, October 26, 1940). Produced and directed by Nat Lichtman; A revue by Alfred Hayes; Sketches by Sam Locke; Music by Alex North and Al Moss; Lyrics by Alfred Hayes; Additional Music and Lyrics by Peter Barry, David Gregory and Richard Lewine; Settings, Carl Kent; Choreography, Esther Junger; Musical director, Alex Saron; Directorial assistant, Paul Roberts; Company manager, E. L. Hardy; Stage director, Chet O'Brien; Stage manager, Saint Arnold Subber
    George Lloyd; Esther Junger; Jerry Munson; Van Kirk; Jack Berry; Sherle Hartt; Mervyn Nelson; Daniel Nagrin; Laura Duncan; Vivian Block; Arno Tanny; Paul Roberts; Alfred Hayes; Saida Gerard; Susan Remos; Bram Vandenberg; Ray Harrison; Jan Zerfing; Alfred and Reese; Virginia Burke; Cappelo and Beatrice; Jane Hoffman
SONGS: You've Got to Have Something to Sing About When You Sing; Lupe; What's Mine Is Thine; Cantata; After Tonight; Ballroom Ballad; The Lady; Hawaiian Ritual; Noises in the Street; 'Tis of Thee; The Rhythm Is Red an' White an' Blue; Tomorrow

'Tis of Thee originated during the summer of 1940 at the Forrest Park, Pa., Unity House of the International Ladies' Garment Workers Union. The revue was called "witless" and, as noted by Gerald Bordman (American Musical Theatre), "The cast was damned as 'untalented,' their material 'poor.'" 'Tis of Thee in no way compared to the International Ladies' Garment Workers Union's 1937 smash-hit revue Pins and Needles, which opened on November 27, 1937, at the Labor Stage Theatre (formerly the 299-seat Princess Theatre) and moved to the larger Windsor Theatre to complete 1,108 performances highlighted by Harold Rome's first Broadway score.

Actors' Equity rebated $60 to the non-Equity cast members of 'Tis of Thee in recognition of their dismal one-performance fiasco and, possibly, so they could maintain their amateur standing. Of greater import than the failed revue was the presence of Saint Arnold Subber as stage manager. Saint-Subber became one of Broadway's leading producers eight years later with the smash hit Kiss Me, Kate and produced, among others, such successes as My Three Angels; The Dark at the Top of the Stairs; Barefoot in the Park: The Odd Couple; and Plaza Suite.

* * *

TOPAZE (Morosco Theatre, December 27, 1947). Produced by Yolanda Mero-Iron; The New Opera Company Production; A revival of a comedy by Marcel Pagnol, adapted by Benn W. Levy; Director, Leo Mittler; Settings, Oliver Smith; Lighting, Peggy Clark; Costumes, Audre; Company manager, Robert Milford; Stage manager, David Jones

Oscar Karlweis (Topaze); Tilly Losch (Suzanne Courtoise); Clarence Derwent (Regis Castel-Benac); Helen Bonfils (Baroness Pitart-Vergniolles); Joe E. Marks (Tamise); Robert Chisholm (Muche); Effie Afton (Ernestine Muche); Philip Robinson (Roger de Berville); Edward Benjamin (Pitart-Vergniolles); Ethel Madsen (Germaine); G. Swayne Gordon (A Venerable Old Man); Kevin Matthews (Cordier); Clifford Sales (Jusserand); Preston Zukor (Tronce-Bobine); Roy Rogers (DeVictor); Sonny Cavell (Durand); David Burke (Ramon); Harold Calvin (Perron); Alan Shay (Blondet); Jan Kindler (Policeman); Lucille Patton (Odette); Jean Saks (Butler)

Topaze, impeccably honest, dedicated Pension Muche professor, refuses to alter a report card of incorrigible Agenor Pitart-Vergniolles, son of the school's wealthy patrons, Baron and Baroness Pitart-Vergniolles, in May of 1910. He is fired. Naive Topaze is befriended by Suzy Courtoise and given a position by her lover, corrupt city councilor Castel-Benac. Clearly aware he is being used as a political dupe, Topaze, emancipated and awakened to the world's realities, greedily embraces and adds new dimensions to political corruption. After being honored for his efforts with the ribbon and palm from the French Academy, Topaze replaces the genius of graft, Castel-Benac, wins the love of his mistress, Suzy, and finds a new maxim: dishonesty does pay.

Topaze opened in Paris at the Théâtre de Variétiés on October 9, 1928, to run for two years. Benn W. Levy's English adaptation of the comedy opened on Broadway at the Music Box Theatre on February 12, 1930, starring Frank Morgan as the wily professor. Critic George Freedley called the play "a masterpiece of satire in its study of unscrupulousness." Raymond Massey was London's Topaze, at the New Theatre on October 8, 1930. The English translations of Pagnol's comedy were not especially successful. The original French version of the play was seen at Broadway's 49th Street Theatre on February 16, 1931, and on December 27, 1947, Topaze was revived yet again, with Oscar Karlweis in the title role. Critics slaughtered the revival and Topaze disappeared after one performance.

* * *

TOTAL ABANDON (Booth Theatre, April 28, 1983). Produced by Elizabeth I. McCann, Nelle Nugent, Ray Larsen, William J. Meloche, Patrick S. Brigham, John Roach; A drama by Larry Atlas; Director, Jack Hofsiss; Setting, David Jenkins; Lighting, Beverly Emmons; Costumes, Julie Weiss; Associate producers, Marc E. Platt, Sander Jacobs, Tommy DeMaio; Production coordinator, May Nealon; Director's assistant, David Rodriguez; Wardrobe, Don Grubler; Production assistant, Maureen Grady; Incidental music, Michael Dansicker; Company manager, Susan Gustafson; Props, Mel Saltzman, Thomas J. Boles; Sound, Louis Shapiro; General management, McCann & Nugent; Stage managers, Ruth E. Rinklin, Mark Schorr

Richard Dreyfuss (Lenny Keller); John Heard (Henry Hirsch); George N. Martin (Walter Bellmon); Clifton James (Ben Hammerstein)

Psychiatrist Henry Hirsch reserves his opinions, but court-appointed lawyer Ben Hammerstein and Midwestern county court psychiatrist Dr. Walter Bellmon are revolted by neurotic Lenny Keller, a misfit jailed for child abuse, disliked by his neighbors, and rejected by his peers. Lenny's battered wife left him to raise his infant son, and he is facing trial for beating his two-year-old son, Tom, into an irreversible coma. Young Tom is considered medically dead although kept alive by a life-support machine. Lenny takes legal action to keep his comatose son on the life-support system, aware that he will be charged with murder should Tom die. Lenny's declaration of his intense love for children, "You just love 'em to death" hardly supports his manic treatment of Tom when, to stop the child's incessant crying, he threw him against a wall. Lenny's appeal to the court is denied and his son dies. Holding his dead son's pajamas, Lenny hysterically sobs, "This is my Boy!"

"Total Abandon," wrote Clive Barnes (New York Post) is "almost a total loss--The play's idea is not a bad one--not good, but not bad" but "far less deep than it can be made to sound. Though the story is horribly conceivable, the writing is strangely banal and unconvincing--You know what is going to happen from the beginning--

and it is somewhat tedious getting to the end." Douglas Watt (Daily News) admired the performance given by Richard Dreyfuss as the psychotic Keller, "Dreyfuss brings everything he has--and it's a great deal--to his amorphous role. But Total Abandon is cheap stuff masquerading as serious-minded drama--Lending a false air of importance to the play's meretricious employment of the subject of child abuse in its arty presentation."

Total Abandon was first produced by Elizabeth I. McCann, Nelle Nugent, and Ray Larsen at the Off-Broadway Perry Street Theatre on June 5, 1982, for twenty-eight performances. Director, Jack Hofsiss; Setting, David Jenkins; Lighting, Beverly Emmond; Costumes, Julie Weiss; Company manager, Mary T. Nealon; Technical director, Paul Everett; Stage managers, Helaine Head, C. Townsend Olcott, II

Jeffrey DeMunn (Lenny Keller); John Heard (Henry Hirsch); Michael Lerner (Ben Hammerstein); W. B. Brydon (Walter Bellmon)

During their seven-year partnership Elizabeth I. McCann and Nelle Nugent produced several notable Broadway hits, in association with Ray Larsen and others. McCann and Nugent presented The American National Theatre and Academy production of Bernard Pomerance's seering drama The Elephant Man on Broadway on April 19, 1979. Co-produced with Richmond Crinkle and directed by Jack Hofsiss, The Elephant Man was the recipient of several awards and played 907 performances. McCann, Nugent, and Larsen brought the revival of Paul Osborn's charming 1939 play Mornings at Seven back to Broadway on April 10, 1980, where the award-winning revival played 564 performances. With the Shubert Organization and Roger S. Berlind, McCann and Nugent presented Peter Shaffer's brilliant play Amadeus on December 17, 1980. In 1981 McCann and Nugent were the producers of Pam Gems's Piaf; Andrew Davies' Rose; Ronald Harwood's drama The Dresser, and Bill C. Davis' hilarious two-character comedy Mass Appeal.

James M. Nederlander, The Shubert Organization, and McCann and Nugent imported David Edgar's The Life and Adventures of Nicholas Nickleby from London to Broadway on October 4, 1981. The beautifully produced and superbly acted Nickleby was the first Broadway show to command an overall ticket price of $100, during its limited engagement of 102 performances. Total Abandon had been fairly well received in its out-of-town tryout, but after seven previews it was abandoned on Broadway after one performance.

Jon Jory's The Actor's Theatre of Louisville, Kentucky, commissioned and produced actor Larry Atlas's one-act monologue The Subject Animal in which an army medical officer graphically describes the unsettling and gruesome experiments made on goats. Playwright Atlas appeared with several regional acting companies in many roles and for several years he was the Captain of "The Spaced Rangers," a skydiving team. Total Abandon was Larry Atlas's first Broadway-produced play.

While Total Abandon was considered less a play and more of "an amorphous smokescreen of filler and endlessly repeated exposition," Richard Dreyfuss's powerful performance as psychotic Lenny Keller was formidable. Thirty-five-year-old Brooklyn-born Richard Dreyfuss attained stardom in a series of Hollywood films (American Graffiti, Jaws, Close Encounters of the Third Kind) and won an Academy Award as Best Actor of the Year for his performance as Elliott Garfield in Neil Simon's 1977 original screenplay The Goodbye Girl. Prior to returning to the Broadway stage, Dreyfuss had played the leading role in the screen version of Brian Clark's 1979 play Whose Life Is It Anyway?

* * *

TOUGH TO GET HELP (Royale Theatre, May 4, 1972). Produced by Sandy Farber and Stanley Barnett in association with Jules Love and Roy Rubin; A comedy by Steve Gordon; Director, Carl Reiner; Setting, Ed Wittstein; Lighting, John Gleason; Costumes, Joseph G. Aulisi; Production assistant, Ron Cummins; Producers assistant, Ken Burros; Associate Producer, Larry Rosen; General manager, Elias Goldin; Stage managers, Lee Murray, Stephen P. Pokart
   John Amos (Luther Jackson); Lillian Hayman (Beulah Jackson); Dick O'Neil (succeeded Jack Cassidy) (Clifford Grant); Billie Lou Watt (Elaine Grant); Abe Vigoda (Abe Lincoln); John Danelle (Leroy Jackson/Young Luther); Chip Fields (Carlotta/Young Beulah); Jimmy Pelham (Pee Wee); Anthony Palmer (Mr. Charlie); Ralph Carter (Boy Ghost)

Leroy Jackson arrives in the Larchmont, New York, home of excessively liberal, if patronizing, white advertising executive Clifford Grant to visit his parents, Luther and Beulah Jackson, Grant's gardener and cook. Leroy proudly proclaims his new militant, destructive life as a member of the Black Bombers, who have just blown up a bank. Luther, well aware of the disadvantages of being black but satisfied with the life he and Beulah have made, resents Leroy's classifying him as an Uncle Tom and is horrified at his son's attempt to turn him into a radical. Luther, however, discovers that Grant's liberalism is masked, hypocritical racism and in his dreams Abe Lincoln encourages him to fight for the black man's rights. Luther and Beulah verbally blast Grant for what he really is and resign, taking with them ten thousand dollars Grant had fraudulently acquired and never reported. They leave for Harlem to join their son and his girl friend, Carlotta.

The excellent performances of Tough to Get Help's cast, especially John Amos, who carried the play and enlivened the script, could not save Steve Gordon's comedy, which was compared with television's long-running series All in the Family. "John Amos is delightful throughout" reported Richard Watts (New York Post) but classifying the play as "The Rebellion of Uncle Tom," added, "If Tough to Get Help had been a serious drama this might have been powerful and striking, but it is intended as a comedy, and it doesn't work." Brendan Gill (The New Yorker) dismissed the play as "a disgusting attempt at comedy."

Clive Barnes (The New York Times) reported Tough to Get Help "tries so hard to be funny that it ought to have succeeded better than it did--When it all started out there might have been a play somewhere around. It got lost." Douglas Watt (Daily News) compared the comedy to a "slickly presented idiocy" which would be "like pure gold to a television producer--The jokes come thick and fast, cleverly constructed and staged and delivered with professional skill" but "As a theater piece, it's simply idiotic--a tasteless joke."

Tough to Get Help began its twenty-two previews on April 14, 1972, starring musical-comedy headliner Jack Cassidy. Cassidy, who burned to death at the age of forty-nine in Los Angeles on December 12, 1976, "withdrew" from the cast and on Tuesday, April 25th Dick O'Neil replaced him as Clifford Grant. The opening of Tough to Get Help was postponed from Saturday, April 29th to Thursday May 4th, when it gave its one and only official performance.

* * *

TRICKS OF THE TRADE (Brooks Atkinson Theatre, November 6, 1980). Produced by Gilbert Cates, in association with Matthew Alexander; A "romantic mystery" by Sidney Michaels; Director, Gilbert Cates; Setting and lighting, Peter Dohanos; Costumes, Albert Wolsky; Incidental music, Charles Fox; Song "My Funny Valentine" by Richard Rodgers and Lorenz Hart; Sound, Peter Berger; Production associate, Tom Folino; Wardrobe, Sally D. Smith; Production associate, Nancy B. Dodds; Assistant to producer, Peggy Griffin; General manager, Paul Libin; Company manager, Sally Campbell; Stage managers, Martin Gold; Carlos Gorbea
    George C. Scott (Dr. August Browning); Trish Van Devere (Diana Woods); Lee Richardson (Howard); Geoffrey Pierson (Paul)

When not active as an agent for the C.I.A., Dr. August Browning has established a psychiatric practice, though he has never attended medical school, and he is in possession of lists of secret agents of the C.I.A. and Russia's K.G.B. His new, mysterious patient, Diana Woods, of bewildering, undetermined neurosis, could be the secret agent seeking both lists or the unknown dangerous spy who killed his C.I.A. partner in Prague the previous year. Dr. Browning feels his life is in jeopardy and he is plagued by persistent, periodic visits from C.I.A. agents Howard and Paul, demanding the secret lists of agents. Dr. Browning surreptitiously films his inconclusive sessions with his strangely mysterious patient Diana, including their erotic love affair. The nemesis of the "Doctor" is finally discovered, and Browning and Diana have fallen in love.

Sidney Michaels "romantic mystery" was neither romantic nor

mysterious, other than it was produced at all and that George C. Scott agreed to play the leading role. "Tricks of the Trade," reported Frank Rich (The New York Times), "is so limp it makes the cold war seem slightly less exciting than 'Bowling for Dollars'--Under Gilbert Cate's static direction, both performances are unusually irritating." Clive Barnes (New York Post) headed his review with "By George, it's a foul 'Trick,'" adding, "if Tricks of the Trade, which unaccountably opened, and must therefore be accountably dealt with --is not the worst play of the season then its vanquisher must be awesomely awful indeed." Douglas Watt (Daily News) called the play "a dog of a thriller--an indigestible stew" which "wouldn't even make a good bad movie."

Playwright Sidney Michaels' play The Plaster Bambino, starring Burgess Meredith and Viveca Lindfors, was produced by the San Francisco Actors' Workshop in 1960 and won the Ford Foundation Playwriting award. Michaels' first Broadway success was his adaptation of François Billetdoux's French comedy Tchin Tchin, starring Anthony Quinn and Margaret Leighton (succeeded by Arlene Francis and Jack Klugman), which opened at the Plymouth Theatre on October 25, 1962, and closed after 222 performances. Alec Guinness starred in Michaels' 1964 play Dylan for 273 performances and, on October 27, 1964, Michaels' book and lyrics set to music by Mark Sandrich for Ben Franklin in Paris headlined Robert Preston, who kept the unexciting book and dreary score alive for 215 performances. Joel Grey starred in Michaels' Goodtime Charley, with music and lyrics by Larry Grossman and Hal Hackady, for 104 performances in 1975. Indecisive Charley never decided whether to be a drama or comedy. Michaels' Tricks of the Trade was a trick played on unsuspecting playgoers but arrived a week late. Hallow'een had also had a one-night stand the previous week.

* * *

TRULY VALIANT (49th Street Theatre, January 9, 1936). Produced by Gustav Blum in association with Ernest W. Mandeville; A drama by Irving Stone; Director, Gustav Blum; Setting, Louis Bromberg
    Margot Stevenson (Berna Bowen); Ian Maclaren (Esa Cranby, Ph.D.); Alan Handley (Dale Cranby); Martha Mayo (Martha Cranby)

California student Berna Bowen, working as a maid in the home of economics professor Esa Cranby to pay her college tuition and expenses, is tutored and seduced by the eminent professor, author, and government consultant for all New Deal financial strategy. The professor's son, Dale, and Berna fall in love but Berna refuses to marry him as she is pregnant with his father's child. Professor Cranby and his wife, Martha, encourage Berna to marry their son, but without telling him the lurid truth. However, Berna confesses to Dale that she is carrying his father's child. Dale furiously strikes his father, then leaves with Berna for St. Louis, resolved to accept her illegitimate child.

Novelist Irving Stone prefaced his first play, Truly Valiant, with a quotation from a far better playwright, William Shakespeare: "He's truly valiant, that can wisely suffer, The worst that man can breathe" (Alcibiades to the Senators, Timon of Athens, Act III, Scene V). Considering the appraisal of Truly Valiant by all the critics, the quotation could have applied to Mr. Stone's initial Broadway effort.

John Mason Brown (The Evening Post) reported "Mr. Stone's four-character play is claptrap of the sorriest, most sententious and absurd sort--There is really nothing else that self-respecting people can do in the presence of such a play as Truly Valiant except laugh nervously and uncomfortably." Richard Lockridge (The Evening Sun) called the play "a distressing error" and, for the valiant cast, added, "To the four members of Equity whose almost unparalleled misfortune it was to be involved in this absurdity my deepest sympathy goes out." Brooks Atkinson (The New York Times) dismissed the play as "a completely humorless exercise" which was badly acted. Gilbert W. Gabriel (The American) found it "undeniably pretty bad" and Percy Hammond (Herald-Tribune) felt a Pulitzer Prize or similar award should be given to the players of Truly Valiant who "gave an exhibition of courage in the face of calamity" in a "ludicrous tragedy." Robert Garland (World-Telegram) found the play to be "One of the most acutely embarrassing theatrical misadventures" and "a disaster in dialogue."

Irving Stone, born Irving Tennenbaum in San Francisco on July 14, 1903, wisely abandoned playwriting after Truly Valiant to become one of America's leading biographical novelists. His novel Lust for Life, based on the life of artist Vincent Van Gogh, was acclaimed in 1934. Sailor on Horseback; the Biography of Jack London appeared in 1938, and his book Immortal Wife, based on Jessie Benton Fremont, was published in 1944. Ten years later, Stone's biography of Mary Todd Lincoln, called Love is Eternal, was published, and in 1961 his lengthy, fictionalized biography of the life of Michaelangelo Buonarroti, The Agony and the Ecstasy, became a great success. David W. Rintels adapted Stone's 1941 biography Clarence Darrow for the Defense to the stage as a solo drama, which opened on March 26, 1974, at the Helen Hayes Theatre, starring the late, great Henry Fonda.

Novelist-biographer Irving Stone, aware of his failure with Truly Valiant, amitted, "I realized two things: one, that I had no talent for dramaturgy; and two, that I liked writing in biographical materials."

* * *

THE UTTER GLORY OF MORRISSEY HALL (Mark Hellinger Theatre, May 13, 1979). Produced by Arthur Whitelaw, Albert W. Selden, H. Ridgely Bullock in association with Marc Howard; A musical with

Book by Clark Gesner and Nagle Jackson; Music and Lyrics by Clark Gesner; Director, Nagle Jackson; Musical numbers and dances staged by Buddy Schwab; Setting and lighting, Howard Bay; Costumes, David Graden; Orchestrations, Jay Blackton, Russell Warner; Musical director, John Lesko; Dance music arrangements, Allen Cohen; Sound, Charles Bellin; Associate conductor, Woody Kessler; Wardrobe, Remigia Marmo; Producer's assistant, Howard P. Lev; Production assistant, Tom Carroll; Associate producer, Sandy Stern; Hairstylist, Vincent of Enrico Caruso; Stage managers, Bryan Young, Gail Pearson, Mark S. Krause

    Celeste Holm (Julia Faysle, Headmistress); Taina Elg (Mrs. Delmonde); Patricia Falkenhain (Foresta Studley); Marilyn Caskey (Elizabeth Wilkins, Secretary); Laurie Franks (Teresa Winkle); Mary Saunders (Carswell); Karen Gibson (Miss Newton); John Wardell (Mr. Weyburn, Groundskeeper); Gina Franz (Vickers); Jill P. Rose (Dale); Adrienne Alexander (Boody); Kate Kelly (Dickerson); Polly Pen (Haverfield); Cynthia Parva (Alice); Becky McSpadden (Helen); Dawn Jeffory (Frances); Bonnie Hellman (Angela); Anne Kaye (Marjorie); Lauren Shub (Mary); Willard Beckham (Richard Tidewell); John Gallogly (Charles Hill); Robert Lanchester (Mr. Osgood); John Lesko (Miss Potts)

SONGS: Promenade; Proud, Erstwhile, Upright, Fair; Elizabeth's Song; Way Back When; Lost; The Letter; Morning; Oh Sun; Give Me That Key; Duet; Interlude and Gallop; See the Blue; You Will Know When the Time Has Arrived; You Would Say; Dance of Resignation; Reflection; The War; The Ending

    Eccentric headmistress Julia Faysle, of an English school for girls called Morrissey Hall, is besieged, bedeviled, and bewildered by the lunatic antics of her pupils. Girls of the 6th Form declare war on the girls of the 5th Form. Dancing teacher Mrs. Delmonde, communicating only from the fifth position and in dance, finally arabesques her resignation. The warfare between the young ladies of Morrissey Hall climaxes in the use of a battle tank and cannon.

    The Utter Glory of Morrissey Hall was reminiscent of the manic girls and addled staff of Ronald Searle's comic strip Belles of St. Trinians, which was filmed in 1954 and far out-distanced the youthful awakening of the Scottish girls in The Prime of Miss Jean Brodie. The adolescent antics of the girls of Morrissey Hall was created and set to music by Clark Gesner, originally produced in 1977 by Michael Kahn, producing director of Princeton's McCarter Theatre, by arrangement with Arthur Whitelaw, Albert W. Selden, H. Ridgely Bullock, and Arthur MacKenzie. The musical opened November 3, 1977. Director, Nagle Jackson; Settings and lighting, Howard Bay; Costumes, David Graden; Musical direction, Jay Blackton; Stage manager, Elizabeth Caldwell; Choreography, Michael Maurer

    Patricia Falkenhain (replaced Eileen Heckart) (Julia Faysle, Headmistress); Catherine Wolf (Mrs. Delmonde); Margaret Jilton (Foresta Studley); Marilyn Caskey (Elizabeth Wilkins, Secretary); Lois De Banzie (Teresa Winkle); Betsey Baird (Felicia Carswell); Diane

Tarleton (Miss Newton); Daniel Keyes (Mr. Weyburn); Gina Franz (Louise Vickers); Jill P. Rose (Eleanor Dale); Kathleen Swan (Pauline Boody); Kate Kelly (Florence Dickerson); Polly Pen (Mary Haverfield); Jane Rose (Emily Stokes, Former Headmistress); Cynthia Parva (Alice Stillwell); Mary Carney (Helen Wells-Morton); Dawn Jeffory (Frances Eaves); Meryl Goodfader (Angela Sutfin); Anne Kaye (Marjorie Wheatley); Lauren Shub (Mary Moley); Bonnie Hellman (Katherine Holly); Alice Nagel (Phoebe Hatch); Daniel Arden (Charles Hill); Gary Beach (Adult); Jeffrey Jones (Tom); Robert Henderson (Richard Tidewell)
SONG: "Whose Little Bird Are You" was dropped from the Broadway production.

The Utter Glory of Morrissey Hall was quickly deglorified by the critics. "It is relentlessly arch and silly, and not a single word uttered or sung in the course of it failed to ring false," reported Brendan Gill in The New Yorker. Clive Barnes (New York Post) wrote, "What was good in this musical can be summed up in two words, Celeste Holm, who was celestial even if not at home--A peculiarly tedious musical." Douglas Watt (Daily News) added, "A musical came to the Hellinger last evening without the slightest justification of being there.... This leaden affair seemed to cast a pall over most of the performers as well as the audience. And utterly lost in its utter dullness was Celeste Holm, its star." Richard Eder (The New York Times) found "It takes off at times in a chain of delightful absurdities; the chain breaks frequently, leaving a great many limp and uncertain intervals--The songs by Mr. Gesner--he wrote the lyrics and music, as well as collaborating on the book--vary from agreeable to undistinguished. Morrissey Hall is untidy, uneven and often a mess; yet, despite the crucial failure in the casting of its central role, it has a charm and sprightliness that are never quite extinguished."

Arthur Whitelaw (with Gene Persson) had produced John Gordon's comedy You're a Good Man, Charlie Brown, based on Charles M. Schulz's comic strip Peanuts, with music and lyrics by Clark Gesner, creator of The Utter Glory of Morrissey Hall. You're a Good Man, Charlie Brown opened Off-Broadway on March 7, 1967, at Theatre 80 St. Marks, with Gary Burghoff (later "Radar" of television's long-running series M*A*S*H) as Charlie Brown. The following year, four companies of You're a Good Man, Charlie Brown were trundling around America, with Wendell Burton, Alan Lofft, Jim Ricketts, and Gary Burghoff in the title role. When Charlie Brown closed on February 14, 1971, the Peanuts characters had accumulated 1,597 performances. Alas, Morrissey Hall's tenancy on Broadway was a one-night stand and seven previews.

* * *

A WARM BODY (Cort Theatre, April 15, 1967). Produced by Jeff Britton; A comedy by Lonnie Coleman; Director, Peter Van Zandt (replaced Charles Bowden); Setting and Lighting, Robert T. Williams;

Costumes, Anna Hill Johnstone; Production assistant, Gerald Thomas; General manager, Al Goldin; Stage managers, David Lipsky, Marian Graham, M. J. Boyer

Kevin McCarthy (Homer Jackson); Lois Markle (replaced Dina Merrill) (Kate Moorehead); Evelyn Russell (Audrey Brewer); Will Gregory (Alan Tomlinson); Franklin Cover (replaced Michael Sivy) (Charles Moorehead); Doris Rich (Mrs. Finn); Rita McLaughlin (Sally Moorehead); Anthony Loder (Benjamin Donleavy); Dorothy Sefton (replaced Anne Meacham) (Lola Jackson)

Middle-aged anthropologist Homer Jackson, an authority on pgymies and director of the Museum of Natural History, escorts Audrey Brewer to a small cocktail party in the Manhattan apartment of Kate Moorehead. Kate is writer of a newspaper column called "Solitary Bliss" or "How to live alone and like it." Audrey leaves the party with Alan, and Homer remains alone with Kate. Having failed at two marriages, Homer is presently avoiding his bitchy second wife, who is eager for alimony, and accepts Kate's offer to spend the weekend. For sixteen years, Kate has been agonizing over having given her illegitimate child away, while Homer attributes his current loneliness to becoming merely another substitute person or a warm body. Homer and Kate realize they can recapture happiness by staying together.

The reviews for A Warm Body would have been more appropriate for a cold one awaiting burial. Walter Kerr (The New York Times) wrote, "It's a drop-in play. You feel that you've dropped in unexpectedly on the performers, or they've dropped in on you, but you're not sure which. This creates a social problem: Who should leave first?" Herbert Kupferberg (World Journal Tribune) reported, "'I'm a substitute person,' remarks Kevin McCarthy--and in much the same way the play itself is a substitute comedy." Douglas Watt (Daily News) considered "A Warm Body ... the kind of play an actor is lucky to come out of alive," and that "Peter Van Zandt has directed A Warm Body as if he'd fallen asleep listening to it." New York Post's Richard Watts, Jr. dismissed A Warm Body as "one of the most forgettable little plays imaginable."

A Warm Body premiered at the Royal Poinciana Playhouse in Palm Beach, Florida, on February 20, 1967, for a one-week tryout. Broadway previews were scheduled to begin on March 27th at the Cort Theatre, but Lois Markle's replacement of the suddenly ill Dina Merrill postponed previews until April 11th. After five previews, A Warm Body opened and closed on April 15, 1967.

Playwright Lonnie Coleman's previous Broadway effort was an adaptation of his novel Adams' Way, retitled Jolly's Progress, which opened on December 6, 1959, at the Longacre Theatre. Produced by The Theatre Guild and Arthur Loew, Jolly's Progress featured Eartha Kitt, Wendell Corey, and Anne Revere for nine performances. April must be the cruelest month. Three years later, Coleman's seven-year-old comedy, retitled A Place for Polly, gave one performance on Broadway, on April 18, 1970.

* * *

THE WATERING PLACE (Music Box Theatre, March 12, 1969). Produced by Gene Persson and James Walsh; A drama by Lyle Kessler; Director, Alan Schneider; Setting, Robin Wagner; Lighting, Jules Fisher; Costumes, Jeanne Button; Associate producer, Rick Hobard; Production assistant, Carolyn Kapla; General Manager, Marvin A. Krauss; Stage managers, Frederic DeWilde, John Actman; Assistant to producers, Charlotte Solomon; Song, "When the Red, Red, Robin Comes Bob, Bob, Bobbin' Along" by Harry Woods
    Ralph Waite (replaced Robert F. Simon) (The Father, William Young); William Devane (Sonny); Shirley Knight (Janet); Vivian Nathan (replaced Tresa Hughes) (The Mother, Margaret Young)

    Sonny, a soldier home from the Vietnam conflict, visits the family of a comrade who died in a North Vietnamese prison camp. William Young, the stern, disciplinarian father of the deceased soldier, is a vigorous, sixty-seven-year-old veteran of two wars, who plays nine innings of baseball every Sunday and heartily disliked his overly protected, weak son, pampered by his neurotic mother, Margaret. The mother has never recovered from the loss of her beloved son and she secludes herself in their dismally darkened home, placating her sorrow with anticipation of the birth of her son's child. Her over-sexed daughter-in-law, Janet, despised her now-dead husband but she encourages Margaret's fantasy by wearing a pillow under her clothing, simulating pregnancy for fifteen months. Sonny rapes and impregnates Janet, breaks William's arm in a brawl, then leaves the despairing family to wallow in their individual miseries.

    Whitney Bolton (The Morning Telgraph) reported The Watering Place "turns out to be very dry bones. It is laden, larded and lathered with more messages than Western Union conveniently could handle in the compass of 24 hours." Clive Barnes (The New York Times) also found "no shortage of messages. It is only the messenger he lacks. The expression of the play is as labored as the ideas are obvious--The play is intended to be strong, but instead it lurches from one nadir of bathos to the next."

    Rehearsals for The Watering Place began on January 6, 1969, directed by Michael Langham, former British director of Canada's Shakespeare Festival and many Broadway Shakespearean revivals, who had also directed the successful 1968 Broadway production of Jay Presson Allen's delightful play The Prime of Miss Jean Brodie. Hollywood character actor Robert F. Simon, cast as the father, William, was coached in baseball techniques and background by New York Mets pitcher Al Jackson, and Tresa Hughes was assigned the role of the mother, Margaret. Simon was replaced during rehearsals by Ralph Waite, a former United Church of Christ minister who became a fine actor and later played John, the father of television's The Waltons for several years, beginning in 1972. Tresa Hughes was replaced by Vivian Nathan as the mother, Margaret, and Alan Schneider, the prestigious director of a long line of Broadway successes, replaced director Langham.

Thirty-three-year-old Philadelphia playwright Lyle Kessler left Temple University as a pre-med student to become an actor. He studied with and became a director at Lee Strasberg's Actors' Studio. Kessler wrote and directed his first play, The Viewing, a one-act drama coupled with Curtis Zahn's play Conditioned Reflex, which was given two performances Off-Broadway at the Theatre De Lys on January 9th and 10th in 1967, and in March 1967 he completed his first full-length play, The Watering Place.

The playwright described The Watering Place as "Not naturalistic. It's extended a little beyond realism. The action takes place in the home and it does not refer to the war but it's about man's inheritance--whatever that means. Man's survival. The survival of the strong. It's a drama, but very funny. Hopefully the audience will laugh and cry." The audience did not cry but they did laugh. As Clive Barnes noted, "Little by way of humor was--I think-- intended, yet the play got more laughs than the last three Broadway comedies put together."

The Watering Place had twenty-five previews and "the survival of the strong" survived one performance.

* * *

WILD AND WONDERFUL (Lyceum Theatre, December 7, 1971). Produced by Rick Hobard in association with Raymonde Weil; A "Big City Fable" musical, based on a story by Bob Brotherson and Bob Miller; Book by Phil Phillips; Music and Lyrics by Bob Goddman; Director, Burry Fredrik; Setting, Stephen Henrickson; Lighting, Neil Peter Janpolis; Costumes, Frank Thompson; Musical direction, Vocal arrangements, Dance music composed and arranged by Thom Janusz; Orchestrations, Luther Henderson; Hairstylist, Nino Raffaello; Dances and musical numbers staged by Ronn Forella; Associate producer, John C. O'Regan; General manager, William Carver; Company manager, Stanley Brody; Stage managers, Robert Keegan, Louis Pulvino, Philip Killian

Laura McDuffie (Jenny); Walter Willison (Charlie); Robert Burr (Lionel Masters); Ted Thurston (Father Desmond); Larry Small (Brother John); Yveline Baudez, Pam Blair, Mary Ann Brunning, Carol Conte, Bob Daley, Anna Maria Fanizzi, Marcelo Gamboa, Adam Grammis, Patti Haine, Ann Reinking, Jimmy Roddy, Steven Vincent, Eddie Wright, Jr. (Ensemble)

SONGS: Wild and Wonderful; Moment Is Now; Desmond's Dilemma; My First Moment; I Spy; Something Wonderful Can Happen; She Should Have Me; Jenny; Fallen Angels; Dance; Petty Crime; Come a Little Closer; Little Bits and Pieces; Is This My Town?; You Can Reach the Sun; Wait for Me; Chances.

   West Point dropout Charlie, son of a millionaire, becomes a C.I.A. agent assigned to infiltrate and investigate the prevalent radicalism of youth. When young New Jersey runaway Jenny tosses her schoolbooks off the George Washington Bridge, Charlie and his obtuse C.I.A. superior Lionel Masters believe her to be a terrorist-type bomb hurler. Charlie takes Jenny to a youth shelter, run by alcoholic Father Desmond and Brother John, where smoking pot and free love flourish. Charlie and Jenny fall in love and Jenny happily leaves the youth shelter and the C.I.A. loses an agent.

   <u>Wild and Wonderful</u> was neither wonderful nor wild but after nine previews and one performance, it became one of Broadway's bombs. Clive Barnes (<u>The New York Times</u>) viewed <u>Wild and Wonderful</u> as "The kind of show that sends you back to television--or, if that is too radical, at least back to television commercials--This is a show that insults the intelligence--a terrible and witless show." Richard Watts (<u>New York Post</u>) found the show "a little tame for Broadway" and it "isn't at all wild and is considerably less than wonderful." Douglas Watt (<u>Daily News</u>) reported "<u>Wild and Wonderful</u> is a pathetic musical" which "had the audacity to open--The book defies description--the music, lacking any style of its own, borrows from several other sources." Leonard Harris (WCBS) called the limited gross production surpassed "by the modesty of its talents" and "demonstrates that a Broadway musical doesn't have to be big to be bad."

*   *   *

THE WOMEN HAVE THEIR WAY (Shubert Theatre, December 7, 1935). Produced and directed by Eva Le Gallienne; A comedy by Serafin and Joaquin Alvarez-Quintero, translated by Helen and Harley Granville-Barker; Setting, Aline Bernstein; Costumes, Emma Cashin; Stage managers, Walter Tupper, Thelma Carpenter
   Richard Waring (Adolfo Adalid); Eva Le Gallienne (Juanita La Rosa); Florida Friebus (Angela); Genevieve Frizell (Santita); Hugh Buckler (Don Julian Figueredo); Eva Leonard Boyne (Dieguilla); Leona Roberts (Concha Puerto); Sayre Crawley (Don Cecilio); Pedro Galvan (Guitarra); Marion O'Neil (Pilar); William S. Phillips (Pepe Lora); Marion Evensen (Doña Helen Zurita); Walter Beck (The Sacristan of San Antonio); Amy Chandler (A Young Peasant Girl)

   Women outnumber men five to one in a small Andalusian village in Spain. Young Madrid lawyer Adolfo Adalid arrives on business and the village women decide he would be an excellent husband for their village beauty, Juanita La Rosa. Juanita's duenna, Doña Helen Zurita, and the anxious women connive and secretly arrange meetings between Adolfo and Juanita, who unexpectedly fall in love. Instead

of returning to Madrid the young lawyer decides to stay in the village
and marry Juanita. The women once again have had their way.

Gregorio Martinez-Sierra and Serafin and Joaquin Alverez-Quintero
were considered the high priests of Spanish sentimentalism. The
Alverez-Quintero brothers wrote many delightful comedies, of which The
Women Have Their Way was one filled with "piquant local color and
fine good humor." Eva Le Gallienne revived the brothers' The
Women Have Their Way, preceded by their one-act comedy A Sunny
Morning, at the Shubert Theatre in 1935 but the two short plays
lasted but one performance.

The New York Times appraised The Women Have Their Way
as a "charming vignette rather than a full bodied comedy" and "a
good humored spoof of village types," but "the forlorn little plot
seems very flimsy indeed."

Edward Chodorov later rewrote Serafin and Joaquin Alverez-
Quintero's comedy, updating the trifle to post-World War II and retitling the piece Signor Chicago.

Eva Le Gallienne first produced Serafin and Joaquin Alverez-
Quintero's play at her Civic Repertory Theatre on January 27, 1930
for twenty-five performances, preceded by Alfred Sutro's one-act
play The Open Door.

Produced by The Civic Repertory Theatre; Director, Eva Le
Gallienne; Setting, Aline Bernstein, executed by Cleo Throckmorton,
Inc.; Costumes, Aline Bernstein, assisted by Irene Sharaff; Trans-
lation by Helen and Harley Granville-Barker
  Donald Cameron (Adolfo Adalid); Eva Le Gallienne (Juanita La
  Rosa); Egon Brecher (Don Julian Figueredo); Leona Roberts
  (Concha Puerto); Robert Ross (Pepe Lora); Sayre Crawley (Don
  Cecilio); Mary Ward (Santita); Paula Miller (Dieguilla); J. Edward
  Bromberg (Guitarra); Josephine Hutchinson (Pilar); Rita Mooney
  (Angela); Walter Beck (The Sacristan of San Antonio); Elizabeth
  Shelly (A young peasant girl); Merle Maddern (Dona Helen Zurita)

J. Brooks Atkinson (The New York Times) admired the excep-
tional playwriting talent of the Alvarez-Quintero brothers, Serafin
and Joaquin, but said of The Women Have Their Way, "It is not a
play, but a sketch in two acts. It is not a plot, but merely an impression of life in a small town." Still, "For group acting and direction, for grace of costuming and setting, and for a pleasantly silly
evening that has sufficient common sense under its skin, The Women
Have Their Way has its own way also in the theatre." Time magazine's appraisal of the leisurely, gentle comedy, in which the Alvarez-
Quintero brothers "realize that when there are no big things to be
dramatic small things become so" in their "glancing, fragile but
wholly affecting art," was that "The Civic Repertory company inter-
prets it admirably."

Alfred Sutro's one-act play was considered pretentious and "a stuffy piece of artificial playmaking." During the Civic Repertory company's tour Sutro's The Open Door was replaced by a one-act curtain raiser by the Alvarez-Quinteros called A Sunny Morning, translated by Lucretia Zavier Floyd. For the 1935 one-performance revival of The Women Have Their Way, Eva Le Gallienne again used A Sunny Morning to precede the Alvarez-Quintero's two-act comedy, using a translation by Helen and Harley Granville-Barker.

Playwright Edward Chodorov's first Broadway success was his adaptation of Hugh Walpole's thrilling story The Silver Casket, titled Kind Lady. Chodorov's play Cue for Passion (1940) survived only 12 performances and his Those Endearing Young Charms in 1943 completed 61 performances. His excellent drama Common Ground closed in 1945 after 69 performances, whereas his own produced drama Decision was classified as one of the ten best plays of the year in 1944, running twenty weeks. Edward Chodorov rewrote the brothers Alvarez-Quintero's comedy The Women Have Their Way in 1949, retitling it Signor Chicago. The Chodorov version never reached Broadway.

Signor Chicago (Opened November 3, 1949, New Haven, Conn.; Closed, November 19, 1949, Philadelphia, Pa.). Produced by Joseph M. Hyman; A comedy by Edward Chodorov, based on the Granville-Barker version of a play by the Alvarez-Quinteros, The Women Have Their Way; Director, John Burrell; Setting and lighting, Samuel Leve; Costumes, Morton Haack; Incidental music, Lehman Engel; General manager, Al Goldin; Stage managers, Sterling Mace, Elizabeth Sutton

> Alfred Ryder (Alfredo); Anne Shaw (Flavia); Guy Kibbee (Dr. Bacchelli); Edith King (Carolina); Joe E. Marks (Father Giovanni); Josephine Brown (Donna Clarice); Grace Mills (Sabina); Enid Pulver (Gina); Richard Bengali (Carolina's Servant); Lucyle Harmantas (Magdelena); Paula Trueman (Esperanza Prezzolini); Rosana (Rita) Moreno (Angela); Joe Verdi (Bobadilla); Wanda Sponda (Maria); Arny Freeman (Marienetti); Charles Mendlick (Ugo Bracco); Lee Graham (A Little Girl)

U.S. army captain Alfredo visits his ancestral home in a small, remote village in Italy after World War II, to settle the financial affairs of his aunt before returning home to Chicago. The village is devoid of young male population and handsome Captain Alfredo becomes the prime prospect for matrimony to the village matriarchy. Alfredo casually admires the village beauty, Flavia, and the matrons immediately arrange a wedding for "Signor Chicago." Dr. Bacchelli, having met a similar fate when he arrived in the village thirty years before on a house call, tries to divert the matriarchal maneuvering, as does meek little priest Father Giovanni. Dr. Bacchelli and Father Giovanni lose the battle of the sexes. Alfredo and Flavia discover they are really in love and eager to marry. The triumphant village matrons have had their way. Again.

BOMBS IN SEASON: CHRONOLOGICAL INDEX

1923-1924

Road Together, The

1925-1926

Beyond Evil

1929-1930

Mystery Moon

1931-1932

Destruction

1932-1933

Hummin' Sam
Marilyn's Affairs
Masks and Faces
Raw Meat

1933-1934

Strange Orchestra

1934-1935

Reprise

1935-1936

Satellite
Truly Valiant
Women Have Their Way, The

1936-1937

Money Mad
Timber House

1937-1938

Bridal Crown, The
Fickle Women
Reunion

1938-1939

Stop Press
Tell My Story

1939-1940

Once Upon a Time

1940-1941

'Tis of Thee

1941-1942

Good Neighbor

210 / Bombs in Season: Chronological Index

1943-1944

According to Law
Strange Play, A

1947-1948

Topaze

1951-1952

Hook 'n Ladder

1953-1954

Pin to See the Peepshow, A
Starcross Story, The

1958-1959

Masquerade

1960-1961

Julia, Jake and Uncle Joe
Once There Was a Russian

1961-1962

Garden of Sweets, The

1962-1963

Moon Besieged, The
On an Open Roof
Step on a Crack

1963-1964

Abraham Cochrane
Bicycle Ride to Nevada
Have I Got a Girl for You!
Murderer Among Us, A
Once for the Asking
Sunday Man, The

1964-1965

Kelly

1965-1966

First One Asleep, Whistle
Mating Dance
Me and Thee

1966-1967

Natural Look, The
Warm Body, A

1967-1968

Happiness Is Just a Little Thing
    Called a Rolls Royce
Here's Where I Belong
Johnny No-Trump

1968-1969

Billy
Cuban Thing, The
Mother Lover, The
Teaspoon Every Four Hours, A
Watering Place, The

1969-1970

Blood Red Roses
Brightower
Gantry
Place for Polly, A
Strada, La

1970-1971

Father's Day
Frank Merriwell
Johnny Johnson

1971/1972

Children! Children!
Heathen!
Ring Round the Bathtub
Tough to Get Help
Wild and Wonderful

1972-1973

Let Me Hear You Smile
No Hard Feelings
Status Quo Vadis

1973-1974

Rainbow Jones

1974-1975

Don't Call Back
Fame
Mourning Pictures

1975-1976

Home Sweet Homer

1976-1977

Something Old, Something New

1977-1978

November People, The
Stages

Break a Leg
Broadway Musical, A
Goodbye People, The
Gorey Stories
Meeting by the River, A
Utter Glory of Morrissey Hall, The

1980-1981

Animals
Broadway Follies
Frankenstein
I Won't Dance
Moony Shapiro Songbook, The
Onward Victoria
Tricks of the Trade

1981-1982

Cleavage
Little Johnny Jones
Ned and Jack
Play Me a Country Song
Ritz, The
Special Occasions

1982-1983

Dance a Little Closer
Guys in the Truck, The
Moose Murders
Total Abandon

ACTOR INDEX

ACKERMAN, LESLIE
  Mourning Pictures
AFTON, EFFIE
  Topaze
ALBERT, EDDIE
  No Hard Feelings
ALDREDGE, TOM
  Stages
ALLEN, BILLIE
  Teaspoon Every Four Hours, A
ALTMAN, FRIEDA
  Timber House
AMES, KENNETH
  Play Me a Country Song
AMOS, JOHN
  Tough to Get Help
ANSON, A. E.
  Road Together, The
ANTONIO, LOU
  Garden of Sweets, The
APPEL, ANNA
  Good Neighbor
APPELL, DON
  According to Law
ASHLEY, ELIZABETH
  Ring Round the Bathtub
ASTOR, MARY
  Starcross Story, The
AUBERJONOIS, RENE
  Break a Leg
AUSTIN, BETH
  Onward Victoria

BAIN, CONRAD
  Cuban Thing, The
BANG, CHARLES
  Hook 'n Ladder

BANNERMAN, MARGARET
  Starcross Story, The
BARBER, ELLEN
  Fame
BARCROFT, JUDITH
  Mating Dance
BARRETT, EDITH
  Strange Orchestra
BARTLETT, MARTINE
  Garden of Sweets, The
BATTISTA, LLOYD
  Guys in the Truck, The
BAVAN, YOLANDE
  Heathen!
BAXTER, KEITH
  Meeting by the River, A
BEACH, GARY
  Moony Shapiro Songbook, The
BEAL, JOHN
  Billy
BEBAN, GEORGE, JR.
  Tell My Story
BECK, THOMAS
  Raw Meat
BECK, VINCENT
  Moon Besieged, The
  Strada, La
BELL, RALPH
  Stop Press
BELLAVER, HARRY
  Tell My Story
BELT, MADELINE
  Hummin' Sam
BENIADES, TED
  Garden of Sweets, The
BENNETT, CARLYLE
  Satellite
BERGERE, LEE
  Happiness Is Just a Little Thing Called a Rolls Royce

BERLIN, ALEXANDRA
   Happiness Is Just a Little
     Thing Called a Rolls
     Royce
BERLINGER, WARREN
   Broadway Musical, A
BERNARDI, HERSCHEL
   Goodbye People, The
BEVANS, PHILLIPA
   Starcross Story, The
   Stop Press
BILLINGS, JAMES
   Johnny Johnson
BLACKWOOD, GEORGE
   Reprise
BLAIR, MARY
   Beyond Evil
BLYDEN, LARRY
   Mother Lover, The
BONELLI, WILLIAM
   Marilyn's Affairs
BONFILS, HELEN
   Topaze
BONNEY, AURORA
   Bridal Crown, The
BORUFF, JOHN
   Bicycle Ride to Nevada
BOSCO, PHILIP
   Stages
BOSLEY, TOM
   Murderer Among Us, A
BOSTICK, CYNTHIA
   Something Old, Something New
BOXLEITNER, BRUCE
   Status Quo Vadis
BRAMBELL, WILFRID
   Kelly
BRASWELL, CHARLES
   Me and Thee
BRENNAN, MAUREEN
   Little Johnny Jones
BRIGGS, DON
   Julia, Jake and Uncle Joe
BRITTON, BARBARA
   Me and Thee
BRODERICK, JAMES
   Johnny No-Trump
   Let Me Hear You Smile
BROOKS, DAVID
   Sunday Man, The
BROOKS, GERALDINE
   Brightower

BROOKS, HILDY
   Happiness Is Just a Little
     Thing Called A Rolls Royce
BROWN, KIRK
   Destruction
BROWN, MURRAY
   Fickle Women
BRYNNER, YUL
   Home Sweet Homer
BUCKLER, HUGH
   Women Have Their Way, The
BURR, ROBERT
   Wild and Wonderful
BUSCH, ROBERT
   Once Upon a Time
BYERS, CATHERINE
   Don't Call Back
BYRD, SAM
   Good Neighbor

CALVERT, PATRICIA
   Strange Orchestra
CAMERON, DONALD
   Timber House
CANNON, ALICE
   Johnny Johnson
CANNON, J. D.
   Mating Dance
CARIOU, LEN
   Dance a Little Closer
CARLSON, PHILIP
   Mourning Pictures
CARRADINE, JOHN
   Frankenstein
CARSON, JEANIE
   Blood Red Roses
CARTER, RALPH
   Tough to Get Help
CARYL, BERNICE
   Money Mad
CASKEY, MARILYN
   Utter Glory of Morrissey Hall,
     The
CASTAGNA, S. MARIO
   Fickle Women
CHANNING, STOCKARD
   No Hard Feelings
CHARLES, LEWIS
   Good Neighbor
CHASE, NORMAN
   Johnny Johnson

214 / Actor Index

CHASTIAN, DON
  Dance a Little Closer
CHISHOLM, ROBERT
  Topaze
CHRISTMAS, ERIC
  Once There Was a Russian
CHRISTOPHER, DENNIS
  Brothers
CLANTON, RALPH
  Strange Play, A
CLARENDON, JEAN
  Raw Meat
CLARK, ALEXANDER
  Julia, Jake and Uncle Joe
CLEMENTE, RENE
  Play Me a Country Song
CLYMER, JOHN
  Raw Meat
COCO, JAMES
  Here's Where I Belong
COLBERT, CLAUDETTE
  Julia, Jake and Uncle Joe
CONGDON, JAMES
  Moon Besieged, The
CONRIED, HANS
  Something Old, Something New
CONVERSE, FRANK
  Brothers
  First One Asleep, Whistle
CONVERSE-ROBERTS, WILLIAM
  Frankenstein
CONWAY, ROBERT C.
  Strange Orchestra
COOK, DONALD
  Masquerade
COOPER, MARILYN
  Teaspoon Every Four Hours, A
COSSART, VALERIE
  Strange Orchestra
COSTA, KATHLEEN
  Destruction
COVER, FRANKLIN
  Warm Body, A
COX, GERTRUDE "BABY"
  Hummin' Sam
CRAIG, NOEL
  Dance a Little Closer
CRAWLEY, SAYRE
  Women Have Their Way, The
CUMMINGS, VICKI
  Hook 'n Ladder

CUNNINGHAM, ZAMAH
  Reprise

DABDOUB, JACK
  Moose Murders
DAMON, CATHRYN
  Place for Polly, A
DANA, LEORA
  Mourning Pictures
DANELLE, JOHN
  Tough to Get Help
DANIELS, CAROLAN
  Me and Thee
DANSON, TED
  Status Quo Vadis
DARDEN, SEVERN
  Murderer Among Us, A
D'ARMS, TED
  On an Open Roof
DAVID, DANIEL
  Cleavage
DAVILA, DIANA
  Home Sweet Homer
  Stages
DAVIS, MICHAEL ALLEN
  Broadway Follies
DEIGHTON, ANN
  Masks and Faces
DE LAPPE, GEMZE
  Gorey Stories
DENNIS, SANDY
  Let Me Hear You Smile
DERE, ANN
  Timber House
DERWENT, CLARENCE
  Topaze
DEVANE, WILLIAM
  Watering Place, The
DEVLIN, JOHN
  Billy
DIENER, JOAN
  Home Sweet Homer
DIETRICH, DENA
  Here's Where I Belong
DITTMANN, DEAN
  Sunday Man, The
DIXON, BEVERLY
  No Hard Feelings
DONHOWE, GWYDA
  Broadway Musical, A

DONOVAN, CASEY
    Ritz, The
DONOVAN, LINDA
    Frank Merriwell
DRAKE, RONALD
    Blood Red Roses
DREYFUSS, RICHARD
    Total Abandon
DRISCOLL, KAWRIE
    Fame
DUELL, WILLIAM
    Stages
DUFF-MacCORMICK, CARA
    Animals
DUKES, DAVID
    Frankenstein
DUNN, RALPH
    Once for the Asking

EASON, MYLES
    Julia, Jake and Uncle Joe
EDWARDS, LYNN
    Marilyn's Affairs
EIKENBERRY, JILL
    Onward Victoria
ELCAR, DANA
    Murderer Among Us, A
ELDEN, EMILIE
    Fickle Women
ELG, TAINA
    Utter Glory of Morrissey Hall, The
ELIAS, TOM
    Cleavage
ELLERBE, HARRY
    Strange Orchestra
ELLIOTT, VIRGINIA
    Fickle Women
ELLIS, LARRY
    Frank Merriwell
ELSTON, ROBERT
    Garden of Sweets, The
EMERY, IAN
    Strange Orchestra
EVANS, SCOTT
    Moose Murders
EWING, GEOFFREY C.
    Guys in the Truck, The

FABRAY, NANETTE
    No Hard Feelings
FALKENHAIN, PATRICIA
    Utter Glory of Morrissey Hall, The
FARRELL, GLENDA
    Masquerade
FAYE, JOEY
    Ritz, The
FIELDS, CHIP
    Tough to Get Help
FLANAGAN, PAULINE
    Step on a Crack
FLANINGAM, LOUISA
    Play Me a Country Song
FLEMING, ALLAN
    Once Upon a Time
FORKUM, DEHNER
    Bridal Crown, The
FOSTER, DONALD
    Masks and Faces
FOX, ANDREW J., JR.
    Reunion
FOX, JANET
    Once for the Asking
FRANCINE, ANNE
    Broadway Musical, A
FRANCIS, ARLENE
    Don't Call Back
FRANCIS, NOEL
    Satellite
FRANCKS, DON
    Kelly
FREITAG, DOROTHEA
    Gantry
FRENCH, VALERIE
    Mother Lover, The
FRIEBUS, FLORIDA
    Women Have Their Way, The
FRIZELL, GENEVIEVE
    Women Have Their Way, The
FULLER, PENNY
    Moon Besieged, The

GABLE, JUNE
    Moose Murders
GAINES, MARJORIE
    Mystery Moon
GALLOWAY, JANE
    Little Johnny Jones

GENEST, EDMOND
    Onward Victoria
GILBERT, LEWIS
    Stop Press
GILLETTE, ANITA
    Kelly
GION, RUTH
    Destruction
GLEASON, JAMES
    Guys in the Truck, The
GLOVER, JOHN
    Frankenstein
GOETZ, PETER MICHAEL
    Ned and Jack
GOLDBLUM, JEFF
    Moony Shapiro Songbook, The
GOLONKA, ARLENE
    I Won't Dance
GORCEY, BERNARD
    Satellite
GORDON, DON
    On an Open Roof
GORDON, G. SWAYNE
    Topaze
GORDON, RICHARD
    Strange Play, A
GORRIN, MICHAEL
    Have I Got a Girl for You!
GREENHOUSE, MARTHA
    Garden of Sweets, The
GREER, MICHAEL
    Ritz, The
GREGORY, WILL
    Warm Body, A
GRIFFIES, ETHEL
    Natural Look, The
GRIFFIN, SEAN
    Ned and Jack
GRIGGS, JOHN
    Abraham Cochrane
GROVER, STANLEY
    Don't Call Back
GUARDINO, LAWRENCE
    Guys in the Truck, The

HACKMAN, GENE
    Natural Look, The
HAILEY, MARION
    Mating Dance
HAINES, A. LARRY
    No Hard Feelings
HANDLEY, ALAN
    Truly Valiant
HARAN, RONNIE
    Step on a Crack
HARDING, ANN
    Abraham Cochrane
HAREWOOD, DORIAN
    Don't Call Back
HARRINGTON, PAT
    Happiness Is Just a Little
    Thing Called a Rolls Royce
HARRIS, EDNA MAE
    Good Neighbor
HARRIS, JULIE
    Break a Leg
HARRIS, ROBERT H.
    Tell My Story
HARRISON, ROBERT
    According to Law
HATFIELD, MARGARET
    Raw Meat
HAYES, ALFRED
    'Tis of Thee
HAYES, HERBERT
    Strange Play, A
HAYES, MARGARET
    Step on a Crack
HAYMAN, LILLIAN
    Tough to Get Help
HAYNES, TIGER
    Broadway Musical, A
HAYS, KATHRYN
    Moon Besieged, The
HEARD, JOHN
    Total Abandon
HECKART, EILEEN
    Mother Lover, The
HEGEZ, ROBERT
    Don't Call Back
HENRITZE, BETTE
    Here's Where I Belong
HICKEY, WILLIAM
    Step on a Crack
HINGLE, PAT
    Johnny No-Trump
HINNANT, BILL
    Frank Merriwell
HOBEL, MARA
    Moose Murders

HODES, GLORIA
  Gantry
HODGES, ANN
  Heathen!
HOFFMAN, JANE
  Murderer Among Us, A
  'Tis of Thee
HOLM, CELESTE
  Utter Glory of Morrissey Hall, The
HOOKS, DAVID
  Gantry
HORTON, CLAUDE
  Pin to See the Peepshow, A
HUBBARD, ELIZABETH
  Children! Children!
  Dance a Little Closer

IRVING, GEORGE S.
  Murderer Among Us, A
IVES, ANN
  Masquerade

JAFFE, SAM
  Meeting by the River, A
JAMES, CLIFTON
  Total Abandon
JANNEY, LEON
  Kelly
JANIS, CONRAD
  No Hard Feelings
JENKIN, ALFRED
  Raw Meat
JENS, SALOME
  First One Asleep, Whistle
JEROME, TIMOTHY
  Moony Shapiro Songbook, The
JOCHIM, KEITH
  Frankenstein
JOHNS, CLAY
  Johnny Johnson
JOHNSON, VAN
  Mating Dance
JONES, ROBERT EARL
  Moon Besieged, The
JORDAN, RICHARD
  Bicycle Ride to Nevada
JOYCE, DOROTHEA
  Mourning Pictures

JULIA, RAUL
  Cuban Thing, The
JUNGER, ESTHER
  'Tis of Thee

KANE, CAROL
  Ring Round the Bathtub
KARLWEIS, OSCAR
  Topaze
KARR, PATTI
  Broadway Musical, A
KASTNER, PETER
  Rainbow Jones
KAY, GERALDINE
  Status Quo Vadis
KAYE, JUDY
  Moony Shapiro Songbook, The
KEARNEY, EILEEN
  Ring Round the Bathtub
KELLY, KITTY
  Mystery Moon
KERCHEVAL, KEN
  Father's Day
  Here's Where I Belong
KERT, LARRY
  Strada, La
KILTY, JEROME
  Pin to See the Peepshow, A
KING, EDITH
  Murderer Among Us, A
KING, JOSEPH
  Destruction
KIRBY, DURWARD
  Me and Thee
KIRBY, RANDY
  Me and Thee
KLAR, GARY
  Brothers
  Guys in the Truck, The
KNIGHT, SHIRLEY
  Watering Place, The
KOLOGI, MARK
  Don't Call Back
KURNITZ, JULIE
  Gorey Stories

LAMPERT, ZOHRA
  Natural Look, The

218 / Actor Index

LANCE, ROBERT J.
   Reunion
LANDON, DANIEL
   Mourning Pictures
LANE, LENITA
   Timber House
LANSING, ROBERT
   Brightower
LASKAWY, HARRIS
   Guys in the Truck, The
LATHAN, BOBBI, JO
   Guys in the Truck, The
LAWRENCE, CHARLES
   Mystery Moon
LAWRENCE, ELIZABETH
   Moon Besieged, The
LAWRENCE, PAULA
   Have I Got a Girl for You!
LEACHMAN, CLORIS
   Masquerade
LEE, IRVING ALLEN
   Broadway Musical, A
LE GALLIENNE, EVA
   Starcross Story, The
   Women Have Their Way, The
LEIBMAN, RON
   Bicycle Ride to Nevada
LEONARD-BOYNE, EVA
   Pin to See the Peepshow, A
LESTER, BARBARA
   Johnny No-Trump
LICHTERMAN, MARVIN
   Goodbye People, The
   Happiness Is Just a Little
      Thing Called a Rolls Royce
LINDEN, MARTA
   Starcross Story, The
LLOYD, GEORGE
   'Tis of Thee
LODER, ANTHONY
   Warm Body, A
LOFTUS, CECILIA
   Strange Orchestra
LOSCH, TILLY
   Topaze
LUMMIS, DAYTON
   According to Law
LYONS, GENE
   Masquerade

McCARTHY, KEVIN
   Warm Body, A
McCLELLAND, DONALD
   Hook 'n Ladder
McDERMOTT, KEITH
   Meeting by the River, A
McDUFFIE, LAURA
   Wild and Wonderful
McGINN, WALTER
   Here's Where I Belong
McGIVER, JOHN
   Happiness Is Just a Little
      Thing Called a Rolls Royce
McGRATH, PAUL
   Bicycle Ride to Nevada
   Brightower
McGREEVEY, ANNIE
   Moony Shapiro Songbook, The
McGUIRE, BIFF
   Father's Day
McKAY, SCOTT
   Once for the Asking
McKENNA, SIOBHAN
   Meeting by the River, A
McLAREN, IAN
   Truly Valiant
McLAUGHLIN, RITA
   Warm Body, A
McNAMARA, MAGGIE
   Step on a Crack
McNAMARA, PAT
   Brothers
McNEELY, ANNA
   Little Johnny Noes
MacRAE, HEATHER
   Here's Where I Belong
MADDEN, DONALD
   Step on a Crack
MALLORY, BURTON
   According to Law
MANSON, ALAN
   No Hard Feelings
   Place for Polly, A
MARGULIES, DAVID
   Break a Leg
MARKLE, LOIS
   Something Old, Something New
   Warm Body, A
MARKS, JOE E.
   Topaze

MARLOW, DAVID
  No Hard Feelings
MARLOWE, STANLEY
  Marilyn's Affairs
MARRIOTT, JOHN
  Bicycle Ride to Nevada
MARSHALL, LARRY
  Broadway Musical, A
MARSHALOV, BORIS
  Julia, Jake and Uncle Joe
MARTIN, CHARLES G.
  Hook 'n Ladder
MARTIN, GEORGE N.
  Total Abandon
MARTIN, VIVIENNE
  Sunday Man, The
MASON, JACKIE
  Teaspoon Every Four Hours, A
MATHEWS, CARMEN
  Ring Round the Bathtub
MATTES, BARBARA
  Step on a Crack
MATTHAEI, KONRAD
  Place for Polly, A
MATTHAU, WALTER
  Once There Was a Russian
MAXWELL, FRANK
  Stop Press
MAYO, MARTHA
  Truly Valiant
MAYRON, MELANIE
  Goodbye People, The
MERCER, MARIAN
  Place for Polly, A
MEREDITH, LEE
  Teaspoon Every Four Hours, A
MERRILL, GARY
  Step on a Crack
MERRIMAN, DAN
  Heathen!
MICHAEL, PAUL
  Johnny Johnson
MICHALSKI, JOHN
  Gorey Stories
MILLER, JOAN
  Pin to See the Peepshow, A
MILTON, DAVID
  Money Mad
MINTURN, HARRY
  Road Together, The

MITCHELL, CAMERON
  November People, The
MOFFAT, DONALD
  Father's Day
MOORE, ROGER
  Pin to See the Peepshow, A
MOORE, VERA
  Teaspoon Every Four Hours, A
MORENO, RITA
  Gantry
MULLIGAN, RICHARD
  Mating Dance
  Ring Round the Bathtub
  Special Occasions
MUNSON, JERRY
  'Tis of Thee

NAISMSITH, LAURENCE
  Billy
NATHAN, VIVIAN
  Watering Place, The
NELSON, GORDON
  Tell My Story
NELSON, JEAN
  Sunday Man, The
NELSON, MERVYN
  'Tis of Thee
NEWMAR, JULIA
  Once There Was a Russian
NICHOLS, JOSEPHINE
  On an Open Roof
NILES, RICHARD
  Don't Call Back
NYPE, RUSSELL
  Once for the Asking

OAKLAND, SIMON
  Have I Got a Girl for You!
O'CONNOR, CARROLL
  Brothers
O'CONNOR, UNA
  Starcross Story, The
OLAF, PIERRE
  Murderer Among Us, A
OLIVER-SMITH, GERALD
  Strange Orchestra
O'NEIL, DICK
  Tough to Get Help

O'NEILL, BARBARA
  Reprise
ORBACH, JERRY
  Natural Look, The
ORFALY, ALEXANDER
  Johnny Johnson
ORTEGA, SANTOS
  Marilyn's Affairs
O'SHEA, TESSIE
  Broadway Follies
OSMOND, DONNY
  Little Johnny Jones

PATRICK, DENNIS
  Children! Children!
PALMER, ANTHONY
  Tough to Get Help
PARNAHAY, ALICIA
  Strange Play, A
PATSTON, DORIS
  Starcross Story, The
PATTERSON, DICK
  Something Old, Something New
PAXINOU, KATINA
  Garden of Sweets, The
PAXTON, MARIE
  Pin to See the Peepshow, A
PEARL, BARRY
  Teaspoon Every Four Hours, A
PEARLMAN, STEPHEN
  Strada, La
PELHAM, JIMMY
  Tough to Get Help
PERSSON, RUBY
  Rainbow Jones
PETERS, BERNADETTE
  Johnny No-Trump
  Strada, La
PETERS, LAURI
  Murderer Among Us, A
PICON, MOLLY
  Something Old, Something New
PIERSON, GEOFFREY
  Tricks of the Trade
PLESHETTE, SUZANNE
  Special Occasions

PLUMMER, CHRISTOPHER
  Starcross Story, The
POLLOCK, NANCY R.
  Have I Got a Girl for You!
POTTER, DON
  Moose Murders
  Ritz, The
POWERS, LEONA
  Bicycle Ride to Nevada
  Once for the Asking
PRATT, JUDSON
  Hook 'n Ladder
PRICE, PAUL B.
  Let Me Hear You Smile

RAMBEAU, EDWARD
  Heathen!
RAMBEAU, MARJORIE
  Road Together, The
RANDOLPH, DONALD
  Reprise
RAVELLE, NAOMI
  Fickle Women
RAYMOND, GUY
  Hook 'n Ladder
REARDON, NANCY
  Fame
REED, PAMELA
  November People, The
REED, TAYLOR
  Ritz, The
REEVES-SMITH, H.
  Road Together, The
RICH, DORIS
  Warm Body, A
RICHARDS, GORDON
  Masks and Faces
RICHARDSON, LEE
  Tricks of the Trade
RICHMAN, MARK
  Masquerade
RIFKIN, RON
  Goodbye People, The
ROBBINS, GIL
  Rainbow Jones
ROBBINS, GREGORY
  According to Law
ROBERTS, DORIS
  Natural Look, The

ROBERTS, LEONA
　Women Have Their Way, The
ROBERTS, PAUL
　'Tis of Thee
ROBERTSON, LIZ
　Dance a Little Closer
ROBINSON, PHILIP
　Topaze
RODGERS, EILEEN
　Kelly
ROGERS, PAUL
　Here's Where I Belong
ROLFING, TOM
　Little Johnny Jones
ROOS, CASPER
　Here's Where I Belong
ROSAY, FRANCOISE
　Once There Was a Russian
ROSE, GEORGE
　Dance a Little Closer
ROSELLE, WILLIAM
　Masks and Faces
ROSS, ANTHONY
　Starcross Story, The
ROSS, MARTIN
　Once for the Asking
ROWLETTE, MILDRED
　Fickle Women
RUMAN, SIG
　Once There Was a Russian
RUSSELL, EVELYN
　Place for Polly, A
　Warm Body, A

SABIN, DAVID
　Dance a Little Closer
SALES, CLIFFORD
　Topaze
SALMI, ALBERT
　Once There Was a Russian
SALT, JENNIFER
　Father's Day
SALVIO, ROBERT
　Billy
SANCHEZ, EDUARDO
　Beyond Evil
SANDER, ALFRED
　On an Open Roof
SANDS, DOROTHY
　Once for the Asking

SATZ, LUDWIG
　Money Mad
SAUNDERS, WARDELL
　According to Law
SCARDINO, DON
　Johnny No-Trump
SCOTT, DONNA
　Once for the Asking
SCOTT, GEORGE C.
　Tricks of the Trade
SCRUGGS, SHARON TROYER
　Cleavage
SEALE, DOUGLAS
　Frankenstein
SEFTON, DOROTHY
　Warm Body, A
SELBY, DAVID
　I Won't Dance
SELDES, MARIAN
　Father's Day
SHACKT, GUSTAV
　Good Neighbor
SHAFFER, LOUISE
　First One Asleep, Whistle
SHANNON, FRANK
　Mystery Moon
SHAUGHNESSY, MICKEY
　Kelly
SHAW, LEON
　Gorey Stories
SHAW, ROBERT
　Gantry
SHAWN, PETER
　Frank Merriwell
SHAYNE, ROBERT
　Timber House
SHEA, LORETTO
　Marilyn's Affairs
SHEFFIELD, DICK
　Cleavage
SHELLEY, FRANCES
　Mystery Moon
SHELLEY, GLADYS
　Money Mad
SHERWOOD, MADELEINE
　Garden of Sweets, The
SHERWOOD, WAYNE
　Johnny Johnson
SHIELDS, HELEN
　Moon Besieged, The
SHIELDS, ROBERT
　Broadway Follies

SMALL, LARRY
  Wild and Wonderful
SMALL, NEVA
  Frank Merriwell
SMITH, LOIS
  Bicycle Ride to Nevada
  Stages
SMITH, LORING
  Murderer Among Us, A
SMITH, SAMMY
  Goodbye People, The
SMITH, SPEEDY
  Hummin' Sam
SMITH, STANLEY
  Satellite
SMITH, WINCHELL
  Good Neighbor
SOHMERS, BARBARA
  Ned and Jack
SOREL, LOUISE
  Happiness Is Just a Little
    Thing Called a Rolls
    Royce
SORVINO, PAUL
  Mating Dance
SPINDELL, AHVI
  Something Old, Something
    New
STARR, MIKE
  Guys in the Truck, The
STERLING, JAN
  November People, The
  Once for the Asking
STERNE, MORGAN
  Garden of Sweets, The
STERNER, MARTHA JEAN
  Onward Victoria
STEVENS, HOUSELEY
  Stop Press
STEVENSON, MARGOT
  Truly Valiant
STRICKLAND, GAIL
  I Won't Dance
  Status Quo Vadis
STRIKER, JOSEPH
  Satellite
SUTORIUS, JAMES
  November People, The
SWEET, DOLPH
  Billy
  Natural Look, The

SYMINGTON, DONALD
  Mourning Pictures

TAPLEY, ROSE
  Satellite
TAYLOR, HOLLAND
  Moose Murders
  Something Old, Something
    New
TAYLOR, REBECCA
  Status Quo Vadis
TCHOR, LUDMILLA
  Julia, Jake and Uncle Joe
THACKER, RUSS
  Heathen!
  Home Sweet Homer
THOMPSON, SADA
  Johnny No-Trump
THURSTON, TED
  Gantry
  Onward Victoria
  Wild and Wonderful
TIPPIT, WAYNE
  Gantry
TOBIN, MATTHEW
  Something Old, Something
    New
TONE, FRANCHOT
  Bicycle Ride to Nevada
TONSICK, CLAUDE
  Destruction
TORN, RIP
  Cuban Thing, The
TRAVERS, BILL
  Abraham Cochrane
TRENHOLME, HELEN
  Strange Orchestra
TROUTMAN, IVY
  Road Together, The
TRUEMAN, PAULA
  Sunday Man, The
TRUMBULL, ROBERT
  Guys in the Truck, The
TUCCI, MARIA
  Cuban Thing, The
TUCKER, LORENZO
  Hummin' Sam
TUMARIN, BORIS
  Garden of Sweets, The

TYNER, CHARLES
  Moon Besieged, The

UECKER, JOHN
  November People, The
UNDERWOOD, DORIS
  Money Mad
UTTRY, ARTHUR
  Mystery Moon

VACCARO, BRENDA
  Father's Day
  Natural Look, The
VAN DER VILS, DIANA
  On an Open Roof
VAN DEVERE, TRISH
  Tricks of the Trade
VAN FLEET, JO
  Garden of Sweets, The
VAN GRIETHUYSEN, TED
  Moon Besieged, The
VAN NORDEN, PETER
  Little Johnny Jones
VAN PATTEN, DICK
  Have I Got a Girl for You!
VERDON, GWEN
  Children! Children!
VICKERY, JOHN
  Ned and Jack
VIGODA, ABE
  Tough to Get Help
VITELLA, SEL
  Gorey Stories

WAITE, RALPH
  Watering Place, The
WALKER, KATHRYN
  Mourning Pictures
WALKER, SYDNEY
  Blood Red Roses
WARD, SIMON
  Meeting by the River, A
WARDEN, JACK
  Stages

WARING, RICHARD
  Women Have Their Way, The
WARRINER, FREDERIC
  Pin to See the Peepshow, A
WATT, BILLIE LOU
  Tough to Get Help
WEEKS, BARBARA
  Satellite
WESTON, JACK
  Break a Leg
WHITE, A. COURTNEY
  Once Upon a Time
WHITE, JANE
  Cuban Thing, The
WHITE, JESSE
  Kelly
WICK, DODEE
  Reunion
WICKWIRE, NANCY
  Abraham Cochrane
  Here's Where I Belong
WIEST, DIANNE
  Frankenstein
WILLIAMS, RALPH
  Johnny Johnson
WILLISON, WALTER
  Wild and Wonderful
WILSON, EDITH
  Hummin' Sam
WINTERS, MARION
  Mating Dance
WOODLAWN, HOLLY
  Ritz, The
WYNN-OWEN, MEG
  Meeting by the River, A

YARNELL, LORENE
  Broadway Follies

ZASLOW, MICHAEL
  Onward Victoria
ZERBE, ANTHONY
  Moon Besieged, The
ZIMMET, MARYA
  First One Asleep, Whistle

CHOREOGRAPHER INDEX

AILEY, ALVIN
    Strada, La

BAYES, SAMMY
    Heathen!
    Rainbow Jones

CAREY & DAVIS
    Hummin' Sam
CHAMPION, GOWER
    Broadway Musical, A

DALE, GROVER
    Billy

FAISON, GEORGE
    Moony Shapiro Songbook, The
FARIA, ARTHUR
    Broadway Follies
FORELLA, RON
    Wild and Wonderful
FULLER, LARRY
    Blood Red Roses

GENO, ALTON
    Cleavage

JUNGER, ESTHER
    'Tis of Thee

KENYON, Neal
    Frank Merriwell

MARRE, ALBERT
    Home Sweet Homer
MORDENTE, TONY
    Here's Where I Belong

ROSS, HERBERT
    Kelly

SAPPINGTON, MARGO
    Play Me a Country Song
SCHWAB, BUDDY
    Utter Glory of Morrissey Hall, The
SHAWN, MICHAEL
    Onward Victoria
SIRETTA, DAN
    Little Johnny Jones

WELDON, BUNNY
    Mystery Moon
WHITE, ONNA
    Gantry
WILSON, BILLY
    Dance a Little Closer

COMPOSER INDEX

AIN, SUSAN
   Mourning Pictures
ALDRICH, DAVID
   Gorey Stories

BARRY, PETER
   'Tis of Thee
BART, LIONEL
   Strada, La
BRIGGS, JOHN R.
   Play Me a Country Song

CARLO and SANDERS
   Mystery Moon
CHARLAP, MOOSE
   Kelly
COHAN, GEORGE M.
   Little Johnny Jones

DANTE, RON
   Billy

FRANK, LARRY
   Frank Merriwell

GESNER, CLARK
   Utter Glory of Morrissey Hall, The
GODDMAN, BOB
   Wild and Wonderful
GREGORY, DAVID
   'Tis of Thee

HERRMANN, KEITH
   Onward Victoria
HILL, ALEXANDER
   Hummin' Sam

LEBOWSKY, STANLEY
   Gantry
LEIGH, MITCH
   Home Sweet Homer
LEWINE, RICHARD
   'Tis of Thee

MAGOON, EATON, JR.
   Heathen!
MARKS, WALTER
   Broadway Follies
MOSS, AL
   'Tis of Thee

NORMAN, MONTY
   Moony Shapiro Songbook, The
NORTH, ALEX
   'Tis of Thee

POKRASS, SAMUEL
   Satellite

REDWINE, SKIP
   Frank Merriwell

SHEFFIELD, BUDDY
   Cleavage

STROUSE, CHARLES
  Broadway Musical, A
  Dance a Little Closer

VALENTI, MICHAEL
  Blood Red Roses

WALDMAN, ROBERT
  Here's Where I Belong
WEILL, KURT
  Johnny Johnson
WILLIAMS, JILL
  Rainbow Jones

COSTUME DESIGNER INDEX

ALDRIDGE, THEONI V.
  Billy
  Break a Leg
  First One Asleep, Whistle
  No Hard Feelings
  Onward Victoria
AUDRE
  Once for the Asking
  Starcross Story, The
  Topaze
AULISI, JOSEPH G.
  November People, The
  Ring Round the Bathtub
  Tough to Get Help

BALIEFF, MADAME
  Bridal Crown, The
BARCELO, RANDY
  Broadway Musical, A
BAY, HOWARD
  Home Sweet Homer
BEL GEDDES, EDITH LYTENS
  Bicycle Ride to Nevada
BLAUSEN, WHITNEY
  Don't Call Back
  Mourning Pictures
BLIGH-WHITE, MARILYN
  Animals
BOXHORN, JERRY
  Hook 'n Ladder
BROOKS, DONALD
  Dance a Little Closer
BROOKS COSTUME CO.
  Hummin' Sam
  Mystery Moon
BUTTON, JEANNE
  Watering Place, The

CAMPBELL, PATTON
  Natural Look, The
CARTIER, DEIDRE
  Blood Red Roses
CASHIN, EMMA
  Women Have Their Way, The
COLT, ALVIN
  Broadway Follies
CUSTER, MARIANNE
  Meeting by the River, A

DIFFEN, RAY
  Home Sweet Homer

EVANS, CHARLES
  Me and Thee

FALABELLA, JOHN
  Guys in the Truck, The
FLETCHER, ROBERT
  Johnny Johnson
  Moon Besieged, The
FOX, FREDERICK
  Julia, Jake and Uncle Joe

GRADEN, DAVID
  Utter Glory of Morrissey Hall
  The
GREENWOOD, JANE
  Mother Lover, The

HANNINGTON, CLARA
  Raw Meat

HARRIS, JAMES BERTON
  Rainbow Jones
HARROW, BRUCE
  Heathen!

JOHNSTONE, ANNA HILL
  Warm Body, A

KIM, WILLA
  Have I Got a Girl for You!
KING, LAWRENCE
  Something Old, Something New
KLOTZ, FLORENCE
  Mating Dance
  On an Open Roof

LEE, FRANNE
  Moony Shapiro Songbook, The

MACKINTOSH, ROBERT
  Masquerade
MANNING, MILDRED
  Money Mad
MILLER, JAMES M.
  Cleavage
MORELY, RUTH
  Here's Where I Belong
  Pin to See the Peepshow, A
MORTON, WINN
  Teaspoon Every Four Hours, A
MOSS, JEFFREY B.
  Fame
MURIN, DAVID
  Gorey Stories
  Ned and Jack
MURRAY-WALSH, MERRILY
  Brothers

ODITZ, CAROL
  Play Me a Country Song

PAKLEDINAZ, MARTY
  I Won't Dance

PALMER, ELIZABETH
  Goodbye People, The
POTTS, GEORGE
  Ritz, The
POTTS, NANCY
  Strada, La

RITMAN, WILLIAM
  Johnny No-Trump
ROBBINS, CARRIE F.
  Frankenstein
  Let Me Hear You Smile
RODRIGUEZ, DOMINGO A.
  Abraham Cochrane
ROTH, ANN
  Children! Children!
  Father's Day
  Gantry
  Happiness Is Just a Little Thing Called a Rolls Royce

STEIN, JANE
  Animals
STUART, PATRICIA QUINN
  Cuban Thing, The
SULLIVAN, JOHN CARVER
  Moose Murders

TAYLOR, NOEL
  Brightower
THOMPSON, FRANK
  Frank Merriwell
  Place for Polly, A
  Wild and Wonderful
TOSER, DAVID
  Little Johnny Jones
  Status Quo Vadis
TOWNER, MARY
  Bridal Crown, The

USKINSKY, STASY
  Bridal Crown, The

VOELPEL, FRED
  Murderer Among Us, A

VON FURSTENBERG, EGON
  Don't Call Back
  Ritz, The
VON MAYRHAUSER, JENNIFER
  Special Occasions

WALTON, TONY
  Once There Was a Russian
WEISS, JULIE
  Total Abandon
WEISS, MARC B.
  Animals

WITTOP, FREDDY
  Kelly
WOLSKY, ALBERT
  Tricks of the Trade

YEARGAN, MICHAEL
  Something Old, Something New

ZIPPRODT, PATRICIA
  Garden of Sweets, The
  Stages
  Step on a Crack

SET DESIGNER INDEX

ARONSON, BORIS
   Garden of Sweets, The

BALLIF, ARIEL
   Pin to See the Peepshow, A
BARRATT, WATSON
   Starcross Story, The
BAY, HOWARD
   Bicycle Ride to Nevada
   Home Sweet Homer
   Utter Glory of Morrissey Hall, The
BENNETT, HARRY
   According to Law
   Strange Play, A
BERNSTEIN, ALINE
   Women Have Their Way, The
BROMBERG, LOUIS
   Truly Valiant
BROWN, JACK
   Heathen!
BURBRIDGE, EDWARD
   Status Quo Vadis
BURLINGAME, LLOYD
   First One Asleep, Whistle

CHAPMAN, DAVID
   Play Me a Country Song
CIRKER & ROBBINS
   Once Upon a Time

DOHANES, PETER
   Tricks of the Trade
DUNHAM, CLARKE
   Place for Polly, A

DUNKEL, EUGENE
   Bridal Crown, The

EDWARDS, BEN
   Mother Lover, The
ELDER, ELDON
   Hook 'n Ladder
   Mating Dance
EVANS, CHARLES
   Me and Thee

FALABELLA, JOHN
   Guys in the Truck, The
FEDER, ABE
   Once for the Asking
FERRER, RICHARD
   Rainbow Jones
FOX, FREDERICK
   Good Neighbor
   Julia, Jake and Uncle Joe

GOREY, EDWARD
   Gorey Stories

HARVEY, PETER
   Johnny Johnson
HAYS, DAVID
   Murderer Among Us, A
HENRICKSON, STEPHEN
   Wild and Wonderful

JACOBSON, JOHN
   Mourning Pictures

JENKINS, DAVID
  Special Occasions
  Total Abandon
JENKINS, GEORGE
  Step on a Crack
JENSEN, DONALD F.
  Sunday Man, The
JOHN, TOM
  Frank Merriwell
JOY, JAMES LEONARD
  Ned and Jack

KELLOGG, MARJORIE BRADLEY
  Moose Murders
KENT, CARL
  'Tis of Thee
KING, LAWRENCE
  Something Old, Something New

LARKIN, PETER
  Break a Leg
  Broadway Follies
  Let Me Hear You Smile
LEE, MING CHO
  Billy
  Here's Where I Belong
  Moon Besieged, The
  Strada, La
LEVE, SAM
  Have I Got a Girl for You!
LOQUASTO, SANTO
  Goodbye People, The
LUNDELL, KERT
  November People, The

MASON, HUGH
  Raw Meat
MENSCHING STUDIOS
  Masks and Faces
MICUNIS, GORDON
  Ritz, The
MIELZINER, JO
  Children! Children!
  Father's Day
MITCHELL, DAVID
  Dance a Little Closer

MITCHELL, ROBERT
  Meeting by the River, A
MORGAN, DICKSON
  Road Together, The
MORRISON, PAUL
  Masquerade
MUNN, TOM
  Brightower

OENSLAGER, DONALD
  Timber House
O'HEARN, ROBERT
  Abraham Cochrane

PEARSON, GEORGE
  Reunion

RADOMSKY, SAUL
  Moony Shapiro Songbook, The
RANDOLPH, ROBERT
  Little Johnny Jones
  No Hard Feelings
  Teaspoon Every Four Hours, A
REHLING, LARRY
  Happiness Is Just a Little Thing Called a Rolls Royce
RITMAN, WILLIAM
  Johnny No-Trump
  Onward Victoria
ROSENTHAL, JEAN
  On an Open Roof

SCHMIDT, DOUGLAS W.
  Fame
  Frankenstein
  Stages
SHARPE, ROBERT REDINGTON
  Strange Orchestra
SMITH, OLIVER
  Don't Call Back
  Kelly
  Topaze
STABILE, BILL
  I Won't Dance
STAGECRAFT STUDIOS
  Money Mad

STEVENS, JOHN WRIGHT
   Animals
STREET, A. W.
   Satellite

TAYLOR, MORRIS
   Cleavage
THEATRICAL ART STUDIOS
   Mystery Moon

VAIL SCENIC CONSTRUCTION CO.
   Marilyn's Affairs

WAGNER, ROBIN
   Cuban Thing, The
   Gantry
   Watering Place, The

WALSH, THOMAS A.
   Brothers
WALTON, TONY
   Once There Was a Russian
WEXLER, PETER
   Broadway Musical, A
WHITELAW, JOHN BIDDLE
   Reprise
WILLIAMS, ROBERT T.
   Warm Body, A
WITTSTEIN, ED
   Blood Red Roses
   Natural Look, The
   Ring Round the Bathtub
   Tough to Get Help

YEARGAN, MICHAEL
   Something Old, Something New

DIRECTOR INDEX

ADLER, JERRY
  Play Me a Country Song
ALEXANDER, DAVID
  Happiness Is Just a Little
    Thing Called a Rolls Royce

BAKER, RITA
  Cleavage
BAVOR, MICHAEL
  Ritz, The
BERRY, JOHN
  First One Asleep, Whistle
BLACK, DAVID
  Guys in the Truck, The
BLECKNER, JEFF
  Goodbye People, The
BLUM, GUSTAV
  Truly Valiant
BLYDEN, LARRY
  Mother Lover, The
BOWDEN, CHARLES
  Warm Body, A
BOYD, JULIANNE
  Onward Victoria
BROWN, MURRAY
  Fickle Women
BRUSKIN, PERRY
  Me and Thee
BURROWS, ABE
  No Hard Feelings

CAMERON, JOHN
  Satellite
CARIOU, LEN
  Don't Call Back
CARNEY, KAY
  Mourning Pictures

CATES, GILBERT
  Tricks of the Trade
CAULEY, HARRY
  Let Me Hear You Smile
CHAMPION, GOWER
  Broadway Musical, A
COTES, PETER
  Pin to See the Peepshow, A

DENHAM, REGINALD
  Once for the Asking
DeSHEIM, CHARLES
  Stop Press
DEWHURST, COLLEEN
  Ned and Jack
DORE, ALEXANDER
  Sunday Man, The
DRIVER, DONALD
  Broadway Follies
  Status Quo Vadis

EBENHACK, ARTHUR
  Marilyn's Affairs
EDWARDS, ROWLAND G.
  Money Mad
ENDREY, EUGENE
  According to Law
  Strange Play, A
ENTERS, WARREN
  Masquerade

FOREMAN, RICHARD
  Stages
FOSTER, ALLAN K.
  Hummin' Sam

FRANKEL, GENE
  Once There Was a Russian
FREDRIK, BURRY
  Wild and Wonderful
FRIED, MARTIN
  Natural Look, The

GELBER, JACK
  Cuban Thing, The
GRAHAM, RONNIE
  Mating Dance
  Place for Polly, A
GUITIERREZ, GERALD
  Little Johnny Jones

HAMMOND, FREEMAN
  Reunion
HARDY, JOSEPH
  Children! Children!
  Johnny No-Trump
HOFSISS, JACK
  Total Abandon
HOPKINS, CHARLES
  Strange Orchestra
HORNER, JED
  Masquerade

INGRASSIA, ANTHONY J.
  Fame

JACKSON, NAGLE
  Utter Glory of Morrissey Hall, The
JILINSKY, ANDRIUS
  Bridal Crown, The

KAHN, MICHAEL
  Here's Where I Belong
KATSELAS, MILTON
  Garden of Sweets, The
  On an Open Roof
KENYON, NEAL
  Frank Merriwell

LAWRENCE, EDDIE
  Animals
LE GALLIENNE, EVA
  Women Have Their Way, The
LERNER, ALAN JAY
  Dance a Little Closer
LEWIS, SINCLAIR
  Good Neighbor
LICHTMAN, NAT
  'Tis of Thee
LIVINGSTON, ROBERT H.
  Something Old, Something New
LYNN, JONATHAN
  Moony Shapiro Songbook, The

MARRE, ALBERT
  Home Sweet Homer
  Meeting by the River, A
MARTIN, PAUL E.
  Masks and Faces
MASSEY, EDWARD
  Beyond Evil
MITTLER, LEO
  Topaze
MOFFAT, DONALD
  Father's Day
MOORE, TOM
  Frankenstein
MORITZ, AL
  Hook 'n Ladder
MORLEY, VICTOR
  Mystery Moon

O'CONNOR, CARROLL
  Brothers
O'HORGAN, TOM
  I Won't Dance

PERSSON, GENE
  Rainbow Jones

QUINTERO, JOSE
  Johnny Johnson

REILLY, CHARLES NELSON
 Break a Leg
REINER, CARL
 Tough to Get Help
RICHARDS, LLOYD
 Moon Besieged, The
RICHARDSON, DON
 Have I Got a Girl for You!
ROACH, JOHN
 Moose Murders
ROSS, HERBERT
 Kelly

SAKS, GENE
 Special Ocassions
SCHNEIDER, ALAN
 Blood Red Roses
 Strada, La
 Watering Place, The
SEGAL, RICHARD Z.
 Once Upon a Time
SEIDELMANN, ARTHUR A.
 Billy
SHERMAN, ARTHUR
 November People, The
SHUGRUE, J. EDWARD
 Timber House
SHUMLIN, HERMAN
 Bicycle Ride to Nevada
SINCLAIR, HOWARD
 Destruction

STEVENS, JEREMY
 Teaspoon Every Four Hours, A
SOMMES, GEORGE
 Reprise
STONE, HAROLD
 Abraham Cochrane
 Ring Round the Bathtub
STRAUSS, MARCEL
 Tell My Story
SWOPE, HERBERT, JR.
 Step on a Crack

TANNER, TONY
 Gorey Stories

VAN ZANDT, PETER
 Warm Body, A
VICTOR, LUCIA
 Heathen!

WANAMAKER, SAM
 Murderer Among Us, A
WEISER, MEL
 Brightower
WHITE, ONNA
 Gantry
WHORF, RICHARD
 Julia, Jake and Uncle Joe
WILLIAMS, WILLIAM A.
 Raw Meat

LYRICIST INDEX

ADAMS, LEE
   Broadway Musical, A
ALLAN, GENE
   Billy
ANKER, CHARLOTTE
   Onward Victoria

BART, LIONEL
   Strada, La
BROWN, FORMAN
   Home Sweet Homer
BURR, CHARLES
   Home Sweet Homer

CARLO and SANDERS
   Mystery Moon
COHAN, GEORGE M.
   Little Johnny Jones

GESNER, CLARK
   Utter Glory of Morrissey Hall, The
GODDMAN, BOB
   Wild and Wonderful

HAYES, ALFRED
   'Tis of Thee
HILL, ALEXANDER
   Hummin' Sam

KURTZ, MANNY
   Satellite

LAWRENCE, EDDIE
   Kelly
LERNER, ALAN JAY
   Dance a Little Closer
LEWIN, JOHN
   Blood Red Roses

MAGOON, EATON, JR.
   Heathen!
MANFREDINI, HARRY
   Play Me a Country Song
MARKS, WALTER
   Broadway Follies
MOORE, HONOR
   Mourning Pictures
MORE, JULIAN
   Moony Shapiro Songbook, The

PARRISH, MITCHELL
   Satellite

ROSENBERG, IRENE
   Onward Victoria

SHAW, KELLY
   Satellite
SHEFFIELD, BUDDY
   Cleavage

TOBIAS, FRED
   Gantry

UHRY, ALFRED
   Here's Where I Belong

WILLIAMS, JILL
   Rainbow Jones

PLAYWRIGHT INDEX

ACKLAND, RODNEY
   Strange Orchestra
ALSBERG, ARTHUR
   Happiness Is Just a Little
      Thing Called a Rolls Royce
ALVAREZ-QUINTERO, SERAFIN
   and JOAQUIN
   Women Have Their Way, The
ANKER, CHARLOTTE
   Onward Victoria
ARNO, OWEN G.
   Once for the Asking
ATLAS, LARRY
   Total Abandon

BACHARDY, DON
   Meeting by the River, A
BARDOLY, LOUIS S.
   Sunday Man, The
BELLWOOD, PETER
   Gantry
BICKNELL, ARTHUR
   Moose Murders
BJORKMAN, EDWIN
   Bridal Crown, The
BLOCKI, FRITZ
   Money Mad
BOBRICK, SAM
   No Hard Feelings
BORUFF, JOHN
   Timber House
BRISTOL, W. DAINGERFIELD
   Reprise
BROAD, JAY
   Play Me a Country Song
BROWN, MURRAY
   Fickle Women
BROWN, WILLIAM F.
   Broadway Musical, A

CAULEY, HARRY
   Let Me Hear You Smile
CLARK, RON
   No Hard Feelings
CLOSSER, MYLA JO
   Raw Meat
COHAN, GEORGE M.
   Little Johnny Jones
COLEMAN, LONNIE
   Place for Polly, A
   Warm Body, A
COOPER, IRVING
   Have I Got a Girl for You!
CURRENS, STEPHEN
   Gorey Stories

DENKER, HENRY
   Something Old, Something
   New
DRIVER, DONALD
   Status Quo Vadis
DUGAN, LAWRENCE JOSEPH
   Once Upon a Time

EBENHECK, ARTHUR
   Marilyn's Affairs
ELWELL, AMBROSE, JR. (NORMAN H. WHITE, JR)
   Reunion
EVSLIN, BERNARD
   Step on a Crack

FISHER, ROBERT
   Happiness Is Just a Little
      Thing Called a Rolls Royce
FRANK, LARRY
   Frank Merriwell

GARDNER, HERB
  Goodbye People, The
GELBER, JACK
  Cuban Thing, The
GESNER, CLARK
  Utter Glory of Morrissey Hall, The
GIALANELLA, VICTOR
  Frankenstein
GLASSMAN, STEPHEN
  Billy
GORDON, ALEX
  Here's Where I Belong
GORDON, STEVE
  Tough to Get Help
GOREY, EDWARD
  Gorey Stories
GOULD, HEYWOOD
  Frank Merriwell
GREEN, PAUL
  Johnny Johnson

HAILEY, OLIVER
  Father's Day
  First One Asleep, Whistle
  I Won't Dance
HANSEN, WALDEMAR
  Garden of Sweets, The
HARWOOD, H. M.
  Pin to See the Peepshow, A
HAYES, ALFRED
  'Tis of Thee
HELPMANN, ROBERT
  Heathen!
HERENDEEN, FRED
  Mystery Moon
HORINE, CHARLES
  Me and Thee
HORNER, CHARLES
  Hook 'n Ladder
HORRIGAN, JACK
  Children! Children!
HOWARD, ELEANOR HARRIS
  Mating Dance
HUSTON, NOEL
  According to Law

INGRASSIA, ANTHONY J.
  Fame

INLENDER, AVRAHAM
  On an Open Roof
ISHERWOOD, CHRISTOPHER
  Meeting by the River, A

JACKSON, NAGLE
  Utter Glory of Morrissey Hall, The
JAMIAQUE, YVES
  Murderer Among Us, A
JESSE, F. TENNYSON
  Pin to See the Peepshow, A

KESSLER, LYLE
  Watering Place, The
KIBBEE, ROLAND
  Home Sweet Homer

LAWRENCE, EDDIE
  Animals
  Kelly

LERNER, ALAN JAY
  Dance a Little Closer
LEVIN, IRA
  Break a Leg
LEVIN, JACK
  Good Neighbors
LEVY, BENN W.
  Topaze
LEWIN, JOHN
  Blood Red Roses
LITTLE, HOMER
  Raw Meat
LOCKE, SAM
  'Tis of Thee

McAVITY, HELEN
  Mating Dance
McNALLY, TERRENCE
  Ritz, The
MAGOON, EATON, JR.
  Heathen!
MARRE, ALBERT
  Home Sweet Homer
MARTIN, PAUL E.
  Masks and Faces

MASON, JACKIE
   Teaspoon Every Four Hours, A
MERCIER, MARY
   Johnny No-Trump
MICHAELS, SIDNEY
   Tricks of the Trade
MIDDLETON, GEORGE
   The Road Together
MILES, HENRY
   Hook 'n Ladder
MILLER, SIGMUND
   Masquerade
MINOR, A. J.
   Masks and Faces
MITCHELL, JOSEPH
   Satellite
MOORE, HONOR
   Mourning Pictures
MORE, JULIAN
   Moony Shapiro Songbook, The
MORGAN, DIANA
   Starcross Story, The
MORTMAN, MIKE
   Teaspoon Every Four Hours, A

NORMAN, MONTY
   Moony Shapiro Songbook, The
NUTTER, EILEEN
   Hummin' Sam

O'NEIL, RUSSELL
   Don't Call Back
OSTROW, STUART
   Stages

PAGNOL, MARCEL
   Topaze
PECK, CHARLES K., JR.
   Strada, La
PHILLIPS, PHIL
   Wild and Wonderful

REDWINE, SKIP
   Frank Merriwell
REIFSNYDER, HOWARD
   Guys in the Truck, The

ROHMAN, RICHARD
   Tell My Story
ROSEN, SHELDON
   Ned and Jack
ROSENBERG, IRENE
   Onward Victoria

SCHARY, DORE
   Brightower
SCHOCHEN, SEYRIL
   Moon Besieged, The
SHAW, KERRY
   Satellite
SHEFFIELD, BUDDY and DAVID
   Cleavage
SHERRY, JOHN
   Abraham Cochrane
SIBBALD, GEORGE
   Brothers
SLADE, BERNARD
   Special Occasions
SPEARS, PATTI
   Strange Play, A.
SPEWACK, SAM
   Once There Was a Russian
STONE, IRVING
   Truly Valiant
STRADLEY, JOHN
   Stop Press
STRINDBERG, AUGUST
   Bridal Crown, The

TEICHMANN, HOWARD M.
   Julia, Jake and Uncle Joe
THOM, ROBERT
   Bicycle Ride to Nevada
THORNE, DAVID
   Beyond Evil
THUNA, LEONORA (LEE)
   Let Me Hear You Smile
   Natural Look, The
TRAHEY, JANE
   Ring Round the Bathtub

UHRY, ALFRED
   Little Johnny Jones

WEIDMAN, JEROME
   Mother Lover, The
WEILL, GUS
   November People, The
WHITE, GEORGE
   Murderer Among Us, A

WIERNIK, BERTHA
   Destruction
WILLIAMS, JILL
   Rainbow Jones

PRODUCER INDEX

ACTING COMPANY, INC., THE
   Stop Press
ALEXANDER, MATTHEW
   Tricks of the Trade
ALL-STARR PRODUCTIONS
   Ned and Jack
ALMEIDA, LOUIS d'
   Masquerade
AMERICAN CLASSIC PLAYERS
   Destruction
ANAMARK PRODUCTIONS
   Happiness Is Just a Little
      Thing Called a Rolls Royce
ANDREWS, JAMES J. C.
   Fame
ARNOLD, LOUISE
   Moon Besieged, The
AXBELL PRODUCTIONS
   Ned and Jack

BABBIN, JACQUELINE
   Ring Round the Bathtub
BALDING, IVOR DAVID
   Cuban Thing, The
BAMBIC, GENE
   Rainbow Jones
BARNETT, STANLEY
   Frank Merriwell
   Tough to Get Help
BARR, RICHARD
   Johnny No-Trump
BAVAR/CULVER PRODUCTIONS
   Ritz, The
BECHOK, SHELLY
   November People, The
BERUH, JOSEPH
   Broadway Follies
BIZMAN, IRVING E.
   Fickle Women

BLACK, DAVID
   Natural Look, The
BOWDEN, CHARLES
   Don't Call Back
BRIGHAM, PATRICK S.
   Total Abandon
BRISSON, FREDERICK
   Dance a Little Closer
BRITTON, JEFF
   Murderer Among Us, A
   Warm Body, A
BRONFMAN, EDGAR
   Stages
BROWN, SLADE
   Don't Call Back
BROWNE, ROBERT M.
   Onward Victoria
BYRD, SAM
   Good Neighbor
BULLOCK, H. RIDGELY
   On An Open Roof
   Utter Glory of Morrissey Hall, The
BURGIN, JON
   Once For the Asking
BYRON, MICHAEL
   Brightower

CAMERON, JOHN
   Satellite
CANYON PRODUCTIONS
   Strada, La
CARNAN PRODUCTIONS, INC.
   Brothers
CASTAGNA, S. MARIO
   Fickle Women
CATES, GILBERT
   Tricks of the Trade

CATES, JOSEPH
  Gantry
CONLEY, JAMES
  Guys in the Truck, The
CORNELIUS PRODUCTIONS
  Sunday Man, The
COSMI, BRUNO di
  Once for the Asking
CRANE, WARREN
  Special Occasions
CUNNINGHAM, JAMES R.
  Ritz, The
CURRENT PRODUCTIONS
  On an Open Roof

DAVIDOW, EDWARD
  Satellite
DAVIDS, NANCY
  Pin to See the Peepshow, A
DELANCEY PRODUCTIONS
  Me and Thee
DRABINSKY, GARTH G.
  Broadway Musical, A
D'SPAIN, JIM
  November People, The

ENDREY, EUGENE
  According to Law
  Strange Play, A
EXPERIMENTAL THEATRE, INC.
  Bridal Crown, The

FARBER, SANDY
  Frank Merriwell
  Tough to Get Help
FEARS, PEGGY
  Bridal Crown, The
FEINSTEIN, MARTIN
  Home Sweet Homer
FISKE, CLINTON E.
  Timber House
FITE, DAVID E.
  Cleavage
FLETCHER, ROBERT
  Johnny Johnson
FORCE TEN PRODUCTIONS
  Moose Murders
FOSTER, ALLAN K.
  Hummin' Sam

FREEMAN THEATRE GROUP
  Tell My Story
FRIED, WALTER
  Abraham Cochrane
FRIEDMAN, NATE
  Frank Merriwell
FRIEDMAN, STEPHEN R.
  Break a Leg
FRYE, BEN
  Garden of Sweets, The

GASTON, KEN
  Heathen!
  Place for Polly, A
GERARD, BEN
  Children! Children!
GILLIN, PHIL
  Rainbow Jones
GLASGOW, BRAXTON III
  Cleavage
GOLDBERG, LEONARD J.
  Heathen!
  Place for Polly, A
GOLDMAN, LOUIS S.
  Blood Red Roses
GORDON, SIDNEY
  Con't Call Back
GOTTLIEB, MORTON
  Special Occasions
GRAF, JAMES M.
  Mystery Moon
GRAY, TIMOTHY
  Johnny Johnson

HAMMOND, PAUL
  Timber House
HARRISON, SETH
  Children! Children!
HART, JOHN N., JR.
  Onward Victoria
HARVEY, HELEN
  Natural Look, The
HAYWARD, LELAND
  Mother Lover, The
HOBARD, RICK
  Wild and Wonderful
HOLMAN, MORGAN
  Don't Call Back
HOLZER, ADELA
  Something Old, Something New

HOPKINS, CHARLES
   Strange Orchestra
HOWARD, MARC
   Utter Glory of Morrissey Hall, The
HOWARD, MEL
   Once There Was a Russian
HUBBARD, HUGH J.
   Onward Victoria

JACOBSON, HELEN
   Abraham Cochrane
JORDAN, MICHAEL
   Animals

KASHA, LAWRENCE
   Father's Day
   No Hard Feelings
KATSELAS, MILTON
   On an Open Roof
KAUFMAN, DAVID
   Have I Got a Girl for You!
KEAN, NORMAN
   Broadway Musical, A
KEATHLEY, GEORGE
   Status Quo Vadis
KENNEDY CENTER FOR THE PERFORMING ARTS
   Dance a Little Closer
   Home Sweet Homer
   Little Johnny Jones
KEY, LEONARD
   Once There Was a Russian
KIPNESS, JOSEPH
   Father's Day
   Frankenstein
   Have I Got a Girl For You!
   No Hard Feelings
KRAKEUR, RICHARD W.
   Have I Got a Girl For You!
   Masquerade
KRAMER, TERRY ALLEN
   Frankenstein
   Gorey Stories
   Meeting by the River, A
KREBS, DAVID
   Little Johnny Jones
KRELLBERG, SAMUEL S.
   Julia, Jake and Uncle Joe Starcross Story, The

LA GUARDIA, MIDGE
   Johnny Johnson
LANE, STEWART F.
   Frankenstein
LANSBURY, BRUCE
   First One Asleep, Whistle
LANSBURY, EDGAR
   Broadway Follies
   First One Asleep, Whistle
LARSEN, RAY
   Total Abandon
LAUB, KENNETH D.
   Break a Leg
LEBER, STEVEN
   Little Johnny Jones
LEFF, JOEL B.
   Animals
LE GALLIENNE, EVA
   Women Have Their Way, The
LEHMAN, ORIN
   No Hard Feelings
LENNOX ARTS CENTER, THE
   Mourning Pictures
LENNY, JACK
   Status Quo Vadis
LEVINE, JOSEPH E.
   Kelly
   Mother Lover, The
LICHTMAN, NAT
   'Tis of Thee
LOVE, JULES
   Tough to Get Help

McCANN, ELIZABETH
   Total Abandon
MacRAE MICHAEL & BARCLAY
   Let Me Hear You Smile
MAILEY, FREDERICK E.
   Reprise
MANDELL, RICK
   Blood Red Roses
MANDEVILLE, ERNEST W.
   Truly Valiant
MARKINSON, MARTIN
   Ned and Jack
MARSOLAIS, KEN
   Ned and Jack
MARTIN, ELIOT
   Mating Dance
MARTIN, PAUL E.
   Masks and Faces

MATTHEWS, HALE
  Gorey Stories
MELNICK, DANIEL
  Kelly
MELOCHE, WILLIAM J.
  Total Abandon
MERO-IRION, YOLANDA
  Topaze
MERRICK, DAVID
  I Won't Dance
MEYER, IRWIN
  Break a Leg
MEYERS, DAVID
  Place for Polly, A
MILFORD, JIM
  Don't Call Back
MILLER, MITCH
  Here's Where I Belong
MINSKOFF, JEROME
  Dance a Little Closer
MOGULL, ARTHUR
  Break a Leg
MOORE, RAYMOND
  Strange Orchestra
MORITZ, AL
  Hook 'n Ladder
MORR, ALEXANDER
  Home Sweet Homer

NEDERLANDER, JAMES
  Broadway Follies
  Dance a Little Closer
  Frankenstein
  Little Johnny Jones
NUGENT, NELLE
  Total Abandon

O'BRIEN, MORGAN P.
  Cleavage
O'BRIEN, WILLIAM J. III
  Cleavage
ORION TELEVISION, INC.
  Brothers
OSTROW, STUART
  Moony Shapiro Songbook, The
  Stages

PAFFRATH, JOHN, INC.
  Marilyn's Affairs

PEARSON, NOEL
  Brothers
PECK, CHARLES K., JR.
  Strada, La
PERSSON, GENE
  Watering Place, The
PRICE, LOREN E.
  Moon Besieged, The
  Natural Look, The
PROVINCETOWN PLAYHOUSE GUILD
  Raw Meat

RANDALL, DICK
  Once There Was a Russian
RELKIN, EDWIN A.
  Money Mad
RIGBY, HARRY
  Gorey Stories
  Meeting by the River, A
ROACH, JOHN
  Total Abandon
ROBINSON, KENNETH W.
  Reunion
ROLO, FELIX
  Bridal Crown, The
ROSENBERG, BEN
  Special Occasions
ROSENFIELD, MAURICE
  Goodbye People, The
RUBIN, ROY
  Tough to Get Help
RUBINSTEIN, JEROLD J.
  Break a Leg
RUBYKATE, INC.
  Rainbow Jones

SALVATORE, STEVE
  Animals
SALZMAN, HAROLD AARON
  Once Upon a Time
SCHLOSSBERG, JERRY
  Gantry
SCHWARTZ, KENNETH
  Once There Was a Russian
SCHWARTZ, SAMUEL H.
  Mourning Pictures
SEGAL, MORTON
  Once There Was a Russian

SELCH, FREDERICK R.
  Play Me a Country Song
SELDON, ALBERT W.
  Utter Glory of Morrissey Hall, The
SHOCTOR, JOSEPH
  Billy
SHUBERT, JOHN
  Julia, Jake and Uncle Joe
SHUBERT, MESSRS.
  Starcross Story, The
SUMLIN, HERMAN
  Bicycle Ride to Nevada
SLADE, SUSAN
  Natural Look, The
SQUIRES, IRVING
  Garden of Sweets, The
STARK, BRUCE W.
  Billy
STEVENS, ROGER L.
  Bicycle Ride to Nevada
  Dance a Little Closer
  Home Sweet Homer
  Julia, Jake and Uncle Joe
  Step on a Crack
STONE, W. CLEMENT
  On an Open Roof
STURM, JUSTIN
  Once There Was a Russian
SUSSKIND, DAVID
  Kelly
SWANSTROM, BJORN T.
  Blood Red Roses
SWOPE, HERBERT, JR.
  Step on a Crack

THORNE, DAVID
  Beyond Evil
TREBITSCH, PAUL M.
  Mystery Moon
TWENTIETH CENTURY-FOX PRODUCTIONS
  Frankenstein

UP FRONT PRODUCTIONS
  Cleavage

VALL, SEYMOUR
  Blood Red Roses

WALSH, JAMES
  Watering Place, The
WARNER PLAYS, INC.
  Break a Leg
WEBER, BERNARD M.
  A Teaspoon Every Four Hours
WEIL, RAYMONDE
  Wild and Wonderful
WEISER, MEL
  Brightower
WHITELAW, ARTHUR
  Children! Children!
  Utter Glory of Morrissey Hall, The
WILDER, CLINTON
  Johnny No-Trump
WILSON, JOHN C.
  Starcross Story, The
WOLF, JAY
  Ring Round the Bathtub
WOODVILLE, E. PAUL
  Heathen!
WOODWARD, CHARLES, JR
  Johnny No-Trump
WULP, JOHN
  Gorey Stories

ZANETTA, TONY
  Fame
ZATKIN, NATHAN
  Bridal Crown, The

GENERAL INDEX

Abandoned Sock, The 71
Abbott, George 69, 125, 130, 144
Abe Lincoln in Illinois 127
Abel, Ron 165
Abie's Irish Rose xv
Abraham, F. Murray 109, 164, 166
Abraham Cochrane xv, 1, 2
Abraham's House 2
Accent on Youth 162
According to Law 23
Achurch, Janet vii
Ackland, Rodney 185, 186, 187, 188
Act of Love 103
Adair, Jean 135
Adair, Laura 193
Adam and Eva 168
Adams, John Quincy 11
Adams, Julie 48
Adams, Lee 28, 29, 48
Adams, Leslie 193
Adams, Robert 169
Adams, Samuel Hopkins 130
Adam's Way 157, 203
Adaptation 165
Adcock, Joe 190
Adelphi 30
Adler, Jacob P. 122, 123
Adler, Jerry 158
Adler, Luther 13, 16, 91
Adler, Stella 94
Adrian 42
Adventures of Eddie Greshaw, The 5
Aeschylus 83
After My Fashion 22, 178
After the Fall 46

Agate, James 188
Agony and the Ecstasy, The 200
Ah, Wilderness! 67, 163
Ailey, Alvin 184
Albatross, The 7
Albert, Eddie 139, 140
Alcatraz Incident, The 44
Alda, Alan 174
Aldrich, Richard 178
Aldridge, Alan T. 152
Alexander, Daisy 154
Alisi, Art 94
All About Eve 48
All-American 28, 38, 102
All-American Sweepstakes, The 30
All God's Chillun Got Wings 6, 7
All in the Family 29, 30, 197
Allardice, James B. 182
Allbritton, Louise 188
Alleman, Doug 180
Allen, Jay Presson 204
Allen, Karen 80
Allen, Rae 49
Allen, Vera 61, 63
Allen, Viola ix
Allison, Bart 166
Along Came a Blackbird 143
Alsberg, Arthur 73, 74
Alswang, Ralph 24
Altered States 57
Altman, Frieda 192, 193
Alton, John 63
Alvarez-Quintero, Serafin and Joaquin 206, 207, 208
Amadeus 109, 196
Amaya, Carmen 26

248 / General Index

Ameche, Don 76
American Graffiti 197
American Idea, The 107
American in Paris, An 37
American King, An 87
American Musical Theatre 111
American Tragedy, An 61
Amos, John 197
Amphigorey 71
Amphigorey, Too 71
Anania, John 145
And Things That Go Bump in the Night 165
And Where She Stops Nobody Knows 49
Anders, Glenn 116, 178
Anderson, Arthur 66
Anderson, Constance 154
Anderson, Derek 154
Anderson, Georgine 156
Anderson, Judith 125, 126
Anderson, Maxwell xvi, 32
Anderson, May x
Andrews, Ann 8
Andrews, Charlton 167
Andrews, Edward 63
Angela Is Twenty-Two 67
Animal 49
Animals 4, 5
Anker, Charlotte 147
Anna and the King of Siam 82
Annie 38
Annis, Francesca 156
Anthony, Susan B. 149
Any Wednesday 189
Appel, Anna 67
Appell, Don 2, 3
Applause 29, 38, 48
Apple, The 34
Arbuckle, Maclyn x
Arbury, Donald 66
Archibald, William 32
Archie Bunker's Place 29
Arden, Daniel 202
Arden, Eve 130
Argentenita 26
Ari 76
Aris, Ben 166
Arlen, Harold 148
Arling, Charles 88
Armbruster, Richard 171

Armstrong, Betty Coe 94
Armstrong, Louis 130
Arno, Owen G. 142, 143
Arnold, Edward viii, 42
Aronstein, Martin 164
Arrowsmith 60, 67
Art of Living, The 128
Arthur, Julia 87
Arthur Godfrey Show, The 85
Asakawas, Fulice 117
Ascent of F 6, The 121
Asch, Sholem 7
Ashman, Howard 71
Ashton, Herbert, Jr. 30
Asked, Muriel 154
Askin, Leon 41
Astaire, Fred 105
Astor, Elizabeth 187
Astor, Mary 176, 177, 178
At War With the Army 182
Atkinson, Brooks xv, 98, 99, 100
Atkinson, Oriana 98, 99, 100
Atlas, Larry 195, 196
Attenborough, Richard 18
Auden, W. H. 121

Babbin, Jacqueline 162, 163
Babbitt 59, 63, 67
Bacall, Lauren 48
Bachardy, Don 119, 120
Bachelor Father 74
Bachmann, Charles 110, 111
Backus, Charles ix, x
Baclanova, Olga 135
Bad Habits 165
Bad Seed, The 32, 143
Bainter, Fay 174
Baird, Betsey 201
Bajour 48
Baker, Marie 169
Baker, Phil 26
Baker's Wife, The 89
Balderston, John L. 56, 57, 70
Ballard, Kaye 166
Ballet Russe de Monte Carlo 118, 180
Bancroft, Anne 174
Banderol 2, 22
Banham, Sam 147

Banks, Leslie   151
Bannerman, Guy   138
Bannister, Harry   61
Banton, D. A. Joab H.   7, 9
Bara, Frank   172
Barbary Shore   34
Bardoly, Dr. Louis   189
Barefoot in the Park   194
Barkentin, Marjorie   29
Barker, Granville   ix
Barker, Petronella   156
Barlow, Reginald   xi
Barnaby and Mr. O'Malley   143
Barnes, Clive   xvi, 95, 96
Barney, Jay   3
Barnum, P. T.   23
Baron, Helen   154
Barr, Richard   94, 95
Barrett, Minnette   xi
Barrie, Sir James   143
Barrier, Edgar   39
Barry, Arthur   94
Barry, Bobby   112
Barry, John   38
Barry, Wesley   88
Barry, Winifred   61
Barrymore, Ethel   137, 138
Barrymore, John   137, 138, 182
Bart, Lionel   184, 185
Barteaux, Judson   137
Bartlett, Clifford   187
Basehart, Richard   147, 185
Basevi, James   79
Bassett, Charles   x
Baswitz, C.   x
Bathing Girl, The   viii
Battles, John   76
Bauer, Bruce   165
Baum, L. Frank   28
Baumer, Marie   45
Baver, Michael   164, 165
Bax, Clifford   xi
Baxt, George   172
Baxter, Alan   126
Baxter, Anne   48, 80, 125
Bay, Howard   80, 82, 201
Beach, Gary   202
Bean, Orson   143
Beard, Stymie   80
Beastly Baby, The   71
Beaton, Cecil   18

Beatty, John Lee   108, 109
Beautiful Mariposa, The   4, 5
Beauty and the Jacobin   xi
Beauty Part, The   96
Beck, Walter   207
Beckel, Graham   49
Beckhart, Arthur   193
Beckwith, Martin   178
Beecher, Catherine   150
Beecher, Henry Ward   148, 149, 150
Beggar's Opera, The   93
Behind the Mask   87
Behrman, S. N.   178
Belafonte, Harry   24
Bell, Alexander Graham   45
Bell, Derrick   82
Bell, Greg   82
Bell, James   161
Bell, Marion   37
Bell for Adano, A   77, 130
Bellamy, Ralph   100
Belle, La   84
Belle Helene, La   84
Belle of Amherst   20
Belle; or the Ballad of Dr. Crippen   128
Belles of St. Trinians   201
Bellflower, Nellie   80
Bellows, Saul   96
Bells Are Ringing   4, 103
Bellwood, Peter L.   59, 60
Belmore, Lionel   58
Ben Franklin in Paris   199
Benchley, Robert   93
Bender, Jack   120
Benedict, Arnold   viii
Benesch, Isaac   91
Benét, Stephen Vincent   125, 126
Bengali, Richard   208
Bennett, Arnold   viii, xi
Bennett, Faith   188
Bennett, Richard   viii
Benstock, Melvin   193
Bergere, Jane   171
Beringer, Carl   63
Berkeley, Reginald   18
Berkey, Ralph   171
Berle, Milton   69
Berlin, Irving   39, 42, 140

Berlin Stories, The 121
Berlind, Roger S. 196
Bern, Julie 172
Bernard, Barney 123
Bernardi, Herschel 68
Bernhardt, Sarah 103
Bernstein, Leonard 38
Berry, John 51
Berry Brothers 25
Bert, Malcolm 79
Bertelsen, Paul 178
Beruh, Joseph 5, 24
Besier, Rudolph x
Bessell, Ted 173
Best Little Whorehouse in Texas, The 158
Best Plays and the Year Book of Drama in America 153
Best Plays of 1926-1927 8
Bet Your Life 122
Bethel Merriday 67
Between Two Worlds xvi
Bevans, Phillipa 178
Beyond Evil 6, 7
Beyond the Fringe 59
Beyond the Horizon viii
Bicknell, Arthur 129, 130
Bicycle Ride to Nevada 10, 11, 193
Bier, Burt 145
Big Pond, The 168
Bigelow, Susan 148
Billetdoux, François 199
Billington, Ken 120
Billy 11, 12, 13
Billy Budd 11, 13, 14
Billy Budd, Foretopman 13
Binner, Marjorie 154
Binns, Edward 126
Biography 178
Bishop, Thomas Brigham 124
Bittner, Jack 108
Black, David 72
Black Chiffon 151
Blackburn, John 188
Blackmer, Sidney 154
Blackton, Jay 201
Blackwood, George 161
Blair, Mary 6, 7
Blake, Rosemary 156
Blakely, David 155, 156

Blanchar, Pierre 8
Bless You, Sister 62
Blithe Spirit 143
Blitzstein, Marc 93
Blocki, Fritz 121, 122
Blood, James H. 149
Blood of an Englishman, The 18
Blood Red Roses 16, 17, 18, 19
Bloom, Harry 188
Bloomer Girl 148, 189
Bloomingdale, Alfred 69
Blue Angel, The 59
Blyden, Larry 131
Bob Newhart Show 173
Bobrick, Sam 139, 140
Boccelli, Richard 165
Boch, Frederick 87
Bochner, Hart 80
Bodeen, DeWitt 13, 15
Bohnen, Roman 91
Boles, John 58
Bolton, Guy 168
Boniface, George C. 125
Bonney, William H. x
Bonselle, Jesse x
Boone, Richard 126
Borchers, Harry 66
Bordman, Gerald 38, 111, 194
Borgo, Micheline Muselli Posso di 37
Born Free 2
Boruff, John Perry 193
Bostonians, The 183
Bottoms, Sam 80
Bottoms, Timothy 80
Bourdet, Edouard 8
Bowden, Charles 44
Bowery, The xv
Boxleitner, Bruce 80, 180
Boy Meets Girl 144
Boyar, Monica 76
Boyd, Ernest 9
Boyd, Hutcheson xi
Boyd, Juliann 147
Boyd, Ruth O'Day 37
Boyer, Charles 98
Boyle, John 113
Boyne, Eva Leonard xi
Boys from Brazil, The 20
Brady, Alice xi, 62
Brady, "Diamond Jim" 103

General Index / 251

Brady, William A.   61, 62
Braggiotti, Stiano   41
Brambell, Wilfrid   100, 102
Bramwell, Henry Howard   124
Brand, Phoebe   91
Brann, Ruth and Gilbert   53
Break a Leg   19, 20
Breakfast at Tiffany's   59, 89
Brecher, Egon   207
Brecht, Bertolt   4, 93, 104
Breda, Kenneth   156
Breffort, Alexandre   128
Brennan, Maureen   108
Brennan, Tim   xiii, xiv
Brian, Donald   110
Bridal Crown, The   21
Bride of the Lamb   62
Bridges, James   120
Bridges, Lloyd   80
Brieux, Eugene   viii
Brigadoon   37, 189
Bright Boy   193
Brightower   2, 22, 177
Britten, Benjamin   13, 14, 15
Broad, Jay   158
Broadway, Broadway   165
Broadway Follies   23, 24, 25, 26
Broadway Musical, A   28, 29
Broadway Scrapbook   98
Broadway's Beautiful Losers   96
Broderick, James   163
Brodie, Steve   xiii, xiv, xv, 102, 104
Brodin, Charles   173
Brody, Ronnie   166
Bromberg, J. Edward   207
Bronner, Edwin   32
Brookes, Jacqueline   120
Brooks, David   189
Brooks, Mel   104
Brooks, Randy   104
Brooks, Richard   63
Brooks, Victor   156
Brothers   29, 30, 31
Brothers, The   30
Brothers Karamozov, The   30
Brotherson, Eric   145
Brown, Christopher, J.   164, 166
Brown, Clarence   42, 121
Brown, E. S.   176
Brown, Gilmor   188

Brown, John   123, 124, 125, 126, 127
Brown, John J.   167
Brown, Josephine   208
Brown, Louis   41
Brown, Susan   120
Brown, Walter P.   101
Brown, William F.   28
Browne, Porter Emerson   xi
Browne, R. Gore   151
Browning, Kirk   15
Browning, Robert   ix
Bruce, Carol   26
Brydon, W. B.   196
Brynner, Yul   80, 82, 83
Buck and Bubbles   25
Buchanan, Thompson   62
Buckmaster, Charles   186, 187
Buckner, Robert   126
Bug Book, The   71
Bullock, H. Ridgely   141, 201
Bunk of 1926   7
Bunny, John   ix
Buona Sera, Mrs. Campbell   38
Burdick, Rose   61
Burgess, Grover   91
Burghoff, Gary   202
Burns, Robert   128
Burrell, John   208
Burrows, Abe   139, 140, 143
Burrows, James Edward   140
Burstyn, Ellen   173
Burton, Philip   102
Burton, Richard   102
Burton, Wendell   80, 202
Bush, Jonathan   94
Bushkin, Nina   37
Butler, Mayor Dan   40
Butler, Richard   55
Butterworth, Peter   166
Buzzell, Eddie   113
Bye, Bye, Barbara   135
Bye, Bye, Birdie   20, 28, 38
Byrd, Sam   66, 67
Byron, Brook   154
Byron, Lord   xvi
Bywaters, Frederick   152, 153, 155

Cabaret   121

252 / General Index

Cactus Flower 96, 136
Cadell, Jean 188
Cadorette, Paul 94
Caesar, Sid 4
Cage aux Folles, La 118
Cagney, James 107, 108, 109, 113, 114
Cagney, Jeanne 114
Cagney by Cagney 113
Cahn, Sammy 171
Calfa, Don 117
Call, John 122
Call Me Back 45
Call Me Madam 130
Cambridge, Godfrey 172
Camelot 37
Cameron, David 63, 193
Cameron, Donald 207
Cameron, Hope 5
Campbell, Douglas 126
Campbell, Jean 187
Campbell, Mrs. Patrick 186, 187
Can-Can 32, 171
Candida vii, 2
Cannon, J. D. 117
Capone, Clifford 71
Capote, Truman 89
Capra, Frank 62
Captain Lafitte 87
Captive, The 8
Cardigan, Lord 18
Caretaker, The 59
Carey, Timothy 79, 80
Cariou, Len 38, 126
Carleton, Claire 122
Carlo, Monte 135
Carlson, Alan 148
Carlson, Ivan 180
Carmelina 38
Carney, Art 134
Carney, Grace 157
Carney, Mary 202
Carnival 185
Carnovsky, Morris 91
Carr, Alexander 123
Carr, Fatty 113
Carrere, Edward 63
Carroll, Earl 9, 135
Carroll, Nancy 172
Carroll, Paul Vincent 67
Carson, Mindy 143

Carter, Peggy 186
Caruso, Anthony 41
Caruso, Barbara 137
Casartelli, Gabrielle 186
Case of Libel, A 171
Cashel Byron x
Cashel Byron's Profession ix
Caskey, Marilyn 201
Cass, Peggy 157
Cassidy, David 109
Cassidy, Jack 109, 145, 198
Casson, Mary 187
Castle, Yvonne 193
Castro, Fidel 33, 34
Cates, Gilbert 198, 199
Cates, Joseph 60
Cauley, Harry 105, 136
Caulfield, Joan 157
Cavanaugh, Hobart 42
Cave Girl, The 168
Chains xi
Challee, William 91
Champion, Gower 28
Chapman, John 153
Chapman, Lonnie 79
Chapman, Robert 13, 14, 16
Charge of the Light Brigade, The 18
Charlap, Moose 100, 102, 103, 104
Charles, Edgar 122
Charnin, Martin 185
Chase, Mary 163
Chatterton, Ruth 41
Cheating Cheaters 168
Chekhov, Anton 186, 187
Chelton, Joseph 152
Cherry, Charles xi
Chester, Mary 156
Chevalier, Maxine 188
Chew, Bruce 108
Chicago 32
Chickencoop Chinaman, The 35
Chiffon Girl, The 135
Children! Children! 31, 32
Children's Hour, The 31
Chilvers, Colin 166
Chin, Frank 35
Chinese Obelisk, The 71
Chodorov, Edward 45, 207, 208
Chodorov, Jerome 143, 163

General Index / 253

Chomyn, Joseph K.   126
Christie, Agatha   152
Chu Chem   172
Cinderella   143
Cinderella's Brothers   114, 115
Citizen Kane   177
Claborne, Robert   188
Claflin, Tennessee   148, 149, 150
Clarence Darrow for the Defense   200
Clark, Alfred   154
Clark, Brian   197
Clark, Burt G.   87
Clark, Harvey   88
Clark, Ron   139, 140
Clarke, John   122
Clarke, Mae   58
Clear All Wires   144
Cleavage   32, 33
Cleveland, Stephen Grover   149
Clifford, John   154
Clift, Jeanette   163
Clifton, Lola   xiii
Climate of Violence   44
Clive, Colin   56, 58
Clondon, Tony   53
Clork, Harry   69
Close Encounters of the Third Kind   197
Clowes, Richard   188
Cobb, Lee J.   91
Coburn, Charles   x, 42
Coburn, D. L.   174
Coburn, James   38
Coco   38
Coghlan, Rose   83
Cogley, Nick   88
Cohan, George M.   105, 106, 107, 108, 109, 110, 111, 112, 113, 114
Cohan, Helen   110, 114
Cohan, Jerry   110, 114
Cohan, Josephine   110, 114
Cohan and Harris   110, 112
Coke, Richard   152
Colbert, Claudette   97, 98, 99
Colby, Barbara   48
Cole, Jack   26
Coleman, Basil   14
Coleman, Cy   185

Coleman, Lonnie   156, 157, 203
Coleridge, Samuel Taylor   xvi
Colette   37
Collier, William Sr.   113
Collins, Kathleen   31
Collins, Russell   91
Collins, Stephen   164
Collison Course   78, 165
Colt, Alvin   68
Colton, John   168
Colorada, Hortensia   165
Comden and Green   4, 29, 48
Come on Strong   118
Common Ground   208
Compton, Francis   39
Conditioned Reflex   205
Conheim, Martha Morton   x
Conkle, E. P.   3
Connection, The   34, 35
Connery, Sean   152
Connolly, Edward   88
Connor, Barry   37
Conover, Teresa Maxwell   xi
Conquering Hero, The   103
Conried, Hans   170, 171, 172
Continental Divide   49
Converse, Frank G.   51
Converse-Roberts, William   57
Conway, Curt   91
Cook, Carole   48
Cook, Donald   116
Cook, Sir Francis   150
Cook, Ray   128
Cook, Richard   138
Cook for Mr. General, A   2
Cooke, Thomas Potter   55
Cooper, Edward   154
Cooper, Edwin   157
Cooper, Gladys   151, 187
Cooper, Helen   74
Cooper, Irving   74
Coover, Robert   35
Copland, Aaron   78
Corbett, Leonora   186
Corbett-Wilson, Cecily   154
Corey, Wendell   157, 203
Cornell, Gerald   94
Cortez, Patti   63
Corwin, Norman   182
Coryell, Esther Jane   117
Cossart, Ernest   154

Costa, Joseph 167
Costello, Helene 88
Cotes, Peter 152, 153
Cotsirilos, Stephanie 167
Coulouris, George 166
Count Joannes 7
Courtleigh, William ix, 87
Coverly, Robert viii
Cowan, Curtiss 157
Coward, Noel 24, 143, 178
Cowie, Laura 187
Cowles, Chandler 13, 14
Coxe, Lewis O. 13, 14, 16
Coxen, Edward 88
Craig, Michael 156
Crane, Elizabeth G. xi
Crane, Neil 180, 181
Craven, Gemma 128
Crawford, Cheryl 91, 92
Crawley, Sayre 207
Cresson, James 49
Crews, Laura Hope xi, 42
Crier, Gordon 188
Crigler, Lynn 108
Crime and Punishment 188
Crinkle, Richmond 196
Crisis in Heaven 18
Crisscross 49
Critics, The xvi
Critic's Choice 20
Cronyn, Hume 174
Crooker, Earle 37
Crossley, Jim 108
Crothers, Rachel xi
Crothers, Sam 49
Crouse, Russel 39, 116, 163
Crozier, Eric 14
Crucifer of Blood, The 57
Cuba Sí 78, 165
Cuban Thing, The 33, 34, 35
Cue for Passion 208
Cuisine des Anges, La 144
Cumming, Dorothy 88
Cummings, Irving x
Cummings, Robert 135
Cummings, Vicki 84, 85
Cuneo, Fred J. 82
Cunningham, John 49
Cunningham, Zamah 161
Curious Sofa, The 71
Curren, Stephen 71

Curry, Ed xiv
Curtiz, Michael 114, 126
Custer, General George Armstrong 126
Cynara 151

Daddy's Gone-A-Hunting 168
Dadswell, Pearl 152
Dahl, Arlene 48
Dahms, Gail 72
Dailey, Irene 41
Dale, Esther 88
Daly, Arnold vii, x
Daly, James 14
Dames at Sea 52
Damn Yankees 32
Dance a Little Closer 35, 36, 37, 38
Dance with a Stranger 156
Dangerfield, George 10, 11
Dangerfield 10, 11
Daniels, William 42
Dante 83, 177
D'Antonakis, Fleury 117
Dark at the Top of the Stairs, The 194
D'Arms, Ted 141
Darwell, Jane x
Davalos, Richard 79
David, Clifford 48
David, Jon 3
Davies, Andrew 196
Davila, Diana 82
Davis, Bette 182
Davis, Bill C. 196
Davis, Joe 128
Davis, Michael Allen 23, 24
Davis, Robert H. xi
Davis, Sammy, Jr. 28
Day, Alice 113
Day Before Spring, The 37
Dazey, Charles T. 85, 86, 87, 88
Dazey, Frank 87
Dean, Faxon 113
Dean, James 79
Dean, Philip Hayes 20
Deane, Hamilton 55, 56, 70
Deathtrap 20
De Banzie, Lois 201

General Index / 255

De Beauset, Michael 147
De Camp, Rosemary 114
Decision 208
De Cordoba, Pedro xi
Deep, The 59
Deeter, Jasper 147
De Hartog, Jan 174
Deighton, Len 18
Dekker, Albert 79
Delaney, Shelagh 156
DeLaurentis, Dino 84, 185
Delta River Boys 26
DeMarco, Elisa 78
DeMarcos, The 25, 26
Dempsey, Jerome 167
Dempster, Hugh 186
DeMunn, Jeffrey 196
Denham, Reginald 143
Denker, Henry 170, 171, 172
Dennis, Nick 79
Dennis, Sandy 173
Departure, The 2
Deranged Cousins, The 71
Dere Mabel 98
Derwent, Clarence 154
Derwent, Elfrida 154
De Santis, Tony 164, 165, 166
Desperate Hours, The 45
Destazio, Brian 82
Destruction 42, 43
Deutsch, Ernest 8
Develin, John 147
Devil Is a Good Man, The 3
Devil's Profession, The 44
Devon, Larry 78
Dewhurst, Colleen 84, 137, 138
Dexter, Aubrey 152
Dexter, Elliott x
Dexter, John 15
Dial "M" For Murder 45, 143
Dickens, Charles 186, 187
Dickerson, John 78
Dickinson, Emily 20
Dickson, Bettie 152
Diener, Joan 80, 82, 84
Dietz, J. Robert 172
Diffen, Ray 80, 82
Dillea, Herbert x
Dillon, Elizabeth 178
Dilloway, Don 7
Dilman, Hugh 168

Di Maggio, Joe 47
Dinehart, Alan 88
Dinelli, Mel 45
Disengaged x
Dishy, Bob 69
Disraeli, Benjamin xvi
Disrespectful Summons, The 71
Ditrichstein, Leon ix
Divine Comedy, The 83
Dixon, Alfred 182
Dixon, John C. ix
Dr. Wake's Patient x
Dodd, D. A. Charles H. 9
Dodge Boys, The 30
Dog Beneath the Skin, The 121
Doherty, Brian 154
Doll's House, A 148
Donald, James 13, 16
Don Howe, Gwyda 28
Donnellan, Judge 8
Donnelly, Dorothy vii, x, xii
Donovan, Larry xiv
Don't Call Back 44, 45
Doolittle, James A. 48
Doolittle, Jay 44
Dorian Gray 7
Dors, Diana 156
Dostoievski, Fyodor 30, 188
Doubtful Guest, The 71
Dougherty, James 47
Douglas, Hazel 152
Douglas, Kirk 84
Douglas, Melvyn 15
Douglass, Frederick 149
Douglass, Garon 82
Down in the Valley 5
Doyle, Peter 63
Dracula 56, 70
Dr. Cook's Garden 20
Draper, Paul 26
Drat! The Cat 20
Dreigroschenoper, Die 93, 121
Dreiser, Theodore 61
Dresdel, Sonia 178
Dresser, The 196
Dreyfuss, Richard 195, 196, 197
Drinkel, Keith 156
Divas, Robert 164, 165
Driver, Donald 178, 179, 180
Du Brock, Neal 89
Dudley, William 15

256 / General Index

Duerrenmatt, Friedrich   133
Duff, Howard   80
Duff, James   30
Dugan, Lawrence Joseph   146
Dugan, William Francis   7
Dukes, David   55, 57
Du Maurier, Daphne   177
Du Maurier, Gerald   151
Duncan, Stuart   5
DuPont, Paul   91
Dupree, George   177
Duttine, John   156
Dvorak, Ann   154
Dylan   199
Dylln, J. Bernard   110
Dzundza, George   164

Earle, Freddie   166
Early Stages   188
East of Eden   77, 78, 79, 80
Ebb, Fred   121
Ed Sullivan Show   191
Edeson, Arthur   57
Edeson, George   87
Edeson, Robert   ix, 113
Edgar, David   196
Edison, Thomas A.   18
Edmondson, Marjorie   xi
Edward Gorey's Dracula   71
Edwards, Hilton   29
Edwards, Maurice   94
Ehrhardt, Peter M.   108
Eitingon, Molly, Mrs.   93
Elder, Eldon   41
Electra   65
Elephant Man, The   196
Eleventh Episode, The   71
Elic, Josip   5
Eliot, T. S.   132
Ellington, Duke   59, 131
Elliott, Gordon   84
Ellis, Larry   53
Ellis, Ruth   155, 156
Elmer, Billy   ix
Elmer Bloor   60
Elmer Gantry   58, 59, 60, 61, 62, 63
Elmore, Marion   87
Elmore, Steve   101
Elsie   135

Elston, Robert   48
Elvey, Maurice   xi
Elwood, W. H.   87
Emerson, Faye   178
Emmes, David   30
Emmond, Beverly   196
Endrey, Eugene   3
Engel, Lehman   xvi, 14, 91, 208
English Governess at the Siamese Court, The   82
Equus   109
Era of Good Feelings, The   10
Erickson, Leif   126
Erskine, Howard   157
Erskine, John   84
Estabrook, Howard   xi
Eternal Road, The   93
Ethier, Alphonz   ix
Eunson, Dale   31
Euripides   83
Evans, Craig   71
Evans, Edith   18, 188
Evans, Maurice   41
Everett, Rupert   156
Everson, John   54, 164, 166
Evil Garden, The   71
Evslin, Bernard   181, 182, 183
Ewell, Tom   96
Exodus   76
Expresso Bongo   128
Eyes of Youth   168

Fabray, Nanette   139, 140
Fadden, Tom   61, 63
Faison, George   28
Falkenhain, Patricia   201
Fame   45, 46, 47
Fanfare   xv
Far Country, A   171
Faragoh, Francis Edwards   56, 57
Farrell, Anthony B.   13, 14
Farren, Nellie   55
Farrington, Adele   88
Farrow, Mia   174
Fatal Lozenge, The   71
Father's Day   47, 48, 49
Faversham, William   ix
Fawcett, Marion   154
Fay, Frank   25

General Index / 257

Fechit, Stepin 88
Feiffer, Jules 72
Feinstein, Martin 82
Feld, Fritz 42
Feld, Rose C. 65
Fellini, Federico 185
Femme du Boulanger, La 89
Ferguson, David 171
Ferguson, Susan 171
Ferrell, Ron 28
Ferren, Bran 57
Feuer, Cy 68
Fickle Women 49, 50
Fields, Benny 25
Fields, Dorothy 185
Fields, Gracie 26
Fields, Joseph 163
Fig Leaves Are Falling, The 109
Finian's Rainbow 102
Finklehoffe, Fred 25
Fiorello 130
First One Asleep, Whistle 49, 50, 51
Firth, Peter 109
Fischer, Clifford C. 25, 26
Fisher, Robert 73, 74, 108
Fiske-Hammond Players 192
Fitzgerald, Walter 84
Flaiano, Ennio 185
Flanagan, Hallie 94
Flanagan, Pauline 182
Flaningam, Louise 148
Fleming, Atholl 154
Fleming, Bud 78
Fleming, George ix
Flemyng, Robert 154
Flender, Harold 126
Fletcher, Robert 90
Flint, Maggie 156
Flippen, Jay C. 9, 26
Florey, Robert 56, 57
Flynn, Errol 18, 126
Flynn, Gertrude 163
Flynn, Patricia 69
Folies Bergere 25
Follies of 1910, The 85
Follow the Leader 169
Fonda, Henry 174, 200
Fontanne, Lynn 38, 39, 40
For Heaven's Sake, Mother 172
For the Defense viii

For the Use of the Hall 49
For Whom the Bell Tolls 65
Forbes, Kathryn 163
Forbes, Scott 178
Forbes-Robertson, Jean 187
Foreman, Edgar A. x
Foreman, Richard 174, 175
Forman, George 66
Forster, E. M. 14
Fort, Garrett 56, 57
Forty-Five Minutes from Broadway 112
Forty-Ninth Star, The 76
Fosse, Bob 145, 185
Foster, John 122
Foster, Phoebe 151
Four Quartets 136
Fourposter, The 174
Fowler, Marge 63
Francine, Anne 28
Francis, Arlene 43, 44, 199
Francis, Kay 18
Francis, Noel 169
Francks, Don 100, 102, 104
Franco, General 40
Frank, Charles 94
Frank, Doug 46
Frank Fay's Vaudeville 25
Frank Merriwell; or First Days at Fardale 52
Frank Merriwell (Or Honor Challenged) 51, 52, 53, 54
Frank Merriwell's Father 53
Frank Merriwell's School Days 52
Frankenstein 54, 55, 56
Frankenstein; or The Man and the Monster 55
Frankenstein; or The Modern Prometheus 55
Franklin, Lydia 172
Franklyn, Ray 147
Franz, Dennis 30
Franz, Gina 202
Fraser, Hugh 166
Frazer, Dan 5
Fredericks, William xi
Freedley, George 3, 93, 195
Freedley, Vinton 39
Freeman, Arny 208
Frehner, Harry 138

258 / General Index

Fremont, Jessie Benton 200
French, Charles K. 87
French, Leslie 187
French, Pauline 113
French Connection, The 136
Freud, Sigmund 171
Friebus, Florida 120
Friedkin, William 136
Friedman, Bruce Jay 89
Froman, Jane 26
Fry, Christopher 83
Fry, Horace B. x
Frye, Dwight 58
Fugua, V. C. 157
Furber, Douglas 167

Gable, Clark 42
Gallagher, Helen 28
Gallagher, "Skeets" 42
Gallatin, Alberta xi
Gallili, Hal 166
Galloway, Jane 108
Gallows Glorious 125
Gantillon, Simon 9
Gantry 58, 59, 60, 61, 62, 63
García Lorca, Federico 65
Garden of Sweets, The 64, 65
Gardiner, Alice 53
Gardiner, Reginald 154
Gardner, Herb 68, 69
Gardner, William 78
Garfield, James A. 149
Garfield, Jules (John) 91
Garland, Judy 24
Garrett, Michael 48
Garrison, Gerald 94
Gashlycrumb Tinies, The 71
Gaston, Ken 75, 76
Gavin, Gene 78
Gaxton, William 26
Gay, John 93
Gaynes, Edmund 94
Gebest, Charles 110
Geer, Ellen 48
Geese 141
Geidt, Jeremy 167
Gelber, Jack 33, 34, 35
Gem, Pam 196
General Seegar 2, 20

George, Gwilym Lloyd 155
George M. 114
George S. Kaufman: An Intimate Portrait 99
George Washington, Jr. 113
Geranium Hat, The 183
Gerard, Bettina 87
Germon, Effie x
Gershwin, George 17, 105, 146
Gershwin, Ira 17, 105
Gesner, Clark 52, 201, 202
Gethers, Steven 2
Geva, Tamara 40
Ghosts viii, 187
Gialanella, Victor 56, 57
Gianfrancesco, Edward 71
Giannini, Christina 157
Gibbons, Cedric 42
Gibson, Alice 154
Gibson, Michael 148
Gibson, William 174
Gielgud, John 18, 186, 187, 188
Gifford, Gwynne 48
Gigi 37
Gilded Bat, The 71
Gill, Brendan 84
Gill, Jack 128
Gillette, Anita 100, 102
Gilman, Ada viii
Gilman, Larry 164
Gilmore, Frank x, xi
Gilroy, Frank 96
Gilson, Charles E. 113
Gin Game, The 173
Giono, Jean 89
Girardot, Etienne 88
Giraudoux, Jean 84, 133
Girl in the Freudian Slip, The 28
Girl Who Came to Supper, The 24
Girls in 509, The 99
Gish, Dorothy 100
Gish, Lillian 100
Gisondi, John 49
Glass, Everett 63
Glass, Montague 123
Glassman, Stephen 11, 12, 13
Gleason, James 72

Glendinning, Ernest xi
Glendinning, John ix
Glenn, Peter 7
God of Vengeance 7
Goetz, Peter Michael 137
Going Places 130
Goland, Arnold 78
Gold, David 145
Gold, Justice Samuel 104
Goldberg, Leonard J. 75, 76
Golden, Echard viii
Golden, Grace viii
Golden Boy 29, 38
Goldfish, The 168
Goldknopf, Abraham xi
Goldman, William xvi, 96
Goldsmith, Fred 167
Golem, The 67
Golonka, Arlene 88, 89
Gomez, S. Thomas 39
Gomez, Vincente 26
Good Neighbor, The 66
Good Neighbors 67
Good News 169
Good Night, Ladies 167
Goodbye Girl, The 197
Goodbye People, The 68, 69
Goodfader, Meryl 202
Goodtime Charley 199
Goodwill Ambassador 30
Gordon, Alan 152
Gordon, Alex 77, 78
Gordon, Harold 79
Gordon, Michael 91
Gordon, John 52
Gordon, Sidney 44
Gordon, Steve 197
Gore, Christopher 30
Gorey, Edward 56, 70, 71
Gorey Stories 70, 71
Gorman, James 110
Gorrin, John 82
Gott, Barbara 154
Gottfried, Martin xvi
Gottschalk, Ferdinand xi
Gould, Elliott 72, 73
Gould, Richard 54
Gow, Ronald 125
Graden, David 201
Graham, Joseph 63
Graham, Lee 208

Granger, Maude ix
Granny Maumee xii
Grant, Ulysses S. 149
Granville-Barker, Helen and Harley 206, 208
Gray, Stephen 154
Gray, Timothy 90
Grease 56, 57
Greatest Story Ever Told, The 171
Greeley, Horace 149
Green, Johnny 105
Green, Paul 17, 90, 94
Green, Stanley 111
Greene, Leon 166
Greenleaf, Ramon 94
Greenstreet, Sydney 39
Greenwillow 145
Greenwood, Jane 49
Greet, Ben xi
Gregory, Paul 125
Greene, Charles N. x
Grey, Jane xi
Grey, Joel 107, 109, 114, 199
Gribble, Harry Wagstaff 63
Griffies, Ethel 136
Grimes, Tammy 49
Griswald, Grace ix
Grossman, Larry 199
Grundy, Sidney x
Guardino, Lawrence 72
Guerre de Troie n' Aura pas Lieu, La 84
Guest in the House 32, 143
Guilty Conscience, The xi
Guinan, Texas 9
Guinness, Alec 199
Gundersen, Karen 37
Guthrie, Tyrone 126
Gutierrez, Gerald 107, 108
Guys and Dolls 28, 145
Guys in the Truck, The 71, 72, 73
Gypsy x, 130

H. M. S. Pinafore 13
Haag, J. Robert 122
Haak, Morton 208
Hackady, Hal 199
Hacker, John 66

260 / Genral Index

Hackett, Joan 157
Hackett, Raymond 161
Hackman, Gene 136
Hadge, Michael 157
Hadrian VII 48
Hague, Albert 109
Hailey, Elizabeth Forsythe 49
Hailey, Marion 117
Hailey, Oliver D., Jr. 47, 48, 49, 50, 51, 88, 89
Haines, Brian 152
Haldridge, Lee 80
Hale, Louise Closser viii, x
Halévy, Ludovic 84
Haley, Jack 26
Half a Sixpence 59
Hall, Carol 158
Hall, Charles D. 57
Hall, Charles S. 124
Hall, Dorothy 7
Hallat, Henry 55
Halliday, John 174
Halstan, Margaret 188
Hambleton, T. Edward 120
Hamilton, Mahlon 88
Hamilton, W. F. 110
Hamlet 182
Hammerstein, Oscar, II 100, 114
Hammond, Paul 193
Hammond, Ronald T. 66
Hampden, Walter xi, 13, 16
Hampf, Dagmar 66
Hampton, Louise 154
Hanburg, Lily 83
Hansen, Waldemar 64, 65
Hapless Child, The 71
Happiness Is Just a Little Thing Called a Rolls Royce 73, 74
Haran, Ronnie 182
Hard Day's Night, A 166
Hardie, Russell 88
Harding, Ann xv, 1, 2
Hardy, Cherry 178
Hare, Lumsden 61
Harewood, Dorian 43, 44
Hargrave, Roy 193
Haring, Blanche 122, 161
Harlam, Macey ix
Harlem 67
Harlem Cavalcade 26
Harmantas, Lucyle 208

Harney, Jordon C. 157
Harper's Ferry 126
Harrigan, Robert 61
Harrington, C. J. 110, 112
Harris, Barb 167
Harris, Caroline x
Harris, Chris 166
Harris, Donald 120
Harris, Julie 19, 20, 79
Harris, Robert 187, 193
Harris, Rosemary 41
Harris, Sam 110
Harris, Vernon 188
Harrison, Phillip 166
Harrison, Vangie 166
Harrison and Fisher 26
Hart, Harvey 80
Hart, Kitty Carlise 100
Hart, Moss 100
Hart, Walter 193
Hart, William S. x
Hartford, Huntington 116
Hartman, Paul and Grace 26
Harvey, Paul 90
Harvey 163
Harwood, H. M. 151, 153
Harwood, Ronald 196
Has Anybody Here Seen Kelly? 104
Haskell, Judith 148
Hathaway, Gwendolyn 61
Have I Got a Girl for You! 74, 75
Hawaii 76
Hawes, Dean 138
Hawkins, Margaret 63
Hawthorn, Pamela 138
Hayes, Helen 99, 100
Hayes, Joseph 45
Hayes, Margaret 182
Haynes, Tiger 141
Hays, David 68
Hayter, James 188
Hayward, Leland 130
Hayward, Thomas xii
Hayworth, Rita 182
Hazell, Hy 145
Healy, David 128
Heard, John 196
Hearn, Lew 122
Heathen! 75, 76

General Index / 261

Heather Field, The ix
Heatherton, Joey 182
Heckart, Eileen 201
Hedda Gabler ix, 65
Heefner, David Henry 137
Heflin, Van 171
Heilbron, Adelaide 113
Heineman, Eda 192
Heist, Karl 148
Hellman, Bonnie 202
Hellman, Lillian 31, 100
Hello, Dolly! 20, 148
Helms, Natalie 148
Helpmann, Sir Robert 75, 76
Hemingway, Ernest 22, 65
Henderson, Robert 202
Henighen, Bernard 82
Henley, E. J. ix
Henning, Doug 24
Henry, Louise 88
Henry, Richard 55
Hepburn, Katharine 177
Hepton, Bernard 156
Herbert, F. Hugh 163
Herendeen, Fred 134, 135
Here's Love 175
Here's Where I Belong 77, 78, 79
Herman, Jerry 118, 172
Herne, Chrystal 193
Herrmann, Keith 147, 148
Hervieu, Paul x
Hey, You, Light Man! 49, 51
Hickman, Darryl 157
Hickson, Kevin 72
Hidden Hero, The 176
Hiding Place, The 59
High Button Shoes 48
Higher Law, The 87
Hildegarde 26
Hill, Gus xiv
Hill, James 182
Hill, Kenneth xi
Hines, Charles 113
Hines, Johnny 113
Hingle, Pat 96
Hinnant, Bill 52
Hinsdale, Harriet 53
Hirson, Roger O. 18
Hitler, Adolph 40, 42, 102
H.M.S. Pinafore 13

Hoban, Gordon 120
Hoffman, Bill 84
Hoffman, Dustin 180
Hofsiss, Jack 196
Holgate, Danny 82
Holland, Anthony 167
Holly Golightly 59, 89
Holm, Celeste 201, 202
Holm, Hanya 78
Holman, Morgan 44
Holmes, Richard 166
Holmes, Wendell 64
Holtz, Lou 25, 26
Holzer, Adela 164, 165, 171
Home Folks 87
Home Front 30
Home Sweet Homer 80, 81, 84
Homer 81, 83
Homer, Irene 61
Honey 169
Honeymoon, The xi
Hood, Margaret 188
Hook 'N Ladder 84, 85
Hopwood, Avery 166
Hornblow, Arthur, Jr. 8
Horne, Geoffrey 13, 16
Horner, Charles 84, 85
Horner, Harry 41
Horniman, Tina 178
Horrigan, Jack 31, 32
Hossack, Grant 128
Hot Heels 112
Hot September 89
House, Billy 135
House of Artreus, The 65
House of Bernardo Alba, The 65
House of Connelly, The 91
Houseboat on the Styx, The 135
How to Be a Jewish Mother 172
How to Steal an Election 28
How to Succeed in Business Without Even Trying 20, 145
Howard, Elizabeth Harris 116, 117
Howard, Max 180
Howard, Sidney 62, 82
Howard, Willie 26, 122
Howe, Julia Ward 124
Howland, Jobyna ix

262 / General Index

Hudson, Rock   126
Hughes, Howard   35
Hughes, Rupert   viii
Hughes, Tresa   204, 205
Hulce, Thomas   108, 109
Hull, Shelly   xi
Humanitarian, The   150
Hummin' Sam   85, 86
Hundreth Man, The   xi
Hurlburt, William   62
Hurt, Mary Beth   49
Husson, Albert   144
Huston, Noel   3
Huston, Walter   114
Hutcheson, David   187
Hutchinson, Josephine   207
Hutton, Betty   24
Hyman, Mac   20
Hyman, Joseph M.   208

I Am a Camera   121
I Can Get It for You Wholesale   130
I Can't Find It Anywhere   49
I Dream of Jeannie   74
I Picked a Daisy   38
I Remember Mama   163
I Won't Dance   49, 88, 89
Ibsen, Henrik   vii, viii, ix, 65, 148, 157, 187
Idiot's Delight   36, 38, 39, 40, 41, 42
Immortal Wife   200
Imperfect Lover, The   151
Importance of Being Dressed, The   189
Impossible Years, The   74
Improper People   188
In a Balcony   ix
In Abraham's Bosom   92
In Old Kentucky   85, 86, 87
In the Long Run   x
Inanimate Tragedy, The   71
Ince, John   88
Indians   34
Inge, William   89
Ingels, Marty   101
Ingram, Rex   63
Inlender, Avraham   141
Innocents, The   32

Insect God, The   71
Insurrection; or Kansas and Harper's Ferry, The   125
Interlanghi, Franco   84
Interlock   20
International Ladies' Garment Workers Union   194
Interstate 76   30
Intruder, The   32
Irene   113, 171
Irma La Douce   59, 128
Iron Tonic, The   71
Irving, George   x
Irwin, Mrs. Seldwin   87
Irwin, Will   82
Isaacs, Mary K.   163
Isherwood, Christopher   119, 120, 121
It Can't Happen Here   67
It's a Bird--It's a Plane--It's Superman!   29, 52
It's Only a Play   165
Ivanov, Peter   172
Ives, Alice E.   xi
Ives, Burl   79
Ives, Charlotte   xii

Jack Gelber's New Play: Rehearsal   35
Jackson, Al   204
Jackson, Barry   187
Jackson, Nagle   201
Jacobs, George   72
Jacobs, Susan   96
Jaffe, Sam   41
Jagger, Dean   63
James, Francis   186
James, Frank and Jesse   30, 103
James, Henry   x, 32, 183
James, Louis   87
Jamiaque, Yves   133, 134
Janis, Conrad   139, 173
Janis, Elsie   25
Janney, Leon   100, 102, 103, 145
Jansen, Jim   148
Jansen, Richard D.   180
Jaroslow, Ruth   165
Jarvis, Frank   156
Jaws   59, 197

Jaws of Hell 18
Jayhawker, The 67
Jazz 187
Jeakins, Dorothy 63
Jealousy 174
Jeffers, Robinson 46
Jeffory, Dawn 202
Jeffrey, Mary viii
Jeffreys-Goodfriend, Ida viii
Jenkins, David 196
Jensen, Robert F. 125
Jensen, Willard 169
Jerome, Frank E. 124
Jerrold, Mary 188
Jesse, F. Tennyson 151, 152, 153, 155, 156
Jessel, George 26
Jewett, Henry viii
Jilinsky, Andrius 21
Jilton, Margaret 201
Jimmy Shine 180
Jochim, Keith 57
Joffrey, Robert 94
Johanna Ventures, Inc. 48
John Brown 125
John Brown's Body 125, 126, 127
John Gabriel Borkman ix
Johnny Johnson 17, 90, 91, 93, 94
Johnny No-Trump 94, 95, 96
Johnson, Ben xi
Johnson, Crockett 143
Johnson, Frank 61, 63
Johnson, Mike 80
Johnson, Richard 178
Johnson, Samuel xvi
Johnson, Van 117, 118
Jolly's Progress 157, 203
Jonathan 44
Jones, Archer x
Jones, H. Trevor 186, 187
Jones, James Earl 20
Jones, Jeffrey 48, 202
Jones, Shirley 63, 109
Jones, Stanley 79
Joplin, Carol 101
Jordan, Georgiana 180
Jory, Jon 196
Journal of a Novel: The East of Eden Letters 80
Jouvet, Louis 84
Joy, James Leonard 137
Joyce, James 30
Judgement Day xvi
Julia, Jake and Uncle Joe 97, 98
Julius Caesar 151
Junior Miss 163
Juniper and the Pagans 89

Kadish 141, 142
Kael, Pauline 166
Kahan, Joseph 94
Kahn, Florence ix
Kahn, Gus 42
Kahn, Michael 77, 78, 201
Kander, John 121
Kane, Beatrice 178
Kanin, Garson 41, 118
Kaplan, Henry 117
Karloff, Boris 56, 58
Karlweis, Oscar 194, 195
Kasha, Lawrence 47, 48
Kaszner, Kurt 167
Katselas, Milton 64, 141
Kauffmann, Stanley 176
Kaufman, George S. 17, 99, 146, 163
Kaufman and Hart 4, 163
Kaufmann, Maurice 152
Kay, Geraldine 180
Kaye, Anne 202
Kaye, Danny 24
Kazan, Elia 46, 79, 91
Kean, Norman 28
Keane, Doris x
Kearney, Patrick 61, 62
Keathley, George 48, 180
Keating, Lucille 63
Keegan, Howard 63
Keep 'Em Laughing 26
Keeper, Gary 164
Keeper of the Flame 22, 176
Keightley, Cyril xi
Kellard, John E. ix
Kelley, Barry 64
Kellin, Mike 164
Kelly, Kate 202

264 / Genral Index

Kelly, Nancy 182
Kelly xv, 4, 100, 101, 102, 103, 104, 105
Kendrick, Richard 193
Kennedy, Arthur 63
Kennett, Luther 178
Kenney, Marie 161
Kent, Betty 94
Kent, Paul 48
Kenton, Godfrey 188
Kenyon, Neal 52
Kern, Jerome 18
Kerr, Deborah 83
Kerr, Frederick 58
Kerr, Walter 9
Kerwin, Shawn 138
Kessler, Lyle 204, 205
Keyes, Daniel 202
Kibbee, Guy 208
Kibbee, Roland 82
Kid, The 35
Kilbreth, Justice xiv
Killer, The 112
Killing of Sister George, The 6
Kimbrough, Charles 173
Kind Lady 45, 208
King, Austin 193
King, Dave 166
King, Dennis 14
King, Edith 208
King, George 42
King, Lawrence 164, 165
King, Rufus 135
King and I, The 82, 83, 120
King Kong 67
King of Jazz, The 170
King Washington ix
Kingsford, Walter xi
Kipness, Joseph 47, 48, 56, 57
Kippen, Mannart 63
Kirby, Durward 118
Kirby, Randy 118
Kirchner, Ray 78
Kirk, Phyllis 151
Kirtland, Louise 94
Kiss and Tell 163
Kiss Me, Kate 144, 145, 194
Kitchen, The 34
Kitt, Eartha 46, 157, 203
Kittridge, Harry 111, 112
Klaer, Adele 61, 63

Klar, Gary 71, 72
Klaw and Erlanger 110
Klein, Charles 123
Klein, Kathleen 171, 172
Klugman, Jack 199
Knight, Shirley 89
Knott, Frederick 45
Know Thyself x
Kologi, Mark 43, 44
Kolster, Clarence 113
Komisarievsky, Theodore 188
Kool Aid 35
Kopit, Arthur 34
Korla, Kathy 180
Koulias, Arthur 154
Kraber, Tony 91
Kramer, Carol 53
Kramer, (Mrs) Terry Allen 57
Krebs, Eric 30
Krizner, Kathleen 54
Kummer, Clare 178
Kurnitz, Harry 24

Ladd, Hank 26
Ladies and the Man, The 103
Ladies in Retirement 143
Ladies Night in a Turkish Bath 167
Lady with a Lamp 18
Laemmle, Carl, Jr. 57
LaGuardia, Midge 90
Lahr, Bert 4, 96
Lake, Richard 152
Lancaster, Burt 63
Land of Heart's Desire, The ix
Landon, Margaret 82
Lane, Burton 38
Lane, Frances 94
Lane, Stewart F. 57
Lang, Philip J. 145
Lange, Hope 173
Langella, Frank 56
Langham, Michael 204, 205
Langton, Diane 128
Lansbury, Bruce 50, 51
Lansbury, Edgar 5, 24, 50, 51
La Rosa, Julius 28
Larsen, Ray 196
Laskawy, Harris 71, 72, 73
Last Analysis, The 96

General Index / 265

Late George Apley, The   163
Latham, Lewis, H.   104
Laugh Time   25
Laugh, Town, Laugh   26
Laughton, Charles   125, 126
Laurents, Arthur   178
Laurie, Joe, Jr.   25
Lavender Leotard, The   71
Lawlor, Lilian   187
Lawrence, Albert   viii
Lawrence, Beth   46
Lawrence, Charles   135
Lawrence, Eddie   4, 5, 100, 102, 103, 104
Lawrence, Elliott   185
Lawrence, Gerald   83
Lawrence, Gertrude   82
Lawson, Wilfrid   125
Layton, Joe   114
Leachman, Cloris   116
Lear, Norman   29
Leave It to Me   144
Leaves from a Mislaid Album   71
Lebowsky, Stanley   59, 60
Le Comte, Edmond   3
Lee, Barbara   188
Lee, Ming Cho   77, 78, 185
Lee, Robert E.   126
Lee, Ronald S.   44
Lee, Will   91
Le Gallienne, Eva   25, 176, 177, 178, 206, 207
Leger, Fernand   103
Leggatt, Alison   154
Legge, Clayton Mackenzie   x
Lehar, Franz   110
Leigh, Mitch   80, 81, 82, 84
Leighton, Margaret   199
Lemae, Julia   28
Lemmon, Jack   41, 173
Lemmon, John Uhler, III   41
LeMoyne, Mrs. Sarah Cowell   ix
LeMura, Mark   48
Lenya, Lotta   93
Lenz, Rick   117
Leonard, Jack E.   4
Leonard, Robert   123
Leone, Maude   169
Leonowens, Anna   82
Leopold, Thomas   165
Lerner, Alan Jay   35, 36, 37, 38

Lerner, Michael   196
Lerner and Loewe   37
LeRoy, Mervyn   113
Leslie, Fred   55
Leslie, Joseph   110
Lester, Hugh   180
Lester, Richard   166
LeStrange, Philip   171, 172
Let Me Hear You Smile   105, 136
Letter of the Law, The   viii
Leve, Samuel   208
Levene, Sam   172
Levey, Ethel   110, 113
Levin, Ira   2, 19, 20
Levin, Jack   66, 67
Levine, Joseph E.   100, 102
Levis, Charles   167
Levy, Benn W.   195
Levy, Jacques   89
Lewin, John   17, 18
Lewis, Bob   91
Lewis, Catherine   viii
Lewis, Frederick   ix, x
Lewis, Harry   188
Lewis, Jerry   24
Lewis, Lloyd   67
Lewis, Sheldon   x
Lewis, Sinclair   10, 11, 59, 60, 61, 62, 63, 66, 67
Lewis, Tom   110, 112
Lieven, Tatiana   40
Life and Adventures of Nicholas Nickleby, The   196
Life of the Party, The   37
Life with Father   163
Lifton, Robert   69
Light of the World, The   168
Limerick, A   71
Lincoln, Abraham   127
Lincoln, Mary Todd   200
Lindfors, Viveca   199
Lindo, Olea   154
Lindsay, Howard   116, 163
Linklater, Eric   18
Linville, Joanne   94
Lippel, Philip   148
Lipton, Bronna   108
Lipton, James   4
Listing Attic, The   71
Litt, Jacob   86

266 / General Index

Little Brown Jug 45
Little Hussar, The viii
Little Johnny Jones 105, 106, 107, 108, 109, 110, 111, 112, 113, 114
Little Maverick, The 87
Little Millionaire, The 107
Little Murders 72
Little Nelly Kelly 107
Little Night Music, A 38
Littlest Revue, The 28
Littlewood, Joan 17
Litvak, Barry 30
Livingston, Robert H. 171
Loane, George H. x
Lo Bianco, Tony 69
Location 44
Lockhart, Gene 7
Loesser, Frank 28, 145
Loew, Arthur 157, 203
Loewe, Frederick 37
Lofft, Alan 202
Logan, Ella 26, 100, 102, 104
Lolita 38
Lolita, My Love 38
Long, Robert Edgar 62
Long, Long Trail, The 17
Look, We've Come Through 96
Lord, Pauline 62
Losee, Frank 87
Lost Lions, The 71
Loud Red Patrick, The 193
Louis and the Elephant 4, 5
Louisiana Lady 135
Love, Andy 78
Love, Bessie 166
Love Is Eternal 200
Love Life 37
Love Mouse 138
Love, Sidney 49
Love Story 81, 82
Lovely Ladies, Kind Gentlemen 48
Love's Pilgrimage x
Lubin, Sigmund 123
Luce, William 20
Luckinbill, Laurence 120
Lugosi, Bela 56, 135
Lulu Belle 7
Lumley, Molly 154

Lundell, Kert 141
Lunt, Alfred 38, 39
Lunts, The 26, 39
Lust for Life 200
Lute Song 82
Lykins, Virginia 188
Lyle 85
Lynn, Diana 151
Lynn, Jonathan 128
Lynn, Regina 69
Lynne, Gillian 128
Lyon, Professor John H. H. xvi
Lytell, Bert 30

MacArthur, Charles 62
McAvity, Helen 116, 117
Macbeth 78
McCallum, David 16
McCann, Elizabeth I. 195, 196
McCarthy, Eugene J. [Senator] 132
McCarthy, Kevin 203
McClintic, Guthrie 65
McConnell, Lulu 122
McCool, Jean 122
McCord, Ted 79
McCorkle, David 78
McCormick, Langdon viii
McDaniel, Donna Jeanne 125
McDermott, Tom 14
McDevitt, Ruth 143
MacDonald, James 94
McDonald, Joyce 78
McDowall, Roddy 16
McFadden, William 161
McFarland, Eric 167
MacFarlane, Bruce 193
McGinn, Walter 77, 78, 79
McGivern, Tom, Jr. 3
Macgowan, Kenneth 7
Macht, Stephan 121
MacIlveen, Mrs. Oriana Torrey see Atkinson, Oriana
McIntire, John 63
Mack, Willard 168
Mackay, Bill 82
Mackay, W. Gayer x
Mackaye, Steele xiv
MacKeller, Helen viii
McKenney, Ruth 193

MacKenzie, Arthur 201
McKinley, Andrew 15
McKinney, Nina Mae 66
MacLiammóir, Micheal 29
McMackin, Patricia 94
MacMahon, Aline 9
McMahon, Virginia 94
McMartin, John 145
McNally, Terrence 78, 164, 165, 166, 167
McNeeley, Anna 108
McNish, Frank, Jr. 111
McPherson, Aimee Semple 60, 62
McQuarrie, Christina 138
McQueen, Jim 138
McRae, Bruce x
MacRae, Michael and Barclay 105
Macy, Gertrude 121
Madame Capet 169
Mlle. Modiste 113
Madden, Donald 181, 182
Maddern, Merle 207
Madwoman of Chaillot, The 133
Magic Show, The 24
Magoon, Eaton, Jr. 75, 76
Mahoney, John 148
Maibaum, Richard 69
Maiden Voyage 84
Mailer, Norman 34
Main Street 67
Majority of One, A 172
Make Me an Offer 128
Make Momma Happy 172
Malambos, Los 23
Male Animal, The 178
Malleson, Miles 154
Mallory, Louise x
Malone, Elizabeth Saxon 112
Malone, Molly 113
Mamma's Bank Account 163
Man, The 45
Man and His Wife, The ix
Man in Possession, The 151
Man in the Glass Booth, The 59
Man That Corrupted Hadleyburg, The 183
Man Who Came to Dinner, The 4
Man Who Wouldn't Talk, The 177
Maney, Richard xv
Mangano, Silvano 84

Manheim and Shea 63
Manhoff, Bill 89, 174
Mann, Michael 82
Mann, P. J. 82
Mannin, Ethel 60
Manning, Mildred 122
Manon, Marcia 88
Man's Man, A 61
Mansfield, Richard vii
Manson, Alan 157
Mantle, Burns 8, 153
Many Happy Returns 178
Marceau, Marcel 24
March, Nadine 187
Marcus, Frank 6
Marilyn: An American Fable 46
Marilyn's Affairs 114, 115
Maritz, Al 84, 85
Markham, Monte 173
Markle, Lois 203
Marks, Alfred 145
Marks, Joe E. 208
Marks, Owen 79
Marley, John 5
Marlowe, Hugh 63
Maross, Joe 63
Marquand, John P. 163
Marr, Richard 78
Marre, Albert 80, 82, 84, 119, 120
Marriage-Go-Round, The 98
Marshall, Larry 28
Marshall, Herbert 162
Marshall, Mort 145
Marston, Don 180
Martelli, Otello 185
Martin, Dan 72
Martin, Elliot 41
Martin, Ernest 68
Martin, John B. 150
Martin, Mary 82, 100, 103
Martin, Vivienne 189
Martindale, Edward 88
Martinez-Sierra, Gregorio 206, 207, 208
Martyn, Edward ix
Marvin, Lee 14
Marx, Arthur 74
Marx, Harpo 26
Mary's Manoeuvres xi
M*A*S*H 202

268 / General Index

Masina, Giulietta 185
Masks and Faces 115
Mason, Jackie 190, 191
Masquerade 116
Mass Appeal 196
Massey, Raymond 40, 41, 79, 125, 126, 151, 195
Master Builder, The ix
Masteroff, Joe 121
Maston, Boyd 148
Masur, Richard 80
Mata Hari 89
Matchmaker, The 148
Mather, Fank Jewett, Jr. 83
Mathis, June xii
Mating Dance 116, 117, 118
Matlowsky, Samuel 94
Matteotti, Giacomo 191, 192
Matthau, Walter 84, 116
Matthews, W. H. 61
Maugham, W. Somerset 168
Maupassant, Guy de 103
Maurer, Michael 201
Maurette, Marcelle 169
Maverick 151
May, Elaine 165
Maya 9
Mayborn, Amelia x
Mayer, Louis B. 22
Mayhew, Kate xi
Maynard, Gaylord 23
Me and Thee 118, 119
Medea and Jason 46
Medley, Lottie 112
Meehan, John 62
Meehan, William E. 111, 112
Meeting By the River, A 119, 120, 121
Meilhac, Henri 84
Meisner, Sanford 91
Melford, Austin 167
Melford, Marian 156
Melnick, Daniel 100, 102, 104
Melville, Herman 11, 12, 13, 14
Mencken, H. L. 60
Mencken, Helen 8
Mendlick, Charles 208
Menmuir, Raymond 156
Menotti, Gian Carlo 5
Mercer, Johnny 130

Merchant of Yonkers, The 148
Mercier, Mary 94, 95, 96
Meredith, Burgess 29, 42, 134, 199
Meredith, Lucille 193
Merivale, Philip 67, 151
Merkow, Edward 49
Merle and Anthony 55
Merrick, David 17, 20, 89, 90, 193
Merrill, Dina 203
Merrill, Gary 181, 182
Merry Malones, The 108
Merry Widow, The 110
Metamorphoses 143
Metcalf, David 147
Metcalf, Rosalind 147
Meyer, Edgar 180
Meyerhold, Vsevolod 188
Meyer's Room 138
Michael, Kathleen 154
Michaelangelo 200
Michaels, Patricia 46
Michaels, Sidney 198, 199
Michell, Keith 118
Michener, James 76
Mickes, Toby 117
Middleton, George 167, 168, 169
Middleton, Josephine 18, 154
Midnight Frolics 69
Midnight Trail, The 87
Midsummer Night's Dream, A 143
Miles, Henry 84, 85
Milford, David W. 171
Milk and Honey 172
Miller, Ann 24
Miller, Arthur 46, 47, 99
Miller, Flournoy 26
Miller, Gilbert 8
Miller, Hugh 40
Miller, Jason 79
Miller, Joan 152, 153
Miller, Joseph E. 69
Miller, Mitch 77, 78, 79
Miller, Paula 207
Miller, Sigmund 116
Mills, Grace 208
Mills, Harry 63
Mills, Mary 188

Milne, A. A. 177, 186
Milner, H. M. 55
Milo and Roger 23
Milton, Robert 61
Minford, Robert 94
Minnelli, Vincente 89
Minnick, Maurice 147
Minnie's Boys 74
Minotis, Alexis 65
Minton, John 165
Miracle Woman, The 62
Miss Liberty 140
Miss Lonelyhearts 99
Miss Thompson 168
Mr. Frank Merriwell 53
Mr. President 102, 140
Mister Roberts 130
Mrs. Smith's Husband viii
Mitchell, Robert 119, 120
Moffat, Donald 47, 48
Moffet, J. C. 67
Molly 172
Molofsky, Merle 35
Money Mad xiv, 121, 122, 123
Monk, Julius 59
Monk, Robby 137
Monroe, James 11
Monroe, Marilyn 46, 47
Monstre et le Magicien, Le 55
Montel, Michael 48, 120
Montgomery, Frank 112
Montgomery, Mabel 61
Moon Beseiged, The 123, 124
Mooney, Charles 178
Mooney, Rita 207
Moony Shapiro Songbook, The 127, 128
Moor, Robert 48
Moore, Adelia 132
Moore, Daniel 132
Moore, Eileen 178
Moore, George 132
Moore, Honor 131, 132
Moore, Jenny McKean 132
Moore, Mabel xi
Moore, Marian 132
Moore, Patience 132
Moore, Paul, Jr., [Right Reverend] 132
Moore, Paul, III 132
Moore, Roger 151

Moore, Rosemary 132
Moore, Scott 122
Moore, Susanna 132
Moore, Tim 26
Moore, Tom 56, 57
Moore, Victor 26
Moose Murders 128, 129, 130
Moran, James 94
Mordente, Tony 78
More, Julian 127, 128
Morely, Robert 172
Moreno, Rita 60, 164, 166, 208
Morgan, Diana 22, 176, 177, 178
Morgan, Dickson 169
Morgan, Elaine 156
Morgan, Frank xii, 195
Morgenstern, C. V. 8
Moriarty, Michael 126
Morning Star 172
Mornings at Seven 79, 196
Morr, Alexander 82
Morris, Gwladys Evan 186
Morris, Nathan xiv
Mortman, Mike 190
Morton, Clive 154
Moss, Peter 138
Most Beautiful Girls in the World, The 44
Most Happy Fella, The 145
Mostel, Zero 26
Mother Courage 185
Mother Lover, The 130, 131
Motley 41, 187
Mourning Pictures 131, 132
Mousetrap, The 152
Muhlhausen xiii
Mulligan, Richard 117, 173
Mulville, Eva 188
Munier, Ferdinand 169
Munson, Ona 178
Murad, Sirri 120
Murder at the Vanities 135
Murderer Among Us, A 133, 134
Murdock, George 30
Murin, David 137
Murphy, Edna 113
Murray, David ix
Murray, Don 13, 16, 173
Murray, James 88
Murray, Stephen 188
Murray, Vera 161

Music Man, The 118
Mussolini, Benito 40, 191
Muszynski, Jan 138
My Fair Lady 37
My Favorite Husband 74
My Life in Court 171
My Sister Eileen 163
My Three Angels 144, 194
My Wife Won't Let Me x
Myerberg, Michael 100
Mules Aroon 100
Mystery Moon 134, 135
Mysterious Client, The 87

Nabokov, Vladimir 38
Nadrag, A 189
Nadzo, Guido 161
Nagel, Alice 202
Napoli, Jeanne 46
Nast, Thomas 149
Nathan, George Jean 85
Nathan, Vivian 204, 205
Natural Look, The 135, 136
Navarro, Chi Chi 166
Necken, The xi
Ned and Jack 137, 138
Nederlander, James 24, 25, 57, 196
Need, The 44
Needles, Ellanora 188
Nefertiti 30
Neighbors 44
Neilan, Marshall 87
Nettleton, John 156
Neufield, Mace 80
Neville, John 16
New Adventures of Frank Merriwell, The 53
New Faces of 1936 118
New Faces of 1968 28
New Girl in Town 32
New Priorities of 1943 26
Newman, Charles, Jr. 3
Newman, Ellen 72
Newman, Phyllis 145
Newton, H. Chane 55
New York Exchange 7
New York Luck 87
Next 165
Ney, Marie 154

Niblo, Fred 110
Nice Wanton xi
Nielson, Carlotta x
Night Hawk 7
Night They Raided Minsky's, The 103
Nightingale, Florence 17, 18
Nights of Cabiria 185
Nizer, Louis 171
No Hard Feelings 138, 139, 140
No Time for Sergeants 20
Noah's Flood xi
Nobody Likes Stephen Sondheim West of Tenth Avenue 30
Nobody's Girl 87
Nolan, Agnes 110
Nolan, Alice 110
Nolan, Lola 110
Nolte, Charles 13, 14, 16
Noon 78, 165
Norman, James 89
Norman, Monty 127, 128
Norman, Is That You? 140
Norris, Donald 78
Notara, Darrell 145
Novarro, Chi Chi 164
November People, The 140, 141
Nugent, Elliott 178
Nugent, Nelle 195, 196
Nugent, Sir Terence 152
Nunn, Mary 53
Nursery Frieze, The 71

Oakman, Wheeler 113
Oates, Warren 80
Ober, Philip 63
Object Lesson, The 71
O'Brien, Eloise Taylor 172
O'Brien, Eugene xi, xii
O'Brien, Pat 172
O'Brien, Tom 84
O'Casey, Sean 100
O'Connor, Carroll 29, 30
O'Connor, Richard 3
O'Connor, Tim 16
O'Connor, Una 178
O'Dell, Denis 166
Odd Couple, The 194
Odets, Clifford 29
Odlum, Emmett xiii

Odyssey 81, 82, 84
Oedipus 65
Oedipus Tyrannus 65
Oenslager, Donald 91
Offenbach, Jacques 84
Oh, Kay! 113
Oh! Oh! Oh! Nurse! 135
Oh! What a Lovely War 17, 18, 146
Ohman, Christopher 49
O'Horgan, Tom 88, 89
O'Keefe, Walter 26
Olaf, Pierre 41
Old Ladies, The 188
Old Maid and the Thief, The 5
Olive Latimer's Husband x
Oliver, Francis V. S. xiv
Oliver, Roland 7
Olivier, Sir Laurence 100
Olson, Nancy 37
On a Clear Day You Can See Forever 37
On an Open Roof 141, 142
On Borrowed Time 79
On Stage: The Making of a Broadway Play 96
On the Bowery xiv
Once and Future King, The 37
Once for the Asking 142, 143, 144
Once There Was a Russian 144, 145
Once Upon a Time 146, 147
One Bright Day 116
One Night in Brodie's Barroom xiv
One Night Only 135
One-Night Stand, The 89
One of the Family 87
O'Neal, Charles 143
O'Neal, Ryan 143
O'Neil, Dick 197, 198
O'Neil, Russell 43, 44, 45
O'Neill, Eugene vii, viii, 6, 7, 9, 67, 163
Onward Victoria 147, 148, 149, 150
Open Door, The 207, 208
Ord, Robert x
O'Reilly, Rosemary 94

Ortega, Kenny 46
Osbick Bird, The 71
Osborn, Paul 79, 84, 196
Oscar, Henry 154
O'Shea, Tessie 23, 24
Osmond, Alan 106
Osmond, Donny 106, 107, 110, 110
Osmond, Jay 106
Osmond, Jimmy 106
Osmond, Marie 106
Osmond, Merrill 106
Osmond, Tommy 106
Osmond, Virl 106
Osmond, Wayne 106
Ossawattomie Brown 125
Ostrovski, Alexander ix
Ostrow, Stuart 174, 175
Osuna, Jess 69
Our Miss Brooks 74
Our Town 67
Over at Uncle Joe's: Moscow and Me 98
Ovid 143
Owen, Tamara 152
Owl and the Pussycat, The 174

Padlocks, of 1927 9
Padula, Edward 102
Paffrath, John 114
Page, Davis 147
Page, Patti 63
Page, Stan 145
Pagnol, Marcel 89, 194, 195
Paint Your Wagon 37
Painter, Estelle 54
Pakewitz, Irving 125
Pakledinaz, Marty 88
Pal Joey 118
Palmer, Betsy 173
Palmerston, Lord 17
Palminteri, Chazz 72
Pantoliano, Joe 30
Paone, Marion 167
Parents and Children 141
Pariah xi
Paris Is Out! 172
Parker, Althea 152

272 / General Index

Parrish, Elizabeth 94
Parsons, Estelle 35
Patridge Family, The 109
Parva, Cynthia 202
Pascal, John and Fran 114
Pascoe, William H. ix
Paterson, Pat 42
Patinkin, Sheldon 20
Patrick, John 89
Patsy, The 37
Patten, George William 52, 53
Paul, Rick 180
Paul Robeson 20
Pawley, Edward 61, 63
Paxinou, Katina 64
Payne, Sandra 37
Peacock, Kim 154
Peake, Richard Brinsley 55
Peanuts 52, 202
Pearlman, Nan 5
Pears, Peter 13, 15
Pearson, Harry 112
Peck, Charles K, Jr. 185
Peggy Leads the Way 87
Pember, Ron 156
Pemberton, Brock 161
Pen, Polly 202
Pence, Marilela 53
Penfold, Tom 112
Penhallow, Leslie 178
People Like Us 37, 152, 153, 154, 155
People on Second Street, The 132
Perelman, S. J. 96
Perkins, Anthony 44, 109, 174
Perlis, Jack 103
Perry, Frederick xi
Perry, Ray 171
Persecution and Assassination of Jean-Paul Marat as Performed by the Inmates of the Asylum of Charenton under the Direction of the Marquis De Sade 180
Persson, Gene 202
Peter Pan 103, 143
Pevney, Joseph 91
Phelan, Mike xiii
Phillips, Jeff 82
Phillips, Stephen 83

Piaf 196
Picnic 89, 182
Picon, Molly 170, 171, 172
Picture of Dorian Gray, The 7
Pierce, Jack P. 57
Pierce, J. Robert 126
Pierson, Arthur 37
Pilgrim Soul, The 132
Pin to See the Peepshow, A 37, 150, 151, 152, 153, 154, 155, 156
Pincus, Warren 108
Pinelli, Tullio 185
Pins and Needles 194
Pinter, Harold 59
Pious Infant, The 71
Pi-Pa-Ki 82
Pippin 175
Pitkin, William 5
Pitot, Genevieve 78
Place for Polly, A 76, 156, 157, 204
Plaster Bambino, The 199
Platt, Livingston 61
Play Me a Country Song 158
Player Maid, The x
Plaza 9 59
Plaza Suite 194
Pleasure Man 8
Pleasures and Palaces 145
Pleshette, Suzanne 173
Plinge, Walter 66
Plume de Ma Tante, La 48
Poetasters of Ispahan, The xi
Point of No Return 79
Polak, Maralyn Lois 190
Politis, Photos 65
Poll, Martin 48
Pollock, Ernest 61
Pollock, Milton 69
Polly With a Past 168
Pomerance, Bernard 196
Ponazecki, Joe 157
Ponti, Carlo 84, 185
Porter, Cole 144
Porter, Stephen 120
Portnoy, Gary 46
Portrait in Black 143
Post, Guy Bates x
Post, William H. xi
Potash and Perlmutter 123

Potash and Perlmutter, Detectives 123
Pousse-Cafe 59, 131
Power, Harley 30
Power, Tyrone 125, 126
Power, Tyrone, Sr. 83
Powers, Marcella 66
Precht, Bob 191
Prentice, Herbert M. 187
Pressman, Lawrence 48
Preston, Robert 199
Presumption; or The Fate of Frankenstein 55
Previn, Andre 38, 63
Price, Paul B. 164, 166
Prime of Miss Jean Brodie, The 201, 204
Primrose Path 168
Prince, Harold (Hal) 120, 128, 157
Prince Albert 17
Prince Edward 112
Princess April 135
Printz, Edward 94
Prior, Herbert 113
Priorities of '42 26
Prisonnière, La 8
Private Life of Helen of Troy, The 84
Probert, George S. ix
Pryor, Nicholas 80
Pulitzer, Joseph 9
Pullen, William 188
Pulver, Enid 208
Putnam, Christina 148
Pygmalion 37, 186

Qualen, John 64
Quayle, Anthony 188
Queen Elizabeth, II 156
Queen High 169, 170
Queen Victoria 17
Queenie and the Japes 67
Quelque Part dans la Monde 103
Quick Quick Slow 128
Quinn, Anthony 185, 199
Quinn, Arthur Hobson 86
Quinn, Michael 145
Quintero, Jose 90, 91

Radder, Paul 63
Radomsky, Saul 128
Raffael, Jack 112
Raffles, Gerry 17
Raft, George xv, 9
Rafter, Adele 111, 112
Raglan, Lord 17
Railton, Jeremy 120
Rain 168
Rainbow Jones 159
Rainy Day in Newark, A 99
Ralphe, David 30
Rambeau, Marjorie 167, 168
Ramsey, Logan 94, 120
Randall, Muriel 186
Randall, Tony 5, 49, 143
Randolph, Amanda 26
Randolph, Clemence 168
Randolph, Robert 145
Raphaelson, Samson 67, 162
Raquello, Edward 39, 42
Rasbury, Andy H. 68
Rathbone, Basil 8
Rattigan, Terence 24
Ratzenberger, John 166
Ravasco, Mario 185
Raw Meat 159, 160
Ray, Johnny 46
Raymond, Vera Brynner 83
Rea, Alec L. 41
Reagan, Ronald 126
Rebecca 177
Recht, Raymond C. 148
Red Buryl 82
Red Devil Battery Sign, The 89
Red Gloves 102
Red Rover, Red Rover 49
Redemption of Dave D'Arcy, The 87
Redfield, William 157
Redhead 32
Redmond, Marge 5
Redwine, Wilbur "Skip" 53
Reed, Donald 113
Rees, Carol 187
Reeves-Smith, H. 169
Regan, Sylvia 172
Reicher, Frank xi
Reicher, Hedwig xi
Reifsnyder, Howard 72, 72, 73

Reilly, Charles Nelson 19, 20
Reilly, Hugh 154
Reilly, Judd 180
Reimueller, Ross 82
Reiner, Hanne Marie 101, 103
Reinhardt, Max 8, 93
Remembered Visit, The 71
Remme, John 165
Rennie, James 135
Reprise 160, 161
Resnick, Muriel 189
Reunion 161, 162
Reunion in Vienna 39
Revenge; or The Pride of Lillian Le Mar xi
Revere, Ann 157, 202
Revolt 63
Rey, Antonia 165
Reynolds, Gene 126
Reynolds, Owen 154
Reynolds, Quentin 177
Rhodes, Jordan 48
Rice, Elmer viii, xvi
Richard II 78
Richards, Doreen 152
Richardson, Jack 96
Richardson, Lee 5, 49
Richardson, Miranda 156
Richardson, Tony 18
Riches, Arnold 186
Richman, Charles 88
Richman, Harry 26
Ricketts, Jim 202
Riddell, George viii
Riley, Larry 28
Ring Round the Bathtub 162, 163
Rintels, David W. 200
Risdon, Elizabeth xi
Rise of Rosie O'Reilly, The 107
Riskin, Robert 62
Ritter, John 120
Ritter, Louise x
Ritz, The 163, 164, 165, 166, 167, 171
Rivera, Chita 48
Roache, Viola 154
Road Together, The 167, 168
Robards, Jason, Jr. 14, 16
Robbins, Carrie 57
Robert Burns x

Roberts, Leona 207
Roberts, Pernell 5
Robertson, Liz 35, 37
Robertson, T. W. xi
Robeson, Paul 7
Robins, Elizabeth ix
Robinson, Bill 88
Robson, Eleanor ix
Roche, Emeline 41
Rochon, Remere 117
Rodgers, Anton 128
Rodgers, Richard 38, 100, 120
Rodgers, Shev 82
Rodgers and Hammerstein 78, 82
Rodgers and Hart 118, 198
Roebling, John Augustus xiii
Roebling, Washington xiii
Roffman, Rose 117
Rogers, Emmett 41
Rogers, Paul 16, 77, 78
Rogers, Will 88
Rogers Brothers in Paris, The 110
Rohman, Richard 191, 192
Rolfing, Tom 148
Romantic Comedy 173
Rome, Harold 78, 130, 131, 194
Romeo and Juliet 78
Romoff, Woody 145
Room in Red and White, A 193
Rooney, Mickey 24
Rooney, Pat 26
Roosevelt, Franklin Delano 22
Roscoe, Albert 169
Rose, George 154
Rose, Jane 66, 202
Rose, Jill P. 202
Rose 196
Rosemary's Baby 20
Rosen, Sheldon 137, 138
Rosenberg, Irene 147
Rosenman, Leonard 79
Rosenzweig, Barney 80
Roskam, Cathy 147
Ross, Robert 207
Rosse, Herman 57
Rossen, Robert 13, 15
Rosson, Arthur 113
Rost, Elaine 53

Roth, Lillian 9
Roth, Wolfgang 94
Roto, Nino 185
Rovere, Marcella 185
Rowe, Anthony 156
Rush, Barbara 48, 49
Russell, Evelyn 157
Russell, Ken 57
Russell, William Howard 17
Ruth, Carol 48
Rutledge, Arthur 169
Ryan, Robert 15
Ryan, Sam J. 110, 112
Ryder, Alfred 14, 16, 208
Ryskind, Morrie 17, 146

Sacred and Profane Love viii
Sadie Love 168
Sailor on Horseback 200
Saint, Eva Marie 5
Saint, The 151
Saint-Subber 194
Saisson, Pierre 168
Saks, Gene 94
Sally 113
Salt Herring, The 71
Salvation 62
Same Time, Next Year 173
Sanchez, Jaime 5
Sanders, Alma 135
Sanderson, Julia 112
Sandrich, Mark 199
Sands, Diana 143, 174
Sanford, Sallie 63
Santayana, George 19
Sante Fe Trail 126
Santos, Cecile 82
Sartre, Jean-Paul 102
Satellite 169, 170
Satz, Ludwig 121, 122, 123
Saunders, Alice ix
Saville, John 100
Saville, T. G. 186
Saxon, John 48
Schaal, Richard 101, 103
Schackt, Gustav 66
Schaefer, George 41
Scarfe, Alan 138
Schary, Dore 2, 22, 177
Schenck, Joseph xv

Schenck, Nicholas 22
Schildkraut, Joseph 24, 42
Schisgal, Murray 180
Schlesinger, Otto L. 180
Schmidt, Douglas W. 57
Schnabel, Stefan 41
Schneider, Alan 184, 204, 205
Schochen, Seyril 123, 124
Scholz, Willard 66
School xi
Schorer, Mark 11, 61
Schreiber, Avery 101, 103
Schrock, Raymond L. 113
Schulberg, Benjamin P. 162
Schultz, Dwight 137
Schulz, Charles M. 52, 202
Schumann, Walter 125
Schwartz, Maurice 67
Scofield, Paul 128
Scofield, Thomas 193
Scott, Clifford 78
Scott, George C. 2, 198, 199
Scott, Hazel 26
Scott, Raymond 82
Scott, Steve 165
Scott's Royal Boxers 23
Sea Master, The 87
Seale, Douglas 54
Searle, Ronald 201
Season, The xvi, 96
Second Time Around 171
Second Time Around, The 171
Seddon, Margaret 113
Seduced 35
See Here, Private Hargrove 98
See My Lawyer 69
Seff, Richard 172
Segal, Erich 81, 82, 84
Seidelman, Arthur A. 157
Selassie, Haile 40
Selby, David 88, 89
Selden, Albert 201
Sellen, Charles 88
Selwyn, Edgar 83
Sennett, Mack 85
Señor Wences 26
Sepley, Michael 178
Serio, Jay 78
Serrano, Vincent viii
Seven Angry Men 127
1776 175
70 Girls 70 171

276 / General Index

Sewell, Robert 152
Sex 7, 8
Seymour, Jane 80
Seymour, William 110, 112
Shadow and Substance 67
Shaffer, Peter 109, 196
Shakespeare, William 78, 83, 143, 179, 182, 200
Shall We Dance 105
Shannon, Frank 61
Shapiro, Richard 80
Sharp, Michael 44
Shattuck, Truly 110
Shaughnessy, Mickey 100, 103
Shaw, Anne 208
Shaw, Charlotte 99
Shaw, George Bernard vii, ix, 2, 37, 99, 186
Shaw, Robert 59, 60
Shaw, Tom 63
She Didn't Say Yes 157
Shea, Joseph E. 61, 180
Shearer, Norma 42
Sheehan, Ed 112
Sheehan, Paul 94
Sheldon, Edward Brewster 39
Sheldon, Gene 26
Shelley, Elizabeth 207
Shelley, Mary Wollstonecraft 54, 55, 56, 57
Shelton, Kent 129
Shepard, Sam 35
Sherek, Henry 41, 152, 153, 154
Sheridan, Liz 71
Sherman, Allan 109
Sherman, Arthur 141
Sherman, Herrick 63
Sherman, Teddi 188
Sherry! 4, 103
Sherry, John 1, 2
Sherwood, Robert E. 36, 37, 38, 39, 40, 41, 42, 126
Shields, Robert 23, 24
Shoemaker, Ann 61
Shoestring Revue, The 28
Showtime 26
Shub, Lauren 202
Shubert, Messrs. 8, 9, 26, 69
Shubert Organization, The 196

Shugrue, J. Edward 192, 193
Sibbald, George 30
Sibthorpe, Marsha 138
Siddons, Helene 188
Sidney, P. Jay 3
Sidney, Sylvia 162
Sidney Shorr 49
Signor Chicago 207, 208
Siletti, Mario 79
Sillman, Leonard 28
Sills, Milton xi
Silvani, Aldo 185
Silver, Sheldon 148
Silver Casket, The 45, 208
Simmons, Jean 63
Simmons, Michael L. xv
Simmons, Michele 78
Simmons, Stanley 5
Simon, Alfred 108
Simon, John 20
Simon, Neil 157, 185, 197
Simon, Robert F. 204
Simon Says Get Married 173
Simonson, Lee 41
Singer, Pearl 157
Sinking Spell, The 71
Siretta, Dan 108, 109
Sissle, Noble 26
1600 Pennsylvania Avenue 38
Skinner, Otis ix
Skyscraper 20
Slade, Bernard 173, 174
Slade, Jill 173
Slap Happy 26
Sleep 35
Sleeping Prince, The 24
Sloan, Ted 112
Small, Paul 25
Smedley, Morgan 147
Smith, Alfred E. [Governor] 8
Smith, Art 91, 183
Smith, Bernard 63
Smith, Catherine Lee 82
Smith, Lois 79
Smith, Loring 143
Smith, Oliver 104
Smith, Osmond W. 52
Smith, Sammy 69, 145
Smith, Stanley 169
Smith and Dale 25, 26

General Index / 277

Snowden, Carolynne 88
Sokoloff, Sidney 66
Sold and Paid For ix
Solid Gold Cadillac, The 99
Solin, Harvey 5
Solomon, Bessie Ruth xv
Something Old, Something New 170, 171, 172
Son of the South, A 87
Sondheim, Stephen 78
Songbook 127, 128
Soon-Teck-On 80
Sophie 65
Sophie Halenczik, American 65
Sophocles 65, 83
Sorrells, Vance 180
Sorvino, Paul 117
Sound of Music, The 130
Sounding Brass 60
Southward, Paige 171
Sovey, Raymond 154
Spangler, David 30
Spears, Patti 3
Special Occasions 172, 173, 174
Spewack, Bella and Sam 144
Spewack, Samuel 144, 145
Spigelgass, Leonard 172
Spinetti, Victor 128
Sponda, Wanda 208
Square in the Eye 34
Stabile, Bill 88, 89
Stag King 138
Stages 174, 175
Stagg, Elizabeth viii
Stahl, John M. 88
Stamp, Terence 13, 15
Standing, Guy x
Standing, Wyndham 113
Standish, Burt L. 52
Stanley, Frank 80
Stanton, Elizabeth Cady 149
Stanwyck, Barbara 62
Starbuck, Betty 161
Starcke, Walter 121
Starcross Story, The 22, 176, 177, 178
Starr, Mike 72
Starters 35
Startime 25
Stasio, Marilyn 96
State of the Union 130

Status Quo Vadis 178, 179, 180
Stavis, Barrie 126
Stedman, Joel 180
Steele, Marjorie 116
Steffe, William 124, 125
Steiger, Rod 125
Stein, Joseph 38
Steinbeck, John 77, 78, 79, 80
Steiner, Emma viii
Step on a Crack 181, 182, 183
Stepford Wives, The 20
Stephens, R. N. xiv
Stephens, William viii
Steppling, John ix
Stern, Leonard 104
Sterner, Martha Jean 148
Sternhagen, Frances 30
Stevens, Charles 110
Stevens, Leslie 98
Stevens, Roger L. 82
Stevens, Vallory 188
Stevens, Vi 152
Stewart, Anita 88
Stewart, Michael 114
Stickney, Dorothy 143
Stiller, Jerry 164, 166
Stilwell, Richard 15
Sting, The 59
Stoker, Bram 56
Stoker, H. G. 154
Stone, Ezra 69
Stone, Fred 67
Stone, Irving 200
Stone, Paula 42
Stop Press 183
Storm, The viii, ix
Story for Sara 71
Stothart, Herbert 42
Stoudt, Paul 118
Stowe, Harriet Beecher 150
Strachey, Lytton 18
Strada, La 183, 184, 185
Stradley, John 183
Strange Interlude 9
Strange Orchestra 185, 186, 187, 188
Strange Play, A 2, 3
Strasberg, Lee 91, 99, 205
Strasberg, Paula Miller 99, 100
Strasser, Robin 120
Stratton, Chester 41

278 / General Index

Strauss, Wally 41
Strickfaden, Kenneth 57
Strickland, Gail 88, 180
Strike Up the Band 17, 146
Strindberg, August xi, 21
Stromberg, Hunt 42
Stronger, The xi
Strouse, Charles 28, 29, 35, 36, 38, 48
Stuart, J. E. B. 126
Stuart, Jean 178
Stuart, John 152
Stuart, Ralph xi
Studer, Hal 53
Styne, Jule 4
Subject Animal, The 196
Subject Was Roses, The 96
Suburban, The 87
Sugar Babies 24
Sullivan, A. S. 42
Sullivan, Ed 26
Sullivan, Ian 82
Sullivan, John L. 82
Sunday, Billy 60
Sunday Man, The 188, 189
Sunny Morning, A 207, 208
Sunrise at Campobello 22
Susskind, David 16, 100, 102, 103, 104
Sutro, Alfred 207, 208
Swan, Kathleen 202
Swayze, Mrs. J. C. 125
Sweeney Todd 38
Sweet, Blanche 161
Sweet Charity 25, 32, 185
Sweet Eros 78, 165
Sweetie 169
Swing High Sweeney 144
Swit, Loretta 173
Swope, Herbert, Jr. 182
Sydow, Jack 126
Sylvia, Mlle. 8
Symonds, Dusty 166
Szabo, Sandor 41

Tainted Philanthropy xi
Take Me Along 26, 163
Tall Story 171
Tally, Ted 167
Tandy, Jessica 174

Tangerine 135
Tanner, Dolores 147
Tapley, Rose E. x
Tarkington, Booth xi
Tarleton, Diane 201, 202
Tate, Reginald 178
Taub, William L. 154
Taylor, Holland 130
Taylor, John 94
Taylor, Rebecca 180
Tchin Tchin 199
Teaspoon Every Four Hours, A 189, 190, 191
Teichmann, Evelyn 99
Teichmann, Howard M. 97, 98, 99
Tell My Story 191, 192
Tenderloin 130
Tennyson, Alfred, Lord 18
Terentius, Publius 30
Terry, Jonathan 30
Thacker, Russ 82
Thalheimer, Norman 46
Thank Heaven for the Heathen 76
That American 87
That Championship Season 79
Thatcher, Torin 14
Theatre '54 153
There Shall Be No Night 39
These Things Are Mine 168
Thimming, Helen 8
13 Daughters 76
This Is the Life 67
Thom, Robert 10, 11
Thomas, A. E. 168
Thomas, Berte ix
Thomas, Bob 82
Thomas, David 78
Thomas, Ernest 44
Thomas, Frank 94
Thompson, Bob 180
Thompson, Edith 153, 155
Thompson, H. R. 152
Thompson, Percy 152, 153, 155
Thompson, Sada 94
Thompson-Bywaters Case 37, 152, 153, 155
Thomson, Barry 39
Thomson, Evan 148
Thorne, David 6

Thorne, Ken 166
Thorpe, Courtnay viii
Those Endearing Young Charms 208
Those Were the Days! 172
Thousand Clowns, A 69
Thrasher, Evelyn 118
Three-Cornered Moon 163
Three Men on a Horse 76
Three Musketeers, The 166
Threepenny Opera, The 4, 93, 104, 121
Three Sisters, The 47
Three Wishes for Jamie 143
Thropp, Frank viii
Thuna, Leonora 105, 136
Thurber, James 178
Thurston, Adelaide ix
Tiger at the Gates 84
Tilton, Elizabeth Richards 149, 150
Tilton, Theodore 150
Timber House 192, 193
Time Limit! 171
Time of the Cuckoo 178
Timon of Athens 200
'Tis of Thee 193, 194
To Bury a Cousin 141
Tobacco Road xv
Tobias, Fred 59, 60
Tonight at 8:30 178
Tonkonogy, Gertrude 163
Too Many Girls 118
Top Notchers 26
Topaze 194, 195
Torch Song 168
Torn, Rip 33, 34, 35
Torrance, Ridgely xii
Torres, Liz 5
Toser, David 108, 109, 180
Total Abandon 195, 196
Tottenham, Merle 186
Tough to Get Help 197, 198
Touliatos, George 54
Tour 78, 165
Tovarich 59
Tracey, Stella 112
Tracy, Lee 40, 41
Tracy, Spencer 177
Trahey, Jane 162, 163
Trash 166

Traube, Shepard 143
Travers, Bill 1, 2
Travin, Harry F. 30
Tree, Sir Herbert Beerbohm 83
Trehan, Al 26
Trevor, Claire 126
Trevor, Norman 8
Trial of Mary Dugan, The 2, 61
Tribute 173
Tricks of the Trade 198, 199
Trimble, Jessie x
Triumph of Love, The x
Troilus and Cressida 78, 83
Trojan War Will Not Take Place, The 84
Troupe, Tom 48
Trousers, The 189
Troy, Louise 5
Truckline Cafe xvi
Trueman, Paula 208
Truly Valiant 199, 200
Trumbell, Robert 72
Trumbo, Dalton 193
Truth About Blayds, The 177
Tryptich 49
Tubs, The 165, 166
Tucker, Rex 156
Tucker, Richard 169
Tudor, Gladys 178
Tumarin, Boris 64, 65
Turn of the Screw, The 32
Turner, Anna 154
Turner, Lana 46
Turner, Raymond 113
Turoff, Robert Ennes 171
Turtlenecks 89
Tuttle, Frank 63
Twain, Mark 183
Twelfth Night 179
Twinkletoes 113
Two Blind Mice 144
Two for the Seesaw 174
Two Mrs. Carrolls, The 143
Tyler, Edith 110
Tynan, J. Brandon ix
Tynan, Kenneth 34
Tyner, Charles 94
Tyrrell, Susan 49

Uchida, Christine 82

280 / General Index

Uhry, Alfred 77, 78, 108
Ulysses 83, 84
Ulysses in Ithica 83
Ulysses in Nighttown 30
Ulysses' Return 83
Under the Sycamore Tree 144
Unemployed Saint, The 89
Uniform of Flesh 13, 14
Unstrung Harp, The 71
Untitled Book, The 71
Uris, Leon 76
Utter Glory of Morrissey Hall, The 200, 201, 202

Vaccaro, Brenda 69, 136
Vail, Seymour 18, 172
Vale, Michael 167
Valency, Maurice 133
Valentine, William 122
Valor, Henrietta 145
Van Buren, A. H. 122
Vance, Nina 162
Van Dekker, Albert 91
Vanderbilt, Cornelius 149
Vander Noot, Edwin H. 3
Van Druten, John 121, 163
Van Fleet, Jo 79
Van Gogh, Vincent 200
Van Gyseghem, Andre 186
Van Heusen, James 171
Van Norden, Peter 108
Van Patten, Joyce 173
Van Sloan, Edward 58
Van Zandt, Peter 203
Van Zandt, Porter 68
Vasil, Art 5
Vaudeville: From the Honky-Tonks to The Palace 25
Vazules, James 94
Vees, Albert 66
Veillers, Bayard 2, 61
Veloz and Yolanda 26
Venturine, Livi 185
Venus at Large 171
Verdi, Joe 208
Verdon, Gwen 25, 31, 32, 185
Verneuil, Louis 174
Veronica's Room 20
Very Close Family, A 173
Vickery, John 137, 138

Victoria for President 147
Vidnovic, Martin 82
Viewing, The 205
Vigran, Herbert 193
Vinegar Tree, The 79
Vines, William 180
Virgin Man, The 7
Visit, The 133
Von Furstenberg, Betsy 157
Vosper, Frank 152, 154, 155

Waber, Bernard 85
Wadsworth, Andrew, C. 128
Waite, Ralph 204
Walcott, Charles x
Walcott, Fred iii
Walden, Henry 3
Waldman, Robert 77, 78
Wales, Ken 80
Wales, Roger B. [Senator] 9
Wales Padlock Act, The 9
Walker, James J. [Mayor] 7, 8
Walker, Walter viii
Wallace, James 126
Wallace, Laura 48
Wallace, Regina 63
Wallack, James 55
Wallerstein, Rose 63
Wallis, Hal B. 126
Walper, Cicely 178
Walpole, Hugh 45, 188, 208
Walsh, M. Emmett 80
Walsh, Raoul xv
Walter, C. Jervis 154
Walters, Barbara 26
Walters, Eugene 174
Walters, Lou 26, 69
Waltons, The 205
Waltzer, Jack 94
War of Wealth 87
War Song, The 144
Ward, Evelyn 109
Ward, Mary 207
Ward, Simon 119, 120
Ward, Theodore 125
Ware, Frank 113
Warhol, Andy 166
Warm Body, A 202, 203
Warner, Russell 108
Warren, Harry 130

General Index / 281

Warriner, Frederic 167
Warrington, Ann ix
Washington Jitters 193
Watering Place, The 204, 205
Waterman, Ida xi
Waters, Ethel 25
Waterston, Sam 120
Watt, Douglas xvi
Watts, Queenie 156
Wead, Robert Lewis ix
Weather Hen, The ix
Webb, George 113
Weber, Bernard 190
Webling, Peggy 55, 56, 57
Webster, Diana 48
Wedding Day, The x
Weedle, Vernon 80
Weeks, Alan 28
Weeks, Barbara 169
Weidman, Jerome 59, 130, 131
Weill, Gus 140, 141
Weill, Kurt 4, 5, 17, 37, 90, 91, 92, 93, 94, 121
Weiss, Julie 196
Weiss, Peter 180
Weitz, Eric 108, 109
Welch, William 53
Weppner, Christine 49
Werfel, Franz 93
Werner, Fred 145
Wesker, Arnold 34
West, Mae 7, 8
West, Nathaniel 99
Westbrook, John 152
Westman, Nydia 143
Weston, Jack 19, 164, 166
West Wing, The 71
Wetherall, Jack 138
Weyson, Samantha 166
Whale, James 56, 57
Whalen, Michael 63
What Did We Do Wrong? 171
What D'You Call It? 3
Whatmore, A. R. 186
What's Up 37
Wheeler, Bert 25, 26
Wheeler, Hugh 96
Wheeler, Michael 44
When Romance Rides 112
Where Has Tommy Flowers Gone? 165

Where's Charley? 145
Whiffen, Mrs. Thomas xi
White Angel, The 18
White, George 9
White, Jesse 100, 102
White, Norman H., Jr. 161
White, Richard 125
White, Stephen 30
White, Stuart 71
White, T. H. 37
White, Valerie 178
White, William Allen 60
White Man 67
Whitehead, Allen B. 145
Whitelaw, Arthur 201, 202
Whitelaw, John Biddle 161
Whiteley, Charles 154
Whitney, John Jay 93
Whitney, William C. 112
Whiz, The 28
Whoop-Up 59, 103
Whorf, Richard 39
Who's Happy Now? 49
Whose Life Is It Anyway? 197
Wiensko, Robert H. 117
Wiggly Ump, The 71
Wilbur, Crane 62
Wild and Wonderful 205, 206
Wilde, Hagar 31
Wilde, Oscar 7
Wilder, Thornton 67, 100, 148
Wilkes, Thomas 169
Willes, Peter 42
Williams, Fred 110
Williams, Hugh 187
Williams, Jill 159
Williams, John D. vii, viii
Williams, Ralph 90, 91
Williams, Tennessee 65, 89
Williams, Treat 166
Williamson, Bruce 94
Willowdale Handcar, The 71
Wilson, Billy 82
Wilson, David 18, 180
Wilson, Dorothy 88
Wilson, John C. 176, 177
Wilson, Paul 166
Windust, Bretaigne 38, 39
Wingreen, Jason 120
Winkworth, Mark 57

Winston, Alice 94
Winter, Donovan 152
Wiseman, Joseph 16
Within the Law 61
Witness 78, 165
Wittop, Freddy 145
Wolf, Catherine 201
Wolf, Jay 162, 163
Wolf, Dr. Max 168
Wolf Lowry 87
Wolfe, Harrison J. ix
Wolpe, Lenny 108, 148
Womack, George 180
Woman Killed with Kindness, A xii
Woman of Independent Means, A 49
Women Have Their Way, The 206, 207, 208
Wonderful World of Oz, The 28
Wood, Cyrus 167
Wood, G. 126
Wood, Lewis ix
Wood, Tom 138
Woodhull, Byron 149
Woodhull, Dr. Canning 149
Woodhull, Victoria 148, 149, 150
Woodhull, Zulu Maud 149
Woodhull and Claflin's Weekly 150
Woodlawn, Holly 166
Woods, Al H. 123, 167, 168
Woods, Franker 135
World by the Tail, The 151
World of Carl Sandburg, The 182
World of Musical Comedy, The 111
World of Susie Wong, The 79
World War 2½ 18
Wray, Fay 67
Wright, Hugh E. 154

Wright, Jackson 66
Wyatt, Eustace 61, 63
Wylie, Ida Alexa Ross 22, 176
Wyndham, Olive xi
Wynn, Ed 26
Wyspianski, Stanislaw 83

Xmas in Las Vegas 96

Yankee Doodle Dandy 108, 113, 114
Yapp, Cecil xi
Yarnell, Bruce 24
Yarnell, Lorene 23, 24
Yeargen, Michael H. 164, 165, 167
Yeats, William Butler ix, 132
Yield to the Night 156
You Can't Take It with You 163
Young, J. S. 180
Young, Mary 154
Youngman, Henny 26
Yount, Kenneth M. 148
You're a Good Man, Charlie Brown 52, 202
Your Own Thing 179

Zabruskie, Grace 80
Zacherle, John 84
Zagon, Martin 180, 181
Zahn, Curtis 205
Zanuck, Darryl F. xv
Zara, Lee 180
Zaslow, Michael 148
Zerbe, Lawson 53
Ziegfeld, Florenz 9, 69
Ziegfeld Follies 69